# ENGLISH DRAMA,
## 1900-1950

# AMERICAN LITERATURE, ENGLISH LITERATURE, AND WORLD LITERATURES IN ENGLISH: AN INFORMATION GUIDE SERIES

Series Editor: Theodore Grieder, Curator, Division of Special Collections, Fales Library, New York University, New York, New York

Associate Editor: Duane DeVries, Assistant Professor, Polytechnic Institute of New York, Brooklyn, New York

*Other books on English literature in this series:*

ENGLISH DRAMA TO 1660 (EXCLUDING SHAKESPEARE)—*Edited by Frieda Elaine Penninger*

ENGLISH DRAMA, 1660-1800—*Edited by Frederick M. Link*

ENGLISH DRAMA AND THEATRE, 1800-1900—*Edited by L.W. Conolly and J.P. Wearing*

CONTEMPORARY DRAMA IN AMERICA AND ENGLAND, 1950-1970—*Edited by Richard H. Harris*

THE ENGLISH LITERARY JOURNAL TO 1900—*Edited by Robert B. White, Jr.*

ENGLISH-CANADIAN LITERATURE TO 1900—*Edited by R.G. Moyles*

ENGLISH PROSE, PROSE FICTION, AND CRITICISM TO 1660—*Edited by S.K. Heninger, Jr.*

OLD AND MIDDLE ENGLISH POETRY TO 1500—*Edited by Walter H. Beale*

ENGLISH POETRY, 1500-1660—*Edited by S.K. Heninger, Jr.*

ENGLISH POETRY, 1600-1800—*Edited by Christopher Cohane*

ENGLISH ROMANTIC POETRY, 1800-1835—*Edited by Donald H. Reiman*

VICTORIAN POETRY, 1835-1900—*Edited by Ronald E. Freeman*

ENGLISH POETRY, 1900-1950—*Edited by Emily Ann Anderson*

CONTEMPORARY POETRY IN AMERICA AND ENGLAND, 1950-1970—*Edited by Calvin Skaggs*

*in press

---

The above series is part of the

# GALE INFORMATION GUIDE LIBRARY

The Library consists of a number of separate series of guides covering major areas in the social sciences, humanities, and current affairs.

General Editor: Paul Wasserman, Professor and former Dean, School of Library and Information Services, University of Maryland

Managing Editor: Dedria Bryfonski, Gale Research Company

# ENGLISH DRAMA, 1900-1950

## A GUIDE TO INFORMATION SOURCES

*Volume 11 in the American Literature, English Literature, and World Literatures in English Information Guide Series*

### E. H. Mikhail

*Professor of English*
*University of Lethbridge*
*Lethbridge, Alberta*

*Gale Research Company*
*Book Tower, Detroit, Michigan 48226*

$C \cdot 1$

**Library of Congress Cataloging in Publication Data**

Mikhail, E H
    English drama, 1900-1950.

    (American literature, English literature, and world
literatures in English information guide series; v. 11)
(Gale information guide library)
    Includes index.
    1. English drama--20th century--Bibliography.
I. Title.
Z2014.D7M545    [PR736]    016.822'9'1    74-11523
ISBN 0-8103-1216-6

# VITA

E.H. Mikhail is professor of English at the University of Lethbridge, Alberta. He graduated from Trinity College, Dublin, and the University of Sheffield, from which he received his Ph.D.

A Canada Council scholar, Mikhail's publications include THE SOCIAL AND CULTURAL SETTING OF THE 1890s; JOHN GALSWORTHY THE DRAMATIST; COMEDY AND TRAGEDY; SEAN O'CASEY: A BIBLIOGRAPHY OF CRITICISM; A BIBLIOGRAPHY OF MODERN IRISH DRAMA 1899-1970; DISSERTATIONS ON ANGLO-IRISH DRAMA: A BIBLIOGRAPHY OF STUDIES 1870-1970; THE STING AND THE TWINKLE: CONVERSATIONS WITH SEAN O'CASEY; J.M. SYNGE: A BIBLIOGRAPHY OF CRITICISM; CONTEMPORARY BRITISH DRAMA 1950-1976: AN ANNOTATED CRITICAL BIBLIOGRAPHY; J.M. SYNGE: INTERVIEWS AND RECOLLECTIONS; W.B. YEATS: INTERVIEWS AND RECOLLECTIONS; and LADY GREGORY: INTERVIEWS AND RECOLLECTIONS.

He has also contributed to MODERN DRAMA; REVUE DE LITTERATURE COMPAREE; BULLETIN OF BIBLIOGRAPHY; COLBY LIBRARY QUARTERLY; and RESEARCH STUDIES. He is contributing editor for THE SEAN O'CASEY REVIEW.

# CONTENTS

# Contents

# Contents

# PREFACE

Because this book deals with "Modern British Drama," the principal concern is for the drama rather than the stage. Dramatic criticism and theory have been included; strictly theatrical concerns have not. The list of books on dramatic theory and technique, however, includes only those making generous contributions to the topic of modern British drama. Journalistic accounts of theatrical events and memoirs of actors and directors and the like are not listed, nor are reviews of individual plays, although "seasons" of theatrical productions are. Only those histories of particular theatres which contribute to the study of individual plays as drama are included. I have also included a few important studies from the pre-1900 decade because I feel they are essential to the understanding of the later period. All entries have been annotated, unless the title is sufficiently self-explanatory (as, for example, Hugh Hunt, "A Gown for Cinderella: Drama in the Universities and an Examination of Some of its Problems").

Entries are arranged alphabetically within chapters, and chronologically within individual author entries. Readers seeking a list of the works of any dramatist listed in Chapter V will find it in the bibliographies annotated as "primary." Critical material will be found in those bibliographies designated "secondary." Readers are also reminded of the author, title, and subject indexes at the end of the book. This Guide will be particularly useful to those doing research on specific theatre movements or topics, such as the Abbey Theatre, the Dublin Gate Theatre, or censorship. In most instances I have included the place of publication; where I have not, the reader will find that the place of publication is obvious. I have attempted to make the bibliography complete through 1973, although some later studies have been included.

E.H. Mikhail

# ACKNOWLEDGMENTS

In the course of preparing this book I have incurred numerous obligations. Thanks are due to the University of Lethbridge for a research grant as well as a teaching-free semester during the academic year 1974-75; to Bea Ramtej for her patience and skill in typing and preparing the final manuscript; and to Drew Lemen and Nellie Jones for research assistance.

It is also a pleasant duty to record my appreciation to the staff of the University of Lethbridge Library; the British Library, London; the National Library of Ireland, Dublin; Trinity College Library, Dublin; the British Theatre Institute Library, London; and the New York Public Library.

# Chapter 1

# BIBLIOGRAPHIES

1   ABSTRACTS OF ENGLISH STUDIES. Boulder, Colo.: National Council of Teachers of English, 1958-- .

   Gives summaries of articles in periodicals.

2   Adelman, Irving, and Rita Dworkin. MODERN DRAMA; A CHECKLIST OF CRITICAL LITERATURE ON 20th CENTURY PLAYS. Metuchen, N.J.: Scarecrow Press, 1967.

   An index to selected commentaries in books and periodicals on modern playwrights and their plays.

3   Allen, Charles, and Felix Pollak, eds. COMPREHENSIVE INDEX TO ENGLISH-LANGUAGE LITTLE MAGAZINES, 1890-1970. Millwood, N.Y.: Kraus-Thomson, 1975.

   A bibliography of secondary authors, arranged alphabetically by name.

4   AMERICAN DOCTORAL DISSERTATIONS.

   See No. 55.

5   ANNOTATED BIBLIOGRAPHY OF NEW PUBLICATIONS IN THE PERFORMING ARTS. New York: Drama Book Shop, 1973-- .

   A quarterly that catalogues books "as soon as they become generally available in the United States and England."

6   ANNUAL BIBLIOGRAPHY OF ENGLISH LANGUAGE AND LITERATURE. London: Modern Humanities Research Association, 1920-- .

   Lists books and articles.

7   ANNUAL MAGAZINE SUBJECT-INDEX. Boston: F.W. Faxon, 1907-49; rpt. with title CUMULATED MAGAZINE SUBJECT-INDEX, 1907-1949. Boston: G.K. Hall, 1964.

Lists articles in periodicals.

8    Baker, Blanch M. THEATRE AND ALLIED ARTS; A GUIDE TO BOOKS DEALING WITH THE HISTORY, CRITICISM, AND TECHNIC OF THE DRAMA AND THEATRE AND RELATED ARTS AND CRAFTS. New York: H.W. Wilson, 1952; rpt. New York: Benjamin Blom, 1967.

Contains more than 6,000 items published between 1885 and 1945. There is ample cross-referencing and indexing. Completely revised form of the same author's 1933 DRAMATIC BIBLIOGRAPHY.

9    Bateson, F.W., and George Watson, eds. THE CAMBRIDGE BIBLIOGRAPHY OF ENGLISH LITERATURE. 5 vols. Cambridge: At the University Press, 1940-57.

Lists primary writings and selected secondary bibliography for each author. See also No. 192.

10    Batho, Edith Clara, and Bonamy Dobree. THE VICTORIANS AND AFTER, 1830-1914. Introductions to English Literature, vol. IV. General ed. Bonamy Dobree. London: Cresset Press; New York: R.M. McBride, 1938.

A guide for the beginning student.

11    Belknap, S. Yancey. GUIDE TO THE PERFORMING ARTS. New York: Scarecrow Press, 1957-- .

The "first annual index of the performing arts." Lists articles in periodicals.

12    Bell, Inglis F., and Jennifer Gallup. A REFERENCE GUIDE TO ENGLISH, AMERICAN, AND CANADIAN LITERATURE; AN ANNOTATED CHECKLIST OF BIBLIOGRAPHICAL AND OTHER REFERENCE MATERIALS. Vancouver: University of British Columbia Press, 1971.

13    Besterman, Theodore. "Drama and Stage." A WORLD BIBLIOGRAPHY OF BIBLIOGRAPHIES. 5 vols. 4th ed. Lausanne, Switzerland: Societas Bibliographica, 1965-66; rpt. included in MUSIC AND DRAMA: A BIBLIOGRAPHY OF BIBLIOGRAPHIES. Totowa, N.J.: Rowman and Littlefield, 1971.

Annotated and arranged under specific subject matter.

14    BIBLIOGRAPHIC INDEX; A CUMULATIVE BIBLIOGRAPHY OF BIBLIOGRAPHIES. New York: H.W. Wilson, 1937-- .

The standard serial bibliography of bibliographies.

15    Bond, Donald F. A REFERENCE GUIDE TO ENGLISH STUDIES. 2nd ed. Chicago and London: University of Chicago Press, 1971.

Designed "primarily for the use of the graduate student."

16 BOOK REVIEW DIGEST. New York: H.W. Wilson, 1906-- .

An index to reviews, in selected periodicals, of books published in the United States. Some excerpts are included.

17 BOOK REVIEW INDEX. Detroit, Mich.: Gale Research Co., 1965-- .

Lists reviews of books in periodicals.

18 Boston Public Library. A CATALOGUE OF THE ALLEN A. BROWN COLLECTION OF BOOKS RELATING TO THE STAGE IN THE PUBLIC LIBRARY OF THE CITY OF BOSTON. Boston: 1919; rpt. New York: Kraus Reprints, 1970.

Arranged in dictionary form, the catalog contains authors, titles, and subjects in a single alphabet.

19 Breed, Paul F., and Florence M. Sniderman, eds. DRAMATIC CRITICISM INDEX; A BIBLIOGRAPHY OF COMMENTARIES ON PLAYWRIGHTS FROM IBSEN TO THE AVANT-GARDE. Detroit, Mich.: Gale Research Co., 1972.

Its nearly 12,000 entries attempt to cover the English-language books, chapters, and articles relating to each playwright and his works.

20 The British Drama League. THE PLAYERS LIBRARY; THE CATALOGUE OF THE LIBRARY OF THE BRITISH DRAMA LEAGUE. London: Faber, 1950; FIRST SUPPLEMENT. London: 1951; SECOND SUPPLEMENT. London: 1954; THIRD SUPPLEMENT. London: 1956.

The bulk of each volume is taken up with a catalog of plays in the British Drama League Library, but in each there is also a short list of books on the theatre, also indexed by author.

21 BRITISH HUMANITIES INDEX.

See No. 174

22 BRITISH MUSEUM SUBJECT INDEX. London: Trustees of the British Museum, 1881-- .

Includes a section listing books on "Drama and Stage: Great Britain and Ireland."

23 THE BRITISH NATIONAL BIBLIOGRAPHY. London: Council of the British National Bibliography, 1950-- .

"A Subject Catalogue of new books published in the British

Isles ... classified, with modifications, according to the Dewey Decimal Classification."

24    Brockett, Oscar G.; Samuel L. Becker; and Donald C. Bryant. A BIB-LIOGRAPHICAL GUIDE TO RESEARCH IN SPEECH AND DRAMATIC ART. Boston: Scott, Foresman, 1963.

Lists important aids and reference tools in the field.

25    Busfield, Roger M., ed. THEATRE ARTS PUBLICATIONS AVAILABLE IN THE UNITED STATES, 1953-1957: A FIVE YEAR BIBLIOGRAPHY. New York: American Educational Theatre Association, 1964.

Oriented toward production, but a section on English drama is included (pages 80-81).

26    Bush, George E., and Jeanne K. Welcher. "A Check List of Modern Plays Based on Classical Mythic Themes." BULLETIN OF THE NEW YORK PUBLIC LIBRARY, 73 (1969), 525-30.

Concerned solely with modern dramatic versions of classical myths.

27    Byrne, M. St. Clare, ed. "Modern." BRITISH DRAMA: HISTORY AND CRITICISM. London: National Book League, 1950. Pp. 16-18.

Gives selected reading on the subject.

28    CAMBRIDGE BIBLIOGRAPHY OF ENGLISH LITERATURE.

See No. 9.

29    CANADIAN PERIODICAL INDEX. Ottawa: Canadian Library Association, 1938-- .

Includes a section on "Drama."

30    Cant, Monica. "A Bibliography of English Drama from 1890 to 1920." LIBRARY ASSOCIATION RECORD, 24 (February 1922), 41-57.

Lists only published plays.

31    Carlson, Marvin. "Modern Drama: A Selected Bibliography of Bibliographies." MODERN DRAMA, 8 (May 1965), 112-18.

Annotated list of bibliographies devoted in whole or part to critical works.

32    Carpenter, Charles A. "The New Bibliography of Modern Drama Studies." MODERN DRAMA, 12 (May 1969), 49-56.

Survey.

33     . "Modern Drama Studies: An Annual Bibliography." MODERN DRAMA, 17 (March 1974), 67-120.

Intended as "a new, improved version of the old ingroup check-list (by Shedd)." (See Nos. 162-65.)

34     . "Modern Drama Studies: An Annual Bibliography." MODERN DRAMA, 18 (March 1975), 61-116.

See also Nos. 74-75, and 132.

35   Cheshire, David. STAGECRAFT AND THE THEATRE. Readers' Guide Series. London: Library Association; London: County Libraries Group, 1965.

A select list of books, most in print, arranged under broad subject headings.

36     . THEATRE: HISTORY, CRITICISM AND REFERENCE. Readers' Guide Series. London: Clive Bingley; Hamden, Conn.: Archon Books, 1967.

Examines principal or significant works.

37   Chicorel, Marietta. CHICOREL INDEX TO THE SPOKEN ARTS ON DISCS, TAPES AND CASSETTES. New York: Chicorel, 1973.

Lists plays, novels, short stories, speeches, commentaries, conversations, poems, and readings.

38     , ed. CHICOREL THEATER INDEX TO PLAYS IN COLLECTIONS, ANTHOLOGIES, PERIODICALS, AND DISCS. 3 vols. New York: Chicorel, 1970-72.

Indexes plays, playwrights, editors, and play collections.

39     , ed. CHICOREL BIBLIOGRAPHY TO THE PERFORMING ARTS. New York: Chicorel, 1972.

A buying guide that lists entries under subject headings.

40     , ed. CHICOREL THEATER INDEX TO PLAYS IN ANTHOLOGIES, PERIODICALS, DISCS AND TAPES: PLAYS ON DISCS AND TAPES. New York: Chicorel, 1972.

Indexes plays and performers on recorded media.

41   Child, Harold. "Revivals of English Dramatic Works, 1901-1926." REVIEW OF ENGLISH STUDIES, 2 (April 1926), 177-88; 3 (April 1927), 169-85.

Brief record of the revivals of English plays from 1901-25.

42   Clarence, Reginald [H.J. Eldridge]. "THE STAGE" CYCLOPAEDIA: A BIBLIOGRAPHY OF PLAYS. London: THE STAGE, 1909; rpt. New York: Burt Franklin, 1970.

     An alphabetical list of plays, with theatres and dates of first London productions.

43   Clough, Peter H. "A Subject Index to DRAMA SURVEY, 1961-1968." THEATRE DOCUMENTATION, 3 (Fall 1970 and Spring 1971), 81-100.

     A cumulative index arranged under twelve topic headings.

44   Clunes, Alec. BRITISH THEATRE HISTORY. London: National Book League, 1955.

     Gives a selected reading on the subject for the nonspecialist.

45   Coleman, Arthur, and Gary R. Tyler. DRAMA CRITICISM. Vol. I: A CHECKLIST OF INTERPRETATION SINCE 1940 OF ENGLISH AND AMERI-CAN PLAYS. Denver, Colo.: Alan Swallow, 1966.

     Lists studies of plays contained in books and periodicals.

46   Coleman, Edward D., comp. THE JEW IN ENGLISH DRAMA; AN AN-NOTATED BIBLIOGRAPHY. New York: New York Public Library, 1943; rpt., 1970.

     An annotated bibliography of bibliographies, general works, collections, and individual plays from the earliest times to 1938.

47   COMPREHENSIVE DISSERTATION INDEX 1861-1972. 37 vols. Ann Arbor, Mich.: Xerox University Microfilms, 1973.

48   Cornyn, Stan. A SELECTIVE INDEX TO THEATRE MAGAZINE. New York and London: Scarecrow Press, 1964.

     A guide to the articles, authors, subjects, and dramatic works in THEATRE MAGAZINE from 1901-31.

49   CUMULATIVE BOOK INDEX. New York: H.W. Wilson, 1928-- .

     A world list of books in English.

50   Cutler, Bradley D., and Villa Stiles. MODERN BRITISH AUTHORS; THEIR FIRST EDITIONS. New York: Greenberg; London: G. Allen, 1930; rpt. Folcroft, Pa.: Folcroft Press, 1969.

51   Daiches, David. THE PRESENT AGE AFTER 1920. Introduction to English Literature, vol. V. General ed. Bonamy Dobree. London: Cresset

Press; Bloomington: Indiana University Press, 1958.

A guide for the beginning student.

52  Danielson, Henry. BIBLIOGRAPHIES OF MODERN AUTHORS. London: Bookman's Journal, 1921; rpt. Folcroft, Pa.: Folcroft Library Editions, 1972.

Includes bibliographies of John Drinkwater and Lord Dunsany.

53  DESCRIPTIVE CATALOGUE OF PLAYS AND DRAMATIC WORKS. London: Samuel French, annually, 1891(?)-- .

Later called GUIDE TO SELECTING PLAYS.

54  DISSERTATION ABSTRACTS. Ann Arbor, Mich.: University Microfilms, 1938-- .

55  DOCTORAL DISSERTATIONS ACCEPTED BY AMERICAN UNIVERSITIES. Ed. Arnold H. Trotier and Marian Harman. New York: H.W. Wilson, 1933-55. Continued as INDEX TO AMERICAN DOCTORAL DISSERTATIONS. Ann Arbor, Mich.: University Microfilms, for Association of Research Libraries, 1955-- .

56  Drury, Francis K.W. VIEWPOINTS IN MODERN DRAMA. Chicago: American Library Association, 1925.

Part II contains "Books on the Modern Drama."

57  _____. DRURY'S GUIDE TO BEST PLAYS. By James M. Salem. 2nd ed. Metuchen, N.J.: Scarecrow Press, 1969.

Includes synopses of plays and guides for production.

58  Dukore, Bernard F., ed. A BIBLIOGRAPHY OF THEATRE ARTS PUBLICATIONS IN ENGLISH, 1963. Washington, D.C.: American Educational Theater Association, 1965.

Contains both author and subject indexes.

59  Eager, Alan R. "Drama." A GUIDE TO IRISH BIBLIOGRAPHICAL MATERIAL; BEING A BIBLIOGRAPHY OF IRISH BIBLIOGRAPHIES AND SOME SOURCES OF INFORMATION. London: Library Association, 1964. Pp. 208-9.

A "quick reference guide."

60  Edyvean, Alfred R. RELIGIOUS DRAMA PROJECT PLAY LIST. New York: American Educational Theatre Association, n.d.

This mimeographed list of plays suitable for religious drama

7

projects includes author, title, cast requirements, type of play, publisher, and length of play.

61    Enser, A.G.S. FILMED BOOKS AND PLAYS; A LIST OF BOOKS AND PLAYS FROM WHICH FILMS HAVE BEEN MADE, 1928-1967. Elmsford, N.Y.: London House & Maxwell, 1968; London: Andre Deutsch, 1971.

62    ESSAY AND GENERAL LITERATURE INDEX. New York: H.W. Wilson, 1900-- .

Essays in books.

63    ETUDES IRLANDAISES: BULLETIN DE LIAISON DES SPECIALISTES FRAN-COPHONES D'HISTOIRE, CIVILISATION ET LITTERATURE DE L'IRLANDE. Centre d'Etudes et de Recherches Irlandaises--Universite de Lille, 1972-- .

Surveys activities of Irish studies in France and gives bibliographical information on publications and dissertations.

64    Faxon, F.W. DRAMATIC INDEX. Boston, 1909-49; rpt. as CUMULATED DRAMATIC INDEX 1909-1949. Ed. F.W. Faxon, M.E. Bates, and A.C. Sutherland. Boston: G.K. Hall, 1965.

Lists articles on, and illustrations of, theatrical subjects from both American and English periodicals.

65    Fidell, Estelle A. PLAY INDEX.

See No. 139.

66    Foshay, Florence E. "Twentieth Century Drama; English, Irish, American." Part I: "English Dramas," BULLETIN OF BIBLIOGRAPHY, 8 (July 1915), 183-87; Part II: "Irish Dramas," 8 (October 1915), 221-22.

Checklist of plays published between 1900-1915.

67    French, Frances-Jane. THE ABBEY THEATRE SERIES OF PLAYS: A BIB-LIOGRAPHY. Dublin: Dolmen Press; London: Oxford University Press, 1969.

Deals with the original "Abbey Theatre Series" of fifteen volumes and the later "Abbey Theatre Series" of nine unnumbered volumes.

68    Gilder, Rosamond. A THEATRE LIBRARY; A BIBLIOGRAPHY OF ONE HUNDRED BOOKS RELATING TO THE THEATRE. New York: Theatre Arts, for National Theatre Conference, 1932.

For additions to THEATRE LIBRARY, see BOOKLIST, 33 (1937). The LIBRARY was continued by Roy Stallings and Paul Myers as A GUIDE TO THEATRE READING (New York: Theatre

Arts, 1949). This GUIDE adds biographies, dramatic criticism, and technical books not considered by Gilder.

69    Gilder, Rosamond, and George Freedley. THEATRE COLLECTIONS IN LIBRARIES AND MUSEUMS; AN INTERNATIONAL HANDBOOK. New York: Theatre Arts; London: B.F. Stevens and Brown, 1936; rpt. New York: Johnson Reprint, 1970.

See also No. 90.

70    Goetsch, Paul, and Heinz Kosok. "Literatur zum modernen englischen Drama: Eine ausgewahlte Bibliographie." DAS MODERNE ENGLISCHEN DRAMA; INTERPRETATIONEN. Ed. Horst Oppel. 2nd rev. ed. Berlin: Erich Schmidt, 1966. Pp. 371-82.

A selected secondary bibliography.

71    GUIDE TO REFERENCE BOOKS. Chicago: American Library Association, 1902-- .

Includes a section on "English Drama."

71A   GUIDE TO SELECTING PLAYS.

See No. 53.

72    Hall, Lillian Arvilla. CATALOGUE OF DRAMATIC PORTRAITS IN THE THEATRE COLLECTION OF THE HARVARD COLLEGE LIBRARY. 4 vols. Cambridge, Mass.: Harvard University Press, 1930-34.

Provides a descriptive index to the engraved dramatic portraits in the Collection. The approximately 40,000 prints considered in this index are portraits of individuals, most of whom are British and American, whose names are associated with theatre history.

73    Harmon, Maurice. MODERN IRISH LITERATURE, 1800-1967; A READER'S GUIDE. Dublin: Dolmen Press, 1967.

Includes a section on "Drama."

74    Haskell, John D., Jr., and Robert G. Shedd. "Modern Drama: A Selective Bibliography of Works Published in English in 1966." MODERN DRAMA, 10 (September 1967), 202-15.

Lists books and articles.

75    _____. "Modern Drama: A Selective Bibliography of Works Published in English in 1967." MODERN DRAMA, 11 (September 1968), 195-213.

Lists books and articles. See also Nos. 32-33, 132, and 162-65.

76    Hayman, Ronald. ONE HUNDRED YEARS OF DRAMA; A SELECTED LIST. London: National Book League, 1972.

77    Holden, David F. AN ANALYTICAL INDEX TO "MODERN DRAMA" VOLUMES I-XIII, MAY 1958-FEBRUARY 1971. Toronto: Hakkert, 1972.

>    Consists of a general index and indexes to contributors and book reviews.

78    Hornby, Richard, comp. "TDR and Theatre: A Bibliography." TULANE DRAMA REVIEW, 9 (Summer 1965), 179-207.

>    Listing of books published in the United States between 1 February 1964 and 31 January 1965.

79    _____. "TDR Books and Theatre: A Bibliography." TULANE DRAMA REVIEW, 10 (Summer 1966), 239-64.

>    Listing of books published in the United States between 1 February 1965 and 31 January 1966. See also No. 184.

80    Howard, Diana, comp. DIRECTORY OF THEATRE RESEARCH RESOURCES IN GREATER LONDON. London: British Theatre Institute, 1974.

>    A central catalogue of the collections of theatre material in London.

81    Howard-Hill, T.H. BIBLIOGRAPHY OF BRITISH LITERARY BIBLIOGRA-PHIES. Oxford: Clarendon Press, 1969; SUPPLEMENT. Oxford: 1971.

>    Listing of enumerative and descriptive bibliographies appearing in books, portions of books, and periodicals published after 1890.

82    Hunter, Frederick J., ed. A GUIDE TO THE THEATRE AND DRAMA COLLECTIONS AT THE UNIVERSITY OF TEXAS. Austin: University of Texas, 1967.

>    Catalogues some of the materials in the theatre and drama collections at the University of Texas.

83    _____. DRAMA BIBLIOGRAPHY: A SHORT-TITLE GUIDE TO EXTEND-ED READING IN DRAMATIC ART FOR THE ENGLISH-SPEAKING AUDI-ENCE AND STUDENTS IN THEATRE. Boston: G.K. Hall, 1971.

>    Selected lists arranged by subject matter.

84    INDEX TO AMERICAN DOCTORAL DISSERTATIONS.

>    See No. 55.

85 AN INDEX TO BOOK REVIEWS IN THE HUMANITIES. Williamston,
Mich.: Phillip Thomson, 1961-- .

Lists only reviews in English.

86 INDEX TO LITTLE MAGAZINES. Denver, Colo.: Alan Swallow, 1943-- .

An author-subject index of a selected list of American little
magazines.

87 AN INDEX TO ONE-ACT PLAYS. Comp. Hannah Logasa and Winnifred
Ver Nooy. Boston: F.W. Faxon, 1924; SUPPLEMENT 1924-31. Boston:
1932; SECOND SUPPLEMENT 1932-40. Boston: 1941; THIRD SUPPLE-
MENT 1941-48. Boston: 1950; FOURTH SUPPLEMENT 1948-57. Boston:
1958.

Contains titles of one-act plays written in English (or translated
into English from a foreign language) published since 1900.
Author, number of characters, background, and location of
published play are given.

88 INDEX TO THESES ACCEPTED FOR HIGHER DEGREES IN THE UNIVER-
SITIES OF GREAT BRITAIN AND IRELAND. London: ASLIB, 1950-- .

89 International Association for the Study of Anglo-Irish Literature. "Bibliography Bulletin." IRISH UNIVERSITY REVIEW; A JOURNAL OF IRISH
STUDIES. Dublin: 1972-- .

Lists books and articles on Anglo-Irish literature.

90 International Federation of Library Associations (International Section for
Performing Arts Libraries and Museums). BIBLIOTHEQUES ET MUSEES
DES ARTS DU SPECTACLE DANS LE MONDE. Paris: Editions du Centre
National de la Recherche Scientifique, 1960; trans. PERFORMING ARTS
COLLECTIONS: AN INTERNATIONAL HANDBOOK. New York: The-
atre Arts, 1967.

A fully revised and expanded edition of Rosamond Gilder's
THEATRE COLLECTIONS IN LIBRARIES AND MUSEUMS (No.
69). Gives information about collections in the United States,
Canada, Mexico, South America, Europe, and Asia.

91 INTERNATIONAL INDEX TO PERIODICALS. New York: H.W. Wilson,
1907-65. Continued as SOCIAL SCIENCES AND HUMANITIES INDEX.
New York: H.W. Wilson, 1965-- .

Author and subject index to selected world periodicals.

92 Ireland, Norma Olin. AN INDEX TO SKITS AND STUNTS. Boston:
F.W. Faxon, 1958.

Indexes 148 collections by author, title, and subject.

93 _____ . INDEX TO FULL LENGTH PLAYS, 1944-1964. Boston: F.W. Faxon, 1965.

A selective coverage of full-length plays published in English.

94 Johnson, Albert E. "Doctoral Projects in Progress in Theatre Arts." EDU-CATIONAL THEATRE JOURNAL, 1956-- .

Listings furnishing the following information: the researcher's name, title, institution, supervisor, and expected date of completion.

95 _____ . BEST CHURCH PLAYS. London: Pioneer Press, 1968.

A bibliography of religious drama which supplies alphabetical listings, subject matter listings, and addresses of publishers, authors, and agents. Pertinent information is given for each play.

96 JOURNAL OF MODERN LITERATURE. Philadelphia: Temple University, 1970-- .

Contains an annual review number with a section on "Criticism of Drama."

97 Junge, Ewald. "World Drama on Records." THEATRE RESEARCH, 6, no. 1 (1964), 16-49.

A list of complete plays in their original language, published on long-playing records.

98 Kahn, A.M.C. THE BRITISH THEATRE: A SELECTED [BOOK] LIST. North-Western Polytechnic School of Librarianship Occasional Papers, no. 5. London: North-Western Polytechnic, 1955.

A select list compiled for a lecture on the "Literature of the Drama and the Theatre" at the Department of Librarianship.

99 _____ , ed. LIBRARY RESOURCES IN THE GREATER LONDON AREA. NO. 4: THEATRE COLLECTIONS; A SYMPOSIUM. London: Library Association. Reference and Special Libraries Section--South Eastern Group, 1953.

A directory of libraries and institutions, grouped under the headings of national, public, special, and private.

100 Keller, Dean H. INDEX TO PLAYS IN PERIODICALS. Metuchen, N.J.: Scarecrow Press, 1971; SUPPLEMENT. Metuchen, N.J.: 1973.

Author-title index.

101 Knower, Franklin H. "Graduate Theses in Theatre." EDUCATIONAL THEATRE JOURNAL, May 1951-May 1963.

Lists dissertations submitted to American universities, classified by subject matter.

102  Lauterbach, Edward S., and W. Eugene Davis. THE TRANSITIONAL AGE: BRITISH LITERATURE 1880-1920. Troy, N.Y.: Whitston Publishing Co., 1973.

   Lists primary books and selected secondary material.

103  Levitt, Paul M. "The Well-Made Problem Play: A Selective Bibliography." ENGLISH LITERATURE IN TRANSITION, 11, no. 4 (1968), 190-94.

   Includes articles and books.

104  LITERATURE AND PSYCHOLOGY. Floral Park, N.Y.: Fairleigh Dickinson University and William Patterson College of New Jersey, 1951-- .

   Includes an annual "Bibliography" issued as a supplement in the fourth issue.

105  LITERATURE, MUSIC, FINE ARTS: A REVIEW OF GERMAN-LANGUAGE RESEARCH CONTRIBUTIONS ON LITERATURE, MUSIC AND FINE ARTS. Tuebingen, Germany: Institute for Scientific Cooperation, 1968-- .

   Biannual review of selected books and articles.

106  Litto, Frederic M. AMERICAN DISSERTATIONS ON THE DRAMA AND THE THEATRE. Kent, Ohio: Kent State University Press, 1969.

   Contains author, key-word-in-context, and subject indexes.

107  Loewenberg, Alfred. THE THEATRE OF THE BRITISH ISLES EXCLUDING LONDON; A BIBLIOGRAPHY. London: Printed for The Society for Theatre Research, 1950.

   A regional bibliography of theatrical activity containing material arranged alphabetically under places.

108  Longaker, Mark, and Edwin C. Bolles. CONTEMPORARY ENGLISH LITERATURE. New York: Appleton-Century-Crofts, 1953.

   Lists primary books and short, selected secondary bibliography.

109  Lower, Henry Eastman, and George Heron Milne. THE DRAMATIC BOOKS AND PLAYS PUBLISHED DURING 1912-1916. Boston: Boston Book Co., 1913-17.

   Lists only works written in English. Issued as a supplement to F.W. Faxon's DRAMATIC INDEX (No. 64).

110  MacNamara, Brinsley, ed. ABBEY PLAYS 1899-1948. INCLUDING THE PRODUCTIONS OF THE IRISH LITERARY THEATRE. Dublin: At the Sign of the Three Candles, [1949].

Also includes a commentary by MacNamara and an index of playwrights.

111 McNamee, Lawrence F. DISSERTATIONS IN ENGLISH AND AMERICAN LITERATURE: THESES ACCEPTED BY AMERICAN, BRITISH AND GERMAN UNIVERSITIES, 1865-1964. New York and London: R.R. Bowker, 1968; SUPPLEMENT ONE. New York and London: 1969; SUPPLEMENT TWO. New York and London: 1974.

112 Mellown, Elgin. A DESCRIPTIVE CATALOGUE OF THE BIBLIOGRAPHIES OF 20TH CENTURY BRITISH WRITERS. Troy, N.Y.: Whitston Publishing Co., 1972.

Lists primary and secondary bibliographies and checklists of British writers whose work appeared after 1890.

113 Melnitz, William W., ed. THEATRE ARTS PUBLICATIONS IN THE UNITED STATES, 1947-1952; A FIVE YEAR BIBLIOGRAPHY. American Educational Theatre Association Monograph no. 1. New York: American Educational Theatre Association, 1959.

Oriented toward production, but a section on dramatists is included.

114 Mersand, Joseph. INDEX TO PLAYS, WITH SUGGESTIONS FOR TEACHING. New York and London: Scarecrow Press, 1966.

Indexes plays which are designed to be used in schools. Annotations include title, author, anthology in which the play may be found, date of publication, biographical information on the author, and study aids on the play.

115 Mikhail, E.H. A BIBLIOGRAPHY OF MODERN IRISH DRAMA 1899-1970. Intro. William A. Armstrong. London: Macmillan; Seattle: University of Washington Press, 1972.

Lists bibliographies, books, periodical articles, and unpublished material devoted to modern Irish drama in general.

116 _____. COMEDY AND TRAGEDY: A BIBLIOGRAPHY OF CRITICAL STUDIES. Troy, N.Y.: Whitston Publishing Co., 1972.

Lists books and periodical articles.

117 _____. DISSERTATIONS ON ANGLO-IRISH DRAMA: A BIBLIOGRAPHY OF STUDIES 1870-1970. London: Macmillan; Totowa, N.J.: Rowman and Littlefield, 1973.

Lists dissertations on Anglo-Irish drama in general and on individual dramatists.

118 Millett, Fred B. CONTEMPORARY BRITISH LITERATURE; A CRITICAL SURVEY AND 232 AUTHOR BIBLIOGRAPHIES. 3rd ed., enl. (based on the revision by John M. Manly and Edith Rickert). New York: Harcourt, Brace, 1935.

> Includes primary books and a short, selected secondary bibliography of books and periodicals.

119 MLA BIBLIOGRAPHY. New York: Modern Language Association of America, 1919-- .

> Basic reference lists of material in books and periodicals. Since 1969 it has MLA INTERNATIONAL BIBLIOGRAPHY in several parts. British drama is included in volume 1.

120 MODERN DRAMA.

> See Nos. 32-33, 74-75, 132, and 162-65.

121 MODERN DRAMA, 1900-1938: A SELECT LIST OF PLAYS PUBLISHED SINCE 1900, AND OF WORKS ON DRAMATIC THEORY AND OTHER RELATED SUBJECTS. London: Library Association, 1939; SUPPLEMENT, 1939-1945. London: 1946.

> Listing of selected plays from the period with certain works of theory and criticism.

122 Mulliken, Clara A. "Reading List on Modern Dramatists; D'Annunzio, Hauptmann, Ibsen, Maeterlinck, Phillips, Rostand, Shaw and Sudermann." BULLETIN OF BIBLIOGRAPHY, 5 (July 1907), 32-37; 5 (October 1907), 49-53; 5 (January 1908), 69.

> Annotated listing of primary and secondary sources.

123 NEW CAMBRIDGE BIBLIOGRAPHY OF ENGLISH LITERATURE, THE

> See No. 192.

124 New York Public Library. CATALOG OF THE THEATRE AND DRAMA COLLECTIONS. Boston: G.K. Hall, 1967.

> Entries are made under author, subject, title, and other secondary headings.

125 New York Public Library. Reference Department. THEATRE SUBJECT HEADINGS. 2nd ed., enl. Boston: G.K. Hall, 1966.

> The subject headings are intended for use with No. 124.

126 THE NEW YORK TIMES INDEX. New York: New York Times Co., 1913-- .

Arranged under subject headings.

127  Nicoll, Allardyce. WHAT TO READ ON ENGLISH DRAMA. Leeds:
Public Libraries, 1930.

Introductory pamphlet containing selective annotated bibliography.

128  _____. "Handlist of Plays, 1900-1930." ENGLISH DRAMA, 1900-1930:
THE BEGINNINGS OF THE MODERN PERIOD. Cambridge: At the University Press, 1973. Pp. 451-1053.

129  _____. "English Drama 1900-1945." ENGLISH DRAMA (EXCLUDING
SHAKESPEARE); SELECT BIBLIOGRAPHICAL GUIDES. Ed. Stanley Wells.
London: Oxford University Press, 1975. Pp. 268-89.

Provides a critical guide to the period as well as a list giving
bibliographical information about the writings mentioned in the
text.

130  NINETEENTH CENTURY READERS' GUIDE TO PERIODICAL LITERATURE
1890-1899. WITH SUPPLEMENTARY INDEXING 1900-1922. Ed. Helen
Grant Cushing and Adah V. Morris. 2 vols. New York: H.W. Wilson,
1944.

Arranged under subject headings.

131  Norton, Clara. MODERN DRAMA AND OPERA; A READING LIST. Boston: Boston Book Co., 1911.

Selective.

132  Norton, Elizabeth Towne, and Robert G. Shedd. "Modern Drama: A
Selective Bibliography of Works Published in English in 1959." MODERN
DRAMA, 3 (September 1960), 143-61.

Lists books and articles. See also Nos. 32-33, 74-75, and
162-65.

133  O'Donoghue, D.J. THE POETS OF IRELAND; A BIOGRAPHICAL AND
BIBLIOGRAPHICAL DICTIONARY. Dublin: Hodges, Figgis; London: Oxford University Press, 1912.

"I confined myself to the Irish men and women who used the
English language."

134  O'Hegarty, P[atrick]. S[arsfield]. "Bibliographical Notes: The Abbey
Theatre (Wolfhound) Series of Plays." DUBLIN MAGAZINE, 22 (April-
June 1947), 41-42.

Sets down some points in connection with the series.

135 O'Neill, James J. A BIBLIOGRAPHICAL ACCOUNT OF IRISH THEATRI-
CAL LITERATURE. Bibliographical Society of Ireland Publications, vol. I,
no. 6. Dublin: John Falconer, 1920.

Contains "General Theatrical History, Players, and Theatrical
Periodicals."

136 Ottemiller, John H. OTTEMILLER'S INDEX TO PLAYS IN COLLECTIONS;
AN AUTHOR AND TITLE INDEX TO PLAYS APPEARING IN COLLECTIONS
PUBLISHED BETWEEN 1900 AND MID-1970. By John M. Connor and
Billie M. Connor. Metuchen, N.J.: Scarecrow Press, 1971.

The fifth edition of an index to plays appearing in 1,280 published collections. Locates more than 9,000 copies of 3,500
different plays.

137 Palmer, Helen H., and Anne Jane Dyson. EUROPEAN DRAMA CRITICISM.
Hamden, Conn.: Shoe String Press, 1968; SUPPLEMENT I. Hamden,
Conn.: 1970; SUPPLEMENT II. Hamden, Conn.: 1974.

Lists studies of plays in books and periodicals.

138 Patterson, Charlotte A., comp. PLAYS IN PERIODICALS: AN INDEX
TO ENGLISH LANGUAGE SCRIPTS IN TWENTIETH CENTURY JOURNALS.
Boston: G.K. Hall, 1970.

Gives access to "over four thousand plays printed in ninety-
seven English language periodicals published from 1900 thru
1968."

139 PLAY INDEX, 1949-1952. Ed. Dorothy Herbert West and Dorothy Mar-
garet Peake. New York: H.W. Wilson, 1953; PLAY INDEX, 1953-1960.
Ed. Estelle A. Fidell and Dorothy Margaret Peake. New York, 1963;
PLAY INDEX, 1961-1967. Ed. Estelle A. Fidell. New York, 1968.

Indexes plays in volumes.

140 Pogson, Rex. "Bibliography." THEATRE BETWEEN WARS (1919-1939).
Drama Study Books no. 1. Clevedon, Somerset: Triangle Press, 1947.
Pp. 48-50.

Selective.

141 Pohle, Helen Loudora. "The New Drama." BULLETIN OF BIBLIOGRA-
PHY 15 (September-December 1934), 94-95; 15 (January-April 1935),
114-16.

Annotated checklist of critical works.

142 Popkin, Henry. "The Drama." CONTEMPORARY LITERARY SCHOLAR-
SHIP; A CRITICAL REVIEW. Ed. Lewis Leary. New York: Appleton-

Century-Crofts, 1958. Pp. 289-337.

Annotated bibliographical survey.

143 Pownall, David E. ARTICLES ON TWENTIETH CENTURY LITERATURE: AN ANNOTATED BIBLIOGRAPHY 1954-1970. Millwood, N.Y.: Kraus-Thomson, 1973.

"An expanded cumulation of 'Current Bibliography' in the journal TWENTIETH CENTURY LITERATURE, Volume One to Volume Sixteen, 1955 to 1970."

144 Raines, Lester. "Five Years of One-Act Plays 1925-1929." BULLETIN OF BIBLIOGRAPHY, 13 (September-December 1929), 200-201; 14 (September-December 1930), 50-52; 14 (January-April 1931), 78-82.

Paperbound plays are not included unless the volume contains a collection of plays.

145 READERS' GUIDE TO PERIODICAL LITERATURE. New York: H.W. Wilson, 1900-- .

Author and subject indexes to selected world periodicals.

146 RESEARCH IN PROGRESS IN ENGLISH AND HISTORICAL STUDIES IN THE UNIVERSITIES OF THE BRITISH ISLES. London: St. James Press, 1971-- .

Starting 1975, also includes research in progress in Commonwealth universities.

147 REVUE D'HISTOIRE DU THEATRE. Paris: Societe d'Histoire du Theatre, 1948-- .

Includes a "Bibliographie," indexed by subject matter.

148 Roberts, Peter. THEATRE IN BRITAIN. London: Pitman, 1973.

Includes a listing of major theatrical collections.

149 Royal Irish Academy. Committee for the Study of Anglo-Irish Language and Literature. HANDLIST OF WORK IN PROGRESS. Dublin: 1969-- .

Arranged under subject headings and individual writers.

150 _____. IRISH AND ANGLO-IRISH PERIODICALS. Dublin: 1970.

Lists and gives the locations in Ireland of all periodicals likely to be of interest to scholars of Anglo-Irish literature.

151 _____. HANDLIST OF THESES COMPLETED BUT NOT PUBLISHED.

Dublin: 1973-- .

Lists dissertations on Irish writers.

152 Ryan, Pat M., Jr. "'England' and 'Ireland.'" HISTORY OF THE MOD-
ERN THEATRE: A SELECTIVE BIBLIOGRAPHY. Tuscon: University of
Arizona, Department of Drama, 1960. Pp. 19-23.

A reading list.

153 Saddlemyer, Ann. "The Irish School." ENGLISH DRAMA (EXCLUDING
SHAKESPEARE); SELECT BIBLIOGRAPHICAL GUIDES. Ed. Stanley Wells.
London: Oxford University Press, 1975. Pp. 248-67.

Provides a critical guide as well as a list giving bibliographical
information about the writings mentioned in the text.

154 Salem, James M. A GUIDE TO CRITICAL REVIEW. Part III: BRITISH
AND CONTINENTAL DRAMA FROM IBSEN TO PINTER. Metuchen,
N.J.: Scarecrow Press, 1968.

Lists reviews of performances and criticism in periodicals.

155 _____. DRURY'S GUIDE TO BEST PLAYS.

See No. 57.

156 Samples, Gordon. THE DRAMA SCHOLARS' INDEX TO PLAYS AND
FILMSCRIPTS IN SELECTED ANTHOLOGIES, SERIES AND PERIODICALS.
Metuchen, N.J.: Scarecrow Press, 1974.

Lists plays and filmscripts in their original languages or in
translations.

157 Santaniello, A.E. "British Theatre: Nineteenth and Twentieth Century
Drama." THEATRE BOOKS IN PRINT; AN ANNOTATED GUIDE TO THE
LITERATURE OF THE THEATRE, THE TECHNICAL ARTS OF THE THEATRE,
MOTION PICTURES, TELEVISION AND RADIO. 2nd ed. New York:
Drama Book Shop, 1966. Pp. 71-93.

158 Saul, George Brandon. "An Introductory Bibliography in Anglo-Irish Literature." NEW YORK PUBLIC LIBRARY BULLETIN, 58 (September 1954),
429-35.

A "purely selective bibliography"; includes books and periodical
articles.

159 Schoolcraft, Ralph Newman. PERFORMING ARTS BOOKS IN PRINT:
AN ANNOTATED BIBLIOGRAPHY. New York: Drama Book Specialists,
1973.

Revised edition of THEATRE BOOKS IN PRINT, originally pub-

lished in 1963 and revised in 1966. Includes sections on
"Great Britain" and "Ireland."

160 Schwartz, Jacob. 1100 OBSCURE POINTS: THE BIBLIOGRAPHIES OF
25 ENGLISH AND 21 AMERICAN AUTHORS. Bristol, Eng.: Chatford
House Press, 1931; rpt. Bristol: 1969.

Includes bibliographies of works by T.S. Eliot, John Galsworthy,
and W.B. Yeats.

161 Sharp, Harold S., and Marjorie Z. Sharp, comps. INDEX TO CHARAC-
TERS IN THE PERFORMING ARTS; AN ALPHABETICAL LISTING OF 30,000
CHARACTERS. Part I: NON-MUSICAL PLAYS. 2 vols. Metuchen,
N.J.: Scarecrow Press, 1966.

Identifies characters with the plays in which they appear, the
authors of the plays, and the years in which the plays were
written, produced, or published.

162- Shedd, Robert G. "Modern Drama: A Selective Bibliography of Works
65 Published in English in 1960 and 1961." MODERN DRAMA, September
1962, pp. 223-44; "...in 1962," September 1963, pp. 204-17; "...in
1963-64," September 1965, pp. 204-26; "...in 1965," September 1966,
pp. 210-26.

Lists books and articles. See also Nos. 32-33, 74-75, and
132.

166 Shipley, Joseph T. GUIDE TO GREAT PLAYS. Washington, D.C.:
Public Affairs Press, 1956.

Alphabetical listing of 660 masterpieces of world drama.

167 Simons, Eric N. "The Library as a Tool of the Theatre." ASLIB PRO-
CEEDINGS (London), I (November 1949), 271-78.

On sources of information regarding the theatre.

168 Sobel, Bernard, ed. THE NEW THEATRE HANDBOOK AND DIGEST OF
PLAYS. New York: Crown Publishers, 1959.

Includes bibliographies of works on plays and playwrights.

169 SOCIAL SCIENCES AND HUMANITIES INDEX.

See No. 91.

170 Stratman, Carl J. "Unpublished Dissertations in the History and Theory
of Tragedy, 1889-1957." BULLETIN OF BIBLIOGRAPHY, 22 (September-
December 1958), 161-64; 22 (September-December 1959), 237-40; 23
(January-April 1960), 15-20; 23 (January-April 1962), 162-65, 187-92.

Lists entries which treat any phase of the history or theory of tragedy, either in general or in the work of a particular playwright or critic.

171 _____. "Preparing a Bibliography of British Dramatic Periodicals, 1720-1960." BULLETIN OF THE NEW YORK PUBLIC LIBRARY, 66 (1962), 405-8.

From the introduction to the author's A BIBLIOGRAPHY OF BRITISH DRAMATICAL PERIODICALS, 1720-1960 (No. 172).

172 _____, ed. A BIBLIOGRAPHY OF BRITISH DRAMATIC PERIODICALS, 1720-1960. New York: New York Public Library, 1962. Rev. ed. BRITAIN'S THEATRICAL PERIODICALS 1720-1967; A BIBLIOGRAPHY. New York: 1972.

In the original edition, 670 titles are arranged chronologically with notes concerning their locations in libraries in both the United States and Great Britain. The reprint edition represents a major revision, indexing 1,235 English periodicals and supplying descriptive entries.

173 _____, ed. DRAMATIC PLAY LISTS, 1591-1963. New York: New York Public Library, 1966.

Enumerates and evaluates dramatic bibliographies concerned with actual play titles.

174 SUBJECT INDEX TO PERIODICALS, 1915-1961. London: Library Association, 1915-61. Continued as BRITISH HUMANITIES INDEX. London: 1962-- .

Subject and author indexes.

175 Temple, Ruth Z., and Martin Tucker, eds. TWENTIETH CENTURY BRITISH LITERATURE; A REFERENCE GUIDE AND BIBLIOGRAPHY. New York: Frederick Ungar, 1968.

Lists primary books and critical or bibliographical studies for each author.

176 THEATRE QUARTERLY.

See No. 183.

177 THEATREFACTS; INTERNATIONAL THEATRE REFERENCE. London: TQ Publications, 1974-- .

Incorporates and expands the reference material formerly included in THEATRE QUARTERLY (see No. 183).

178   Thomson, Ruth G.  INDEX TO FULL-LENGTH PLAYS:  1895-1925; 1926-1944.  Westwood, Mass.:  F.W. Faxon, 1946, 1956.

     Plays in English are listed with cast requirements, type of play, and set and costume requirements.

179   THE TIMES INDEX.  London, 1790-- .

     Subject index to the London TIMES.

180   THE TIMES LITERARY SUPPLEMENT INDEX.  London, 1962-- .

     Subject index to the London TIMES LITERARY SUPPLEMENT.

181   Trewin, J.C.  "Books on the Theatre 1965-1969."  BRITISH BOOK NEWS, September 1970, pp. 661-65; October 1970, pp. 743-47.

     Annotated selected list.

182   _____, ed.  THE YEAR'S WORK IN THEATRE 1948-1951.  3 vols. London:  Longmans, Green, for the British Council, 1949-51.

183   Trussler, Simon.  "Current Bibliography."  THEATRE QUARTERLY (London), 1971-73.

     A cumulative record of English language books on theatre and related performing arts.  See the continuation of this work, No. 177.

184   TULANE DRAMA REVIEW, 3 (1959) - 11 (1967).

     Includes "Books and Theatre," selected lists of books on drama and the theatre arranged by general subject.  See also Nos. 78-79.

185   TWENTIETH CENTURY LITERATURE.  Los Angeles:  1955-- .

     Contains a quarterly annotated "Current Bibliography" of critical literature in periodicals listed alphabetically by author of article.

186   Ullrich, Kurt, comp.  WHO WROTE ABOUT WHOM; A BIBLIOGRAPHY OF BOOKS ON CONTEMPORARY BRITISH AUTHORS.  Berlin:  Arthur Collignon, 1932.

     A bibliography of the books that deal with British authors published from 1920-31.

187   Underwood, Pierson.  "The Little Theatre."  BOOKMAN (New York), 55 (June 1922), 403-9.

     Annotated bibliography, with a reading list.

188  Veinstein, Andre, ed. PERFORMING ARTS LIBRARIES AND MUSEUMS
OF THE WORLD. 2nd ed., rev. and enl. by Cecil Giteau. Paris:
Editions du Centre National de la Recherche Scientifique, 1967.

Originally published in 1960, this bilingual second edition is
a census of all the known performing arts collections, libraries,
and museums throughout the world.

189  Vowles, Richard B. "Psychology and Drama: A Selected Checklist."
WISCONSIN STUDIES IN CONTEMPORARY LITERATURE, 3, no. 1 (1962),
35-48.

Attempts to list all relevant research and speculation since
1920.

190  Welker, David, ed. "EDUCATIONAL THEATRE JOURNAL": A TEN-
YEAR INDEX: 1949-1958. East Lansing: Michigan State University,
n.d.

Classified index of material published in the first ten volumes
of the EDUCATIONAL THEATRE JOURNAL.

191  West, Dorothy Herbert, and Dorothy Margaret Peake, comps. PLAY IN-
DEX 1949-1952.

See No. 139.

192  Willison, I.R., ed. "Drama." THE NEW CAMBRIDGE BIBLIOGRAPHY
OF ENGLISH LITERATURE. Vol. 4: 1900-1950. Cambridge: At the
University Press, 1972. Cols. 821-80.

For most authors, replaces THE CAMBRIDGE BIBLIOGRAPHY
OF ENGLISH LITERATURE (No. 9).

193  WORLD PREMIERES. Paris: International Theatre Institute, 1949-64.

Lists details of first productions of plays. Incorporated in
WORLD THEATRE (See No. 221).

194  YEAR'S WORK IN ENGLISH STUDIES. London: English Association,
1919-- .

Annotated selective bibliography.

# Chapter 2

# REFERENCE WORKS

195   Adams, W.D. A DICTIONARY OF THE DRAMA; A GUIDE TO THE
PLAYS, PLAYWRIGHTS, PLAYERS, AND PLAYHOUSES OF THE UNITED
KINGDOM AND AMERICA, FROM THE EARLIEST TIMES TO THE PRES-
ENT. Vol. 1: A–G. London: Chatto & Windus; Philadelphia: J.B.
Lippincott, 1904; rpt. New York: Franklin, 1964.

     As comprehensive as the subtitle suggests, but unfortunately
     never continued beyond the first volume.

196   Anderson, Michael, et al. CROWELL'S HANDBOOK OF CONTEMPOR-
ARY DRAMA. New York: Thomas Y. Crowell, 1971; London: Pitman,
1972.

     An alphabetically arranged guide to written drama since World
     War II, with some critical appraisal of plays and playwrights
     as well as factual information.

197   Barnet, Sylvan; Morton Berman; and William Burto. A DICTIONARY OF
LITERARY, DRAMATIC, AND CINEMATIC TERMS. Boston: Little, Brown,
1971.

198   THE BEST PLAYS OF 1919–47. Ed. Burns Mantle. 27 vols. New York:
Dodd, Mead, 1920–47.

     Includes an annual survey of "The London Scene."

199   THE BEST PLAYS OF 1947–50. Ed. John Chapman. 3 vols. New York:
Dodd, Mead, 1947–50.

     Includes an annual survey of "The London Scene."

200   Bowman, Walter Parker, and Robert Hamilton Ball. THEATRE LANGUAGE:
A DICTIONARY OF TERMS IN ENGLISH OF THE DRAMA AND STAGE
FROM MEDIEVAL TO MODERN TIMES. New York: Theatre Arts, 1961.

     Technical and standard nontechnical terms, jargon, cant, and
     slang are defined and cross-referenced.

201 Buchanan-Brown, John, ed. CASSELL'S ENCYCLOPAEDIA OF WORLD LITERATURE. London: Cassell; West Caldwell, N.J.: Morrow, 1973.

202 Burton, E.J. "'Things Old and New' and 'Contemporary Theatre.'" THE STUDENT'S GUIDE TO BRITISH THEATRE AND DRAMA. London: Herbert Jenkins, 1963. Pp. 147-76.

Deals "not only with the literary history of British drama but also the growth of British theatre."

203 Cartmell, Van H., ed. "British Plays." PLOT OUTLINES OF 100 FAMOUS PLAYS. Garden City, N.Y.: Doubleday, 1962. Pp. 83-241.

204 Dooley, Roger B. REVIEW NOTES AND STUDY GUIDE TO MODERN BRITISH AND IRISH DRAMA. New York: Monarch Press, 1964.

Introductory.

205 Downs, Harold, ed. THEATRE AND STAGE; A MODERN GUIDE TO THE PERFORMANCE OF ALL CLASSES OF AMATEUR DRAMATIC, OPERATIC, AND THEATRICAL WORK. 2 vols. London: Pitman, 1934.

206 Drury, Francis K.W. DRURY'S GUIDE TO BEST PLAYS. By James M. Salem. 2nd ed. Metuchen, N.J.: Scarecrow Press, 1969.

Includes synopses of plays and guides for production.

207 ENCICLOPEDIA DELLO SPETTACOLO. 10 vols. and appendix. Rome: Casa Editrice le Maschere, 1954-68.

By far the most comprehensive work on all aspects of the stage, cinema, radio, and all related arts. Includes bibliographies and biographies. Coverage is universal.

208 ENCYCLOPEDIA OF IRELAND. Dublin: Allen Figgis, 1968.

Includes material on Irish drama.

209 Fay, W[illiam]. G[eorge]., comp. A SHORT GLOSSARY OF THEATRICAL TERMS. London and New York: Samuel French, 1930.

Reprinted from DRAMA (London).

210 Fleischmann, Wolfgang Bernard, ed. ENCYCLOPEDIA OF WORLD LITERATURE IN THE 20TH CENTURY. 3 vols. New York: Frederick Ungar, 1969.

211 Gassner, John, and Edward Quinn, eds. THE READER'S ENCYCLOPEDIA OF WORLD DRAMA. New York: Thomas Y. Crowell, 1969.

Gives information on plays and playwrights from all countries
and has an appendix containing "basic documents in dramatic
theory."

212   Granville, Wilfred, comp.   A DICTIONARY OF THEATRICAL TERMS.
London: Andre Deutsch, 1952; American ed. THEATRE DICTIONARY.
New York: Oxford University Press, 1952.

The compiler's aim was "to record the technical, colloquial
and slang terms ... before many phrases used by 'old pros'
died with their passing."

213   GREEN ROOM BOOK: OR WHO'S WHO ON THE STAGE--AN ANNUAL
BIBLIOGRAPHICAL RECORD OF THE DRAMATIC, MUSICAL AND VARIETY
WORLD, 1906-9. London: Pitman, 1906-9. Continued as WHO'S WHO
IN THE THEATRE: A BIOGRAPHICAL RECORD OF THE CONTEMPORARY
STAGE. London: 1912-- .

As well as biographies of all well-known living personalities
in the theatre, includes genealogical tables, obituaries, dates
of notable productions, etc.

214   Grigson, Geoffrey, ed.   THE CONCISE ENCYCLOPEDIA OF MODERN
WORLD LITERATURE.   2nd ed.   New York: Hawthorn Books, 1971.

Contains mini-essays on individual writers.

215   Harmon, Maurice.   MODERN IRISH LITERATURE 1800-1967; A READER'S
GUIDE. Dublin: Dolmen Press, 1967.

"The main intention was to open up the whole of modern Irish
literature for study and exploration."

216   Hartnoll, Phyllis, ed.   THE OXFORD COMPANION TO THE THEATRE.
3rd ed. London: Oxford University Press, 1967.

Particular topics tend to be discussed under broad headings.

217   Harvey, Paul.   OXFORD COMPANION TO ENGLISH LITERATURE.   4th
ed., rev. by Dorothy Eagle. London and New York: Oxford University
Press, 1967.

218   Holden, Michael.   THE STAGE GUIDE; TECHNICAL INFORMATION ON
BRITISH THEATRES. London: Carson and Comerford, 1971.

A new and updated edition of the GUIDE published by THE
STAGE newspaper in 1912 and revised in 1946.

219   Holloway, John.   "The 20th Century: Drama." ENCYCLOPEDIA BRITAN-
NICA. London: Encyclopaedia Britannica, 1970. 8, 594-95.

220  Howard, Diana. LONDON THEATRES AND MUSIC HALLS, 1850-1950. London: Library Association, 1970.

Directory.

221  International Theatre Institute. WORLD PREMIERES. New York: UNESCO, 1949-64.

A list, arranged by country, of first productions of new plays only, giving details of title, author, and cast. Since 1965, this list has been incorporated in the institute's periodical WORLD THEATRE.

222  Kienzle, Siegfried. MODERN WORLD THEATER: A GUIDE TO PRODUCTIONS IN EUROPE AND THE UNITED STATES SINCE 1945. Trans. Alexander and Elizabeth Henderson. New York: Frederick Ungar, 1970.

Some 580 plays are discussed.

223  Kunitz, Stanley J., and Howard Haycraft, eds. TWENTIETH CENTURY AUTHORS: A BIOGRAPHICAL DICTIONARY OF MODERN LITERATURE. New York: H.W. Wilson, 1942; FIRST SUPPLEMENT. New York: 1955.

224  Leyson, Peter. LONDON THEATRES: A SHORT HISTORY AND GUIDE. London: Apollo Publications, 1971.

A handy guide to the main theatres, with brief historical notes.

225  Lounsbury, Warren C. THEATRE BACKSTAGE FROM A TO Z. Seattle and London: University of Washington Press, 1967.

A dictionary of technical terms and methods.

226  MCGRAW-HILL ENCYCLOPEDIA OF WORLD DRAMA. 4 vols. New York: McGraw-Hill, 1972.

227  Mander, Raymond, and Joe Mitchenson. THE THEATRES OF LONDON. London: Rupert Hart-Davis, 1961; New York: Hill & Wang, 1962; rev. and enl. ed. London: New English Library, 1975.

A chronicle of the theatres of London.

228  Matlaw, Myron. MODERN WORLD DRAMA; AN ENCYCLOPEDIA. New York: E.P. Dutton; London: Secker & Warburg, 1972.

229  May, Robin. A COMPANION TO THE THEATRE; THE ANGLO-AMERICAN STAGE FROM 1920. London: Lutterworth Press, 1973.

"While dealing extensively with all the major theatrical genres, the author highlights certain plays and productions that are milestones in the story of the English-speaking theatre."

230  Melchinger, Siegfried. DRAMA ZWISCHEN SHAW UND BRECHT: EIN
LEITFADEN DURCH DAS ZEITGENOSSISCHE SCHAUSPIEL. 2 vols. Bre-
men, Germany: Schunemann, 1957.

A dictionary of both topics and dramatists.

231  _____. THE CONCISE ENCYCLOPEDIA OF MODERN DRAMA. Trans.
George Wellwarth. New York: Horizon Press, 1964; London: Vision,
1966.

The major part of the book is a biographical dictionary of some
800 playwrights. Analyses of plays, discussions of main trends,
extensive glossary, important documents by leading dramatists,
and a chronology of opening nights are provided.

232  Mueller, William R. "English Literature: Modern Drama." MERIT STU-
DENTS ENCYCLOPEDIA. New York: Crowell-Collier Educational Corp.,
1971. Pp. 397-98.

233  Nathan, George Jean. ENCYCLOPAEDIA OF THE THEATRE. New York:
Alfred A. Knopf, 1940; rpt. Rutherford, N.J.: Fairleigh Dickinson University Press, 1970.

"Nathan expressed his knowledge and perceptions of the theatre
in language that is filled with literary allusions and humor."

234  NEW YORK THEATRE CRITICS' REVIEW. New York: Critics' Theatre
Review, 1940-- .

A periodical publication of the reviews of Broadway theatres
reprinted from the seven major New York newspapers. Well
indexed.

235  Noble, Peter. BRITISH THEATRE. Foreword Laurence Olivier. London:
British Yearbooks, 1946.

Surveys the British theatre during the period 1939-46.

236  O'Mahony, Mathew. GUIDE TO ANGLO-IRISH PLAYS. Dublin: Progress House, 1960.

"A survey of Anglo-Irish plays in suitable form for quick reference." An up-to-date elaboration of the author's PLAY GUIDE
FOR IRISH AMATEURS, published in 1947.

237  Pride, Leo B., ed. INTERNATIONAL THEATRE DIRECTORY: A WORLD
DIRECTORY OF THE THEATRE AND PERFORMING ARTS. New York:
Simon & Schuster, 1973.

A list of theatres divided by country and subdivided by city and town.

238 Queant, G. ENCYCLOPEDIE DU THEATRE CONTEMPORAIN, 1850-1950. 2 vols. Paris: Publications de France, 1957-59.

This is not a true encyclopedia, but it contains a great deal of visual material in brilliant color and monochrome.

239 Rae, Kenneth, and Richard Southern, eds. INTERNATIONAL VOCABULARY OF TECHNICAL THEATRE TERMS IN EIGHT LANGUAGES. Brussels: Elsevier; New York: Reinhardt, 1959; Theatre Arts, 1960.

Compiled for the International Theatre Institute. The eight languages are American, Dutch, English, French, German, Italian, Spanish, and Swedish.

240 Roberts, Peter. THEATRE IN BRITAIN; A PLAYGOER'S GUIDE. London: Pitman, 1973.

Contains reference sections "concerned with the practicalities of visiting the theatre and its offshoots."

241 Runes, Dagobert D., and Harry G. Schrikel, eds. ENCYCLOPEDIA OF THE ARTS. New York: Philosophical Library, 1946; rpt. London: P. Owen, 1965.

"A comprehensive survey of all the arts of all times and all places."

242 Salem, James M. DRURY'S GUIDE TO BEST PLAYS.

See No. 57.

243 Schorer, Mark. "Modern Period: Drama." THE ENCYCLOPEDIA AMERICANA. International ed. New York: Americana Corporation, 1972. 10, pp. 452-53.

244 Shank, Theodore J., ed. A DIGEST OF 500 PLAYS: PLOT OUTLINES AND PRODUCTION NOTES. New York: Collier Books; London: Collier-Macmillan, 1966.

245 Sherman, Robert Lowery. ACTORS AND AUTHORS; WITH COMPOSERS AND MANAGERS WHO HELPED TO MAKE THEM FAMOUS: A CHRONOLOGICAL RECORD AND BRIEF BIOGRAPHY OF THEATRICAL CELEBRITIES FROM 1750 TO 1950. Chicago: Privately printed, 1951.

246 Shipley, Joseph T. GUIDE TO GREAT PLAYS. Washington, D.C.: Public Affairs Press, 1956.

Gives a digest of each play in addition to information on famous productions, casts, and reviews.

247 Sobel, Bernard, ed. THE NEW THEATRE HANDBOOK AND DIGEST OF PLAYS. New York: Crown Publishers, 1959.

A revision of the 1940 edition, this volume contains synopses of plays, glossaries of theatre terms, biographies, information on productions, and bibliographies.

248 Spencer, Terence John Bew. "The 20th Century: Drama." CHAMBERS'S ENCYCLOPAEDIA. New rev. ed. Oxford: Pergamon Press, 1966. V, 317.

249 Sprinchorn, Evert, ed. 20TH-CENTURY PLAYS IN SYNOPSIS. New York: Thomas Y. Crowell, 1965.

Act-by-act synopses of 133 representative modern plays, and biographical information about the playwrights.

250 THE STAGE AND TELEVISION TODAY STAGE GUIDE. London: Carson and Comerford, 1912-- .

251 THE STAGE AND TELEVISION TODAY YEAR BOOK. London: Carson and Comerford, 1908-- .

Gives overall picture of the previous year in a few short articles and lists names of managements, professional organizations, etc.

252 Stallman, R.W. "The 1900's: Drama Reborn." THE WORLD BOOK ENCYCLOPEDIA. Chicago: Field Enterprises Educational Corp., 1971. 6, 254d.

253 Taylor, John Russell. THE PENGUIN DICTIONARY OF THE THEATRE. Harmondsworth: Penguin Books, 1966; New York: Barnes & Noble, 1967.

Despite its title, this is really a miniature encyclopedia.

254 THE THAMES AND HUDSON ENCYCLOPAEDIA OF THE ARTS. London: Thames and Hudson, 1966.

Biographies, definitions of technical terms, and brief accounts of movements but no general articles.

255 THEATRE WORLD ANNUAL. London: Barrie and Rockliff, 1949-63; London: Iliffe, 1964-- .

Indexes the plays and players featured in its largely pictorial survey of the major London productions.

256 Ward, A[lfred]. C. LONGMAN COMPANION TO TWENTIETH CENTURY LITERATURE. 2nd ed. London: Longman, 1975.

> A "compact handbook."

257 WHO'S WHO IN THE THEATRE: A BIOGRAPHICAL RECORD OF THE CONTEMPORARY STAGE.

> See No. 213.

258 WORLD THEATRE.

> See No. 221.

# Chapter 3
# CRITICAL BOOKS AND ESSAYS

259 "The Abbey Theatre." THE IRELAND OF TODAY. REPRINTED, WITH
SOME ADDITIONS, FROM THE LONDON TIMES. London: John Murray, 1913; Boston: Small, Maynard, 1915. Pp. 131-37.

Survey.

260 Abdur Rub Choudhury, Khan Sahib. MODERN ENGLISH DRAMA; A
SURVEY FROM 1890 TO THE PRESENT TIME. Dacca, Bengal: A Latif
Choudhury, 1936.

Considers "the dramatic outburst in English Literature towards
the end of the nineteenth century and follows its development
up to recent times."

261 Adcock, A. St. John. GODS OF MODERN GRUB STREET; IMPRESSIONS
OF CONTEMPORARY AUTHORS. London: Low; New York: Stokes,
1923.

Includes impressions of John Drinkwater, John Galsworthy,
John Masefield, George Russell, Somerset Maugham, and A.
A. Milne.

262 _____. THE GLORY THAT WAS GRUB STREET; IMPRESSIONS OF CON-
TEMPORARY AUTHORS. London: Low, 1928.

Includes impressions of Bernard Shaw, Clemence Dane, and
St. John Ervine.

263 Agate, James. BUZZ, BUZZ! ESSAYS OF THE THEATRE. London: Collins, [1918]; rpt. New York: Benjamin Blom, 1969.

Criticisms reprinted in slightly different form from THE MAN-
CHESTER GUARDIAN and THE MANCHESTER PLAYGOER.

264 _____. ALARUMS AND EXCURSIONS. London: Grant Richards; New
York: George H. Doran, 1922.

Articles, including criticism of Bernard Shaw and John Drinkwater.

265 _____. AT HALF-PAST EIGHT; ESSAYS OF THE THEATRE 1921-1922.
London: Jonathan Cape, 1923; rpt. New York: Benjamin Blom, 1969.

Includes notices from THE SATURDAY REVIEW of plays by St.
John Ervine, James Barrie, John Galsworthy, Bernard Shaw,
John Drinkwater, and Somerset Maugham.

266 _____. THE CONTEMPORARY THEATRE, 1923. London: Leonard Parsons, 1924; rpt. New York: Benjamin Blom, 1969.

A collection of articles from the SATURDAY REVIEW and the
SUNDAY TIMES on plays by John Drinkwater, St. John Hankin, Noel Coward, John Masefield, and J.E. Flecker.

267 _____. THE CONTEMPORARY THEATRE, 1924. Intro. Noel Coward.
London: Leonard Parsons, 1925; rpt. New York: Benjamin Blom, 1969.

A collection of articles from the SUNDAY TIMES on plays by
Bernard Shaw, C.K. Munro, Gordon Bottomley, John Galsworthy, Allan Monkhouse, Noel Coward, and Frederick Lonsdale.

268 _____. THE CONTEMPORARY THEATRE, 1925. Intro. C.E. Montague.
London: Leonard Parsons, 1926; rpt. New York: Benjamin Blom, 1969.

A collection of articles from the SUNDAY TIMES on plays by
Sean O'Casey, Lennox Robinson, Noel Coward, A.A. Milne,
Frederick Lonsdale, Bernard Shaw, H. Granville-Barker, and
John Galsworthy.

269 _____. A SHORT VIEW OF THE ENGLISH STAGE, 1900-1926. London:
Herbert Jenkins, 1926; rpt. New York: Benjamin Blom; Freeport, N.Y.:
Books for Libraries Press, 1969.

Includes studies of plays by Bernard Shaw, John Galsworthy,
John Drinkwater, H. Grandville-Barker, St. John Hankin,
Stephen Phillips, and John Masefield.

270 _____. THE CONTEMPORARY THEATRE, 1926. Intro. Arnold Bennett.
London: Leonard Parsons, 1927; rpt. New York: Benjamin Blom, 1969.

A collection of articles from the SUNDAY TIMES on plays by
Sean O'Casey, Noel Coward, and John Galsworthy.

271 _____. PLAYGOING; AN ESSAY. London: Jarrolds, 1927; rpt. New
York: Benjamin Blom, 1969.

Recollections and impressions.

34

272 _____. THEIR HOUR UPON THE STAGE. Cambridge: Mandarin Press, 1930; rpt. New York: Benjamin Blom, 1971.

Collected reviews, 1927-30.

273 _____. MY THEATRE TALKS. London: Arthur Barker, 1933; rpt. New York: Benjamin Blom, 1971.

A collection of B.B.C. talks.

274 _____. FIRST NIGHTS. London: Ivor Nicholson & Watson, 1934; rpt. New York: Benjamin Blom, 1971.

Criticisms from the SUNDAY TIMES, 1930-34.

275 _____. MORE FIRST NIGHTS. London: Victor Gollancz, 1937; rpt. New York: Benjamin Blom, 1969.

Criticisms from the SUNDAY TIMES, 1934-37.

276 _____. THE AMAZING THEATRE. London: George G. Harrap, 1939; rpt. New York: Benjamin Blom, 1969.

Criticisms from the SUNDAY TIMES, 1937-39.

277 _____. RED LETTER NIGHTS; A SURVEY OF THE POST-ELIZABETHAN DRAMA IN ACTUAL PERFORMANCE ON THE LONDON STAGE, 1921-43. London: Jonathan Cape, 1944; rpt. New York: Benjamin Blom, 1969.

A selection from his previous collections.

278 _____. IMMOMENT TOYS; A SURVEY OF LIGHT ENTERTAINMENT ON THE LONDON STAGE, 1920-1943. London: Jonathan Cape, 1945; rpt. New York: Benjamin Blom, 1969.

Criticism from the SUNDAY TIMES on musical plays, revues, silhouettes, pantomimes.

279 _____. THE CONTEMPORARY THEATRE, 1944 AND 1945. London: George G. Harrap, 1946.

A collection of articles from the SUNDAY TIMES.

280 _____. THOSE WERE THE NIGHTS; AN ANTHOLOGY OF CRITICISM 1880-1906. London: Hutchinson; New York: Universal Distributors, 1947; rpt. New York: Benjamin Blom, 1969.

Extracts from two collections of newspaper cuttings.

281 _____. EGO. 9 vols. London: George G. Harrap, 1935-48.

Autobiographical.

282 _____. AN ANTHOLOGY. Ed. Herbert Van Thal. Intro. Alan Dent. London: Rubert Hart-Davis; New York: Hill & Wang, 1961.

283 Aiken, Conrad. A REVIEWER'S ABC. Ed. A. Blanshard. New York: Meridian Books, 1958; London: W.H. Allen, 1961.

Includes criticism of John Galsworthy, D.H. Lawrence, John Masefield, and George Moore.

284 Aldington, Richard. SELECTED CRITICAL WRITINGS, 1928-1960. Ed. Alister Kershaw. Preface Harry T. Moore. Carbondale and Edwardsville: Southern Illinois University Press; London and Amsterdam: Feffer & Simons, 1970.

Includes articles on Somerset Maugham and D.H. Lawrence.

285 Allen, John. MASTERS OF BRITISH DRAMA. London: Dennis Dobson, 1957; rpt. New York: Citadel, 1968.

Chapters on Pinero, Shaw, and O'Casey.

286 Andrews, Charlton. "The British." THE DRAMA TODAY. Philadelphia and London: J.B. Lippincott, 1913. Pp. 105-68.

Survey.

287 Archer, William. PLAY-MAKING: A MANUAL OF CRAFTSMANSHIP. London: Chapman and Hall, 1912; rpt. New York: Dover Publications, 1960.

Uses illustrations from some modern British plays.

288 _____. THE OLD DRAMA AND THE NEW; AN ESSAY IN RE-VALUA-TION. Boston: Small, Maynard, 1923; rpt. New York: Benjamim Blom, 1972.

Includes studies of Bernard Shaw, H. Granville-Barker, John Galsworthy, John Masefield, J.M. Synge, W.B. Yeats, Lennox Robinson, and Stanley Houghton.

289 Archer, William, and H[arley]. Granville-Barker. A NATIONAL THEATRE; SCHEME & ESTIMATES. London: Privately printed, 1904; Duckworth, 1907; rpt. Port Washington, N.Y.: Kennikat Press, 1970.

A detailed scheme for the creation, organization, and management of a National Theatre. See also No. 1827.

290 Armstrong, William A. "The Irish Point of View: The Plays of Sean O'

Casey, Brendan Behan, and Thomas Murphy." EXPERIMENTAL DRAMA. London: G. Bell, 1963; New York: Dufour, 1965. Pp. 79-102.

291 _____. "The Playwright and His Theatre, 1945-62." EXPERIMENTAL DRAMA. London: G. Bell, 1963; New York: Dufour, 1965. Pp. 15-35.

Developments in theatrical politics and economics.

292 _____. "The Irish Dramatic Movement." CLASSIC IRISH DRAMA. Harmondsworth: Penguin, 1964. Pp. 7-15.

Survey.

293 Arns, Karl. GRUNDRISS DER GESCHICHTE DER ENGLISCHEN LITERATUR VON 1832 BIS ZUR GEGENWART. Paderborn, Germany: Schoningh, 1941.

Deals with most modern British dramatists.

294 THE ART OF PLAYWRITING. Philadelphia: University of Pennsylvania Press; London: Oxford University Press, 1928.

Lectures delivered at the University by Jesse Lynch Williams, Langdon Mitchell, Lord Dunsany, Gilbert Emery, and Rachel Crothers.

295 Aylen, Leo. GREEK TRAGEDY AND THE MODERN WORLD. London: Methuen, 1964.

Claims that this is an age when tragedy once again might answer a need in our lives.

296 Bab, Julius. DAS THEATER DER GEGENWART: GESCHICHTE DER DRAMATISCHEN BUEHNE SEIT 1870. Leipzig, Germany: J.J. Weber, 1928.

Includes references to some modern British dramatists.

297- Baker, Denys Val, ed. WRITERS OF TODAY. 2 vols. London: Sidg-
98 wick and Jackson, 1946, 1948.

Volume 1 contains essays on Graham Greene, J.B. Priestley, and T.S. Eliot. Volume 2 deals with Somerset Maugham and W.H. Auden.

299 Baker, George Pierce. DRAMATIC TECHNIQUE. Boston: Houghton Mifflin, 1919.

Lectures, including illustrations from modern British plays.

300 Bakshy, Alexander. THE THEATRE UNBOUND: A PLEA ON BEHALF OF

THE ILL-USED: THE ACTOR, THE STAGE AND THE SPECTATOR. London: Cecil Palmer, 1923; rpt. New York: Benjamin Blom, 1969.

Articles from various periodicals.

301   Balmforth, Ramsden. THE ETHICAL AND RELIGIOUS VALUE OF THE DRAMA. London: George Allen & Unwin, 1925.

Includes chapters on Bernard Shaw and John Galsworthy.

302   _____. THE PROBLEM-PLAY AND ITS INFLUENCE ON MODERN THOUGHT AND LIFE. London: George Allen & Unwin; New York: Henry Holt, 1928.

Makes illustrations from plays by Bernard Shaw, John Galsworthy, St. John Ervine, Stanley Houghton, and Somerset Maugham.

303   Barley, Joseph Wayne. THE MORALITY MOTIVE IN CONTEMPORARY ENGLISH DRAMA. Mexico, Mo.: Missouri Printing and Publishing Company, 1912.

Attempts to take an account of "one phase of the English religious drama of the last ten years, that of the Modern Morality."

304   Barnet, Sylvan; Morton Berman; and William Burto, eds. "The English Theater Since 1660: An Introduction." THE GENIUS OF THE LATER ENGLISH THEATER. New York: New American Library, 1962. Pp. 7-20.

Also contains essays by Max Beerbohm, W.B. Yeats, James Joyce, Frank O'Connor, and Sean O'Casey.

305   Bax, Clifford. WHITHER THE THEATRE? A LETTER TO A YOUNG PLAY-WRIGHT. London: Home & Van Thal, 1945.

Observations on English drama.

306   _____, ed. ALL THE WORLD'S A STAGE; THEATRICAL PORTRAITS. London: Frederick Muller, 1946.

Fifty-two representative players.

307   Baxter, Beverley. FIRST NIGHTS AND NOISES OFF. London and New York: Hutchinson, [1949].

Criticisms from the EVENING STANDARD, 1943-46.

308   _____. FIRST NIGHTS AND FOOTLIGHTS. London: Hutchinson, 1955.

Criticisms from the EVENING STANDARD, 1948-54.

309 Baxter, Kathleen M. SPEAK WHAT WE FEEL: A CHRISTIAN LOOKS AT THE CONTEMPORARY THEATRE. London: SCM Press, 1964. American ed. CONTEMPORARY THEATRE AND THE CHRISTIAN FAITH. Nashville: Tenn.: Abingdon Press, 1964.

> "The aim of this short book is to observe the points at which the 'new' theatre can illuminate some of the problems which Christians face in understanding and communicating their faith."

310 Beach, Joseph Warren. "The Drama in England." ENGLISH LITERATURE OF THE NINETEENTH AND THE EARLY TWENTIETH CENTURIES. New York: Collier Books; London: Collier-Macmillan, 1966. Pp. 216-30.

311 Beatty, Arthur. STUDY OUTLINE ON CONTEMPORARY DRAMA. New York: H.W. Wilson, 1918.

> Introductory survey.

312 Beckerman, Bernard. DYNAMICS OF DRAMA; THE THEORY AND METHOD OF ANALYSIS. New York: Alfred A. Knopf, 1970.

> Makes some illustrations from modern British plays.

313 Beerhohm, Max. AROUND THEATRES, 1898-1910. London: Heinemann, 1924; New York: Alfred A. Knopf, 1930; rpt. London: Rupert Hart-Davis; New York: British Book Centre, 1953.

> Reviews from the SATURDAY REVIEW.

314 _____. "Playgoing." MAINLY ON THE AIR. London and Toronto: Heinemann, 1946. Pp. 63-70.

> Differences between play-going in the Victorian and Edwardian periods and nowadays.

315 _____. MORE THEATRES, 1898-1903. London: Rupert Hart-Davis, 1969.

> Selections from his SATURDAY REVIEW essays.

316 _____. LAST THEATRES, 1904-1910. London: Rupert Hart-Davis, 1970.

317 Bell, Sam H. "Theatre." CAUSEWAY: THE ARTS IN ULSTER. Ed. Michael Longley. Belfast: Arts Council of Northern Ireland, 1971. Pp. 83-94.

> Survey.

318 _____. THE THEATRE IN ULSTER: A SURVEY OF THE DRAMATIC MOVEMENT IN ULSTER FROM 1902 TO THE PRESENT DAY. Totowa,

N.J.: Rowman and Littlefield; Dublin: Gill and Macmillan, 1972.

319 Bentley, Eric. THE PLAYWRIGHT AS THINKER; A STUDY OF DRAMA IN
MODERN TIMES. New York: Reynal & Hitchcock, [1946]. British ed.
THE MODERN DRAMA; A STUDY OF DRAMATISTS AND THE DRAMA.
London: Robert Hale, 1948.

> Chapter on Shaw and several references to other modern British
> dramatists.

320 _____. IN SEARCH OF THEATER. New York: Alfred A. Knopf; Toronto: McClelland & Stewart, 1953; London: Dobson, 1954.

> Contains "Gentility in London," "The Poet in Dublin," "Bernard
> Shaw Dead," and "Yeats's Plays."

321 _____. THEATRE OF WAR; COMMENTS ON 32 OCCASIONS. London:
Eyre Methuen, 1972.

> Reprinted essays.

322 Bergholz, Harry. DIE NEUGESTALTUNG DES MODERNEN ENGLISCHEN
THEATERS, 1870-1930. Berlin: Bergholz, 1933.

> Includes discussions of the English National Theatre and the
> Abbey Theatre.

323 Berthold, Margot. "The Independent Theatre in London." A HISTORY
OF WORLD THEATER. New York: Frederick Ungar, 1972. Pp. 577-80.

> Panoramic survey.

324 Bickley, Francis. "The Irish Theatre." J.M. SYNGE AND THE IRISH
DRAMATIC MOVEMENT. London: Constable, 1912. Pp. 67-73.

> Brief survey.

325 Bishop, George W. BARRY JACKSON AND THE LONDON THEATRE.
Foreword Charles B. Cochran. London: Arthur Barker, 1933.

> Chronicles a record of achievement in the theatre "unequalled
> by any other manager since the War."

326 _____. MY BETTERS. London and Toronto: Heinemann, 1957.

> Includes chapters on Noel Coward, Bernard Shaw, Somerset
> Maugham, and J.B. Priestley.

327 Black, Hester M. THE THEATRE IN IRELAND: AN INTRODUCTORY
ESSAY. Dublin: Trinity College, 1957.

> Survey.

328 Blamires, Harry. "Twentieth-Century Drama." A SHORT HISTORY OF ENGLISH LITERATURE. London: Methuen, 1974. Pp. 391-409.

> Introductory survey.

329 Blistein, Elmer M. COMEDY IN ACTION. Durham, N.C.: Duke University Press, 1964.

> Some references to modern British dramatists.

330 Block, Anita. THE CHANGING WORLD IN PLAYS AND THEATRE. Boston: Little, Brown, 1939.

> A critical study of contemporary American, English and Continental plays. Concerned chiefly with social problems reflected in the drama.

331 Blunt, Jerry. STAGE DIALECTS. San Francisco: Chandler Publishing Co., 1967.

> Includes chapters on standard English, Cockney, Irish, and Scots.

332 Blythe, Ernest. THE ABBEY THEATRE. Dublin: National Theatre Society, [1965].

> A brochure.

333 Bogard, Travis, and William I. Oliver, eds. MODERN DRAMA; ESSAYS IN CRITICISM. New York: Oxford University Press, 1965.

> Essays on T.S. Eliot, Bernard Shaw, and W.B. Yeats.

334 Borsa, Mario. THE ENGLISH STAGE OF TODAY. Trans. Selwyn Brinton. London and New York: John Lane, 1908.

> "His book presents not only a wide but a minute survey of the Stageland of today and yesterday"--William Archer.

335 Bottomley, Gordon. A NOTE ON POETRY AND THE STAGE. Religious Drama Pamphlets no. 7. London: Religious Drama Society, [1944]. Reprinted from LIFE AND LETTERS TODAY, April 1944.

336 Boulton, Marjorie. THE ANATOMY OF DRAMA. London: Routledge & Kegan Paul, 1960.

> Several illustrations from modern British plays.

337 Bourdon, Georges. LES THEATRES ANGLAIS. Preface Edwin O. Sachs. Paris: Bibliotheque-Charpentier, 1903.

338  Bourne, John. "The One-Act Play in England." THE ONE-ACT PLAY
TODAY. Ed. William Kozlenko. New York: Harcourt, Brace, 1938.
Pp. 219-41.

Survey.

339  Boyd, Alice K. THE INTERCHANGE OF PLAYS BETWEEN LONDON AND
NEW YORK 1910-1939: A STUDY IN RELATIVE AUDIENCE RESPONSE.
New York: King's Crown Press; London: Oxford University Press, 1948.

340  Boyd, Ernest A. IRELAND'S LITERARY RENAISSANCE. Dublin: Talbot
Press; New York: John Lane, 1916; New York: Alfred A. Knopf, 1922;
rpt. Dublin: Allen Figgis, 1968.

A study of the Irish dramatic movement.

341  _____. APPRECIATIONS AND DEPRECIATIONS: IRISH LITERARY STUD-
IES. Dublin: Talbot Press, 1917; London: T. Fisher Unwin; New York:
John Lane, 1918; rpt. Freeport, N.Y.: Books for Libraries Press, 1968.

Includes chapters on George Russell, Lord Dunsany, and Bernard
Shaw.

342  _____. THE CONTEMPORARY DRAMA OF IRELAND. Dublin: Talbot
Press; London: T. Fisher Unwin, 1918; Boston: Little, Brown, 1928.

Survey.

343  Bradbrook, M.C. ENGLISH DRAMATIC FORM: A HISTORY OF ITS
DEVELOPMENT. London: Chatto & Windus; New York: Barnes & Noble,
1965.

Chapters on T.S. Eliot and W.B. Yeats.

344  Brahms, Caryl. THE REST OF THE EVENING'S MY OWN. London:
W.H. Allen, 1964.

Collected reviews.

345  Brandt, G.W. "Realism and Parables: From Brecht to Arden." CON-
TEMPORARY THEATRE. Ed. John Russell Brown and Bernard Harris.
Stratford-upon-Avon Studies, no. 4. London: Edward Arnold; New York:
St. Martin's Press, 1962. Pp. 33-35.

Survey.

346  Brawley, Benjamin. "Later Victorian and Contemporary Drama: Analysis
and the Social Impulse." A SHORT HISTORY OF THE ENGLISH DRAMA.
London: George G. Harrap, 1921; rpt. Freeport, N.Y.: Books for Libraries Press, 1969.

"It aims simply to set forth in brief compass the main facts that one might wish to have at hand in his first course in the English Drama."

347 Brewster, Dorothy. EAST-WEST PASSAGE; A STUDY IN LITERARY RELA-TIONSHIPS. London: George Allen & Unwin, 1954.

On the influence of Russian literature on such writers as Bernard Shaw, George Moore, and D.H. Lawrence.

348 Bricker, Herschel Leonard, ed. OUR THEATRE TODAY; A COMPOSITE HANDBOOK ON THE ART, CRAFT, AND MANAGEMENT OF THE CONTEMPORARY THEATRE. New York: Samuel French, 1936.

Anthology.

349 Bridgwater, Patrick. NIETZSCHE IN ANGLOSAXONY: A STUDY OF NIETZSCHE'S IMPACT ON ENGLISH AND AMERICAN LITERATURE. Leicester, Eng.: Leicester University Press, 1972.

Includes discussions of Bernard Shaw and W.B. Yeats.

350 Bridie, James. THE BRITISH DRAMA. British Way Series, no. 12. Glasgow: Craig and Wilson, 1945.

Introductory pamphlet.

351 Brockett, Oscar G. "Realism in the Theatre: England." THE THEATRE: AN INTRODUCTION. New York: Holt, Rinehart and Winston, 1964. Pp. 271-72.

Survey.

352 _____. HISTORY OF THE THEATRE. Boston: Allyn and Bacon, 1968.

Chapters on the English and Irish theatres.

353 Brockett, Oscar G., and Robert R. Findlay. CENTURY OF INNOVA-TION: A HISTORY OF EUROPEAN AND AMERICAN THEATRE AND DRAMA SINCE 1870. Englewood Cliffs, N.J.: Prentice-Hall, 1973.

A new historical survey of major trends in Western theatre and drama.

354 Brook, Donald. WRITER'S GALLERY: BIOGRAPHICAL SKETCHES OF BRITAIN'S GREATEST WRITERS, AND THEIR VIEWS ON RECONSTRUCTION. London: Rockliff, 1944; Port Washington, N.Y., and London: Kennikat Press, 1970.

Includes sketches of Noel Coward, Somerset Maugham, A.A. Milne, J.B. Priestley, and Bernard Shaw.

355 _____. THE ROMANCE OF THE ENGLISH THEATRE. London: Rockliff, 1945.

"This is a book for the 'ordinary' playgoer who is sufficiently interested in drama."

356 Brown, Curtis. CONTACTS. London: Cassell; New York: Harper, 1935.

Includes essays on Bernard Shaw, D.H. Lawrence, John Galsworthy, Clemence Dane, and A.A. Milne.

357 Brown, Ivor. "The Difficulties of Dramatic Criticism." ESSAYS BY DIVERS HANDS. London: Oxford University Press, 1942. XIX, 101-8.

358 _____. "Can There Be a Revival of Poetic Drama in the Modern Theatre?" ESSAYS BY DIVERS HANDS. London: Oxford University Press, 1947. XXIII, 72-82.

"There are obviously two essential conditions of a revival of poetic drama. There must be poets, and there must be an audience prepared to encourage poets."

359 _____. WHAT IS A PLAY? London: Macdonald, 1964.

Dramatic theory, making references to some modern British plays.

360 Brown, John Mason. THE MODERN THEATRE IN REVOLT. New Arts Series. New York: W.W. Norton, 1929.

Traces the course of the development of the theatre during the last hundred years and the contribution of each generation of revolutionists.

361 _____. "London Pride." SEEING MORE THINGS. New York: Whittlesey House, 1948. Pp. 179-220.

Reviews from the SATURDAY REVIEW OF LITERATURE.

362 _____. AS THEY APPEAR. New York: McGraw-Hill, 1952; London: Hamish Hamilton, 1953.

Reviews from the SATURDAY REVIEW OF LITERATURE.

363 _____. DRAMATIS PERSONAE; A RETROSPECTIVE SHOW. New York: Viking Press; London: Hamish Hamilton, 1963.

Reviews from the SATURDAY REVIEW OF LITERATURE.

364 Brown, Malcolm. THE POLITICS OF IRISH LITERATURE: FROM THOMAS DAVIS TO W.B. YEATS. London: George Allen & Unwin; 1972. Seat-

tle: University of Washington Press, 1972.

Touches on a few plays by W.B. Yeats and Lady Gregory.

365 Browne, E. Martin. VERSE IN THE MODERN ENGLISH THEATRE. Cardiff: University of Wales Press, 1963.

The W.D. Thomas Memorial Lecture, delivered at the University College of Swansea on 28 February 1963.

366 _____, ed. "Introduction." FOUR MODERN VERSE PLAYS. Harmondsworth: Penguin Books, 1957.

Anthology.

367 _____, ed. "Introduction." THREE IRISH PLAYS. Harmondsworth: Penguin Books, 1959.

Anthology.

368 Bruestle, Beaumont Schrader. THE "FOOL OF NATURE" IN THE ENGLISH DRAMA OF OUR DAY. Philadelphia: University of Pennsylvania Press, 1932.

"It is the purpose of this work to present those characters in the contemporary English drama ... who may be considered 'fools of nature.'"

369 Bryant, Sophie. "The Gael in Literature." THE GENIUS OF THE GAEL: A STUDY IN CELTIC PSYCHOLOGY AND ITS MANIFESTATIONS. London: T. Fisher Unwin, 1913. Pp. 181-218.

370 Bullough, Geoffrey. "Christopher Fry and the 'Revolt' against Eliot." EXPERIMENTAL DRAMA. Ed. William A. Armstrong. London: G. Bell, 1963; New York: Dufour, 1965. Pp. 56-78.

On poetic drama.

371 Burns, Elizabeth. THEATRICALITY; A STUDY OF CONVENTION IN THE THEATRE AND IN SOCIAL LIFE. London: Longman, 1972.

Makes references to some modern British dramatists.

372 Burton, Richard. "The Modern School." HOW TO SEE A PLAY. New ed. New York: Macmillan, 1929. Pp. 79-102.

Survey.

373 Busfield, Roger M., Jr. THE PLAYWRIGHT'S ART. New York: Harper, 1958; Westport, Conn.: Greenwood Press, 1971.

Some illustrations from modern British plays.

374   Byrne, Dawson. THE STORY OF IRELAND'S NATIONAL THEATRE: THE ABBEY THEATRE, DUBLIN. Dublin: Talbot Press, 1929.

375   Caboche, Lucien. LE THEATRE EN GRANDE-BRETAGNE PENDANT LA SECONDE GUERRE MONDIALE. Paris: Marcel Didier, 1969.

     Survey of English drama during World War II.

376   Calderwood, James L., and Harold E. Toliver, eds. PERSPECTIVES ON DRAMA. New York and London: Oxford University Press, 1968.

     Collection of essays on dramatic theory.

377   Canfield, Curtis, ed. PLAYS OF THE IRISH RENAISSANCE, 1880-1930. London: Macmillan; New York: Ives Washburn, 1929.

     Includes an introduction and notes.

378   _____, ed. PLAYS OF CHANGING IRELAND. New York: Macmillan, 1936.

     Includes introductions and notes.

379   Canfield, Mary Cass. GROTESQUES AND OTHER REFLECTIONS. London: Harper, 1927.

     Includes studies of plays by Bernard Shaw, Sutton Vale, and Noel Coward.

380   Cannan, Gilbert. THE JOY OF THE THEATRE. London: Batsford, 1913.

     Observations on the English theatre.

381   Cannon, Fanny. WRITING AND SELLING A PLAY. New York: Henry Holt, 1915.

     Includes illustrations from some modern British plays.

382   Carpenter, Bruce. THE WAY OF THE DRAMA; A STUDY OF DRAMATIC FORMS AND MOODS. New York: Prentice-Hall, 1929.

     Includes illustrations from some modern British plays.

383   Carroll, Sydney W. SOME DRAMATIC OPINIONS. London: F.V. White, [1924]; rpt. Port Washington, N.Y.: Kennikat Press, 1968.

     Consists principally of essays from the SUNDAY TIMES, including studies of J.M. Synge and J.M. Barrie.

384   Carter, Huntley. "The New Spirit in London." THE NEW SPIRIT IN DRAMA AND ART. London: Frank Palmer, 1912; New York: Mitchell

Kennerley, 1913. Pp. 7-45.

385 _____. "England." THE NEW SPIRIT IN THE EUROPEAN THEATRE, 1914-1924; A COMPARATIVE STUDY OF THE CHANGES EFFECTED BY THE WAR AND REVOLUTION. London: Ernest Benn; New York: George H. Doran, 1925. Pp. 1-119.

386 Chandler, Frank Wadleigh. ASPECTS OF MODERN DRAMA. New York: Macmillan, 1914.

Considers the different types of modern plays and exponents of the types. Includes illustrations from modern British plays.

387 _____. "Twentieth-Century Drama in England." COLUMBIA UNIVER- SITY COURSE IN LITERATURE. New York: United States Publishers As- sociation, 1928-29; rpt. Freeport, N.Y.: Books for Libraries Press, 1969. 15, pp. 460-74.

Survey.

388 Chapman, John, ed. "The London Scene." THE BEST PLAYS OF 1947- 50. 3 vols. New York: Dodd, Mead, 1947-50.

An annual survey.

389 Charques, R.D., ed. FOOTNOTES TO THE THEATRE. London: Peter Davies, 1938.

Contributions on various aspects of the modern English theatre.

390 Chaturvedi, B.N. ENGLISH POETIC DRAMA OF THE TWENTIETH CEN- TURY. Gwalior, India: Kitab Char, 1967.

391 Cheney, Sheldon. "The New English Dramatists." THE NEW MOVE- MENT IN THE THEATRE. New York: Mitchell Kennerley, 1914. Pp. 67-87.

Survey.

392 _____. THE THEATRE; THREE THOUSAND YEARS OF DRAMA, ACTING AND STAGECRAFT. London and New York: Longmans, 1929; rev. and enl. ed., 1952.

Survey.

393 Chesterton, A.K. ADVENTURES IN DRAMATIC APPRECIATION. Lon- don: T. Werner Laurie, 1931.

Includes studies of R.C. Sherriff, Bernard Shaw, Somerset Maugham, and Noel Coward.

394    Chew, Samuel C., and Richard D. Altick. "Modern Drama." THE
       NINETEENTH CENTURY AND AFTER (1789-1939). A LITERARY HISTORY
       OF ENGLAND. Ed. Albert C. Baugh. New York: Appleton-Century-
       Crofts, 1968. IV, 1507-31.

       Survey.

395    Chiari, J. "Poetic Drama." LANDMARKS OF CONTEMPORARY DRAMA.
       London: Herbert Jenkins, 1965; New York: Hillary House, 1966; rpt.
       New York: Gordian Press, 1971. Pp. 81-106.

       Survey.

396    Chisholm, Cecil. REPERTORY; AN OUTLINE OF THE MODERN THEATRE
       MOVEMENT. London: Peter Davies, 1934.

397    Chislett, William, Jr. MODERNS AND NEAR MODERNS. London:
       Grafton Press; New York: Hitchcock, 1928.

       Includes studies of J.M. Synge, Lady Gregory, W.B. Yeats,
       Lord Dunsany and Bernard Shaw.

398    Churchill, R.C. "The Comedy of Ideas: Cross Currents in the Fiction
       and Drama of the Twentieth Century." THE MODERN AGE. Pelican
       Guide to English Literature, no. 7. Ed. Boris Ford. Harmondsworth:
       Penguin Books, 1961. Pp. 221-30.

399    Clark, Barrett H. THE BRITISH AND AMERICAN DRAMA OF TODAY.
       New York: Henry Holt, 1915; rpt. AMS Press, 1971.

       Suggests study outlines of representative modern English and
       Irish plays.

400    _____. THE MODERN DRAMA. Chicago: American Library Associa-
       tion, 1927.

       Includes introductions to plays by Bernard Shaw and J.M.
       Barrie, and to books on modern drama in general.

401    _____. "English Dramatic Criticism of the Nineteenth and Twentieth
       Centuries." EUROPEAN THEORIES OF THE DRAMA. Rev. ed. New
       York and London: D. Appleton, 1930. Pp. 453-81.

       Anthology.

402    _____. "'The English Drama' and 'The Irish Drama.'" A STUDY OF
       THE MODERN DRAMA. New ed. New York and London: D. Appleton-
       Century, 1936. Pp. 219-327, 329-57.

       A study of representative plays.

403 Clark, William S. "The Rise of the Irish Theater and Drama." CHIEF PATTERNS OF WORLD DRAMA: AESCHYLUS TO ANDERSON. Boston: Houghton Mifflin, 1946. Pp. 887-90.

Survey.

404 Clarke, David Waldo. "Some Dramatists of Today." WRITERS OF TO-DAY. Essential English Library Series. London and New York: Longmans, Green, 1956. Pp. 78-85.

Introductory survey.

405 Cleaver, James. "The English Theatre of the Twentieth Century." THE-ATRE THROUGH THE AGES. New York: Hart Publishing Co., 1967. Pp. 295-355.

Survey.

406 Clunes, Alec. "Twentieth Century Theatre--A Progress." THE BRITISH THEATRE. London: Cassell, 1964; New York: A.S. Barnes, 1965. Pp. 155-77.

Introductory.

407 Clurman, Harold. "The Theatre of England." LIES LIKE TRUTH. New York and London: Macmillan, 1958. Pp. 161-94.

Reports on productions and short essays on some leading players.

408 Cohen, Helen Louise. "The Irish National Theater." ONE-ACT PLAYS BY MODERN AUTHORS. New York: Harcourt, Brace, 1921.

Survey.

409 Cohn, Ruby. "English Language Drama." CURRENTS IN CONTEMPO-RARY DRAMA. Bloomington and London: Indiana University Press, 1969. Pp. 3-17.

Survey.

410 Cohn, Ruby, and Bernard F. Dukore, eds. TWENTIETH CENTURY DRAMA: ENGLAND, IRELAND AND THE UNITED STATES. New York: Random House, 1966.

Anthology with editorial material.

411 Cole, Toby, ed. PLAYWRIGHTS ON PLAYWRITING; THE MEANING AND MAKING OF MODERN DRAMA FROM IBSEN TO IONESCO. London: MacGibbon & Kee, 1960; New York: Hill & Wang, 1961.

Anthology.

412   Collins, A.S. "The Drama, 1900 to 1950." ENGLISH LITERATURE OF
THE TWENTIETH CENTURY. London: University Tutorial Press, 1960.
Pp. 281-327.

  Survey.

413   Colum, Mary. LIFE AND THE DREAM. London: Macmillan, 1947; rev.
ed. Dublin: Dolmen Press; London: Oxford University Press, 1966.

  On the Irish theatre.

414   Colum, Padraic. MY IRISH YEAR. London: Mills & Boon, 1912.

  Contains background to Irish drama.

415   _____. THE ROAD ROUND IRELAND. New York: Macmillan, 1926.

  Contains background to Irish drama.

416   Compton-Rickett, Arthur. PORTRAITS AND PERSONALITIES. London:
Selwyn and Blount, 1937.

  Includes studies of J.M. Barrie, Bernard Shaw, and J.B.
Priestley.

417   Cookman, A.V. "The Prose Drama." THEATRE PROGRAMME. Ed. J.C.
Trewin. London: Frederick Muller, 1954. Pp. 31-48.

  Survey since World War II.

418   Cordell, Richard A. HENRY ARTHUR JONES AND THE MODERN DRA-
MA. New York: Ray Long & Richard R. Smith, 1932.

419   Corrigan, Robert W., ed. THEATRE IN THE TWENTIETH CENTURY.
New York: Grove Press, 1963.

  Anthology of criticism from TULANE DRAMA REVIEW.

420   _____, ed. "Introduction" and "England and Ireland." THE MODERN
THEATRE. New York: Macmillan, 1964. Pp. ix-xviii, 877-1072.

  Anthology.

421   _____, ed. "The British Drama in the Twentieth Century." LAUREL
BRITISH DRAMA: THE TWENTIETH CENTURY. New York: Dell, 1965.
Pp. 9-27.

  Survey.

422   _____, ed. "The Irish Dramatic Flair." MASTERPIECES OF THE MODERN

IRISH THEATRE. New York: Collier Books, 1967. Pp. 6-8.

"All evidence indicates that while the Golden Age of the Irish theatre lasted only a short while, the Irishman's age-old capacity to create a language which sings on the stage has not waned."

423 _____, ed. "The Modern British Theatre and the Wide Embrace." MASTERPIECES OF THE MODERN ENGLISH THEATRE. New York: Collier Books, 1967. Pp. 7-10.

Survey.

424 Corrigan, Robert W., and James L. Rosenberg, eds. THE CONTEXT AND CRAFT OF DRAMA; CRITICAL ESSAYS ON THE NATURE OF DRAMA AND THE THEATRE. San Francisco: Chandler Publishing Co., 1964.

Anthology including contributions by British dramatists.

425 Cotes, Peter. NO STAR NONSENSE. London: Rockliff, 1949; New York: Macmillan, 1950.

Makes several references to modern British dramatists.

426 Counsell, John. COUNSELL'S OPINIONS. London: Barrie and Rockliff, 1963.

Autobiography, including references to some modern British plays.

427 Courtney, Marie-Therese. EDWARD MARTYN AND THE IRISH THEATRE. New York: Vantage Press, 1956.

428 Courtney, W.L. "Realistic Drama." OLD SAWS AND MODERN INSTANCES. London: Chapman and Hall, 1918; rpt. Freeport, N.Y.: Books for Libraries Press, 1969. Pp. 161-217. Reprinted from FORTNIGHTLY REVIEW, 93 (1913), 945-61, 1136-53; 94 (1914), 96-110.

"The modern English stage has developed mainly along the lines of realism."

429 Cowell, Raymond. TWELVE MODERN DRAMATISTS. Oxford: Pergamon Press, 1967.

Includes Bernard Shaw, J.M. Synge, and Sean O'Casey.

430 Cox, C.B., and A.E. Dyson, eds. THE TWENTIETH-CENTURY MIND: HISTORY, IDEAS, AND LITERATURE IN BRITAIN. 3 vols. London and New York: Oxford University Press, 1972.

Includes a section on "Drama."

431    Craig, Gordon. ON THE ART OF THE THEATRE. London: Heinemann, 1911.

432    _____. THE THEATRE ADVANCING. London: Constable, 1921.

        Essays.

433    Cunliffe, John W. "The Irish Movement." ENGLISH LITERATURE DURING THE LAST HALF-CENTURY. London and New York: Macmillan, 1919; rpt. Freeport, N.Y.: Books for Libraries Press, 1971.

        Survey.

434    _____. MODERN ENGLISH PLAYWRIGHTS; A SHORT HISTORY OF THE ENGLISH DRAMA FROM 1825. New York and London: Harper, 1927; rpt. Port Washington, N.Y.: Kennikat Press, 1969.

        Includes chapters on J.M. Barrie, John Galsworthy, H. Gran-ville Barker, St. John Hankin, J.M. Synge, St. John Ervine, Stanley Houghton, Allan Monkhouse, John Masefield, John Drinkwater, J.E. Flecker, Lord Dunsany, A.A. Milne, C.K. Munro, Noel Coward, and Sean O'Casey.

435    _____. "The Irish Renaissance." ENGLISH LITERATURE IN THE TWEN-TIETH CENTURY. New York: Macmillan, 1933.

        Survey.

436    Curran, C.P. UNDER THE RECEDING WAVE. London: Gill & Mac-millan, 1970.

        Includes an account of the early years of the Abbey Theatre.

437    Curtis, Anthony, ed. THE RISE AND FALL OF THE MATINEE IDOL; PAST DEITIES OF STAGE AND SCREEN, THEIR ROLES, THEIR MAGIC, AND THEIR WORSHIPPERS. London: Weidenfeld and Nicolson, 1974.

        Contributions by "a spectrum of authors all of whom have been engaged in the theatre" which "focus upon the matinee idol at significant moments in his glorious history."

438    Dace, Letitia. MODERN THEATRE AND DRAMA. New York: Richards Rosen Press, 1973.

        Includes chapters on Bernard Shaw, The Abbey Theatre, T.S. Eliot, and Christopher Fry.

439    Daiches, David. "Drama." THE PRESENT AGE IN BRITISH LITERATURE. Bloomington: Indiana University Press, 1958. Pp. 148-67.

        Survey.

440 _____. "Drama from the Beginning of the Eighteenth Century." A CRITICAL HISTORY OF ENGLISH LITERATURE. London: Secker & Warburg, 1963. II, 1094-112.

Survey.

441 Dalgard, Olav. TEATRET I DET 20. HUNDREARET. Oslo: Norske Samlaget, 1955.

Includes studies of W.B. Yeats, J.M. Synge, Bernard Shaw, John Galsworthy, J.B. Priestley, Sean O'Casey, T.S. Eliot, and Christopher Fry.

442 Dane, Clemence. APPROACHES TO DRAMA. English Association Presidential Address, 1961. London: Oxford University Press, 1961.

Pamphlet dealing with the new "moods in which people go to a play."

443 Darlington, W.A. THROUGH THE FOURTH WALL. London: Chapman and Hall, 1922; New York: Brentano's, 1933.

Notices and essays from DAILY TELEGRAPH.

444 _____. LITERATURE IN THE THEATRE AND OTHER ESSAYS. London: Chapman and Hall, 1925; New York: Henry Holt, 1933.

Essays from FORTNIGHTLY REVIEW and DAILY TELEGRAPH.

445 _____. THE ACTOR AND HIS AUDIENCE. London: Phoenix House, 1949.

Includes references to some modern British dramatists.

446 _____. SIX THOUSAND AND ONE NIGHTS: FORTY YEARS A CRITIC. London: George G. Harrap; New York: Clarke, Irwin, 1960.

A general survey of his long career as critic.

447 Dataller, Roger. DRAMA AND LIFE. London and New York: Thomas Nelson, 1938.

Some illustrations from modern British plays.

448 Daubeny, Peter. STAGE BY STAGE. London: John Murray, 1952.

The author's experience as a producer-manager, with references to some modern British dramatists.

449 _____. "The West End--Lonsdale, Novello, Maugham, Coward." MY WORLD OF THEATRE. London: Joanthan Cape, 1971. Pp. 82-116.

His early London productions brought him into close working contact with such leading writers of the time as Frederick Lonsdale, Somerset Maugham, and Noel Coward.

450 Davidson, H.A. STUDIES IN MODERN PLAYS; A STUDY OUTLINE. New York: H.W. Wilson, 1915.

451 Davison, P.H. "Contemporary Drama and Popular Dramatic Forms." ASPECTS OF DRAMA AND THE THEATRE. Ed. Richard N. Coe et al. Preface A.K. Stout. Sydney: Sydney University Press; London: Methuen, 1965. Pp. 143-97.

Discusses, with many examples, the influence on English drama of music hall, pantomime, radio, and television.

452 Day, Martin S. "English Drama from Shaw to the Present." HISTORY OF ENGLISH LITERATURE 1837 TO THE PRESENT. Garden City, N.Y.: Doubleday, 1964. Pp. 273-98.

453 Dean, Basil. THE THEATRE IN RECONSTRUCTION. Tonbridge, Kent: Tonbridge Printers, 1945.

Considers "the place which the Theatre should occupy in our national life during the years of reconstruction" after World War II.

454 _____. SEVEN AGES; AN AUTOBIOGRAPHY 1888-1927. London: Hutchinson, 1970.

Several references to modern British plays.

455 Dennis, Nigel. DRAMATIC ESSAYS. London: Weidenfeld and Nicolson, 1962.

Includes references to some modern British dramatists.

456 Dent, Alan. PRELUDES AND STUDIES. London: Macmillan, 1942; rpt. Port Washington, N.Y.: Kennikat Press, 1970.

Collected essays and reviews.

457 _____. NOCTURNES AND RHAPSODIES. London: Hamish Hamilton, 1950.

Collected essays and reviews.

458 Deseo, Lydia Glover, and Hulda Mossberg Phipps. LOOKING AT LIFE THROUGH DRAMA. New York: Abingdon Press, 1931.

Shows that the simple reading of worth-while plays opens the way to "sympathetic understanding of the persons and issues involved in the modern conflicts portrayed."

459  Dickinson, P.L. "The Theatre." THE DUBLIN OF YESTERDAY. London: Methuen, 1929. Pp. 82-98.

On Irish drama.

460  Dickinson, Thomas H. AN OUTLINE OF CONTEMPORARY DRAMA. Boston: Houghton Mifflin, 1927; rpt. New York: Biblo and Tannen, 1969.

"While providing a background for modern drama, the work studies, in part three, the twentieth century drama in detail."

461  _____. THE CONTEMPORARY DRAMA OF ENGLAND. Boston: Little, Brown, 1931.

A history of the English drama from the Victorian theatre to the free theatre, with a glance into the future.

462  Dietrich, Margret. DAS MODERNE DRAMA: STROMUNGEN--GESTALTEN--MOTIVE. Stuttgart, Germany: Alfred Kroner, 1961.

Includes studies of W.H. Auden, Gordon Bottomley, Noel Coward, T.S. Eliot, St. John Ervine, Christopher Fry, John Galsworthy, Christopher Isherwood, Somerset Maugham, Sean O'Casey, J.B. Priestley, Terence Rattigan, Bernard Shaw, J.M. Synge, and W.B. Yeats.

463  Disher, M. Willson. PLEASURES OF LONDON. London: Robert Hale, 1950; New York: Macmillan, 1951.

Includes chapters on the important theatres in London, with references to some productions.

464  Dobbs, Brian. DRURY LANE: THREE CENTURIES OF THE THEATRE ROYAL, 1663-1971. London: Cassell, 1972.

Survey.

465  Dobree, Bonamy. TIMOTHEUS; THE FUTURE OF THE THEATRE. London: Kegan Paul, Trench, Trubner; New York: E.P. Dutton, 1925.

Booklet.

466  Donaldson, Frances. THE ACTOR MANAGERS. London: Weidenfeld and Nicolson, 1970.

Several references to modern British plays.

467 Donoghue, Denis. THE THIRD VOICE; MODERN BRITISH AND AMERICAN VERSE DRAMA. Princeton, N.J.: Princeton University Press; London: Oxford University Press, 1959.

> History of the revival of verse drama with detailed criticism of many dramatists.

468 Dooley, Roger B. MODERN BRITISH AND IRISH DRAMA. Monarch Review Notes & Study Guide Series, no. 624. New York: Thor Publications, 1964.

> Introductory.

469 Downer, Alan S. "The Revival of the Drama." THE BRITISH DRAMA; A HANDBOOK AND BRIEF CHRONICLE. New York: Appleton-Century-Crofts, 1950. Pp. 299-334.

> "It is intended as a guide and companion to those undertaking for the first time a study of the drama."

470 Downs, Harold. THEATREGOING. London: Thrift Books, 1951.

> "A book for all who enjoy seeing plays and also for those who think they might enjoy them more."

471 _____. THE CRITIC IN THE THEATRE. Foreword Neville Cardus. London: Pitman, 1953.

> Includes many references to modern British plays.

472 _____. APPRAISING A PLAY. London: Herbert Jenkins, 1955.

> Includes references to some British dramatists.

473 Drew, Elizabeth. DISCOVERING DRAMA. New York: W.W. Norton; London: Jonathan Cape, 1937.

> References to some modern British plays.

474 Drinkwater, John. THE GENTLE ART OF THEATRE-GOING. London: Robert Holden, 1927; American ed. THE ART OF THEATRE-GOING. Boston and New York: Ernest Benn, 1927.

> References to some modern British plays.

475 Driver, Tom F. ROMANTIC QUEST AND MODERN QUERY; A HISTORY OF THE MODERN THEATER. New York: Delacorte Press, 1970.

> References to some modern British plays.

476 Duggan, G.C. THE STAGE IRISHMAN; A HISTORY OF THE IRISH PLAY

AND STAGE CHARACTERS FROM THE EARLIEST TIMES. Dublin and Cork: Talbot Press; London: Longmans, 1937.

Survey.

477 Dukes, Ashley. "England." MODERN DRAMATISTS. London: Frank Palmer, 1911; rpt. Freeport, N.Y.: Books for Libraries Press, 1967. Pp. 114-50.

Essays on Bernard Shaw, Harley Granville-Barker, and John Galsworthy.

478 _____. THE YOUNGEST DRAMA; STUDIES OF FIFTY DRAMATISTS. London: Ernest Benn, 1923; Chicago: Charles H. Sergel, 1924; rpt. Folcroft, Pa.: Folcroft Press, 1969.

Includes essays on J.M. Barrie, John Galsworthy, H. Granville-Barker, John Masefield, Somerset Maugham, Bernard Shaw, J. M. Synge, St. John Ervine, C.K. Munro, A.A. Milne, John Drinkwater, and J.E. Flecker.

479 _____. THE WORLD TO PLAY WITH. London: Oxford University Press, 1928.

Essays on various aspects of the theatre and the play.

480 _____. THE SCENE IS CHANGED. London: Macmillan, 1942.

Modern British drama in retrospect.

481 Dukore, Bernard F., ed. "Nineteenth and Twentieth-Century England and Ireland." DRAMATIC THEORY AND CRITICISM: GREEKS TO GROTOW-SKI. New York: Holt, Rinehart and Winston, 1947. Pp. 577-672.

Contributions by Wilde, Shaw, Yeats, Synge, Murray, Archer, and Esslin.

482 Duncan, Barry. THE ST. JAMES'S THEATRE; ITS STRANGE AND COM-PLETE HISTORY 1835-1957. London: Barrie and Rockliff, 1964.

483 Duncan, G.A. IRELAND'S ABBEY THEATRE. Dublin: Privately printed, 1963.

484 Dunsany, Lord Edward John Moreton Drax Plunkett. "Drama." THE DONNELLAN LECTURES 1943. London: Heinemann, 1945. Pp. 46-66.

Dramatic theory.

485 Eastman, Fred. CHRIST IN THE DRAMA; A STUDY OF THE INFLUENCE OF CHRIST ON THE DRAMA OF ENGLAND AND AMERICA. New York:

Macmillan, 1947.

>Examines plays by Bernard Shaw, John Galsworthy, John Mase-
field, and Emlyn Williams.

486  Eastwood, Wilfred, and John Thompson Good. SIGNPOSTS: A GUIDE
TO MODERN ENGLISH LITERATURE. Cambridge: At the University Press,
for the National Book League, 1960.

>Includes a survey of general trends in drama since 1900.

487  Eaton, Walter Prichard. PLAYS AND PLAYERS; LEAVES FROM A CRITIC'S
SCRAPBOOK. Cincinnati: Stewart & Kidd, 1916.

>Reprinted reviews and essays including some on modern British
plays.

488  _____. THE DRAMA IN ENGLISH. New York: Scribner's, 1930. Pp.
237-92.

>Traces the development of English drama from the beginnings
to the late 1920s and includes studies of Bernard Shaw, J.M.
Barrie, John Galsworthy, J.M. Synge, and Sean O'Casey.

489  Edwards, Hilton. THE MANTLE OF HARLEQUIN. Preface and two de-
signs by Michael MacLiammoir. Dublin: Progress House, 1958.

>On the Dublin Gate Theatre.

490  Eglinton, John. IRISH LITERARY PORTRAITS. London: Macmillan, 1935.

>Includes chapters on W.B. Yeats, George Russell, George
Moore, and James Joyce.

491  Egri, Lajos. HOW TO WRITE A PLAY. New York: Simon & Schuster,
1942. Rev. ed. THE ART OF DRAMATIC WRITING. New York: Simon
& Schuster, 1946; London: Pitman, 1950.

>Some references to modern British plays.

492  Eliot, T.S. "The Possibility of a Poetic Drama." THE SACRED WOOD;
ESSAYS ON POETRY AND CRITICISM. London: Methuen, 1920; New
York: Alfred A. Knopf, 1921. Pp. 54-63.

493  _____. "A Dialogue on Dramatic Poetry." SELECTED ESSAYS. 3rd
enl. ed. London: Faber and Faber, 1951. Pp. 43-58.

494  _____. POETRY AND DRAMA. Cambridge, Mass.: Harvard University
Press; London: Faber and Faber, 1951; rpt. included in ON POETRY AND
POETS. London: Faber and Faber, 1957. Pp. 72-88.

The first Theodore Spencer Memorial Lecture delivered at Harvard University.

495 _____. "Five Points on Dramatic Writing." AN ASSESSMENT OF TWENTIETH CENTURY LITERATURE. Ed. Jacob Isaacs. London: Secker & Warburg, 1951. Pp. 159-60.

Reprinted from TOWNSMAN: A QUARTERLY REVIEW, July 1938, p. 10. Extract from a letter to Ezra Pound.

496 _____. RELIGIOUS DRAMA: MEDIAEVAL AND MODERN. New York: House of Books, 1954.

An address delivered in 1937.

497 Ellehauge, Martin. STRIKING FIGURES AMONG MODERN ENGLISH DRAMATISTS. Copenhagen: Levin and Munksgaard; London: Williams and Norgate, 1931; rpt. Folcroft, Pa.: Folcroft Library Editions, 1971.

Chapters on J.M. Synge, John Galsworthy, Harley Granville-Barker, Gilbert Cannan, John Drinkwater, Lascelles Abercrombie, John Masefield, Gordon Bottomley, and J.M. Barrie.

498 Ellis-Fermor, Una. THE IRISH DRAMATIC MOVEMENT. London: Methuen, 1939; rpt. London: University Paperbacks, 1967.

499 _____. THE FRONTIERS OF DRAMA. London: Methuen, 1945; rpt. London: University Paperbacks, 1964.

References to some modern British plays.

500 Ellmann, Richard, ed. EDWARDIANS AND LATE VICTORIANS. New York: Columbia University Press, 1960.

Includes studies of Bernard Shaw, W.B. Yeats, and George Moore.

501 Elsom, John. EROTIC THEATRE. London: Secker & Warburg, 1973.

Contrasts the treatment of sex in the theatre during two periods --1890-1910 and 1950 to the present.

502 Elton, Oliver. "Living Irish Literature." MODERN STUDIES. London: Edward Arnold, 1907.

Survey.

503 Enck, John J.; Elizabeth T. Foster; and Alvin Whitley, eds. THE COMIC IN THEORY & PRACTICE. New York: Appleton-Century-Crofts, 1960.

Anthology including writings by and references to some modern

British dramatists.

504 Ervine, St. John. SOME IMPRESSIONS OF MY ELDERS. London: George Allen & Unwin, 1923.

Includes chapters on George Russell, John Galsworthy, George Moore, Bernard Shaw, and W.B. Yeats.

505 _____. THE ORGANISED THEATRE; A PLEA IN CIVICS. London: George Allen & Unwin, 1924.

"The English theatre is, at the moment, under a cloud."

506 _____. HOW TO WRITE A PLAY. London: George Allen & Unwin, 1928.

Includes references to some modern British plays.

507 _____. THE THEATRE IN MY TIME. London: Rich & Cowan, 1933; New York: Barrows Mussey, 1934.

"In my lifetime . . . I have seen . . . a revolution in the world of entertainment."

508 Evans, Sir [B.] Ifor. A SHORT HISTORY OF ENGLISH DRAMA. Harmondsworth: Penguin, 1948; rev. ed. London: Staples Press, 1950; rev. and enl. ed. Boston: Houghton Mifflin, 1965.

Survey.

509 Fallon, Gabriel. THE ABBEY AND THE ACTOR. Dublin: National Theatre Society, 1969.

"The aim of this booklet is to set out in essay form the historical background to what has come to be known as 'the Abbey Theatre acting tradition'."

510 _____, ed. ABBEY THEATRE 1904-1966. Dublin: National Theatre Society, 1966.

Brochure to mark the opening of the New Abbey Theatre in 1966.

511 Faulkner, J.W.H. THE THEATRE: IDEAS AND IDEALS. London: Arthur H. Stockwell, 1924.

Reflections on various aspects of the drama and the theatre.

512 Fay, Frank J. TOWARDS A NATIONAL THEATRE: THE DRAMATIC CRITICISM OF FRANK J. FAY. Ed. with intro. Robert Hogan. Irish

Theatre Series, no. 1. Dublin: Dolmen Press; London: Oxford University Press, 1970.

Reprinted reviews and essays on the Irish dramatic movement.

513 Fay, Gerard. "The Irish Theatre--A Decline and Perhaps, in the End, a Fall." THEATRE IN REVIEW. Ed. Frederick Lumley. Edinburgh: Richard Paterson, 1956. Pp. 80-89.

It is questionable "whether such a thing as 'the Irish theatre' now exists."

514 _____. THE ABBEY THEATRE, CRADLE OF GENIUS. Dublin: Clonmore & Reynolds; London: Hollis & Carter, 1958.

Survey.

515 Fay, William George. MERELY PLAYERS. London: Rich & Cowan, 1932.

Background to Irish drama by a leading Irish actor.

516 Fay, William George, and Catherine Carswell. THE FAYS OF THE ABBEY THEATRE; AN AUTOBIOGRAPHICAL RECORD. Foreword James Bridie. London: Rich & Cowan; New York: Harcourt, Brace, 1935.

Also contains "List of First Productions, with Casts."

517 Fechter, Paul. DAS EUROPAISCHE DRAMA: GEIST UND KULTUR IM SPIEGEL DES THEATRES. 3 vols. Mannheim, Germany: Bibliographisches Institut Ag., 1956-58.

Includes studies of J.B. Priestley, Noel Coward, Laurence Housman, Sean O'Casey, T.C. Murray, T.S. Eliot, Christopher Fry, W.B. Yeats, Bernard Shaw, J.M. Synge, John Galsworthy, Somerset Maugham, and John Van Druten.

518 Fergusson, Francis. THE HUMAN IMAGE IN DRAMATIC LITERATURE. Garden City, N.Y.: Doubleday Anchor Books, 1957.

Includes essays on T.S. Eliot and James Joyce's EXILES.

519 Figgis, Darrel. STUDIES AND APPRECIATIONS. London: J.M. Dent; New York: E.P. Dutton, 1912.

Includes two chapters on J.M. Synge and one on "The Vitality of Drama."

520 Filon, Augustin. THE ENGLISH STAGE; BEING AN ACCOUNT OF THE VICTORIAN DRAMA. London: John Milne; New York: Dodd, 1897; rpt. Port Washington, N.Y.: Kennikat Press, 1970.

Background to the beginnings of modern British drama.

521  Finch, Robert. HOW TO WRITE A PLAY. New York: Greenberg, 1948.

"This book is intended as an introduction, and to suggest a practical way to make a beginning as a playwright."

522  Findlater, Richard. THE UNHOLY TRADE. London: Victor Gollancz; Toronto: Longmans, 1952.

An assessment of modern British drama.

523  _____. THE FUTURE OF THE THEATRE. London: Fabian Society, 1959.

Pamphlet examining the state of the English theatre and suggesting some measures which must be taken.

524  _____. BANNED! A REVIEW OF THEATRICAL CENSORSHIP IN BRITAIN. London: MacGibbon & Kee, 1967.

525  _____. COMIC CUTS. London: Andre Deutsch, 1970.

A "bedside sampler of censorship in action."

526  Flanagan, Hallie. SHIFTING SCENES OF THE MODERN EUROPEAN THEATRE. New York: Coward-McCann, 1928; London: George G. Harrap, 1929.

Dramatic diary of a year spent in European theatres.

527  Flannery, James W. MISS ANNIE F. HORNIMAN AND THE ABBEY THEATRE. Irish Theatre Series, no. 3. Dublin: Dolmen Press; London: Oxford University Press, 1970.

Booklet.

528  Fluchere, Henri. "The Function of Poetry in Drama." ENGLISH STUDIES TODAY. Ed. C.L. Wrenn and G. Bullough. London: Oxford University Press, 1951. Pp. 22-34.

Makes references to a few modern British plays.

529  Ford, Ford Madox. PORTRAITS FROM LIFE. Boston and New York: Houghton Mifflin; Chicago: Henry Regnery, 1937; British ed. MIGHTIER THAN THE SWORD. London: George Allen & Unwin, 1938.

Includes memories and criticisms of D.H. Lawrence and John Galsworthy.

530  Fornelli, Guido. TENDENZE E MOTIVI NEL DRAMMA INGLESE MOD-

ERNO E CONTEMPORANEO. Florence: Vallecchi, 1930.

Survey.

531 Fowell, Frank, and Frank Palmer. CENSORSHIP IN ENGLAND. London: Frank Palmer, 1913; rpt. New York: Benjamin Blom, 1969.

Survey.

532 Franc, Miriam Alice. IBSEN IN ENGLAND. Boston: Four Seas Co., 1919; rpt. Folcroft, Pa.: Folcroft Press, 1970.

533 Franzen, Erick. FORMEN DES MODERNEN DRAMAS; VON DER ILLU-SIONSBUEHNE ZUM ANTITHEATER. Munich: C.H. Beck, 1961.

Includes references to T.S. Eliot, Christopher Fry, Bernard Shaw, and W.B. Yeats.

534 Fraser, G.S. "The Drama." THE MODERN WRITER AND HIS WORLD. Rev. ed. London: Andre Deutsch, 1964. Pp. 200-226.

Includes a chapter on "The Irish Dramatic Revival" and another on "The Revival of Poetic Drama."

535 Freedley, George. "England and Ireland." A HISTORY OF MODERN DRAMA. Ed. Barrett H. Clark and George Freedley. New York: Appleton-Century-Crofts, 1947. Pp. 160-216.

Outline.

536 Freedley, George, and John A. Reeves. "The Irish National Theatre (1899-1940)." A HISTORY OF THE THEATRE. 3rd rev. ed. New York: Crown Publishers, 1968. Pp. 481-94.

537 _____. "England--Napoleon to the Battle of Britain (1815-1940)." A HISTORY OF THE THEATRE. 3rd rev. ed. New York: Crown Publishers. 1968. Pp. 553-82.

538 Freedman, Morris, ed. ESSAYS IN THE MODERN DRAMA. Boston: D.C. Heath, 1964.

Includes essays by various hands on Bernard Shaw, Arthur Pinero, Henry Arthur Jones, Sean O'Casey, T.S. Eliot, and Christopher Fry.

539 _____. THE MORAL IMPULSE: MODERN DRAMA FROM IBSEN TO THE PRESENT. Carbondale and Edwardsville: Southern Illinois University Press; London and Amsterdam: Feffer & Simon, 1967.

Includes essays on Bernard Shaw and Sean O'Casey.

540  Frenz, Horst. DIE ENTWICKLUNG DES SOZIALEN DRAMAS IN ENG-
LAND VOR GALSWORTHY. Bleicherode-am-Harz: Carl Nieft, 1938.

The development of social drama in England before Galsworthy.

541  Freyer, Grattan. "The Irish Contribution." THE MODERN AGE. Peli-
can Guide to English Literature no. 7. Ed. Boris Ford. Harmondsworth:
Penguin, 1961.

Survey.

542  Fricker, Robert. DAS HISTORISCHE DRAMA IN ENGLAND VON DER
ROMANTIK BIS ZUR GEGENWART. Swiss Studies in English. Bern: A.
Francke Verlag, 1940.

Survey from 1780 to 1937.

543  _____. DAS MODERNE ENGLISCHE DRAMA. Gottingen, Germany:
Vandenhoeck & Ruprecht, 1964.

Includes studies of W.H. Auden, J.M. Barrie, Lawrence Durrell, T.S. Eliot, Christopher Fry, John Galsworthy, H. Granville-Barker, Christopher Isherwood, Denis Johnston, James
Joyce, Somerset Maugham, Charles Morgan, Sean O'Casey,
J.B. Priestley, Bernard Shaw, Stephen Spender, J.M. Synge,
and W.B. Yeats.

544  Fry, Christopher. AN EXPERIENCE OF CRITICS. London: Perpetua,
1952; New York: Oxford University Press, 1953.

Dramatic criticism. First delivered as an address to the Critics' Circle on 28 April 1952, at The Arts Theatre, London.

545  GAIETY THEATRE, DUBLIN. 1871-1971: ONE HUNDRED YEARS OF
GAIETY. Dublin: Gaiety Theatre, 1971.

546  Galsworthy, John. "Some Platitudes Concerning Drama." THE INN OF
TRANQUILITY; STUDIES AND ESSAYS. London: Heinemann, 1912. Pp.
189-202.

Dramatic theory.

547  _____. "Anglo-American Drama and Its Future." ANOTHER SHEAF.
London: Heinemann; New York: Scribner's, 1919. Pp. 112-39.

Partially reprinted from the HIBBERT JOURNAL for 1910.

548  Gascoigne, Bamber. TWENTIETH-CENTURY DRAMA. London: Hutchinson, 1962; New York: Barnes & Noble, 1968.

According to the TIMES LITERARY SUPPLEMENT reviewer, this

is "the best introduction to the subject yet written."

549 Gaskell, Ronald. DRAMA AND REALITY: THE EUROPEAN THEATRE SINCE IBSEN. London: Routledge & Kegan Paul, 1972.

Includes essays on J.M. Synge and T.S. Eliot.

550 Gassner, John. MASTERS OF THE DRAMA. 3rd rev. and enl. ed. New York: Dover Publications, 1954.

Includes chapters on J.M. Synge, Bernard Shaw, T.S. Eliot, and Christopher Fry.

551 _____. THE THEATRE IN OUR TIMES; A SURVEY OF THE MEN, MATERIALS AND MOVEMENTS IN THE MODERN THEATRE. New York: Crown Publishers, 1954.

Includes many essays on various aspects of modern British drama.

552 _____. FORM AND IDEA IN MODERN THEATRE. New York: Holt, Rinehart and Winston, 1956.

See No. 553.

553 _____. DIRECTIONS IN MODERN THEATRE AND DRAMA. New York: Holt, Rinehart and Winston, 1965.

An expanded edition of FORM AND IDEA IN MODERN THEATRE (No. 552). Essays on various aspects of modern drama, making several references to modern British dramatists.

554 _____. DRAMATIC SOUNDINGS. New York: Crown Publishers, 1968.

Essays and reviews including some on modern British drama.

555 Gassner, John, and Ralph G. Allen. THEATRE AND DRAMA IN THE MAKING. Boston: Houghton Mifflin, 1964.

Anthology on dramatic method including contributions by W.B. Yeats and J.M. Synge.

556 George W.L. DRAMATIC ACTUALITIES. London: Sidgwick & Jackson, 1915.

Essays from various periodicals.

557 Gielgud, John. EARLY STAGES. London: Macmillan, 1939; rev. ed. London: Falcon Press, 1948; rev. ed. London: Heinemann, 1974.

Throws light on life in the English theatre during the '20s and '30s. The 1974 edition contains four new excerpts added to fill in briefly the years to 1952.

558 _____. STAGE DIRECTIONS. London: Heinemann, 1963; New York: Random House, 1964; London: Mercury Books, 1965.

Collection of unrelated articles.

559 Gielgud, Val. BRITISH RADIO DRAMA, 1922-1956. Foreword Sir William Haley. London and Toronto: George G. Harrap, 1957.

The author served as head of BBC drama for twenty-nine years.

560 Gilder, Rosamond, et al., eds. THEATRE ARTS ANTHOLOGY; A RECORD AND A PROPHECY. New York: Theatre Arts Books, 1950.

Includes articles on W.B. Yeats, Somerset Maugham, Sean O' Casey, and Bernard Shaw.

561 Gilliatt, Penelope. UNHOLY FOOLS: WITS, COMICS, DISTURBERS OF THE PEACE--FILM AND THEATRE. London: Secker & Warburg; New York: Viking Press, 1973.

A "compendium of her film and theater writing, drawn from more than a decade's reviewing and reportage on both sides of the Atlantic."

562 Glover, Halcott. DRAMA AND MANKIND; A VINDICATION AND A CHALLENGE. London: Ernest Benn, 1923; Boston: Small, Maynard, 1924.

Reflections on various aspects of drama.

563 Godfrey, Philip. BACK-STAGE; A SURVEY OF THE CONTEMPORARY ENGLISH THEATRE FROM BEHIND THE SCENES. London: George G. Harrap, 1933.

"It is this background which must be examined to understand how the theatre really functions."

564 Goetsch, Paul, ed. ENGLISH DRAMATIC THEORIES: 20TH CENTURY. English Texts no. 13. General ed. Theo Stemmler. Tuebingen, Germany: Max Niemeyer, 1972.

An anthology of dramatic writings by Bernard Shaw, W.B. Yeats, J.M. Synge, John Drinkwater, T.S. Eliot, Somerset Maugham, Sean O'Casey, W.H. Auden, Christopher Fry, Terence Rattigan, James Bridie, and J.B. Priestley.

565 Gogarty, Oliver St. John. AS I WAS GOING DOWN SACKVILLE STREET. London: Reynal; New York: Ryerson Press, 1937; rpt. London: Sphere Books, 1968.

Includes reflections on the Irish drama.

566 Goldman, Emma. THE SOCIAL SIGNIFICANCE OF THE MODERN DRA-
MA. Boston: Richard G. Badger; Toronto: Copp Clark, 1914.

Chapters on Bernard Shaw, John Galsworthy, Stanley Houghton,
Githa Stowerby, W.B. Yeats, Lennox Robinson, and T.C.
Murray.

567 Gowda, H.H. Anniah. THE REVIVAL OF ENGLISH POETIC DRAMA.
(IN THE EDWARDIAN & GEORGIAN PERIODS). Bangalore, India: Government Press, 1963.

Survey.

568 Gozenpud, A. PUTI I PEREPUT'YA. ANGLIISKAYA I FRANTSUZSKAYA
DRAMATURGIYA XX V [Roads and cross-roads. English and French 20th
century drama]. Leningrad: Iskusstvo, 1967.

Includes studies of J.M. Barrie, James Bridie, John Galsworthy,
James Joyce, Noel Coward, Somerset Maugham, Sean O'Casey,
J.B. Priestley, Christopher Fry, Bernard Shaw, and T.S. Eliot.

569 Granville-Barker, Harley. THE EXEMPLARY THEATRE. London: Chatto
& Windus, 1922; rpt. New York: Benjamin Blom, 1969.

"This book is a plea for the recognition of the theatre as an
educational force."

570 _____. A NATIONAL THEATRE. London: Sidgwick & Jackson, 1930.

571 _____. ON DRAMATIC METHOD: BEING THE CLARK LECTURES FOR
1930. London: Sidgwick & Jackson, 1931; rpt. New York: Hill &
Wang Dramabooks, 1956.

A "rediscovery of the laws of the theater."

572 _____. THE STUDY OF DRAMA. Cambridge Miscellany, XVI. Cambridge: At the University Press; New York: Macmillan, 1934.

"The ordinary theatre today exists by catering to the public
appetite for sensation and novelty."

573 _____. ON POETRY IN DRAMA. Romanes Lecture, 1937. London:
Sidgwick & Jackson, 1937.

574 _____. THE USE OF THE DRAMA. Princeton Books in the Humanities.
Princeton, N.J.: Princeton University Press, 1945; London: Sidgwick &
Jackson, 1946.

Discussion of various aspects of drama, making some references to modern British dramatists.

575 Graves, A.P. "Anglo-Irish Literature." THE CAMBRIDGE HISTORY OF ENGLISH LITERATURE. Ed. A.W. Ward and A.R. Waller. Cambridge: At the University Press, 1964. XIV, 329-30.

Survey.

576 Greene, Graham. BRITISH DRAMATISTS. London: William Collins; New York: Chanticleer Press, 1942.

Introductory survey.

577 Greenwood, Ormerod. THE PLAYWRIGHTS; A STUDY OF FORM, METHOD, AND TRADITION IN THE THEATRE. London: Pitman, 1950.

Makes illustrations from some modern British plays.

578 Gregory, Lady Isabella Augusta. OUR IRISH THEATRE. New York and London: G.P. Putnam, 1914; rpt. New York: Capricorn Books, 1965; new enl. ed. with foreword by Roger McHugh. New York: Oxford University Press, 1973.

579 _____. JOURNALS 1916-1930. Ed. Lennox Robinson. London: G.P. Putnam, 1946; New York: Macmillan, 1947.

Includes material on Irish drama.

580 _____, ed. IDEALS IN IRELAND. London: At the Unicorn, 1901.

A collection of articles by various hands which show "in what direction thought is moving in Ireland."

581 Greig, J.Y.T. THE PSYCHOLOGY OF LAUGHTER AND COMEDY. London: George Allen & Unwin; New York: Dodd, Mead, 1923; rpt. New York: Cooper Square Publishers, 1969.

Makes references to some modern British dramatists.

582 Grein, J.T. PREMIERES OF THE YEAR. London: John Macqueen, 1900; rpt. New York: Benjamin Blom, 1971.

Reprinted reviews and articles.

583 _____. DRAMATIC CRITICISM. London: Greening, 1902; rpt. New York: Benjamin Blom, 1969.

Collection of reviews.

584 _____. THE WORLD OF THE THEATRE; IMPRESSIONS AND MEMOIRS, MARCH 1920-1921. London: Heinemann, 1921.

585 _____. THE NEW WORLD OF THE THEATRE, 1923-1924. Preface G. K. Chesterton. London: Martin Hopkinson, 1924.

586 Groom, Bernard. A LITERARY HISTORY OF ENGLAND. London and New York: Longmans, 1929.

   Includes studies of Bernard Shaw, John Masefield, John Galsworthy, J.M. Barrie, and J.M. Synge.

587 Grundy, Sydney. THE PLAY OF THE FUTURE BY A PLAYWRIGHT OF THE PAST: A GLANCE AT "THE FUTURE OF THE THEATRE" BY JOHN PALMER. London: Samuel French, 1914.

588 Guenther, Margarete. DER ENGLISCHE KRIEGSROMAN UND DAS ENGLISCHE KRIEGSDRAMA 1919 BIS 1930. Neue Deutsche Forschungen, Band 59. Berlin: Junker und Duennhaupt, 1936.

   A historical survey examining the impact of World War I on English drama.

589 Guerrero Zamora, Juan. HISTORIA DEL TEATRO CONTEMPORANEO. 4 vols. Barcelona: Juan Flors, 1961.

   Includes chapters on T.S. Eliot, Christopher Fry, W.B. Yeats, J.M. Synge, J.B. Priestley, Sean O'Casey, and Bernard Shaw.

590 Guthke, Karl S. MODERN TRAGICOMEDY: AN INVESTIGATION INTO THE NATURE OF THE GENRE. New York: Random House, 1966.

   Includes some references to modern British plays.

591 Guthrie, John. THE CHAMBER DRAMA; BEING AN INTRODUCTORY TREATISE ON THE PRESENTATION OF A NEW FORM OF DRAMATIC ART. Flansham, Sussex: Pear Tree Press, 1930.

   "The key-notes of the Chamber Drama are simplicity and directness."

592 Guthrie, Tyrone. THEATRE PROSPECT. London: Wishart, 1932.

   Reflections on various aspects of the theatre.

593 _____. A LIFE IN THE THEATRE. London: Hamish Hamilton; New York: McGraw-Hill, 1960.

   Includes chapters on "West End" and "Ireland."

594 _____. IN VARIOUS DIRECTIONS: A VIEW OF THEATRE. London: Michael Joseph; New York: Macmillan, 1965.

Discussions on many theatrical topics including some references to modern British dramatists.

595 Gywnn, Denis. "The Irish Literary Theatre." EDWARD MARTYN AND THE IRISH REVIVAL. London: Jonathan Cape, 1930.

Survey.

596 Gwynn, Stephen. "The Gaelic League and the Irish Theatre." TODAY AND TOMORROW IN IRELAND; ESSAYS ON IRISH SUBJECTS. Dublin: Hodges, Figgis; London: Macmillan, 1903. Pp. 87-96.

597 _____. "The Irish Theatre." IRISH LITERATURE. Ed. Justin MacCarthy. Chicago: John D. Morris, 1904.

Survey.

598 _____. "Beginnings of the Irish Drama." IRISH LITERATURE AND DRA-MA IN THE ENGLISH LANGUAGE; A SHORT HISTORY. London: Thomas Nelson, 1936; rpt. Folcroft, Pa.: Folcroft Press, 1969.

Survey.

599 Hale, Edward Everett, Jr. DRAMATISTS OF TODAY. New York: Henry Holt; London: G. Bell, 1905.

Includes chapters on Arthur Pinero, Bernard Shaw, and Stephen Phillips.

600 Hale, Lionel. THE OLD VIC, 1949-50. London: Evans, 1950.

601 Hamilton, Clayton. "The Irish National Theatre." STUDIES IN STAGE-CRAFT. London: Grant Richards; New York: Henry Holt, 1914. Pp. 123-44.

Reprinted from THE BOOKMAN (New York), 34 (January 1912), 508-16. Discusses the aims and achievements of the Irish National Theatre Society.

602 _____. PROBLEMS OF THE PLAYWRIGHT. New York: Henry Holt, 1917.

Includes some illustrations from modern British plays.

603 _____. CONVERSATIONS ON CONTEMPORARY DRAMA. London and New York: Macmillan, 1924.

Includes studies of Bernard Shaw, J.M. Barrie, and John Galsworthy.

604 _____. "SO YOU'RE WRITING A PLAY!" Boston: Little, Brown, 1935;
London: Pitman, 1936.

Technical aspects of playwriting making some references to
modern British plays.


605 _____. THE THEORY OF THE THEATRE AND OTHER PRINCIPLES OF
DRAMATIC CRITICISM. New York: Henry Holt, 1939.

This consolidated edition includes THE THEORY OF THE THE-
ATRE, STUDIES IN STAGECRAFT, PROBLEMS OF THE PLAY-
WRIGHT, and SEEN ON THE STAGE.


606 Hamilton, Cosmo. PEOPLE WORTH TALKING ABOUT. New York: R.M.
McBridie, 1933; London: Hutchinson, 1934.

Includes studies of Bernard Shaw, J.M. Bridie, John Galsworthy, and Noel Coward.


607 Haney, J.L. ENGLISH LITERATURE. New York: Harcourt, Brace, 1920.

Includes discussions of Stephen Phillips, John Masefield, Bernard Shaw, J.M. Barrie, W.B. Yeats, J.M. Synge, and Lord
Dunsany.


608 Hardwicke, Sir Cedric. THE DRAMA TOMORROW. Rede Lecture, 1936.
Cambridge: At the University Press; New York: Macmillan, 1936.

In the author's judgment, "the drama has a tomorrow."


609 _____. A VICTORIAN IN ORBIT; THE IRREVERENT MEMOIRS OF SIR
CEDRIC HARDWICKE AS TOLD TO JAMES BROUGH. London: Methuen;
New York: Doubleday, 1961.

Makes references to some modern British dramatists.


610 Harker, Joseph. STUDIO AND STAGE. Intro. Sir Johnston Forbes-
Robertson. London: Nisbet, 1924.

Random memories of fifty years' work in the theatre.


611 Harris, Frank. CONTEMPORARY PORTRAITS. Four Series. New York:
Privately printed, 1915-23.

Includes Bernard Shaw, George Moore, Lord Dunsany, John
Galsworthy, and J.M. Barrie.


612 Hartmann, Alfons. DER MODERNE ENGLISCHE EINAKTER. Leipzig,
Germany: Noske, 1936.

The modern English one-act play.

613 Hartnoll, Phyllis. "The Modern Theatre." A CONCISE HISTORY OF
THE THEATRE. London: Thames and Hudson, 1968; paperback ed., 1971.
Pp. 240-62.

A history of the theatre "in the widest sense."

614 Hatlen, Theodore. ORIENTATION TO THE THEATER. 2nd ed. New
York: Appleton-Century-Crofts, 1972.

A study of various aspects of the drama making some references
to modern British plays.

615 Heilman, Robert B. TRAGEDY AND MELODRAMA; VERSIONS OF EX-
PERIENCE. Seattle and London: University of Washington Press, 1968.

Includes some illustrations from modern British plays.

616 _____. THE ICEMAN, THE ARSONIST, AND THE TROUBLED AGENT;
TRAGEDY AND MELODRAMA ON THE MODERN STAGE. Seattle: University of Washington Press; London: George Allen & Unwin, 1973.

Examination of tragic and melodramatic styles begun in TRAG-
EDY AND MELODRAMA (No. 615).

617 Henderson, Archibald. EUROPEAN DRAMATISTS. Cincinnati: Stewart &
Kidd, 1913; rev. ed. New York and London: D. Appleton, 1926; rpt.
Freeport, N.Y.: Books for Libraries Press, 1971.

Includes chapters on Bernard Shaw, Harley Granville-Barker,
and John Galsworthy.

618 _____. THE CHANGING DRAMA; CONTRIBUTIONS AND TENDEN-
CIES. London: Grant Richards; New York: Henry Holt, 1914; Cincinnati: Stewart & Kidd, 1919.

An analysis of the contribution of the modern school of dramatists and of the various trends of dramatic art, with references
to some modern British dramatists.

619 Henderson, W.A. 1909: THE IRISH NATIONAL THEATRE MOVEMENT.
A YEAR'S WORK AT THE ABBEY THEATRE. Dublin: Privately printed,
1909.

Told in press-cuttings.

620 Henn, T.R. THE HARVEST OF TRAGEDY. London: Methuen, 1956;
University Paperbacks, 1966; New York: Barnes & Noble, 1966.

Includes chapters on Bernard Shaw, T.S. Eliot, and the Irish
tragedy.

621  Hewitt, Barnard. HISTORY OF THE THEATRE FROM 1800 TO THE PRES-
ENT. New York: Random House, 1970.

> Survey.

622  Hickey, Des, and Gus Smith. A PALER SHADE OF GREEN. London:
Leslie Frewin, 1972; American ed. FLIGHT FROM THE CELTIC TWILIGHT.
Indianapolis: Bobbs-Merrill, 1973.

> Mirrors "the significant events in theatrical and cinematic his-
> tory which have been influenced by the Irish since the turn
> of the century."

623  Hinchliffe, Arnold P. "Drama." THE TWENTIETH-CENTURY MIND:
HISTORY, IDEAS, AND LITERATURE IN BRITAIN, VOL. III--1945-1965.
Ed. C.B. Cox and A.E. Dyson. London and New York: Oxford Univer-
sity Press, 1972. Pp. 414-39.

> Survey.

624  Hind, C.L. AUTHORS AND I. London: John Lane, 1921.

> Includes essays on J.M. Barrie, John Galsworthy, and John
> Masefield.

625  _____. MORE AUTHORS AND I. London: John Lane, 1922.

> Includes essays on St. John Ervine and J.M. Synge.

626  Hobson, Bulmer, ed. THE GATE THEATRE, DUBLIN. Dublin: Gate
Theatre, 1934.

> On the productions of the Gate Theatre since 1928.

627  Hobson, Harold. THEATRE. London and New York: Longmans, 1948.

> Reviews reprinted from the SUNDAY TIMES and the CHRISTIAN
> SCIENCE MONITOR.

628  _____. THEATRE 2. London and New York: Longmans, 1950.

> Reviews reprinted from the SUNDAY TIMES, 1948-49.

629  _____. VERDICT AT MIDNIGHT; SIXTY YEARS OF DRAMATIC CRITI-
CISM. London and New York: Longmans, 1952.

> Survey.

630  _____. THEATRE. Pleasures of Life Series. London: Burke, 1953.

> A bedside book.

631 _____. THE THEATRE NOW. London and New York: Longmans, 1953.
Reviews reprinted from the SUNDAY TIMES, 1949-52.

632 Hodson, James Landsdale. "Some Dramatists." NO PHANTOMS HERE.
London: Faber and Faber, 1932. Pp. 147-89.

633 Hogan, Robert. AFTER THE IRISH RENAISSANCE; A CRITICAL HISTORY
OF THE IRISH DRAMA SINCE "THE PLOUGH AND THE STARS". Minne-
apolis: University of Minnesota Press, 1967; London: Macmillan, 1968.

An "informal critical account."

634 _____. "Where Have All the Shamrocks Gone?" ASPECTS OF THE
IRISH THEATRE. Ed. Patrick Rafroidi, Raymonde Popot, and William
Parker. Lille, France: Publications de l'Universite de Lille; Paris: Editions
Universitaires, 1972. Pp. 261-71.

Argues that the Irishness of Irish drama will become extinct.

635 Hogan, Robert, and James Kilroy, eds. "Introduction." LOST PLAYS OF
THE IRISH RENAISSANCE. Newark, Del.: Proscenium Press; Gerrards
Cross, Buckinghamshire: Colin Smythe, 1970. Pp. 9-16.

This volume exemplifies "the chief alternatives that were arising
to challenge Yeats' idea of a poetic drama."

636 Holloway, Joseph. JOSEPH HOLLOWAY'S ABBEY THEATRE; A SELEC-
TION FROM HIS UNPUBLISHED JOURNAL "IMPRESSIONS OF A DUBLIN
PLAYGOER." Ed. Robert Hogan and Michael J. O'Neill. Carbondale
and Edwardsville: Southern Illinois University Press; London and Amsterdam: Feffer & Simons, 1967.

The history of Dublin and the Abbey Theatre . . . "has been
considerably enlivened by the fact that Mr. Holloway trundled
home every day to record in detail his reactions to plays and
players and his comments about and conversations with literary
and theatrical people."

637 _____. JOSEPH HOLLOWAY'S IRISH THEATRE, 1926-1944. 3 vols.
Ed. Robert Hogan and Michael J. O'Neill. Dixon, Calif.: Proscenium
Press, 1968-70.

Selections from the later years of Holloway's journal.

638 Hooper, W.E. THE STAGE IN THE YEAR 1900. London: Spottiswoode,
1901.

A collection of photogravure plates, portraying the leading
players and playwrights of the day.

639 Hope-Wallace, Philip. "Theatre, Music and Ballet." THE BALDWIN AGE. Ed. John Raymond. London: Eyre & Spottiswoode, 1960; Chester Springs, Pa.: Dufour Editions, 1961.

Survey of British drama from 1923 to 1937.

640 Hormann, Wilhelm. ENGLISCHE LITERATUR IM 20 JAHRUNDERT. Bern: A. Francke Verlag, 1965.

Deals with Noel Coward, Sean O'Casey, Denis Johnson, Bernard Shaw, T.S. Eliot, J.B. Priestley, and Christopher Fry.

641 Houghton, Norris. THE EXPLODING STAGE; AN INTRODUCTION TO TWENTIETH CENTURY DRAMA. New York: Weybright and Talley, 1971; Delta Books, 1973.

Includes illustrations from some modern British plays.

642 Howarth, Herbert. THE IRISH WRITERS, 1880-1940: LITERATURE UNDER PARNELL'S STAR. London: Rockliff, 1958; New York: Hill & Wang, 1959.

Survey.

643 Howe, P.P. THE REPERTORY THEATRE: A RECORD AND A CRITICISM. London: Martin Secker, 1910.

Chapter 2 deals with the Abbey Theatre.

644 Hoy, Cyrus. THE HYACINTH ROOM; AN INVESTIGATION INTO THE NATURE OF COMEDY, TRAGEDY AND TRAGICOMEDY. London: Chatto & Windus; New York: Alfred A. Knopf, 1964.

Includes a few illustrations from modern British plays.

645 Hubbell, Jay B., and John O. Beaty. "Irish Dramatists." AN INTRODUCTION TO DRAMA. New York: Macmillan, 1929. Pp. 522-24.

646 Hudson, Lynton. THE TWENTIETH-CENTURY DRAMA. London: George G. Harrap, 1946.

Includes discussions of most modern British dramatists.

647 _____. "A Dose of Paregoric." LIFE AND THE THEATRE. London: George G. Harrap, 1949. Pp. 172-86.

Reflections on modern British drama.

648 _____. THE ENGLISH STAGE 1850-1950. London: George G. Har-

rap, 1951.

"This is a history of the English theatre over the past century rather than of the drama itself during that period."

649  Hughes, Glenn. "Revolt in the English Theatre." THE STORY OF THE THEATRE; A SHORT HISTORY OF THEATRICAL ART FROM ITS BEGINNING TO THE PRESENT DAY. New York and London: Samuel French, 1928. Pp. 308-9.

650  _____. THE PATH TO THE MODERN DRAMA. Claremont, Calif.: Scripps College, 1930.

Summarizes the new technique in the theatre which is forward-looking and which he calls "Expressionism, not an attempt to reproduce life but to comment upon life."

651  Huneker, James Gibbons. THE PATHOS OF DISTANCE; A BOOK OF A THOUSAND AND ONE MOMENTS. New York: Scribner's, 1913.

Includes studies of George Moore, J.M. Synge, and W.B. Yeats.

652  Hunt, Elizabeth R. THE PLAY OF TODAY; STUDIES IN PLAY-STRUCTURE. New York: John Lane, 1913; new and rev. ed. New York: Dodd, 1924.

Illustrations from some modern British plays.

653  Hunter, G.K. "English Drama 1900-1960." HISTORY OF LITERATURE IN THE ENGLISH LANGUAGE. Vol. 7: THE TWENTIETH CENTURY. Ed. Bernard Bergonzi. London: Sphere Books, 1970. Pp. 310-35.

Survey.

654  Hurt, James, ed. FOCUS ON FILM AND THEATRE. Englewood Cliffs, N.J.: Prentice-Hall, 1974.

Anthology making a few references to modern British plays.

655  Hyman, Alan. THE GAIETY YEARS. London: Cassell, 1975.

On the productions at the Gaiety Theatre, London.

656  Isaacs, J. "T.S. Eliot and Poetic Drama." AN ASSESSMENT OF TWENTIETH-CENTURY LITERATURE. London: Secker & Warburg, 1951. Pp. 133-60.

Also makes references to other verse dramatists.

657  Jacquot, Jean, ed. LE THEATRE MODERNE; HOMMES ET TENDANCES.

Paris: Editions du Centre National de la Recherche Scientifique, 1958.
Includes discussion of T.S. Eliot and Sean O'Casey.

658 James, D.G., ed. THE UNIVERSITIES AND THE THEATRE. London: George Allen & Unwin, 1952.

Papers read at the symposium on the responsibility of the universities to the theatre, April 1951.

659 Jameson, Storm. MODERN DRAMA IN EUROPE. London: Collins; New York: Harcourt, Brace, 1920.

Includes discussions of the leading modern British dramatists.

660 Jeans, Ronald. WRITING FOR THE THEATRE. London: Edward Arnold; New York: Longmans, 1949.

Primarily about "craftsmanship as applied to the modern, realistic play."

661 Jellicoe, Ann. SOME UNCONSCIOUS INFLUENCES IN THE THEATRE. Judith Wilson Lecture, 1967. Cambridge: At the University Press, 1967.

Pamphlet.

662 Jennings, Humphrey. "The Theatre." THE ARTS TODAY. Ed. Geoffrey Grigson. London: John Lane, 1935. Pp. 189-216.

Reflections.

663 Jones, Henry Arthur. THE FOUNDATIONS OF A NATIONAL DRAMA. London: Chapman and Hall; New York: George H. Doran, 1913; rpt. Freeport, N.Y.: Books for Libraries, 1967.

A collection of lectures, essays, and speeches, delivered and written in the years 1896-1912.

664 _____. TALKS WITH PLAYGOERS. London: G. Bell, 1913.

Municipal and repertory theatres.

665 _____. THE THEATRE OF IDEAS. London: Chapman and Hall, 1915.

A burlesque allegory.

666 Jordon, John. "The Irish Theatre -- Retrospect and Premonition." CONTEMPORARY THEATRE. Ed. John Russell Brown and Bernard Harris. Stratford-upon-Avon Studies, no. 4. London: Edward Arnold, 1961; New York: St. Martin's Press, 1962. Pp. 165-83.

Survey.

667  Joyce, James. "The Day of the Rabblement." THE GENIUS OF THE IRISH THEATRE. Ed. Sylvan Barnet, Morton Berman, and William Burto. New York: New American Library, 1960.

Attacks the Irish dramatic movement.

668  Jurak, Mirko. GLAVNA PROBLEMSKA OBMOCJA V ANGLESKI POETICNO-POLITICNI DRAMATIKI V LETIH 1930-1940. Ljublijana, Yugoslavia: University of Ljublijana, 1968.

Deals with problems in the English politico-poetic drama 1930-40.

669  Kain, Richard M. DUBLIN IN THE AGE OF WILLIAM BUTLER YEATS AND JAMES JOYCE. Norman: University of Oklahoma Press, 1962; rpt. Norman: 1967.

Background to Irish drama.

670  Kavanagh, Peter. THE IRISH THEATRE: BEING A HISTORY OF THE DRAMA IN IRELAND FROM THE EARLIEST PERIOD UP TO THE PRESENT DAY. Tralee, Ireland: Kerryman, 1946.

Survey.

671  _____. THE STORY OF THE ABBEY THEATRE, FROM ITS ORIGINS IN 1899 TO THE PRESENT. New York: Devin Adair, 1950.

Survey.

672  Kelly, Blanche Mary. "Stage Directions." THE VOICE OF THE IRISH. New York: Sheed & Ward, 1952. Pp. 253-76.

Survey of the Irish dramatic movement.

673  Kennedy, Andrew. SIX DRAMATISTS IN SEARCH OF A LANGUAGE: STUDIES IN DRAMATIC LANGUAGE. Cambridge: At the University Press, 1975.

Includes discussions of Bernard Shaw and T.S. Eliot.

674  Kennedy, David. "The Drama in Ulster." THE ARTS IN ULSTER; A SYMPOSIUM. Ed. Sam Hanna Bell et al. London: George G. Harrap, 1951. Pp. 47-68.

Survey.

675  Kennedy, J.M. ENGLISH LITERATURE 1880-1905. London: Stephen Swift, 1912.

Includes sections on Bernard Shaw and W.B. Yeats.

676 Kenny, Herbert A. "Modern Times." LITERARY DUBLIN; A HISTORY. Dublin: Gill & Macmillan; New York: Taplinger, 1974. Pp. 243-318.

Survey.

677 Kernodle, George R. INVITATION TO THE THEATRE. New York: Harcourt, Brace & World, 1967.

Considers all major forms of theatre, with several illustrations from modern British plays.

678 Kerr, Alfred. DAS NEUE DRAMA. Berlin: G. Fischer, 1905.

Includes references to some modern British dramatists.

679 Kerr, Walter. HOW NOT TO WRITE A PLAY. New York: Simon & Schuster, 1955; London: Reinhardt, 1956.

Makes a few illustrations from modern British plays.

680 _____. PIECES AT EIGHT. New York: Simon & Schuster, 1957; London: Reinhardt, 1958.

Reprinted articles, making a few references to modern British plays.

681 _____. TRAGEDY AND COMEDY. New York: Simon & Schuster, 1967; London: Bodley Head, 1968.

Includes some illustrations from modern British plays.

682 _____. THIRTY PLAYS HATH NOVEMBER; PAIN AND PLEASURE IN THE CONTEMPORARY THEATER. New York: Simon & Schuster, 1969.

Reprinted essays, making some references to modern British plays.

683 Knight, G. Wilson. THE GOLDEN LABYRINTH; A STUDY OF BRITISH DRAMA. London: Phoenix House; New York: W.W. Norton, 1962.

684 Knoblock, Edward. "The Playwright's Progress." KISMET AND OTHER PLAYS. London: Chapman and Hall, 1957. Pp. 8-14.

Reprinted from THE LISTENER (London), 53 (2 June 1955), 981, 983. Practical notes on playwriting.

685 Knowles, Dorothy. THE CENSOR: THE DRAMA AND THE FILM 1900-1934. Preface Hubert Griffith. London: George Allen & Unwin, 1934.

Survey.

686  Kraft, Irma. "England--The Conservative." PLAYS, PLAYERS, PLAY-HOUSES: INTERNATIONAL DRAMA OF TODAY. New York: George Dobsevage, 1928. Pp. 129-45.

687  Kronenberger, Louis. THE THREAD OF LAUGHTER; CHAPTERS ON ENGLISH STAGE COMEDY FROM JONSON TO MAUGHAM. New York: Alfred A. Knopf, 1952; New York: Hill & Wang Dramabook, 1970.

   Includes chapters on Bernard Shaw, J.M. Synge, and Somerset Maugham.

688  Krutch, Joseph Wood. "MODERNISM" IN MODERN DRAMA; A DEFINI-TION AND AN ESTIMATE. Ithaca, N.Y.: Cornell University Press, 1953; London: Oxford University Press, 1954.

   Includes chapters on Bernard Shaw and J.M. Synge.

689  Lambert, J.W. "The Verse Drama." THEATRE PROGRAMME. Ed. J.C. Trewin. London: Frederick Muller, 1954. Pp. 49-72.

   Survey since World War II.

690  Lamm, Martin. MODERN DRAMA. Trans. Karin Elliott. Oxford: Basil Blackwell, 1952; New York: Philosophical Library, 1953; rpt. Folcroft, Pa.: Folcroft Library Editions, 1971.

   Includes chapters on Bernard Shaw, John Galsworthy, and the Irish drama.

691  Langner, Lawrence. THE PLAY'S THE THING. New York: G.P. Put-nam, 1960.

   Makes references to some modern British dramatists.

692  Lauterbach, Edward S., and W. Eugene Davis. "Drama." THE TRANSI-TIONAL AGE: BRITISH LITERATURE 1880-1920. Troy, N.Y.: Whitston Publishing Co., 1973. Pp. 45-58.

   Survey.

693  Law, Hugh Alexander. "Dramatists." ANGLO-IRISH LITERATURE. Fore-word A.E. George Russell. Dublin: Talbot Press; London: Longmans, 1926. Pp. 250-71.

   Survey.

694  Lawson, John Howard. THEORY AND TECHNIQUE OF PLAYWRITING. New York: G.P. Putnam, 1949; New York: Hill & Wang Dramabook, 1960.

   Includes several references to modern British dramatists.

695  Leech, Clifford. THE DRAMATIST'S EXPERIENCE; WITH OTHER ESSAYS IN LITERARY THEORY. London: Chatto & Windus; New York: Barnes & Noble, 1970.

Includes some references to modern British dramatists.

696  Levin, Harry, ed. PERSPECTIVES OF CRITICISM. Cambridge, Mass.: Harvard University Press, 1950.

Includes studies of W.B. Yeats and J.M. Synge.

697  Lewis, Allan. THE CONTEMPORARY THEATRE; THE SIGNIFICANT PLAY-WRIGHTS OF OUR TIME. New York: Crown Publishers, 1962.

Includes chapters on Bernard Shaw, T.S. Eliot, and Sean O' Casey.

698  Lewis, B. Roland. THE TECHNIQUE OF THE ONE-ACT PLAY; A STUDY IN DRAMATIC CONSTRUCTION. Boston: John W. Luce, 1918.

Includes some references to modern British one-act plays.

699  Lewisohn, Ludwig. "The Renaissance of the English Drama." THE MODERN DRAMA; AN ESSAY IN INTERPRETATION. New York: B.W. Huebsch, 1915; London: Secker, 1916; New York: Viking Press, 1931. Pp. 166-219.

Studies modern dramatic tendencies and methods by examining works of individual dramatists.

700  _____. THE DRAMA AND THE STAGE. New York: Harcourt, Brace, 1922; rpt. New York: Johnson Reprint, 1968.

Includes essays, reprinted from THE NATION, on Bernard Shaw, J.M. Barrie, and Somerset Maugham.

701  Lindsay, Ann. THE THEATRE. London: Bodley Head, 1948.

Introductory booklet.

702  LITERARY IDEALS IN IRELAND. London: T. Fisher Unwin, 1899.

Includes: John Eglinton, "What Should be the Subjects of a National Drama?"; W.B. Yeats, "A Note on National Drama"; John Eglington, "National Drama and Contemporary Life"; and A.E. [George Russell], "Literary Ideals in Ireland."

703  Littlewood, S.R. DRAMATIC CRITICISM. Foreword Sir Barry Jackson. London: Pitman, 1939; rev. and enl. ed. entitled THE ART OF DRAMA-TIC CRITICISM. Foreword Sir Barry Jackson. London: Pitman, 1952.

Survey and reflections by a professional dramatic critic.

704    "The London Season." THE BEST PLAYS OF 1919-1950. 30 vols. New York: Dodd, Mead, 1920-50.

      Each volume is an annual survey.

705    Long, William J. "The Celtic Revival." ENGLISH LITERATURE: ITS HISTORY AND ITS SIGNIFICANCE FOR THE LIFE OF THE ENGLISH SPEAKING WORLD. Boston: Ginn, 1964. Pp. 610-20.

      Introductory survey.

706    Longaker, Mark, and Edwin C. Bolles. "The Drama: 1890-1950." CONTEMPORARY ENGLISH LITERATURE. New York: Appleton-Century-Crofts, 1953. Pp. 386-421.

      Introductory, dealing with individual playwrights.

707    LONGFORD PRODUCTIONS: DUBLIN GATE SOUVENIR, 1939. Dublin: Corrigan & Wilson, 1939.

      Brochure.

708    Lucas, F.L. THE DRAMA OF CHEKOV, SYNGE, YEATS, AND PIRANDELLO. London: Cassell; New York: Dufour, 1963.

      Chapters on individual plays.

709    Lumley, Frederick. TRENDS IN 20TH CENTURY DRAMA: A SURVEY SINCE IBSEN AND SHAW. London: Barrie and Rockliff, 1956; rev. ed., 1960; updated ed. entitled NEW TRENDS IN 20TH CENTURY DRAMA: A SURVEY SINCE IBSEN AND SHAW. London: Barrie and Rockliff; New York: Oxford University Press, 1967.

      Comprehensive survey.

710    _____, ed. THEATRE IN REVIEW. Edinburgh: Richard Paterson, 1956.

      Collection of essays on various aspects of the modern British theatre.

711    Lunari, Gigi. IL MOVIMENTO DRAMMATICO IRLANDESE (1899-1922). Bologna: Cappelli, 1960.

      Survey of the Irish dramatic movement.

712    Lynd, Robert. "Literature and Music." HOME LIFE IN IRELAND. London: Mills & Boon, 1909. Pp. 305-17.

      Reflections on Irish drama.

713    _____. OLD AND NEW MASTERS. London: T. Fisher Unwin; New

York: Scribner's, 1919; rpt. Freeport, N.Y.: Books for Libraries Press, 1970.

Includes chapters on J.M. Synge, Bernard Shaw, W.B. Yeats, and Lady Gregory.

714 Mabley, Edward. DRAMATIC CONSTRUCTION; AN OUTLINE OF BASIC PRINCIPLES. Philadelphia: Chilton Book Co., 1972.

Analysis of plays by dramatists including Bernard Shaw and Sean O'Casey.

715 MacAnna, Thomas. "Nationalism from the Abbey Stage." THEATRE AND NATIONALISM IN TWENTIETH-CENTURY IRELAND. Ed. Robert O'Driscoll. Toronto: University of Toronto Press, 1971. Pp. 89-101.

716 McBrien, Peter F. HIGHER ENGLISH: DRAMA. Dublin: Intermediate & University College, n.d.

Textbook of literary appreciation with many illustrations from modern British plays.

717 McCaan, Sean, ed. THE STORY OF THE ABBEY THEATRE. A Four Square Book. London: New English Library, 1967.

Contents: Sean McCaan, "The Beginnings"; Anthony Butler, "The Guardians"; Sean McCaan, "The Theatre Itself"; Catherine Rynne, "The Playwrights"; Gabriel Fallon, "The Abbey Theatre Acting Tradition"; Donal Dorcey, "The Big Occasions."

718 MacCarthy, Desmond. THE COURT THEATRE, 1904-1907. London: A.H. Bullen, 1907; rpt. Coral Gables, Fla.: University of Miami Press, 1966.

Appraisal of the Court Theatre under the management of John E. Vedrenne and Harley Granville-Barker during the years which were a turning point in the English theatre.

719 _____. DRAMA. London and New York: G.P. Putnam, 1940; rpt. New York: Benjamin Blom, 1971.

A selection of his reviews in the NEW STATESMAN from 1913-35. See also No. 720.

720 _____. THEATRE. London: MacGibbon & Kee, 1954; New York: Oxford University Press, 1955.

An expanded form of his DRAMA (No. 719).

721 McCarthy, Mary. THEATRE CHRONICLES 1937-1962. New York: Farrar, Straus, 1963.

Collected essays and reviews. Much of the material was included in SIGHTS AND SPECTACLES, 1937-1958 (New York: Farrar, Straus; London: Heinemann, 1959).

722 McCollom, William G. "Tragedy for the Time Being." TRAGEDY. New York: Macmillan, 1957. Pp. 227-49.

Includes illustrations from some modern British tragedies.

723 _____. THE DIVINE AVERAGE; A VIEW OF COMEDY. Cleveland and London: Press of Case Western Reserve University, 1971.

Includes illustrations from some modern British plays.

724 MacDonagh, Thomas. LITERATURE IN IRELAND; STUDIES IRISH AND ANGLO-IRISH. Dublin: Talbot Press; New York: Stokes, 1916; rpt. Port Washington, N.Y.: Kennikat Press, 1970.

Survey.

725 MacGowan, Kenneth. THE THEATRE OF TOMORROW. New York: Boni and Liveright, 1921; London: T. Fisher Unwin, 1923.

Describes the new playhouse and the new play, with references to some modern British dramatists.

726 _____. A PRIMER OF PLAYWRITING. New York: Random House, 1951.

Includes illustrations from some modern British plays.

727 MacGowan, Kenneth, and William [W.] Melnitz. LIVING STAGE; A HISTORY OF THE WORLD THEATER. Englewood Cliffs, N.J.: Prentice-Hall, 1955.

Considers various aspects of the modern British theatre. See also No. 728.

728 _____. GOLDEN AGES OF THE THEATER. A Spectrum Book. Englewood Cliffs, N.J.: Prentice-Hall, 1959.

Condensed version of their LIVING STAGE (No. 727).

729 McHenry, Margaret. THE ULSTER THEATRE IN IRELAND. Philadelphia: University of Pennsylvania, 1931.

Survey.

730 MacKenna, Stephen. JOURNAL AND LETTERS. Ed. E.R. Dodds. London: Constable, 1936.

Includes background to Irish drama.

731    McLeod, Stuart R.   MODERN VERSE DRAMA.   Salzburg:   University of
Salzburg, 1972.

>    Includes discussions of W.B. Yeats, T.S. Eliot, Christopher
>    Fry, and W.H. Auden.

732    MacLiammoir, Micheal.   ALL FOR HECUBA; AN IRISH THEATRICAL
AUTOBIOGRAPHY.   London:   Methuen, 1946; Dublin:   Progress House,
1961.

>    Relates the story of the Dublin Gate Theatre.

733    _____.   THEATRE IN IRELAND.   Dublin:   Three Candles, for the Cultural Relations Committee of Ireland, 1950; rpt. ed. with "Sequel," 1964.

>    A monograph describing the rise of Irish theatre movements
>    other than the Abbey.

734    _____.   EACH ACTOR ON HIS ASS.   London:   Routledge & Kegan
Paul, 1961.

>    Diaries.

735    _____.   "Dramatic Accidents."   THEATRE 72.   Ed. Sheridan Morley.
London:   Hutchinson, 1972.   Pp. 37–49.

>    The Irish theatre in the twentieth century, viewed by its most
>    distinguished actor-manager.

736    Macqueen-Pope, W.   THEATRE ROYAL, DRURY LANE.   London:   W.H.
Allen, 1945.

>    Chronicle of the Theatre Royal from the time it opened in
>    1963 to the present.

737    _____.   CARRIAGES AT ELEVEN:   THE STORY OF THE EDWARDIAN
THEATRE.   London:   Hutchinson, 1947; rpt. Port Washington, N.Y.:
Kennikat Press, 1970; London:   Hale, 1972.

>    Survey.

738    _____.   GAIETY; THEATRE OF ENCHANTMENT.   London:   W.H. Allen,
1949.

>    The story of the Gaiety Theatre from its opening in 1868 to
>    its closing in 1939.

739    _____.   ST. JAMES'S; THEATRE OF DISTINCTION.   London:   W.H.
Allen, 1958.

>    Affectionate and "carefully detailed book."

740    _____. THE FOOTLIGHTS FLICKERED. London: Herbert Jenkins, 1959.
On the theatre in London, 1920-29.

741    Mais, S.P.B. "Modern Drama." FROM SHAKESPEARE TO O. HENRY.
Rev. ed. London: Grant Richards, 1923. Pp. 161-78.
Survey.

742    _____. SOME MODERN AUTHORS. London: Grant Richards, 1923;
rpt. Freeport, N.Y.: Books for Libraries Press, 1970.
Includes chapters on Harley Granville-Barker, J.M. Barrie,
Clemence Dane, St. John Ervine, John Galsworthy, Somerset
Maugham, Arthur Pinero, Bernard Shaw, and Alfred Sutro.

743    Malevinsky, Moses L. THE SCIENCE OF PLAYWRITING. New York:
Brentano's, 1925.
Includes some illustrations from modern British plays.

744    Malone, Andrew E. THE IRISH DRAMA. London: Constable; New York:
Scribner's, 1929; rpt. New York: Benjamin Blom, 1965.
Survey.

745    Malye, Jean. LA LITTERATURE IRLANDAISE CONTEMPORAINE. Paris:
Bibliotheque Internationale d'Edition, 1913.
Includes the Irish dramatic movement.

746    Mandel, Oscar. A DEFINITION OF TRAGEDY. New York University
Press, 1961.
Includes references to T.S. Eliot and J.M. Synge.

747    Mander, Raymond, and Joe Mitchenson. "The Twentieth Century (1901-
1957)." A PICTURE HISTORY OF THE BRITISH THEATRE. Hulton Picture
Histories. London: Hulton Press, 1957. Pp. 390-538.

748    Mantle, Burns, ed. "The London Scene." THE BEST PLAYS OF 1919-49.
27 vols. New York: Dodd, Mead, 1920-47.
An annual survey.

749    _____. THE THEATRE. London: George G. Harrap, 1931.
Introductory survey.

750    _____. MODERN DRAMA. London and New York: Thomas Nelson,
[1934].

Introductory survey.

751 _____, ed. ONE-ACT PLAYS OF TODAY. London: George G. Harrap, 1924.

Includes "Foreword" and introductions to each play.

752 _____, ed. GREAT MODERN BRITISH PLAYS. London: George G. Harrap, 1929.

Anthology including "Preface" and introductions to each play.

753 Marshall, Norman. THE OTHER THEATRE. London: John Lehmann, 1947.

"This book is about the experimental theatre in England during the last quarter of a century."

754 Martin, Wallace. "The 'New Drama.'" THE NEW AGE UNDER ORAGE; CHAPTERS IN ENGLISH CULTURAL HISTORY. Manchester, Eng.: Manchester University Press; New York: Barnes & Noble, 1967. Pp. 61-80.

Examines the criticisms of the drama which appeared in THE NEW AGE between 1908-10.

755 Martz, Louis L. "The Saint as Tragic Hero: SAINT JOAN and MURDER IN THE CATHEDRAL." TRAGIC THEMES IN WESTERN LITERATURE. New Haven, Conn. and London: Yale University Press, 1955. Pp. 150-78.

Explores the problem of whether a saint's play can ever be truly tragic.

756 Marx, Milton. THE ENJOYMENT OF DRAMA. New York: F.S. Crofts, 1940; 2nd rev. ed. New York: Appleton-Century-Crofts, 1961.

Includes references to some modern British plays.

757 Mason, A.E.W. SIR GEORGE ALEXANDER AND THE ST. JAMES THEATRE. London: Macmillan, 1935; rpt. New York: Benjamin Blom, 1969.

Record of the plays produced during Alexander's tenancy.

758 Mason, Eugene. CONSIDERED WRITERS, OLD AND NEW. London: Methuen, 1925.

Includes J.E. Flecker, John Masefield, John Drinkwater, and W.B. Yeats.

759 Matthews, Brander. A STUDY OF THE DRAMA. Boston: Houghton Mif-

flin, 1910.

Includes a few illustrations from modern British plays.

760 _____. "Irish Plays and Irish Playwrights." THE PRINCIPLES OF PLAY-MAKING AND OTHER DISCUSSIONS OF THE DRAMA. New York: Scribner's, 1919. Pp. 196–213.

Survey.

761 May, Robin, comp. THE WIT OF THE THEATRE. Prologue J.C. Trewin. London: Leslie Frewin, 1969.

Selective anthology.

762 Meier, Erika. REALISM AND REALITY: THE FUNCTION OF THE STAGE DIRECTIONS IN THE NEW DRAMA FROM THOMAS WILLIAM ROBERTSON TO GEORGE BERNARD SHAW. Cooper Monographs on English and American Literature, no. 12. Bern: A Francke Verlag, 1967.

Includes chapters on Arthur Pinero, Henry Arthur Jones, and Bernard Shaw.

763 Merchant, W. Moelwyn. CREED AND DRAMA; AN ESSAY IN RELIGIOUS DRAMA. London: Society for Promoting Christian Knowledge, 1965.

Includes chapters on T.S. Eliot and Christopher Fry.

764 Mercier, Vivian. THE IRISH COMIC TRADITION. London and New York: Oxford University Press, 1962; paperback ed., 1969.

The first sustained attempt to show that an unbroken comic tradition may be traced in Irish literature from approximately the ninth century down to the present day.

765 Mercier, Vivian, and David H. Greene, eds. "Introduction." 1000 YEARS OF IRISH PROSE: THE LITERARY REVIVAL. New York: Devin Adair, 1952; Grosset & Dunlap, 1961.

Includes background material.

766 Metwally, Abdalla A. STUDIES IN MODERN DRAMA. Vol. I. Beirut: Beirut Arab University, 1971.

Includes essays on Bernard Shaw, J.M. Synge, and T.S. Eliot.

767 Miller, Anna Irene. THE INDEPENDENT THEATRE IN EUROPE, 1887 TO THE PRESENT. New York: Ray Long and Richard R. Smith, 1931; rpt. New York: Benjamin Blom, 1966.

Includes chapters on "The Independent Theatres of England,"

"The National Theatre of Ireland," and "The Dramatic Awakening of Scotland and Wales."

768 Miller, J. William. MODERN PLAYWRIGHTS AT WORK. London and New York: Samuel French, 1968.

Includes chapters on Bernard Shaw and John Galsworthy.

769 Miller, Nellie Burget. THE LIVING DRAMA; HISTORICAL DEVELOPMENT AND MODERN MOVEMENTS VISUALIZED. New York and London: Century, 1924.

Includes discussions of the leading modern British dramatists.

770 Millett, Fred B. READING DRAMA; A METHOD OF ANALYSIS WITH SELECTIONS FOR STUDY. New York: Harper; London: Hamish Hamilton, 1950; rpt. Freeport, N.Y.: Books for Libraries Press, 1970.

Includes commentaries about plays by J.M. Barrie, W.B. Yeats, and J.M. Synge.

771 Millett, Fred B., and Gerald Eades Bentley. THE ART OF THE DRAMA. New York and London: D. Appleton-Century, 1935; rpt., 1963.

Includes some references to modern British plays.

772 Moderwell, Hiram Kelly. THE THEATRE OF TODAY. Intro. John Mason Brown. New York: Dodd, Mead, 1914.

Survey of British dramatic literature, 1890-1914.

773 Monahan, Michael. NOVA HIBERNIA: IRISH POETS AND DRAMATISTS OF TODAY AND YESTERDAY. New York: Mitchell Kennerley, 1914.

Includes studies of W.B. Yeats and J.M. Synge.

774 Montague, C.E. DRAMATIC VALUES. London: Methuen, 1911; rev. ed. Garden City, N.Y.: Doubleday, 1925.

Includes chapters on J.M. Synge, Bernard Shaw, and John Masefield.

775 Moody, William Vaughan, and Robert Morss Lovett. "Drama." A HISTORY OF ENGLISH LITERATURE. 8th ed. Ed. Fred B. Millett. New York: Scribner's, 1964. Pp. 391-401, 451-67.

Introductory survey.

776 Moore, George. HAIL AND FAREWELL. 3 vols. London: Heinemann; New York: D. Appleton, 1911-14.

Includes background to Irish drama.

777  Morgan, A.E. TENDENCIES OF MODERN ENGLISH DRAMA. London: Constable; New York: Scribner's, 1924; rpt. Freeport, N.Y.: Books for Libraries Press, 1969.

> Includes chapters on Bernard Shaw, H. Granville-Barker, St. John Hankin, John Galsworthy, W.B. Yeats, Edward Martyn, Lady Gregory, J.M. Synge, Stanley Houghton, Padraic Colum, Lennox Robinson, T.C. Murray, St. John Ervine, J.M. Barrie, John Masefield, John Drinkwater, Lord Dunsany, J.E. Flecker, and Gordon Bottomley.

778  Morgan, Louise. WRITERS AT WORK. London: Chatto & Windus, 1931.

> Includes chapters on W.B. Yeats and Somerset Maugham.

779  Morley, Malcolm. "Plays of Near Today." THE THEATRE. Art and Life Series. London: Pitman, 1935. Pp. 52-64.

> Survey.

780  Morris, Lloyd R. "The Drama." THE CELTIC DAWN: A SURVEY OF THE RENAISSANCE IN IRELAND 1889-1916. New York: Macmillan, 1917; rpt. New York: Cooper Square Publications, 1970. Pp. 88-172.

> Survey.

781  Morrison, G.E. THE RECONSTRUCTION OF THE THEATRE. Foreword Henry Arthur Jones. London: Simpkin, Marshall, Hamilton, Kent, for The Critics' Circle, 1919.

> Articles on the current state of the theatre from THE MORNING POST.

782  Muir, Kenneth. "Verse and Prose." CONTEMPORARY THEATRE. Ed. John Russell Brown and Bernard Harris. Stratford-upon-Avon Studies, no. 4. London: Edward Arnold; New York: St. Martin's Press, 1962. Pp. 97-115.

> Survey of poetic drama.

783  Munro, C.K. WATCHING A PLAY. London: Gerald Howe, 1933.

> In this discussion of dramatic technique, references are made to a few modern British dramatists.

784  Nathan, George Jean. TESTAMENT OF A CRITIC. New York and London: Alfred A. Knopf, 1931.

> Makes references to some modern British dramatists.

785  _____. SINCE IBSEN; A STATISTICAL HISTORICAL OUTLINE OF THE

POPULAR THEATRE SINCE 1900. New York: Alfred A. Knopf, 1933.

786    _____. "The Playwrights." THE THEATRE OF THE MOMENT; A JOUR-
NALISTIC COMMENTARY. New York and London: Alfred A. Knopf,
1936. Pp. 279-310.

>    Includes discussions of Noel Coward, J.B. Priestley, Dodie
>    Smith, and Bernard Shaw.

787    _____. "Foreword." FIVE GREAT MODERN IRISH PLAYS. New York:
Modern Library, 1941. Pp. ix-xiii.

>    Reflections on Irish drama.

788    _____. "The Contribution of the Irish." THE ENTERTAINMENT OF A
NATION. New York: Alfred A. Knopf, 1942. Pp. 68-75.

>    Argues that, except for Sean O'Casey, "the quondam rich vein
>    appears to have run dry."

789    _____. "Sample British Imports." THE THEATRE IN THE FIFTIES. New
York: Alfred A. Knopf, 1953. Pp. 124-60.

>    An impression of British drama in the 1950s.

790    _____. THE MAGIC MIRROR; SELECTED WRITINGS ON THE THEATRE.
Ed. with intro. Thomas Quinn Curtiss. New York: Alfred A. Knopf,
1960.

>    Includes essays on Bernard Shaw, Sean O'Casey, John Gals-
>    worthy, and Noel Coward.

791    Nevinson, Henry Woodd. BOOKS AND PERSONALITIES. London
and New York: John Lane, 1905.

>    Includes studies of some Irish plays.

792    Newman, Evelyn. THE INTERNATIONAL NOTE IN CONTEMPORARY
DRAMA. New York: Kingsland Press, 1931.

>    Survey since the pre-War years.

793    Nichols, Beverley. ARE THEY THE SAME AT HOME? London: Jonathan Cape; New York: Doubleday, 1929.

>    Includes chapters on Frederick Lonsdale, Somerset Maugham,
>    George Moore, and Sean O'Casey.

794    Nicoll, Allardyce. THE THEORY OF DRAMA. London: George G.
Harrap; New York: Thomas Y. Crowell, 1931; rpt. New York: Benjamin
Blom, 1966.

Makes illustrations from some modern British dramatists.

795 _____. FILM AND THEATRE. London: George G. Harrap; New York: Thomas Y. Crowell, 1936.

Makes references to some modern British plays.

796 _____. "The Modern Period." THE ENGLISH THEATRE; A SHORT HISTORY. London: Thomas Nelson, 1936. Pp. 176-211.

Survey.

797 _____. BRITISH DRAMA; AN HISTORICAL SURVEY FROM THE BEGINNINGS TO THE PRESENT TIME. 4th rev. ed. London: George G. Harrap, 1947.

Survey.

798 _____. WORLD DRAMA FROM AESCHYLUS TO ANOUILH. London: George G. Harrap, 1949; New York: Harcourt, Brace, 1950.

"This book attempts to provide a general conspectus of the drama's development."

799 _____. HISTORY OF ENGLISH DRAMA. Vol. 5: LATE NINETEENTH CENTURY DRAMA, 1850-1900. Cambridge: At the University Press, 1959.

Includes the beginnings of modern British drama.

800 _____. "Somewhat In a New Dimension." CONTEMPORARY THEATRE. Ed. John Russell Brown and Bernard Harris. Stratford-upon-Avon Studies, no. 4. London: Edward Arnold; New York: St. Martin's Press, 1962. Pp. 77-95.

Comparison between the dramatists of the fifties and those of the Edwardian and Georgian eras.

801 _____. THE THEATRE AND DRAMATIC THEORY. London: George G. Harrap, 1962.

Includes some references to modern British plays.

802 _____. "The Modern Drama." ENGLISH DRAMA: A MODERN VIEWPOINT. London: George G. Harrap; New York: Barnes & Noble, 1968. Pp. 104-25.

Survey.

803 _____. ENGLISH DRAMA 1900-1930; THE BEGINNINGS OF THE MOD-

ERN PERIOD. Cambridge: At the University Press, 1973.

Survey.

804 Nic Shiubhlaigh, Maire. THE SPLENDID YEARS: RECOLLECTIONS OF MAIRE NIC SHIUBHLAIGH, AS TOLD TO EDWARD KENNY. Foreword Padraic Colum. Dublin: James Duffy, 1955.

Covers Irish drama from 1899-1916.

805 Noble, Peter. BRITISH THEATRE. Foreword Laurence Olivier. London: British Yearbooks, 1946.

Surveys the British theatre during the period 1939-46.

806 Norman, C.H. "English Drama of Revolt." THE REVOLUTIONARY SPIRIT IN MODERN LITERATURE AND DRAMA AND THE CLASS WAR IN EUROPE, 1918-36. London: Blue Moon Press, 1937; rpt. Folcroft, Pa.: Folcroft Press, 1970; Port Washington, N.Y.: Kennikat Press, 1971. Pp. 23-26.

Surveys the plays that indict the social system.

807 O'Casey, Sean. THE FLYING WASP; ESSAYS ON THE MODERN THE-ATRE. London: Macmillan, 1937.

The subtitle reads: "A Laughing Look-Over of What Has Been Said about the Things of the Theatre by the English Dramatic Critics, with Many Merry and Amusing Comments Thereon, with Some Shrewd Remarks by the Author on the Wise, Delicious, and Dignified Tendencies in the Theatre of Today."

808 _____. AUTOBIOGRAPHIES. 6 vols. in 2. London: Macmillan, 1963.

Contains background to Irish drama.

809 _____. BLASTS AND BENEDICTIONS; ARTICLES AND STORIES. Selected with intro. Ronald Ayling. London: Macmillan; New York: St. Martin's Press, 1967.

Writings between 1926, when he first came to England, and 1964, the year of his death.

810 O'Connor, Frank. "All the Olympians." THE BACKWARD LOOK; A SURVEY OF IRISH LITERATURE. London: Macmillan, 1967. Pp. 183-93; American ed. A SHORT HISTORY OF IRISH LITERATURE; A BACK-WARD LOOK. New York: G.P. Putnam, 1967; Capricorn Books, 1968. Pp. 183-93.

Reprinted from SATURDAY REVIEW (10 December 1966, pages 30-32, 99), the essay includes discussion of J.M. Synge, W. B. Yeats, and Lady Gregory.

811 _____. "The Abbey Theatre." MY FATHER'S SON. London: Macmillan, 1968. Pp. 145-78.

Recollections.

812 O'Connor, Norreys Jephson. CHANGING IRELAND: LITERARY BACK-GROUNDS OF THE IRISH FREE STATE, 1889-1922. London: Oxford University Press; Cambridge, Mass.: Harvard University Press, 1924.

Includes background to Irish drama and studies of W.B. Yeats, Lord Dunsany, and Lady Gregory.

813 O'Donnel, F[rank]. Hugh. THE STAGE IRISHMEN OF THE PSEUDO-CELTIC DRAMA. London: John Long, 1904.

814 O'Driscoll, Robert, ed. THEATRE AND NATIONALISM IN TWENTIETH-CENTURY IRELAND. Toronto: University of Toronto Press; London: Oxford University Press, 1971.

"This book is about the writers who moulded the mind of modern Ireland."

815 O'Hagan, Thomas. "The Irish Dramatic Movement." ESSAYS ON CATHOLIC LIFE. Baltimore: John Murphy, 1916; rpt. Freeport, N.Y.: Books for Libraries Press, 1965. Pp. 57-73.

Survey.

816 OhAodha, Micheal. THE ABBEY--THEN AND NOW. Dublin: Abbey Theatre, 1969.

A monograph bringing the Abbey Theatre's history up to 1969.

817 _____. THEATRE IN IRELAND. Oxford: Basil Blackwell; Totowa, N.J.: Rowman and Littlefield, 1974.

Traces the formative processes which have shaped Irish drama from the opening of the first theatre in Ireland in 1637 to the reopening of the Gate Theatre on a subsidized basis in 1971.

818 Oliver, D.E. "The Present Day Stage." THE ENGLISH STAGE; ITS ORIGINS AND MODERN DEVELOPMENTS. 2nd ed. London: John Ouseley, 1912. Pp. 71-142.

Survey.

819 Olson, Elder. TRAGEDY AND THE THEORY OF DRAMA. Detroit, Mich.: Wayne State University Press, 1966.

Makes a few illustrations from modern British plays.

820 O'Neill, James J. IRISH THEATRICAL HISTORY: A BIOGRAPHICAL ES-SAY. Dublin: Browne & Nolan, 1910.

Survey.

821 Oppel, Horst, ed. DAS MODERNE ENGLISCHE DRAMA: INTERPRETA-TIONEN. Berlin: Erich Schmidt, 1963.

Includes studies of plays by Bernard Shaw, W.B. Yeats, J.M. Synge, John Galsworthy, Sean O'Casey, W.H. Auden, Chris-topher Isherwood, T.S. Eliot, and Christopher Fry.

822 Oppenheimer, George, ed. THE PASSIONATE PLAYGOER; A PERSONAL SCRAPBOOK. New York: Viking Press, 1958.

Includes some references to modern British dramatists.

823 Ould, Hermon. THE ART OF THE PLAY. London: Pitman, 1938.

Includes discussions of T.S. Eliot, Noel Coward, Bernard Shaw, John Galsworthy, and Sean O'Casey.

824 Owen, Harrison. THE PLAYWRIGHT'S CRAFT. London and New York: Thomas Nelson, 1940.

Makes illustrations from some modern British plays.

825 Palmer, D.J. "Drama." THE TWENTIETH-CENTURY MIND: HISTORY, IDEAS, AND LITERATURE IN BRITAIN. Ed. C.B. Cox and A.E. Dyson. Vol. I: 1900-1918. London and New York: Oxford University Press, 1972. Pp. 447-74.

Includes discussion of Bernard Shaw and J.M. Synge.

826 Palmer, John. THE CENSOR AND THE THEATRES. London: T. Fisher Unwin, 1912; New York: Mitchell Kennerley, 1913.

Chapter IV, "The Dramatic Authors," deals with the attitude of the modern British dramatists toward censorship.

827 _____. THE FUTURE OF THE THEATRE. London: G. Bell, 1913.

Discusses the current state of British drama.

828 Paul-Dubois, L. "The Literary Awakening." CONTEMPORARY IRELAND. Dublin: Maunsel; New York: Baker & Taylor, 1908. Pp. 420-30.

Includes survey of Irish drama.

829 Peacock, Ronald. THE POET IN THE THEATRE. New York: Harcourt, Brace; London: Routledge, 1946; rpt. New York: Hill & Wang, 1960.

Includes chapters on T.S. Eliot, Bernard Shaw, J.M. Synge, and W.B. Yeats.

830 _____. THE ART OF DRAMA. London: Routledge & Kegan Paul, 1957; rpt. Westport, Conn.: Greenwood Press, 1974.

Makes references to some modern British dramatists.

831 Pearson, Hesketh. MODERN MEN AND MUMMERS. London: George Allen & Unwin, 1921.

Includes studies of Bernard Shaw, Stephen Phillips, and Harley Granville-Barker.

832 _____. THE LAST ACTOR-MANAGERS. London: Methuen, 1950; New York: Harper, 1951; rpt. London: White Lion Publishers, 1974.

Includes some references to modern British plays.

833 _____. LIVES OF THE WITS. London: Heinemann; New York: Harper, 1962.

Contains essays on Max Beerbohm and Bernard Shaw.

834 Pellizzi, Camillo. ENGLISH DRAMA: THE LAST GREAT PHASE. Trans. Rowan Williams. London: Macmillan, 1935.

835 Percy, Edward. THE ART OF THE PLAYWRIGHT. London: English Theatre Guild, 1949.

A lecture delivered at the London Polytechnic on 13 November 1947, with added excerpts from the author's own work illustrating his methods.

836 Perry, Henry Ten Eyck. "Modern Times." MASTERS OF DRAMATIC COMEDY AND THEIR SOCIAL THEMES. Cambridge, Mass.: Harvard University Press, 1939; rpt. Port Washington, N.Y.: Kennikat Press, 1968.

Deals with W.B. Yeats, Lady Gregory, J.M. Synge, and Bernard Shaw.

837 Phelps, William Lyon. THE TWENTIETH CENTURY THEATRE; OBSERVATIONS ON THE CONTEMPORARY ENGLISH AND AMERICAN STAGE. New York: Macmillan, 1918; rpt. Port Washington, N.Y.: Kennikat Press, 1968.

Analyzes the conditions and tendencies of the stage in England and America since 1900, and points out the merits and defects of the modern play.

838 _____. ESSAYS ON MODERN DRAMATISTS. New York: Macmillan, 1921; rpt. Books for Libraries Press, 1970.

Papers on six outstanding leaders of the drama including Barrie, Shaw, and Galsworthy.

839 _____. AS I LIKE IT. New York: Scribner's, 1923.

Articles from SCRIBNER'S MAGAZINE.

840 Platt, Agnes. THE STAGE IN 1902. London: Simpkin, Marshall, 1903.

Reviews and essays from the LONDON MUSICAL COURIER.

841 Playfair, Nigel. THE STORY OF THE LYRIC THEATRE, HAMMERSMITH. London: 1925; rpt. New York: Benjamin Blom, 1969.

Includes some references to modern British plays.

842 Poel, William. WHAT IS WRONG WITH THE STAGE; SOME NOTES ON THE ENGLISH THEATRE FROM THE EARLIEST TIMES TO THE PRESENT DAY. London: George Allen & Unwin, 1920.

Pamphlet attributing the poor condition of current British drama to "commercialism" and suggesting "some necessary reforms."

843 Pogson, Rex. THEATRE BETWEEN WARS (1919-1939). Drama Study Books, no. 1. Clevedon, Somerset: Triangle Press, 1947.

Brief survey.

844 Pollock, John. CURTAIN UP. London: Peter Davies, 1958.

Notes on the theatre, making references to some modern British dramatists.

845 Porter, Raymond J., and James D. Brophy, eds. MODERN IRISH LITERATURE; ESSAYS IN HONOR OF WILLIAM YORK TINDALL. New York: Twayne Publishers, 1972.

Includes essays on W.B. Yeats and Lady Gregory.

846 Power, Patrick C. A LITERARY HISTORY OF IRELAND. Cork: Mercier Press, 1969.

Includes introductory survey of Irish drama.

847 Priestley, J.B. THEATRE OUTLOOK. London: Nicholson & Watson, 1947.

Reflections on the modern English theatre.

848 _____. THE ART OF THE DRAMATIST; A LECTURE TOGETHER WITH APPENDICES AND DISCURSIVE NOTES. London: Heinemann, 1957; Boston: The Writer, 1958.

Makes some references to modern British plays.

849 _____. MARGIN RELEASED; A WRITER'S REMINISCENCES AND RE-FLECTIONS. London and Toronto: Heinemann, 1962.

Includes references to many modern British dramatists.

850 Prior, Moody E. THE LANGUAGE OF TRAGEDY. New York: Columbia University Press, 1947; Bloomington and London: Indiana University Press, 1966.

Includes some references to modern British tragedies.

851 Rafroidi, Patrick; Raymonde Popot; and William Parker, eds. ASPECTS OF THE IRISH THEATRE. Lille, France: Publications de l'Universite de Lille; Paris: Editions Universitaires, 1972.

Anthology of critical articles.

852 Raphaelson, Samson. THE HUMAN NATURE OF PLAYWRITING. New York: Macmillan, 1949.

Makes references to some modern British plays.

853 Reaske, Christopher R. HOW TO ANALYZE DRAMA. New York: Thor Publications, 1964.

Introductory booklet.

854 Reynolds, Ernest. MODERN ENGLISH DRAMA; A SURVEY OF THE THE-ATRE FROM 1900. Foreword Allardyce Nicoll. London: George G. Harrap; New York: British Book Centre, 1949; Norman: University of Oklahoma Press, 1951.

Deals with "varying tendencies within the theatre as well as with individual authors and plays."

855 Rickword, Edgell, ed. SCRUTINIES. London: Wishart, 1928.

Includes articles from SCRUTINY on J.M. Barrie, John Galsworthy, John Masefield, and Bernard Shaw.

856 Rivoallan, Anatole. LITTERATURE IRLANDAISE CONTEMPORAINE. Paris: Hachette, 1939.

Chapter 6 is a survey of Irish drama.

857 Robinson, Lennox. CURTAIN UP: AN AUTOBIOGRAPHY. London: Michael Joseph, 1942.

Contains background to Irish drama.

858 _____. TOWARDS AN APPRECIATION OF THE THEATRE. Dublin: Metropolitan Publishing Co., 1945.

Makes some illustrations from modern British plays.

859 _____. PICTURES IN A THEATRE; A CONVERSATION PIECE. Dublin: Abbey Theatre, [1947].

Contains background to Irish drama.

860 _____. IRELAND'S ABBEY THEATRE; A HISTORY 1899-1951. London: Sidgwick & Jackson, 1951; rpt. Port Washington, N.Y.: Kennikat Press, 1968.

Survey.

861 _____, ed. THE IRISH THEATRE: LECTURES DELIVERED DURING THE ABBEY THEATRE FESTIVAL HELD IN DUBLIN IN AUGUST 1938. London: Macmillan, 1939; rpt. New York: Haskell House, 1971.

Contents: Andrew E. Malone, "The Early History of the Abbey Theatre"; Frank O'Connor, "Synge"; Lennox Robinson, "Lady Gregory"; F.R. Higgins, "Yeats and Poetic Drama in Ireland"; Andrew E. Malone, "The Rise of the Realistic Movement"; T.C. Murray, "George Shiels, Brinsley Mac Namara, etc."; Walter Starkie, "Sean O'Casey"; and Ernest Blythe, "Gaelic Drama."

862 Rodgers, W.R., ed. IRISH LITERARY PORTRAITS. London: British Broadcasting Corp., 1972.

Broadcast conversations with those who knew some of the greatest Irish writers, including W.B. Yeats, J.M. Synge, and Bernard Shaw.

863 Roston, Murray. "The Modern Era." BIBLICAL DRAMA IN ENGLAND FROM THE MIDDLE AGES TO THE PRESENT DAY. London: Faber and Faber; Evanston, Ill.: Northwestern University Press, 1968. Pp. 233-306.

Includes discussions of J.M. Barrie, James Bridie, Christopher Fry, D.H. Lawrence, Bernard Shaw, and W.B. Yeats.

864 Rowe, Kenneth Thorpe. WRITE THAT PLAY. New York and London: Funk & Wagnalls, 1939; rpt., 1968.

Detailed analysis of A NIGHT AT AN INN, by Lord Dunsany,

and RIDERS TO THE SEA, by J.M. Synge.

865 _____. A THEATRE IN YOUR HEAD. New York: Funk & Wagnalls, 1960.

Makes illustrations from some modern British plays.

866 Rowell, George. "The Era of Society Drama." THE VICTORIAN THEATRE; A SURVEY. London and New York: Oxford University Press, 1956. Pp. 103-50.

Considers the work done in the English theatre up to 1914.

867 _____, ed. VICTORIAN DRAMATIC CRITICISM. London: Methuen, 1971.

Anthology including contributions by William Archer, Max Beerbohm, Desmond MacCarthy, and Bernard Shaw.

868 Roy, Emil. BRITISH DRAMA SINCE SHAW. Carbondale: Southern Illinois University Press; London and Amsterdam: Feffer & Simons, 1972.

Includes chapters on Bernard Shaw, W.B. Yeats, J.M. Synge, Sean O'Casey, T.S. Eliot, and Christopher Fry.

869 Rubinstein, H.F. WHAT ISN'T WRONG WITH THE DRAMA. London: Ernest Benn, 1927.

An address delivered to the Interlude Theatre Guild on 13 January 1927.

870 _____. "The Restoration of Roundhead Drama." THE ENGLISH DRAMA. London: Ernest Benn, 1928. Pp. 63-79.

Introductory survey.

871 Russell, Caro Mae Green. MODERN PLAYS AND PLAYWRIGHTS; WITH SOME NOTES ON THE THEATER AND SCREEN BY PAUL GREEN. University of North Carolina Liberal Extension Publications, vol. 2, no. 6. Chapel Hill: University of North Carolina Press, 1936.

Includes a chapter on Lennox Robinson and Sean O'Casey.

872 Russell, Diarmuid, ed. "Introduction." THE PORTABLE IRISH READER. New York: Viking Press, 1946. Pp. xi-xxx.

Includes useful background.

873 Russell, Sir Edward. THE THEATRE AND THINGS SAID ABOUT IT. Liverpool: Henry Young, 1911.

A paper read before the Literary and Philosophical Society of

Southport on 2 March 1911, making references to some modern British dramatists.

874  Rust, Adolf. BEITRAEGE ZU EINER GESCHICHTE DER NEU-KELTISCHEN RENAISSANCE. Bueckeburg, Germany: Grimme, 1922.

Includes studies of W.B. Yeats, Edward Martyn, Alice Milligan, George Moore, Douglas Hyde, and J.M. Synge.

875  Ryan, W.P. "Ireland at the Play." THE POPE'S GREEN ISLAND. London: Nisbet, 1912. Pp. 299-307.

Reflections on Irish drama.

876  Sahal, N. SIXTY YEARS OF REALISTIC IRISH DRAMA (1900-1960). Bombay: Macmillan, 1971.

Comprehensive survey.

877  Saint-Denis, Michel. THEATRE; THE REDISCOVERY OF STYLE. Intro. Laurence Olivier. London and Toronto: Heinemann, 1960.

Lectures on aspects of the theatre, with some references to the British theatre.

878  Salerno, Henry F., ed. "Introduction." ENGLISH DRAMA IN TRANSITION 1800-1920. New York: Pegasus, 1968. Pp. 11-22.

Survey prefixed to an anthology.

879  Samachson, Dorothy, and Joseph Samachson. THE DRAMATIC STORY OF THE THEATRE. London: Abelard-Schuman, 1955.

Exciting pictures of the English and Irish theatres.

880  Saul, George Brandon. "Introduction." AGE OF YEATS: THE GOLDEN AGE OF IRISH LITERATURE. New York: Dell, 1964.

Background to Irish drama.

881  Sawyer, Newell W. THE COMEDY OF MANNERS FROM SHERIDAN TO MAUGHAM. Philadelphia: University of Pennsylvania Press, 1931; rpt. New York: A.S. Barnes, 1961.

Survey.

882  Schelling, Felix E. "English Drama Since Sheridan." ENGLISH DRAMA. London: J.M. Dent; New York: E.P. Dutton, 1914; rpt. Delhi: S. Chand, 1963. Pp. 309-32.

Survey.

883 Scott, Clement. THE DRAMA OF YESTERDAY AND TODAY. 2 vols. London: Macmillan, 1899.

"Result of forty years of keen observation."

884 Scott, Dixon. MEN OF LETTERS. London and New York: Hodder and Stoughton, 1916.

Includes studies of Bernard Shaw, J.M. Barrie, Harley Granville-Barker, and John Masefield.

885 Scott, Nathan A., Jr., ed. THE CLIMATE OF FAITH IN MODERN LIT-ERATURE. New York: Seaburg Press, 1964.

Includes two articles: "Being and Faith in the Contemporary Theater," by Kay Baxter, and "The Christian Presence in the Contemporary Theater," by E. Martin Browne.

886 Scott-James, R.A. PERSONALITY IN LITERATURE. London: Secker, 1931; New York: Henry Holt, 1932.

Includes studies of Bernard Shaw and J.M. Synge.

887 _____. FIFTY YEARS OF ENGLISH LITERATURE 1900-1950. WITH A POSTSCRIPT--1951 TO 1955. London: Longmans, 1956.

Includes introductory survey.

888 Sell, Henry Blackman. WHAT IS IT ALL ABOUT? A SKETCH OF THE NEW MOVEMENT IN THE THEATRE. Chicago: Laurentian Publishers, 1914.

Introductory pamphlet.

889 Seltzer, Daniel, ed. THE MODERN THEATRE: READINGS AND DOCU-MENTS. Boston: Little, Brown, 1967.

Anthology of articles on various aspects of the theatre.

890 Setterquist, Jan. IBSEN AND THE BEGINNINGS OF ANGLO-IRISH DRAMA. Upsala Irish Studies. Dublin: Hodges, Figgis; Cambridge, Mass.: Harvard University Press, 1952.

On the influence of Ibsen.

891 Shank, Theodore [J.]. THE ART OF DRAMATIC ART. Belmont, Calif.: Dickenson, 1969.

"In this book I have attempted to provide an understanding of dramatic art as a single, unique fine art, distinct from litera-ture and the other arts with which it is something associated."

892 Shanks, Edward. SECOND ESSAYS ON LITERATURE. London: Collins, 1927.

> Includes essays on John Galsworthy, D.H. Lawrence, and J. E. Flecker.

893 Sharp, E. Farquharson. A SHORT HISTORY OF THE ENGLISH STAGE FROM ITS BEGINNINGS TO THE SUMMER OF THE YEAR 1908. London: Walter Scott, 1909.

894 Sharp, William L. LANGUAGE IN DRAMA; MEANINGS FOR THE DIRECTOR AND THE ACTOR. Scranton, Pa.: Chandler Publishing Co., 1970.

> Makes references to some modern British plays.

895 Shaw, Bernard. DRAMATIC OPINIONS AND ESSAYS. New York: Brentano's, 1906.

> Contributions to the London SATURDAY REVIEW.

896 _____. A NOTE ON THE IRISH THEATRE BY THEODORE ROOSEVELT AND AN "INTERVIEW" ON THE IRISH PLAYERS IN AMERICA. New York: Mitchell Kennerley, 1912.

> On the occasion of the Irish Players' first American tour.

897 _____. PLAYS AND PLAYERS; ESSAYS ON THE THEATRE. Selected with intro. A[lfred]. C. Ward. London: Oxford University Press, 1952.

> Selections from his SATURDAY REVIEW assessments.

898 _____. THE MATTER WITH IRELAND. Ed. with intro. David H. Greene and Dan H. Laurence. London: Rupert Hart-Davis; New York: Hill & Wang, 1962.

> Includes material on Irish drama.

899 Short, Ernest. THEATRICAL CAVALCADE. London: Eyre & Spottiswoode; Toronto: Collins, 1942; London: Woman's Book Club, 1943.

> Deals with most modern British dramatists.

900 _____. FIFTY YEARS OF VAUDEVILLE, 1895-1945. London: Eyre & Spottiswoode, 1946.

> Survey of the genre.

901 _____. INTRODUCING THE THEATRE; TOGETHER WITH A DISCUSSION ON THE FACTORS WHICH MAKE FOR "GOOD THEATRE." London:

Eyre & Spottiswoode, 1949; New York: British Book Centre, 1950.

Review of "the plays and theatrical entertainments of the past half-century or so."

902 _____. SIXTY YEARS OF THEATRE. London: Eyre & Spottiswoode, 1951.

Includes material from THEATRICAL CAVALCADE and FIFTY YEARS OF VAUDEVILLE (Nos. 899 and 900).

903 Short, Ernest, and Arthur Compton-Rickett. RING UP THE CURTAIN: BEING A PAGEANT OF ENGLISH ENTERTAINMENT COVERING HALF A CENTURY. London: Herbert Jenkins, 1938.

Survey.

904 Skelton, Robin, and David R. Clark, eds. IRISH RENAISSANCE; A GATHERING OF ESSAYS, MEMOIRS, AND LETTERS FROM "THE MASSA-CHUSETTS REVIEW". Dublin: Dolmen Press; London: Oxford University Press, 1965.

Includes essays on W.B. Yeats, Lady Gregory, J.M. Synge, Bernard Shaw, and Sean O'Casey.

905 Skelton, Robin, and Ann Saddlemyer, eds. THE WORLD OF W.B. YEATS: ESSAYS IN PERSPECTIVE. Victoria, B.C.: Adelphia Bookshop, for University of Victoria, 1965; rev. ed. Seattle: University of Washington Press, 1967.

Includes articles on W.B. Yeats, the Abbey Theatre, poetic drama in Yeats' time, Lady Gregory, Edward Martyn, and J. M. Synge.

906 Skinner, R. Dana. OUR CHANGING THEATRE. New York: Dial Press; Toronto: Longmans, 1931.

Collected reviews from THE COMMONWEAL indicating general trends and the writer's conviction that there is a "transition through ultra-realism back to the old magic of the theatre of make-believe."

907 Slater, Derek. PLAYS IN ACTION; A SIX-TERM COURSE IN DRAMA. Oxford: Pergamon Press, 1964.

Includes close study of THE DEVIL'S DISCIPLE, by Bernard Shaw, and THE PLAYBOY OF THE WESTERN WORLD, by J. M. Synge.

908 Slater, Guy, ed. BEST THEATRE STORIES. London: Faber and Faber, 1968.

Includes contributions by Somerset Maugham and Noel Coward.

909  Snider, Rose. SATIRE IN THE COMEDIES OF CONGREVE, SHERIDAN, WILDE AND COWARD. Orono:  University of Maine Studies, 1937; rpt. New York:  Phaeton Press, 1972.

910  Sorell, Walter. FACETS OF COMEDY.  New York:  Grosset & Dunlap, 1972.

Makes some illustrations from modern British plays.

911  Spanos, William V. THE CHRISTIAN TRADITION IN MODERN BRITISH VERSE DRAMA:  THE POETICS OF SACRAMENTAL TIME.  Foreword E. Martin Browne.  New Brunswick, N.J.:  Rutgers University Press, 1967.

Includes discussions of Gordon Bottomley, T.S. Eliot, John Masefield, Christopher Fry, Charles Williams, and Christopher Hassall.

912  Speaight, Robert. DRAMA SINCE 1939.  The Arts in Britain Series. London:  Longmans, Green, for The British Council, 1947.

Booklet.

913  _____. THE CHRISTIAN THEATRE.  Faith and Fact Books, no. 118. London:  Burns & Oates; Englewood Cliffs, N.J.:  Hawthorn Books, 1960.

Survey of modern religious British drama.

914  Speer, Rev. J.C. THE ETHICAL OUTLOOK OF THE CURRENT DRAMA. Toronto:  William Briggs, 1902.

A paper read before the Toronto General Ministerial Association, 1902.

915  S[pence]., E.F. OUR STAGE AND ITS CRITICS.  London:  Methuen, 1910.

Articles from the WESTMINSTER GAZETTE on the current state of the British theatre.

916  Spencer, Theodore [J.].  "Man's Spiritual Situation As Reflected in Modern Drama."  SPIRITUAL PROBLEMS IN CONTEMPORARY LITERATURE; A SERIES OF ADDRESSES AND DISCUSSIONS.  Ed. Stanley Romaine Hopper.  New York:  Harper, 1952.  Pp. 45-58.

Illustrations from Bernard Shaw and T.S. Eliot.

917  Spinner, Kaspar. DIE ALTE DAME SAGT:  NEIN! DREI IRISCHE DRA-MATIKER:  LENNOX ROBINSON, SEAN O'CASEY, DENIS JOHNSTON.

Swiss Studies in English. Bern: A. Francke Verlag, 1961.

Detailed study of their plays.

918    Stamm, Rudolf. GESCHICHTE DES ENGLISCHEN THEATERS. Bern: A. Francke Verlag, 1951.

Chapter IX contains a survey of modern British drama.

919    _____. ZWISCHEN VISION UND WIRKLICHKEIT. Bern: A. Francke Verlag, 1964.

Includes essays on Bernard Shaw, W.B. Yeats, T.S. Eliot, and Christopher Fry.

920    Stanford, Derek, ed. LANDMARKS. London and Camden, N.J.: Thomas Nelson, 1969.

Includes plays, with introductory notes, by Christopher Fry and T.S. Eliot.

921    Starkie, Enid. "Drama." FROM GAUTIER TO ELIOT; THE INFLUENCE OF FRANCE ON ENGLISH LITERATURE, 1851-1939. London: Hutchinson University Library; New York: Humanities Press, 1960. Pp. 202-10.

Survey.

922    Stein, Walter. "Drama." THE TWENTIETH-CENTURY MIND: HISTORY, IDEAS, AND LITERATURE IN BRITAIN. Ed. C.B. Cox and A.E. Dyson. Vol. II: 1918-1945. London and New York: Oxford University Press, 1972. Pp. 417-56.

Includes discussions of Bernard Shaw, Sean O'Casey, and T. S. Eliot.

923    Steiner, George. THE DEATH OF TRAGEDY. New York: Alfred A. Knopf, 1961; Hill & Wang Dramabook, 1963.

Makes some illustrations from modern British plays.

924    Stewart, J.I.M. EIGHT MODERN WRITERS. Oxford History of English Literature, vol. XII. London and New York: Oxford University Press, 1963.

Includes chapters on complete bibliographies of Bernard Shaw, W.B. Yeats, James Joyce, D.H. Lawrence, and Joseph Conrad.

925    Streatfeild, G.S. THE MODERN SOCIETY PLAY. London: Society for Promoting Christian Knowledge, 1915.

Pamphlet.

926　Strong, L.A.G. COMMON SENSE ABOUT DRAMA. London: Thomas Nelson; New York: Alfred A. Knopf, 1937.

Makes references to some modern British dramatists.

927　_____. PERSONAL REMARKS. London: Peter Nevill; New York: Liveright, 1953.

Includes chapters on W.B. Yeats and J.M. Synge.

928　_____. "Plays." THE WRITER'S TRADE. London: Methuen, 1953. Pp. 52-59.

Problems of playwriting.

929　_____. "Stage Plays." INSTRUCTIONS TO YOUNG WRITERS. London: Museum Press, 1958. Pp. 76-78.

Introductory.

930　Styan, J.L. THE ELEMENTS OF DRAMA. Cambridge: At the University Press, 1960.

Includes close analyses of plays by J.M. Synge, Bernard Shaw, T.S. Eliot, Sean O'Casey, and Christopher Fry.

931　_____. THE DARK COMEDY; THE DEVELOPMENT OF MODERN COMIC TRAGEDY. Cambridge: At the University Press, 1962; 2nd ed., 1968.

Includes studies of Bernard Shaw, J.M. Synge, and Sean O' Casey.

932　_____. THE DRAMATIC EXPERIENCE. Cambridge: At the University Press, 1965.

Introduction to drama, making some references to modern British plays.

933　_____. DRAMA, STAGE AND AUDIENCE. Cambridge: At the University Press, 1975.

Makes illustrations from some modern British plays.

934　Sutton, Graham. SOME CONTEMPORARY DRAMATISTS. London: Leonard Parsons, 1924; New York: George H. Doran, 1925; rpt. Port Washington, N.Y.: Kennikat Press, 1967.

Includes chapters on Harley Granville-Barker, Clemence Dane, John Drinkwater, St. John Ervine, Somerset Maugham, A.A. Milne, A.N. Monkhouse, and C.K. Munro.

935  Swinnerton, Frank. A LONDON BOOKMAN. London: Secker, 1930.

>   Includes studies of H. Granville-Barker and Bernard Shaw.

936  Symons, Arthur. PLAYS, ACTING AND MUSIC; A BOOK OF THEORY. London: Constable, 1909.

>   Includes discussions of Harley Granville-Barker, Bernard Shaw, and W.B. Yeats.

937  Synge, J.M. COLLECTED WORKS. Vol. 2: PROSE. Ed. Alan Price. London: Oxford University Press, 1966.

>   Includes material on Irish drama.

938  Talbot, A.J. CRAFT IN PLAY-WRITING. London: Frederick Muller, 1939.

>   Makes illustrations from some modern British plays.

939  Taylor, Alison. THE STORY OF THE ENGLISH STAGE. London and New York: Pergamon Press, 1967.

>   Introductory survey.

940  Taylor, Estella Ruth. THE MODERN IRISH WRITERS; CROSS CURRENTS OF CRITICISM. Lawrence: University of Kansas Press, 1954; rpt. New York: Greenwood Press, 1969.

>   Includes essays on Bernard Shaw and W.B. Yeats.

941  Taylor, George. WRITING A PLAY. Practical Stage Handbooks. London: Herbert Jenkins, 1957.

>   Makes illustrations from some modern British plays.

942  Taylor, John Russell. THE RISE AND FALL OF THE WELL-MADE PLAY. London: Methuen; New York: Hill & Wang, 1967.

>   Includes chapters on Bernard Shaw, Harley Granville-Barker, John Galsworthy, Frederick Lonsdale, Noel Coward, and Terence Rattigan.

943  Tennyson, G.B. AN INTRODUCTION TO DRAMA. New York and London: Holt, Rinehart and Winston, 1967.

>   Makes few references to modern British dramatists.

944  Thomas, Geoffrey. THE THEATRE ALIVE. London: Christopher Johnson, 1948.

>   A study of some topics in drama, with references to many modern British plays.

945 Thompson, E.R. PORTRAITS OF THE NEW CENTURY; THE FIRST TEN YEARS. London: Ernest Benn; Garden City, N.Y.: Doubleday, Doran, 1928.

>Includes studies of Bernard Shaw, John Galsworthy, Stephen Phillips, and J.M. Barrie.

946 Thompson, William Irwin. THE IMAGINATION OF AN INSURRECTION: DUBLIN, EASTER 1916; A STUDY OF AN IDEOLOGICAL MOVEMENT. New York: Oxford University Press, 1967.

>Includes chapters on W.B. Yeats, George Russell, and Sean O'Casey.

947 Thorndike, Ashley H. ENGLISH COMEDY. New York: Macmillan, 1929; rpt. New York: Cooper Square Publishers, 1965.

>Survey.

948 Thouless, Priscilla. MODERN POETIC DRAMA. Oxford: Basil Blackwell, 1934; rpt. Freeport, N.Y.: Books for Libraries Press, 1968.

>Includes chapters on Stephen Phillips, James Elroy Flecker, Laurence Binyon, John Masefield, Wilfred Wilson Gibson, John Drinkwater, Lascelles Abercrombie, John Davidson, Thomas Hardy, Arthur Symons, W.B. Yeats, Gordon Bottomley, and Sturge Moore.

949 Tindall, William York. FORCES IN MODERN BRITISH LITERATURE 1885-1956. Vintage Books. New York: Random House, 1956.

>"My concern has been not only with history, but also with meanings and values."

950 Trewin, J.C. THE ENGLISH THEATRE. London: Paul Elek, 1948.

>A "sketch of the plays and playwrights of the last quarter of a century."

951 _____. WE'LL HEAR A PLAY. London: Carroll & Nicholson, 1949.

>Articles from various periodicals.

952 _____. DRAMA 1945-1950. London: Longmans, Green, for The British Council, 1951.

>A "brief account of five years of the Drama in Britain."

953 _____. THE THEATRE SINCE 1900. London: Andrew Dakers; Toronto: Saunders, 1951.

>Survey.

954 _____. A PLAY TONIGHT. London: Elek Books, 1952.

Collection of criticism.

955 _____. DRAMATISTS OF TODAY. London: Staples Press, 1953.

British dramatists from 1900 to date.

956 _____. VERSE DRAMA SINCE 1800. Cambridge: At the University Press, for the National Book League, 1956.

Survey.

957 _____. THE NIGHT HAS BEEN UNRULY. London: Robert Hale, 1957.

Recalls "some of the most catastrophic first nights ever experienced."

958 _____. THE GAY TWENTIES; A DECADE OF THE THEATRE. Foreword Noel Coward. London: Macdonald, 1958.

Year-by-year survey.

959 _____. THE TURBULENT THIRTIES; A FURTHER DECADE OF THE THEATRE. Foreword Emlyn Williams. London: Macdonald, 1960.

Year-by-year survey.

960 _____. LONDON'S THEATRELAND. London: Perfecta Publications, 1971.

Pamphlet containing a survey of London's West End theatres.

961 _____, ed. THE YEAR'S WORK IN THE THEATRE 1948-1949. London: Longmans, Green, for The British Council, 1949.

Review of the year in the theatre.

962 _____, ed. THE YEAR'S WORK IN THE THEATRE 1949-1950. London: Longmans, Green, for The British Council, 1950.

Review of the year in the theatre.

963 _____, ed. THE YEAR'S WORK IN THE THEATRE 1950-1951. London: Longmans, Green, for The British Council, 1951.

Review of the year in the theatre.

964 _____, ed. THEATRE PROGRAMME. London: Frederick Muller; Toronto: Saunders, 1954.

Collection of essays by various authors on the British drama since World War II.

965    Tucker, S.M., ed. MODERN AMERICAN AND BRITISH PLAYS. New York: Harper, 1931.

> An anthology with a critical introduction on the influences and types of contemporary American and British drama.

966    Tucker, S.M., and Alan S. Downer, eds. TWENTY-FIVE MODERN PLAYS. 3rd ed. New York and London: Harper, 1953.

> An anthology including plays, with introductions, by Arthur Pinero, J.M. Synge, Sean O'Casey, T.S. Eliot, and St. John Ervine.

967    Tynan, Katharine. TWENTY-FIVE YEARS: REMINISCENCES. London: John Murray, 1913.

> Includes background to Irish drama.

968    Tynan, Kenneth. HE THAT PLAYS THE KING. London: Longmans, 1950.

> Records of actors at the height of their immediately post-war powers.

969    _____. PERSONA GRATA. London: Allan Wingate, 1953; New York: G.P. Putnam, 1954.

> Impressions of some famous people including Noel Coward, Christopher Fry, and Somerset Maugham.

970    _____. "The British Theatre." CURTAINS. New York: Atheneum; London: Longmans, 1961. Pp. 3-244.

> Reprinted play reviews and essays on general themes.

971    _____. TYNAN ON THEATRE. Harmondsworth: Penguin, 1964.

> A revised selection from CURTAINS.

972    _____. A VIEW OF THE ENGLISH STAGE. London: Davis-Poynter, 1975.

> Reprinted reviews of performances between 1946 and 1960.

973    Ure, Peter, and C.J. Rawson, eds. YEATS AND ANGLO-IRISH LITERA-TURE. New York: Harper, 1974.

> Covers W.B. Yeats, Bernard Shaw, and George Moore.

974 Ussher, Arland. THREE GREAT IRISHMEN: SHAW, YEATS, JOYCE. London: Victor Gollancz, 1952.

975 Van Doren, Carl, and Mark Van Doren. AMERICAN AND BRITISH LITERATURE SINCE 1890. New York: Appleton-Century-Crofts, 1967.

Introductory survey.

976 Van Druten, John. PLAYWRIGHT AT WORK. London: Hamish Hamilton; New York: Harper, 1953.

Discusses "characterisation, plot, dialogue and the art of 'holding an audience' with many examples from modern plays."

977 Vargas, Luis. GUIDEBOOK TO THE DRAMA. London: English Universities Press; New York: Dover Publications, 1960.

Introductory survey.

978 Vernon, Frank. THE TWENTIETH-CENTURY THEATRE. Intro. John Drinkwater. London: George G. Harrap; Boston: Houghton Mifflin, 1924.

Discusses trends in modern British drama since the 1890s.

979 Vines, Sherard. A HUNDRED YEARS OF ENGLISH LITERATURE. London: Duckworth, 1950; New York: Macmillan, 1951.

Includes a survey of modern British drama (pages 133-53) and one of modern Irish drama (pages 215-19).

980 Walbrook, H.M. NIGHTS AT THE PLAY. London: W.J. Ham-Smith, 1911.

Reprinted reviews.

981 _____. A PLAYGOER'S WANDERINGS. London: Leonard Parsons, 1926.

Articles from various periodicals.

982 Walkley, A.B. DRAMATIC CRITICISM; THREE LECTURES DELIVERED AT THE ROYAL INSTITUTION. London: John Murray, 1903.

Contents: "The Ideal Spectator"; "The Dramatic Critic"; "Old and New Criticism."

983 _____. DRAMA AND LIFE. London: Methuen, 1907; New York: Brentano's, 1908; rpt. Freeport, N.Y.: Books for Libraries Press, 1967.

Articles from the TIMES.

984 _____. "A Theatrical Forecast." PASTICHE AND PREJUDICE. London: Heinemann; New York: Alfred A. Knopf, 1921. Pp. 138-43.

One or two "guesses for next season."

985 _____. "Sympathy." MORE PREJUDICE. London: Heinemann; New York: Alfred A. Knopf, 1923. Pp. 153-57.

986 _____. STILL MORE PREJUDICE. London: Heinemann; New York: Alfred A. Knopf, 1925.

Articles from the TIMES.

987 Ward, A[lfred]. C., ed. SPECIMENS OF ENGLISH DRAMATIC CRITICISM XVII-XX CENTURIES. London: Oxford University Press, 1945.

Includes reviews of some British plays.

988 _____. "Playwrights." TWENTY-CENTURY ENGLISH LITERATURE 1901-1960. London: Methuen, 1964. Pp. 90-142.

Survey.

989 Warnock, Robert. "Modern British Drama." REPRESENTATIVE MODERN PLAYS: BRITISH. Chicago: Scott, Foresman, 1953. Pp. 1-19.

Introductory survey prefixed to an anthology.

990 Wauchope, George Armstrong. THE NEW IRISH DRAMA. Bulletin of the University of South Carolina, no. 168. Columbia: University of South Carolina, 1925.

Survey.

991 Weales, Gerald. "The Edwardian Theater and the Shadow of Shaw." EDWARDIANS AND LATE VICTORIANS. English Institute Essays, 1959. Ed. Richard Ellmann. New York: Columbia University Press, 1960. Pp. 160-87.

Reveals that the Edwardian theatre was unusually unified in its purposes and methods.

992 _____. RELIGION IN MODERN ENGLISH DRAMA. Philadelphia: University of Pennsylvania Press; London: Oxford University Press, 1961.

Shows that the successful production of religious plays on the English commercial stage in the years since World War II "is not an isolated phenomenon in the history of modern English drama."

993 _____. "Introduction." EDWARDIAN PLAYS. New York: Hill &

Wang, 1962. Pp. vii–xviii.

Survey prefixed to an anthology.

994 _____. A PLAY AND ITS PARTS. New York: Basic Books, 1964.

Makes illustrations from some modern British plays.

995 Webb, Kaye, ed. AN EXPERIENCE OF CRITICS. London: Perpetua, 1952.

Contains an essay by Christopher Fry, "An Experience of Critics," together with contributions on their approaches to dramatic criticism by W.A. Darlington, Ivor Brown, Alan Dent, Harold Hobson, Philip Hope-Wallace, Eric Keown, J.C. Trewin, and T.C. Worsley.

996 Welland, Dennis. "Some Post-War Experiments in Poetic Drama." EXPERIMENTAL DRAMA. Ed. William A. Armstrong. London: G. Bell, 1963; New York: Dufour, 1965. Pp. 36–55.

997 Weygandt, Cornelius. IRISH PLAYS AND PLAYWRIGHTS. London: Constable; Boston and New York: Houghton Mifflin, 1913; rpt. Port Washington, N.Y.: Kennikat Press, 1966.

Survey.

998 _____. TUESDAYS AT TEN: A GARNERING FROM THE TALKS OF THIRTY YEARS ON POETS, DRAMATISTS, AND ESSAYISTS. Philadelphia: University of Pennsylvania Press, 1928; London: Oxford University Press, 1929.

Includes talks on Lord Dunsany, W.B. Yeats, and John Masefield.

999 White, Terence de Vere. THE ANGLO-IRISH. London: Victor Gollancz, 1972.

Stresses the literary figures of 1900–20.

1000 Whitfield, George. AN INTRODUCTION TO DRAMA. 2nd ed. London and New York: Oxford University Press, 1963.

Includes discussions of plays by Bernard Shaw and T.S. Eliot.

1001 Whiting, Frank M. "The Spirit of Realism in England" and "Ireland." AN INTRODUCTION TO THE THEATRE. 3rd ed. New York and London: Harper, 1969. Pp. 92–98, 98–100.

Surveys.

1002 Whiting, John. JOHN WHITING ON THEATRE. LONDON MAGA-

ZINE Editions, no. 4. London: Alan Ross, 1966.

Reviews from the LONDON MAGAZINE.

1003 Whitworth, Geoffrey. THE THEATRE OF MY HEART. London: Victor Gollancz, 1938.

On the National Theatre.

1004 _____. THE THEATRE AND THE NATION. London: Quality Press, 1939.

A lecture delivered at the Royal Institution, London, December 1938.

1005 _____. THE MAKING OF A NATIONAL THEATRE. London: Faber and Faber, 1951.

Survey.

1006 Wieczorek, Hubert. IRISCHE LEBENSHALTUNG IM NEUEN IRISCHEN DRAMA. Breslau, Poland: Priebatsch, 1937.

Deals with Irish attitude in the new Irish drama.

1007 Wild, Friedrich. DIE ENGLISCHE LITERATUR DER GEGENWART SEIT 1870: DRAMA UND ROMAN. Wiesbaden, Germany: Dioskuren-Verlag, 1928.

Includes chapters on Bernard Shaw, J.M. Barrie, John Galsworthy, and Anglo-Irish drama.

1008 Wilde, Percival. THE CRAFTSMANSHIP OF THE ONE-ACT PLAY. Boston: Little, Brown, 1923.

1009 Williams, Harold. "Literary and Intellectual Drama in England." MODERN ENGLISH WRITERS: BEING A STUDY OF IMAGINATIVE LITERATURE 1890-1914. London: Sidgwick & Jackson, 1925; rpt. Port Washington, N.Y.: Kennikat Press, 1970. Pp. 223-70.

Survey.

1010 Williams, Raymond. DRAMA FROM IBSEN TO ELIOT. London: Chatto & Windus, 1952; rev. ed. entitled DRAMA FROM IBSEN TO BRECHT. London: Chatto & Windus, 1968; Harmondsworth: Penguin Books, 1973.

Includes chapters on the Irish dramatists, T.S. Eliot, Auden and Isherwood, Christopher Fry, and Bernard Shaw.

1011 _____. MODERN TRAGEDY. London: Chatto & Windus; Stanford, Calif.: Stanford University Press, 1966.

Makes references to some modern British tragedies.

1012 _____. "Modern Experimental Drama." DRAMA IN PERFORMANCE. New ed. London: C.A. Watts, 1968; New York: Basic Books, 1969. Pp. 134-58.

Includes discussion of T.S. Eliot and Samuel Beckett.

1013 Williams, Stephen. PLAYS ON THE AIR; A SURVEY OF DRAMA BROAD-CASTS. London and New York: Hutchinson, 1951.

A selection from weekly articles written for the RADIO TIMES as introductions to plays broadcast on BBC, including many modern British plays.

1014 Williams, T.G. "Revival of Drama." ENGLISH LITERATURE; A CRITI-CAL SURVEY. London: Pitman, 1951. Pp. 203-7.

1015 Williamson, Audrey. THEATRE OF TWO DECADES. London: Rockliff, 1951.

Includes discussions of J.B. Priestley, James Bridie, Emlyn Williams, Ronald Mackenzie, Peter Ustinov, Terence Rattigan, Rodney Ackland, Bernard Shaw, T.S. Eliot, Stephen Phillips, Christopher Fry, and W.H. Auden.

1016 Wilson, A.E. POST-WAR THEATRE. London: Home and Van Thal, with Dewynters, 1949.

Year by year survey, 1945-49.

1017 _____. EDWARDIAN THEATRE. London: Arthur Barker, 1951; New York: Macmillan, 1952.

Comprehensive survey.

1018 _____. PLAYGOER'S PILGRIMAGE. Foreword Dame Sybil Thorndike. London and New York: Stanley Paul, n.d.

"This is the life story ... of a dramatic critic."

1019 Wilson, N. Scarlyn. EUROPEAN DRAMA. London: Ivor Nicholson and Watson, 1937.

Includes discussions of John Galsworthy, Bernard Shaw, "The Pre-War Drama in England," and "The Post-War Drama in England."

1020 Wimsatt, W.K., Jr., ed. ENGLISH STAGE COMEDY. English Institute Essays, 1954. New York: Columbia University Press, 1955.

Includes essays on Bernard Shaw and T.S. Eliot.

1021 Worsley, T.C. THE FUGITIVE ART; DRAMATIC COMMENTARIES 1947-1951. London: John Lehmann, 1952.

Reprinted from BRITAIN TODAY and NEW STATESMAN AND NATION.

1022 _____. "The Author and the Theatre." THE CRAFT OF LETTERS IN ENGLAND; A SYMPOSIUM. Ed. John Lehmann. London: Cresset Press, 1956; Boston: Houghton Mifflin, 1957. Pp. 122-39.

Reveals that only in the theatre has creative activity seemed to flag.

1023 Worth, Katharine J. REVOLUTIONS IN MODERN ENGLISH DRAMA. London: G. Bell; Toronto: Clarke, Irwin, 1973.

Includes essays on T.S. Eliot, Bernard Shaw, W.H. Auden, Christopher Isherwood, and Sean O'Casey.

1024 Wright, Edward A., and Lenthiel H. Downs. A PRIMER FOR PLAY-GOERS. 2nd ed. Englewood Cliffs, N.J., and London: Prentice-Hall, 1959.

Makes some references to modern British plays.

1025 Yamamoto, Shuji. AIRURANDO ENGEKI KENKYU. Kyoto: Aporon-sha, 1968.

The story of the Irish drama.

1026 Yeats, W[illiam]. B[utler]. "A Note on National Drama." LITERARY IDEALS IN IRELAND. London: T. Fisher Unwin, 1899.

1027 _____. "The Literary Movement in Ireland." IDEALS IN IRELAND. Ed. Lady [Isabella Augusta] Gregory. London: Unicorn, 1901. Pp. 87-102.

1028 _____. THE CUTTING OF AN AGATE. London and New York: Macmillan, 1912; rpt. included in ESSAYS. London: Macmillan, 1924; and in ESSAYS AND INTRODUCTIONS. London: Macmillan, 1961.

1029 _____. "The Irish Movement." PLAYS AND CONTROVERSIES. London: Macmillan, 1923. Pp. 1-218.

1030 _____. "The Celtic Element in Literature." ESSAYS. London: Macmillan, 1924. Pp. 213-31; rpt. included in ESSAYS AND INTRODUCTIONS. London: Macmillan, 1961. Pp. 173-89.

1031 _____. ESSAYS. New York: Macmillan, 1924.

1032 _____. THE IRISH NATIONAL THEATRE. Rome: Reale Academia d' Italia, 1935.

1033 _____. DRAMATIS PERSONAE. London: Macmillan, 1936; rpt. included in AUTOBIOGRAPHIES. London: Macmillan, 1955.

1034 _____. AUTOBIOGRAPHIES. London: Macmillan, 1955.

1035 _____. "Advice to Playwrights Who are Sending Plays to the Abbey, Dublin." THE GENIUS OF THE IRISH THEATER. Ed. Sylvan Barnet, Morton Berman, and William Burto. Mentor Books. New York: New American Library, 1960. Pp. 349-50.

1036 _____. EXPLORATIONS. London: Macmillan, 1962.

1037 _____, ed. BELTAINE; THE ORGAN OF THE IRISH LITERARY THEATRE, MAY 1899-APRIL 1900. Ed. B.C. Bloomfield. London: Frank Cass, 1970.

  Reprint of the periodical which contains much of the early history of the Irish Literary Theatre.

1038 _____, ed. SAMHAIN, OCTOBER 1901-NOVEMBER 1908. Ed. B.C. Bloomfield. London: Frank Cass, 1970.

  Reprint of the periodical which contains the early history of the Irish Literary Theatre.

1039 Young, Ella. "Eire." FLOWERING DUSK; THINGS REMEMBERED ACCURATELY AND INACCURATELY. New York: Longmans, 1945; London: Dennis Dobson, 1947. Pp. 3-200.

  Background to Irish drama.

1040 Young, Stark. THE THEATRE. New York: George H. Doran, 1927; rpt. New York: Hill & Wang Dramabooks, 1959.

  Presents his philosophy of dramatic art as a whole.

1041 _____. IMMORTAL SHADOWS; A BOOK OF DRAMATIC CRITICISM. New York and London: Scribner's, 1948; London: MacGibbon & Kee, 1958.

  Play reviews from NEW REPUBLIC.

# Chapter 4

# PERIODICAL ARTICLES

1042 Aas, L. "Tre engelske Dramatikere." TILSKUEREN, 46 (May 1929), 355-63.

Discusses H. Granville-Barker, St. John Ervine, and John Drinkwater.

1043 "The Abbey Theatre." THEATRE ARTS MONTHLY (New York), 16 (September 1932), 692, 695.

Announcing the Abbey Theatre's new American tour.

1044 "The Abbey Theatre." IRISH TIMES (Dublin), 28 July 1944, p. 3.

Correspondence on the general condition of the Irish National Theatre.

1045 "The Abbey Theatre: Its Origins and Accomplishments." TIMES (London), Irish number, 17 (March 1913), 15.

Survey.

1046 "Abbey Theatre Subsidy." LITERARY DIGEST (New York), 86 (12 September 1925), 29-30.

Discussion of subsidy by the Irish Free State.

1047 "Abbey's New Policy." EVENING HERALD (Dublin), 13 August 1935, p. 7; rpt. LITERARY DIGEST (New York), 1 June 1935, p. 24.

Some of the best classical, Continental, and American drama will be given when new Irish plays are not available.

1048 Abercrombie, Lascelles. "The Function of Poetry in the Drama." POETRY REVIEW, 1 (1912), 107-18.

A play written in prose "is a thing essentially fantastic, unreal, bizarre--in fact, a tour de force."

1049 Adams, J. Donald. "The Irish Dramatic Movement." HARVARD MONTH-
LY, November 1911, pp. 44-48.

Survey.


1050 Agate, James. "What Is Wrong with the Theatre?" BOOKMAN (London),
73 (December 1927), 167-68.

Nine-tenths of the audience "like rubbish and will support that
rubbish."


1051 _____. See also his regular contributions to SUNDAY TIMES (London)
from 1923-47 and the critical collections cited in this bibliography (Nos.
263-82).


1052 Alldridge, John. "What's Wrong with the Abbey?" IRISH DIGEST (Dublin), 24 (February 1948), 17-19.

The Abbey Theatre "is a 'national' theatre in name only."


1053 Allen, Percy. "Ulster Drama; Modern Developments." DAILY TELE-
GRAPH (London), 25 March 1926, p. 65; rpt. as "The Theatre in Ulster."
LIVING AGE (Boston), 329 (29 May 1926), 467-69.

Survey.


1054 Allensworth, Josephine. "The Effectiveness of the One-Act Play." QUAR-
TERLY JOURNAL OF SPEECH, 26 (1940), 269-74.

The one-act play can be used effectively for the development
of oral reading, to form principles of clear thinking, and to
improve the speaking voice.


1055 "The Americanized British Stage." LITERARY DIGEST, 99 (December
1928), 26.


1056 Anderson, John. "This Year's Theater." SATURDAY REVIEW OF LITERA-
TURE (New York), 27 (2 April 1938), 14-15.

Review article.


1057 Andreades, A. "Les Theatres a Londres." LES ANNALES POLITIQUES
ET LITTERAIRES, 83 (20 March 1927), 314.

Survey of new plays.


1058 Andrews, Irene Dwen. "The Irish Literary Theatre." POET-LORE (Boston), 39 (Spring 1928), 94-100.

Striking features of modern Irish drama.

1059 Angus, William. "Expressionism in the Theatre." QUARTERLY JOURNAL OF SPEECH, 29 (November 1933), 477-92.

Expressionism has been "a considerable influence."

1060 Ansorge, Peter. "Ireland." PLAYS AND PLAYERS (London), 15 (May 1968), 60-62.

On the Abbey Theatre's offering at the World Theatre Season in London.

1061 Archer, William. "Plays of the New Season." FORTNIGHTLY REVIEW, 84 (October 1908), 676-86; rpt. LIVING AGE, 259 (7 November 1908), 329-38.

1062 _____ . "The Theatrical Situation." FORTNIGHTLY REVIEW, n.s. 88 (October 1910), 736-50.

1063 _____ . "Recent London Productions." NATION (New York), 98 (14 May 1914), 581-83.

1064 _____ . "The London Season." NATION (New York), 98 (25 June 1914), 764-65.

1065 _____ . "A Persistent Season." NATION (New York), 99 (6 August 1914), 171-72.

1066 _____ . "London Drama in War-Time." NATION (New York), 99 (5 November 1914), 559-60.

Survey.

1067 _____ . "The Stage in London--A Season of Quantity Rather Than Quality." NATION (New York), 100 (20 May 1915), 575-76.

1068 _____ . "New Productions in London." NATION (New York), 101 (28 October 1915), 526-27.

1069 _____ . "War Plays in London." NATION (New York), 104 (24 May 1917), 638-40.

1070 _____ . "The Drama in London." NATION (New York), 105 (4 October 1917), 377-79.

Survey.

1071 _____ . "The Drama in London." NATION (New York), 105 (29 November 1917), 601-3.

Survey.

1072 _____. "Impecunious Idealism." REVIEW (New York), 1 (11 October 1919), 479-80.

On bodies supporting drama.

1073 _____. "On the London Stage." REVIEW (New York), 2 (10 January 1920), 38, 40.

Survey.

1074 _____. "The Unreviving London Stage and Its Revivals." REVIEW (New York), 2 (1 May 1920), 465-66.

"The British drama is making a very slow recovery."

1075 _____. "Opening of the London Season." WEEKLY REVIEW (New York), 3 (13 October 1920), 326-28.

Survey.

1076 _____. See also his regular contributions to WORLD (1900-06), DAILY CHRONICLE (1900-10), MORNING LEADER (1901-12), TRIBUNE (1906-08), NATION (London; 1908-10), NATION (New York; 1914-18), and his critical works cited in this bibliography (Nos. 287-89).

1077 Armstrong, William A. "Modern Developments in the British Theatre." NEUPHILOLOGISCHE MITTEILUNGEN, 51 (February 1950), 19-34.

Survey.

1078 Arnold, Sidney. "The Abbey Theatre." ARTS AND PHILOSOPHY (London), Summer 1950, pp. 25-30.

1079 Arns, Karl. "Englische Theatermisstaende und Reformplaene." ZEIT-SCHRIFT FUER FRANZOESISCHEN UND ENGLISCHEN UNTERRICHT, 20 (1921), 232-42.

English theatrical ill-humor and reform plans.

1080 _____. "Neues zur englischen Theaterreform." ZEITSCHRIFT FUER FRANZOESISCHEN UND ENGLISCHEN UNTERRICHT, 23 (1923), 161-70.

New English theatre forms.

1081 _____. "Neue englische Dramen." ENGLISCHE STUDIEN (Leipzig)

59, no. 1 (1925), 62-77.

Survey.

1082 _____. "Reformen und Reformplaene im englischen Theaterwesen." ZEIT-SCHRIFT FUER FRANZOESISCHEN UND ENGLISCHEN UNTERRICHT, 24 (1926), 385-94.

Reforms and the reform of plans in the English theatre.

1083 _____. "Moderne englische Dramaturgie und Theaterkritik." ZEIT-SCHRIFT FUER FRANZOESCHEN UND ENGLISCHEN UNTERRICHT, 25 (1926), 54-61.

Modern English drama and dramatic criticism.

1084 _____. "Englische Theaterchronik 1933/34." RHEINISCH-WESTFAELISCHE ZEITUNG, 355 (1934).

1085 "At Last." DRAMA (London), Autumn 1962, p. 17.

The announcement on 4 July that a National Theatre is at last to be built.

1086 Atkinson, Brooks. "All Over Hell's Kitchen. Or, A Great Deal about Nonsense." THEATRE ARTS MONTHLY (New York), 11 (January 1927), 69-72.

Reflections on drama.

1087 "Au Revoir to the Abbey Theatre." SUNDAY TIMES (London), 25 January 1959, p. 9.

To preserve a record of the Abbey Theatre before it is pulled down for rebuilding, some of its former illustrious members visited it to make a film.

1088 Auden, W.H. "The Outlook for 'Poetic Drama.'" FRANCE-GRANDE BRETAGNE, 22 (1939), 226-34.

Address to a conference at the Sorbonne, Paris, on 8 December 1938.

1089 B. "The Irish Players." T.P.'S WEEKLY (London), 16 June 1911, p. 744.

The Irish National Theatre Society season at the Court Theatre, London.

1090 _____. "Miss Horniman's Season at the Court." SPECTATOR (London), 110 (31 May 1913), 924-25.

1091 Baker, George Pierce. "Narrative in the Drama." READER MAGAZINE (Indianapolis), 9 (January 1907), 211-17.

1092 _____. "Rhythm in Recent Dramatic Dialogue." YALE REVIEW, 19 (1929), 116-33.

> It is to the "importance of rhythmic flow . . . that we have been waking in our modern drama."

1093 Bakshy, Alexander. "The Theatre Unbound." ENGLISH REVIEW, 34 (February 1922), 159-62.

> The theatre must "forget its dreamy wanderings in the far-off realms of the playwrights' imagination, and come back to its own world--its Performance, its Showmen, its Stage-boards, and its Spectators."

1094 Barbor, H.R. "The War in the Theatre; The Case for The Actors' Association." NATION AND THE ATHENAEUM (London), 34 (18 October 1924), 110-11.

> The present condition of the theatre "offers tremendous opportunities to the actors as a class to exercise the greatest measure of control over the future development of British drama."

1095 Barnes, J.H. "The Drama of Today and the Public's Attitude Thereto." NINETEENTH CENTURY, 63 (February 1908), 305-10.

1096 _____. "The Drama of Today." NINETEENTH CENTURY, 93 (June 1923), 893-97.

> "There is not a new play, or even a revival, on the London stage which will be remembered in twelve months' time."

1097 Bartholeyns, A. O'D. "Our National Drama." WESTMINSTER REVIEW, 162 (October 1904), 444-49.

> English drama "is merely a pastime for the frivolous."

1098 Baughan, E.A. "The Irish Players." DAILY NEWS AND LEADER (London), 14 July 1913, p. 6.

> No progress has been made either in the writing or acting of these Irish plays."

1099 Bax, Clifford. "Plays in Performance." DRAMA (London), Winter 1948, pp. 8-11.

> Survey.

1100 Beers, Henry A. "The English Drama of Today." NORTH AMERICAN

REVIEW, 180 (May 1905), 746-57.

"The dramatic output of the last quarter-century outweighs that of any other quarter-century since 1700."

1101 _____. "Retrospects of the Drama." NORTH AMERICAN REVIEW, 186 (July 1907), 623-34.

Literary drama has been paralyzed because "England has lost the dramatic habit."

1102 Benavente, Jacinto. "The Playwright's Mind." YALE REVIEW, 13 (1923), 43-62.

The playwright "must detach himself from any consideration of moral ends as he studies the characters which he creates."

1103 Bentley, Eric. "The Drama at Ebb." KENYON REVIEW, 7 (Spring 1945), 169-84.

"As to Britain, drama is there reduced to the status of opera; all the best energy goes into revivals of classics."

1104 _____. "Drama Now." PARTISAN REVIEW, 12 (Spring 1945), 244-51.

Review article.

1105 _____. "Theory and Theatre." THEATRE ARTS MONTHLY (New York), 31 (1947), 44-45.

Review article.

1106 _____. "A Traveler's Report." THEATRE ARTS (New York), 33 (April 1949), 32-36.

"The talent of the English theatre . . . goes chiefly into revivals."

1107 _____. "World Theatre: 1900-1950." THEATRE ARTS (New York), 33 (December 1949), 22-27.

"As a tortured century reaches midpoint, in what direction is our theatre moving?"

1108 _____. "Irish Theatre: Splendeurs et Miseres." POETRY (Chicago), 79 (January 1952), 216-32; rpt. included in IN SEARCH OF THEATER. New York: Vintage Books, 1953. Pp. 307-21.

Survey.

1109 Bernstein, Henri. "Women and the Theatre." SATURDAY REVIEW (London), 29 August 1931, p. 262.

"The changes that have taken place with regard to the importance attached to women in the present-day world are visible
in the theatre of today."

1110 Bewley, Charles. "The Irish National Theatre." DUBLIN REVIEW, 152
(January 1913), 132-44; rpt. LIVING AGE (Boston), 276 (15 February
1913), 410-18.

"To those of us who entertained high hopes of a native Irish
school of drama the present state of the Abbey Theatre is a
continuous source of disappointment."

1111 Billington, Michael. "All Our Yesterdays--1936." PLAYS AND PLAYERS
(London), 13 (July 1966), 62-63.

"It wasn't a year for great new plays or playwrights."

1112 _____. "All Our Yesterdays--1946." PLAYS AND PLAYERS (London),
13 (September 1966), 62-63.

"Takes a look at this boom year in the theatre when Shafts-
bury Avenue was able to offer a temporary escape from the
realities of rationing and restriction."

1113 Birch, Frank. "The London Theatre." NATION AND THE ATHENAEUM
(London), 33 (21 July 1923), 525-26.

There is no attempt "at something dramatically decent."

1114 Birmingham, George A. "The Literary Movement in Ireland." FORT-
NIGHTLY REVIEW (London and New York), n.s. 82 (December 1907),
947-57.

The last part of the article deals with the Irish dramatic movement.

1115 Birrell, Francis. "The Last Theatrical Season." NATION AND ATHE-
NAEUM (London), 37 (25 July 1925), 514-15.

"Last season seems to have been less of a torture than the ones
that went before."

1116 _____. "The Proposed National Theatre." NATION AND ATHENAEUM
(London), 45 (20 July 1929), 535-36.

The theatre is obviously in special need of "safeguarding."

1117 Bishop, W.J. "The Theatre of Tomorrow." MILLGATE, January 1938,
pp. 191-93.

The real hope for the "theatre of tomorrow" lies in the work of the repertory companies.

1118 Bissing, Toska. "Dublin Gate Theatre Productions." THEATRE ARTS (New York), 25 (January 1941), 49-52.

Survey.

1119 Blake, Warren Barton. "Irish Plays and Players." INDEPENDENT (New York), 74 (6 March 1913), 515-19.

Review article.

1120 Blau, Herbert. "A Character Study of the Drama." JOURNAL OF AESTHETICS AND ART CRITICISM, 13 (1954), 52-68.

Examines the relationship between poetry and drama, and the operation of poetry within the dramatic form.

1121 _____. "Language and Structure in Poetic Drama." MODERN LANGUAGE QUARTERLY, 18 (1957), 27-34.

In the drama, "it is by means of words that the activity of conscious agents is informed and evaluated."

1122 Boas, Frederick S. "The Malvern Theatrical Festival: 1929-1939." QUEEN'S QUARTERLY, 47 (Summer 1940), 219-30.

An account of the development of the festival and of some of its significant features.

1123 Bonner, George H. "The Present State of the Drama." NINETEENTH CENTURY AND AFTER (London), 97 (May 1925), 746-55.

Declares that plays are becoming more intellectual, with an atmosphere of questioning, of skepticism, of the overthrowing of established beliefs and methods.

1124 Borinski, Ludwig. "Shaw und die Stilexperimente des fruehen 20. Jahrhunderts." DIE NEUEREN SPRACHEN, 5 (1956), 361-71.

Shaw and the experimentation of style in the early twentieth century.

1125 Bottomley, Gordon. "Poetry Seeks a New Home." THEATRE ARTS MONTHLY (New York), 13 (1929), 920-26.

"I conceive that in future those who desire dramatic poetry will seek it in places set apart for it, as they seek operatic music and symphonic music."

1126 _____. "Poetry and the Contemporary Theatre." ESSAYS AND STUDIES (Oxford), 19 (1933), 137-47.

"If poetry is to regain its right of entry to the theatre it must learn again to base itself upon contemporary speech-rhythms."

1127 _____. "Choric Speech and the Stage." THEATRE ARTS MONTHLY (New York), 19 (July 1935), 531-34.

A note on a modern development.

1128 Bourdet, Edouard. "Playwriting as a Profession." THEATRE ARTS MONTHLY (New York), 15 (February 1931), 125-33.

"One does not learn how to write plays."

1129 Bowen, Elizabeth. "What We Need in Writing." SPECTATOR (London), 157 (20 November 1936), 901-2.

A more natural approach to life is needed in the theatre.

1130 Bowker, Gordon. "All Our Yesterdays." PLAYS AND PLAYERS (London), 13 (April 1966), 60-61, 70.

Looks at the theatre in 1921.

1131 _____. "All Our Yesterdays--1931." PLAYS AND PLAYERS (London), 13 (June 1966), 60-61.

Traces the theatre's reflection of changes in a decade.

1132 Boyd, Ernest A. "The Irish National Theatre; A Criticism." IRISH TIMES (Dublin), 27 December 1912, p. 5.

"Unless good plays are produced and past successes revived, the Abbey Theatre will continue to decline until it is scarcely distinguishable from the ordinary commercial theatre."

1133 _____. "The Abbey Theatre." IRISH REVIEW (Dublin), 2 (February 1913), 628-34.

Some radical change must be made in the conduct of the Abbey Theatre.

1134 _____. "Le theatre irlandais." REVUE DE PARIS, 5 (1 September 1913), 191-205.

Survey.

1135 Brahms, Caryl. "Today's Theatre of Disenchanted Classless Writers." TIMES (London), 18 April 1968, p. 9.

Comparison between the thirties and now.

1136 Bregy, Katherine. "Aspects of Recent Drama in England." CATHOLIC
WORLD, 106 (January 1918), 445-50; (February 1918), 654-60; (March
1918), 764-71; 107 (April 1918), 88-95.

1137 Brereton-Barry, R. "The Need for a State Theatre." IRISH STATESMAN
(Dublin), 3 (25 October 1924), 210-12.

In Ireland.

1138 Bridges-Adams, W. "A National Theatre." DRAMA (London), Winter
1958, pp. 27-30.

Review article on the Abbey Theatre.

1139 _____. "When Did Respectability Begin?" DRAMA (London), Winter
1962, pp. 26-28.

On the social status of the actor.

1140 Bridie, James. "The Theatre in Scotland." SPECTATOR (London), 148
(28 May 1932), 758.

Survey.

1141 _____. "A National Theatre." PAPERS OF THE ROYAL PHILOSOPHI-
CAL SOCIETY (Glasgow), 64 (1940), 23-39.

Paper delivered before the Society on 23 November 1938.

1142 _____. "The Play of Ideas." NEW STATESMAN AND NATION (London), 39 (11 March 1950), 270-71.

A reply by F. Hall appears in NEW STATESMAN AND NA-
TION, 39 (18 March 1950); 301.

1143 Brighouse, Harold. "News of the European Theatre: England." DRAMA
(Chicago), 21 (October 1930), 11; (November 1930), 13-14; (December
1930), 14-16; (January 1931), 16-17; (February 1931), 16-17; (March
1931), 16; (April 1931), 15; (May 1931), 13-14; (June 1931), 11.

Survey.

1144 "British Drama." TIMES LITERARY SUPPLEMENT (London), 12 August 1939,
p. 479.

Editorial.

1145 Brook, Peter. "The Contemporary Theatre; The Vitality of the English

Stage." LISTENER (London), 4 May 1950, pp. 781-82.

1146 Brosnan, Gerald. "Dublin's Abbey--the Immortal Theatre." THEATRE ARTS (New York), 35 (October 1951), 36-37.

Recollections by a playwright who happened to be in Dublin and to see the ruins of the Abbey Theatre, which went up in flames on 18 July 1951.

1147 Brown, Ivor. "The London Scene--1925." THEATRE ARTS MONTHLY, 10 (January 1926), 47-52.

"It was interesting but rather 'anarchic.'"

1148 _____. "Enduring Passion." SATURDAY REVIEW (London), 146 (29 December 1928), 874-75.

"1928 has been undoubtedly a poor year."

1149 _____. "The Spirit of the Age in Drama." FORTNIGHTLY REVIEW, 134 (November 1930), 596-605.

"Argues that shapeliness of writing is distinctly out of fashion."

1150 _____. "Small Talk and Great." NEW STATESMAN AND NATION (London), 7 (31 March 1934), 483-84.

On dialogue in modern drama.

1151 _____. "National and Provincial." NEW STATESMAN AND NATION (London), 7 (30 June 1934), 994-95.

"The English theatre is ceasing to be English and becoming an aspect of London only."

1152 _____. "Left Theatres." NEW STATESMAN AND NATION (London), 9 (6 April 1935), 487-88.

A reply by B. Dixon appears in the 13 April 1935 issue of NEW STATESMAN AND NATION (p. 520). "As far as the manual worker is concerned there is no English theatre."

1153 _____. "The Muse Mendicant." NEW STATESMAN AND NATION (London), 9 (20 April 1935), 553-54.

On the National Theatre.

1154 _____. "British Comedy." THEATRE ARTS MONTHLY, 19 (August 1935), 585-93.

British comedy has been "obstinately realistic."

1155 _____. "The English Drolls." THEATRE ARTS MONTHLY (New York), 22 (September 1938), 649-56.

On English music-halls.

1156 _____. "The Serious Theatre and Its Critics." NEW STATESMAN AND NATION (London), 17 (21 January 1939), 88.

Letter to the editor.

1157 _____. "The Theatre in Wartime." NEW STATESMAN AND NATION (London), 18 (23 December 1939), 926-27.

1158 _____. "Dramatic Criticism--Is It Possible?" THEATRE ARTS MONTHLY (New York), November 1940, pp. 803-7; rpt. included in THEATRE ARTS ANTHOLOGY. New York: Theatre Arts Books, 1950.

Brown answers the title question in the negative because a dramatic critic "is dealing with a cooperative venture which has a complicated secret history."

1159 _____. "Troubles of the Time." DRAMA (London), Spring 1955, pp. 21-23.

"The London theatres get clogged up with the Show Business productions and also with long-running rough-and-tumble comedies."

1160 _____. "The Press and the Theatre." DRAMA (London), Spring 1957, pp. 30-32.

Dramatic criticism "dwindles while theatre gossip and 'stories of the Stars' increase."

1161 _____. "Forty Years Back." DRAMA (London), Spring 1959, pp. 25-27.

A balance-sheet of theatrical gains and losses during the forty years since the British Drama League was founded.

1162 _____. "From Blood to Mud." DRAMA (London), Winter 1959, pp. 29-31.

"The theatre of today . . . has its own excess of ugliness."

1163 _____. "Theatre, Press and Public." DRAMA (London), Winter 1960, pp. 28-30.

Comparison between dramatic criticism now and forty years ago.

1164 _____. "The New Bardolatry." DRAMA (London), Spring 1962, pp.

34-36.

"Bardolatry flourishes as it certainly did not between the wars."

1165 _____. "All Mixed Up." DRAMA (London), Summer 1970, pp. 43-45.

"The theatre, with or without partition by a curtain, is a great mixer."

1166 _____. "The Real Thing." DRAMA (London), Summer 1972, pp. 42-45.

Comparison between realism in the contemporary theatre and in the Edwardian and Georgian theatres.

1167 See also Brown's regular contributions to MANCHESTER GUARDIAN (1919-35), SATURDAY REVIEW (London; 1923-30), OBSERVER (London; 1929-54), ILLUSTRATED LONDON NEWS (1935-40), and the critical works cited in this bibliography (Nos. 357-59).

1168 Browne, E. Martin. "The Church and the Drama." CHURCH QUARTERLY REVIEW, 113 (October 1931), 66-70.

Argues that "it is now possible to get dramatists with theatrical experience to understand the needs of the church."

1169 _____. "The One-Act Play in English Repertories." THEATRE ARTS MONTHLY (New York), 21 (July 1937), 528-32.

1170 _____. "Poetry in the English Theatre." PAPERS OF THE ROYAL INSTITUTE OF GREAT BRITAIN, 34 (1949), 287-93.

"There is a barrier between the poet and the audience of to-day."

1171 _____. "Religious Drama Since 1939." NATIONAL AND ENGLISH REVIEW, March 1952, pp. 160-62.

Survey.

1172 _____. "The British Drama League." EDUCATIONAL THEATRE JOURNAL, 5 (October 1953), 203-6.

A survey of the League's activities by its director.

1173 _____. "Drama's Return to Religion." THEATRE ARTS MONTHLY (New York), 41 (August 1957), 18-19, 92-93.

Survey of religious drama in England from John Masefield to the present.

1174 Browne, Maurice. "The New Rhythmic Drama." DRAMA (Chicago), 16 (1914), 616-30.

Makes special reference to dramatic form and principle.

1175 Bullough, Geoffrey. "Poetry in Modern English Drama." CAIRO STUDIES IN ENGLISH, 1959, pp. 26-42.

Survey.

1176 Burnham, David. "Busman's Holiday." COMMONWEAL, 35 (10 April 1942), 620-21.

British drama is "experiencing today a noticeable decline."

1177 Cannan, Gilbert. "A Short History of the Decline and Fall of the English Theatre." POETRY AND DRAMA (London), 2 (1914), 413-15.

Theatre-managers have lost sight of the tradition of the theatre.

1178 _____. "The English Theatre during and after the War." THEATRE ARTS, 4 (January 1920), 21-24.

The theatre cannot compete with the music-hall.

1179 _____. "Hope for the Drama." SEWANEE REVIEW, 30 (October 1922), 385-89.

A dramatist must turn "to the buffoons and let his imagination learn from them the art of dealing with a modern audience."

1180 _____. "All Eyes on the Theatre (1924)." SEWANEE REVIEW, 32 (1924), 130-38.

"Our immediate concern is with the theatre of Western Europe, which as a social entity is just beginning to attain consciousness in spite of or perhaps owing to the confusion and distraction due to the financial difficulties of the various national governments."

1181 Capek, Karel. "The English Theatre." SATURDAY REVIEW (London), 138 (2 August 1924), 115-16.

The manager of a London theatre "must cater for the taste of his visitors or else his trade is doomed."

1182 Carr, Philip Comyns. "The London Theatre in 1900." LISTENER (London), 41 (6 January 1949), 26-27.

From a talk prepared for the BBC Third Programme.

1183 Carric, Allen. "The English Stage in 1911." MASK, 1 (1911), 181-84.

> "There is nothing good to be said about it."

1184 Carroll, Paul Vincent. "Can the Abbey Theatre Be Restored?" THEATRE ARTS (New York), 36 (January 1952), 18-19, 79.

> The Abbey Theatre has been "in retreat" as a result of: 1. "unofficial interference of the Government"; 2. "very powerful unofficial clerical censorship"; 3. "deplorable policy of the Abbey Directorate."

1185 Carroll, Sydney W. "Prospects of a National Theatre." ADULT EDUCATION (London), June 1935, pp. 303-7.

1186 Carter, Huntley. "About the Theatre in London." THEATRE ARTS, 4 (July 1920), 217-19.

> On the influence of the Moscow Art Theatre.

1187 Caswell, Robert W. "Unity and the Irish Theatre." STUDIES; AN IRISH QUARTERLY REVIEW (Dublin), 159 (Spring 1960), 63-67.

> Suggests that various theatres in Dublin which maintain a more or less homogeneous group of actors and actresses should unite in some effective way.

1188 "A Celtic Theatre." FREEMAN'S JOURNAL (Dublin), 22 March 1900, p. 4.

> Editorial.

1189 "The Censorship of Plays." LIVING AGE, 7 December 1907, pp. 632-34.

> Reprinted from SPECTATOR.

1190 Chambers, E.K. "The Experiments of Mr. Yeats." ACADEMY AND LITERATURE (London), 64 (9 May 1903), 465-66.

> On plays given by the Irish National Theatre Society at the Queen's Gate Hall. See Yeats's reply, "Irish Plays and Players," which appears as a letter to the editor in the 16 May 1903 issue of the same periodical (p. 495).

1191 Chanel. "The Deserted Abbey." LEADER (Dublin), 12 (28 April 1906), 151-52.

> Discusses reasons for poor attendance.

1192 "The Claims of a National Theatre." SPECTATOR (London), 154 (4 January 1935), 5-6.

"This moment of economic improvement ought to be the right one for a strenuous effort to turn this long-cherished dream into a reality."

1193 Clark, Barrett H. "The Early London Season." DRAMA (Chicago), November 1913, pp. 187-93.

"The English drama of the present day is surpassed in originality and ideas by that of no other country."

1194 _____. "Contemporary English Dramatists." ENGLISH JOURNAL, 15 (September 1926), 490-98; (October 1926), 569-79; (November 1926), 649-58; (December 1926), 728-37.

Survey.

1195 Clark, James M. "The Irish Literary Movement." ENGLISCHE STUDIEN (Leipzig), 49 (July 1915), 50-98.

The last part of the article deals with the modern Irish theatre.

1196 Clarke, Austin. "The Problem of Verse Drama Today." LONDON MERCURY, 33 (November 1935), 34-38.

"The problem involves the contemporary relations between poetry and speech itself."

1197 Clarke, Michael. "The Abbey Theatre." IRISH TIMES (Dublin), 11 August 1944, p. 3.

Letter to the Editor on the "disintegration" of the theatre.

1198 Clurman, Harold. "The Subject Is Not Roses; or, The Grandeur and Misery of Repertory." THEATRE, 2 (1965), 111-21.

Deals with the British National Theatre and other repertory companies.

1199 "'Coarse and Cynical' Plays." LITERARY DIGEST, 104 (1 March 1930), 21.

1199A Coffey, Brian. "In Dublin." COMMONWEAL (New York), 46 (3 October 1947), 597-98.

Survey.

1200 Cohen, Helen Louise. "The Irish National Theatre." SCHOLASTIC (Pittsburgh), 24 (17 March 1934), 7-8.

Survey.

1201 Cole, Alan. "The Gate Influence on Dublin Theatre." DUBLIN MAGA-
ZINE, 29 (July–September 1953), 6–14.

 The influence of the Dublin Gate Theatre established by Micheal
 MacLiammoir and Hilton Edwards in 1928.

1202 Coleman, John. "A National Theatre; An Appeal to the London County
Council." NINETEENTH CENTURY, 50 (December 1901), 991–1000.

1203 Colum, Padraic. "The Irish Literary Movement." FORUM (New York
and London), 53 (January 1915), 133–48.

 The last part of the article surveys the modern Irish theatre.

1204 _____. "Youngest Ireland." SEVEN ARTS MAGAZINE (New York),
2 (September 1917), 608–23.

 The last part of the article deals briefly with the Irish theatre.

1205 _____. "The Abbey Theatre Comes of Age." THEATRE ARTS MONTHLY
(New York), 10 (September 1926), 580–84.

 Survey.

1206 _____. "Ibsen in Irish Writing." IRISH WRITING (Cork), February
1949, pp. 66–70.

 Ibsen does not seem to have had much influence on Irish dramatists.

1207 "The Complimentary Dinner to Mr. J.E. Vedrenne and Mr. H. Granville-
Barker: A Transcript of the Proceedings." SHAW REVIEW, 2 (May 1959),
17–34.

 Includes speeches by Vedrenne, Granville-Barker, Shaw, Beerbohm Tree, Gilbert Murray, Wynne Matthison, Sir Oliver
 Lodge, and William Archer.

1208 Conacher, W.M. "The Irish Literary Movement." QUEEN'S QUARTERLY,
45 (1938), 56–65.

 Calls attention to certain marked characteristics.

1209 Connolly, James. "National Drama." UNITED IRISHMAN (Dublin), 10
(24 October 1903), 2.

 On the Irish National Theatre.

1210 Conolly, L.W. "The Abolition of Theatre Censorship in Great Britain:
The Theatres Act of 1968." QUEEN'S QUARTERLY, 75 (1968), 569–83.

Survey of the function which had been exercised by the Lord Chamberlain since 1737.

1211 Constance, Jennie M. "Some Tendencies of the English-Speaking Drama." POET LORE, 33 (September 1922), 385-94.

Treats the modern drama in its revolt from the past both in matter and in form.

1212 Cookman, A.V. "The Theatre of 1935." LONDON MERCURY, 33 (February 1936), 427-28.

Survey.

1213 Cooper, Bryan. "The Drama in Ireland." IRISH REVIEW (Dublin), 3 (May 1913), 140-43.

Examines the Abbey as a repertory theatre.

1214 Corbin, John. "Play-Going in London." SCRIBNER'S, 35 (April 1904), 395-410.

"A London first night is far more of an event than a first night in New York."

1215 Cordell, William H., and Kathryn C. Cordell. "The Future Theatre of the Air." SEWANEE REVIEW, 44 (October-December 1936), 405-19.

The BBC's drama programs have been hailed as "the true National Theatre of Great Britain."

1216 Cotes, Peter. "Decentralising the Theatre." THEATRE WORLD, June 1948, pp. 30-31.

1217 Coulter, John. "The Canadian Theatre and the Irish Exemplar." THEATRE ARTS MONTHLY (New York), 22 (July 1938), 503-9.

Argues that the Candian theatre should emulate the example of the Abbey Theatre.

1218 Courtneidge, Robert. "The Future of the Theatre." QUARTERLY REVIEW, 260 (April 1933), 228-40.

Discusses the theatre and the cinema in their struggle for supremacy and tells what the stage proper can do for itself.

1219 Courtney, W.L. "Modern Social Drama As Influenced by the Novel." FORTNIGHTLY REVIEW, 77 (1902), 666-74; rpt. LIVING AGE, 15 (17 May 1902), 396-403.

A lecture delivered at the Birmingham Midland Institute in

February 1902.

1220 _____. "Realistic Drama." FORTNIGHTLY REVIEW, 93 (1913), 945-61, 1136-53; 94 (1914), 96-110; rpt. included in OLD SAWS AND MODERN INSTANCES. London: Chapman & Hall, 1918; Freeport, N.Y.: Books for Libraries Press, 1969. Pp. 161-217.

"The modern English stage has developed mainly along the lines of realism."

1221 Cox, H. Bartle. "What the English Theatre Needs." NEW WORLD (London), April 1921, pp. 45-53.

Discusses the need for state aid.

1222 Craig, Gordon. "Some Evil Tendencies of the Modern Theatre." MASK, 1 (1908), 149-54.

1223 _____. "On Tolerance in Dramatic Criticism." MASK, 1 (1909), 243-45.

1224 _____. "The English Theatre Today." DRAMA (London), Summer 1956, pp. 30-31.

Impressions.

1225 Crawfurd, H.E. "The King's English and the National Theatre." SATURDAY REVIEW (London), 159 (1 June 1935), 690.

The National Theatre "would be a stronghold" of English.

1226 Crocker, Lionel. "Will the One-Act Play Endure?" QUARTERLY JOURNAL OF SPEECH, 14 (February 1928), 64-71.

Explains why one-act plays are more popular in England than in America.

1227 Crockett, John. "Theatre Leadership." NEW STATESMAN AND NATION (London), 37 (8 January 1949), 33.

1228 "The Curtain Goes Up." CANADIAN FORUM, 28 (May 1948), 28.

On the National Theatre.

1229 Cusack, Cyril. "In Terms of Theatre." IRIS HIBERNIA (Fribourg, Switzerland), 4, no. 3 (1960), 20-26.

Comments on the Irish theatre, past and present.

1230 Cusack, Dymphna. "The English Theatre." MEANJIN, 9 (Autumn 1950),

36-38.

> "The London stage seems to be given up to the actor and the producer."

1231 _____. "What Is Wrong with the English Playwright?" MEANJIN, 9 (Winter 1950), 127-30.

> The English playwright "has no intelligible coherent view of the contemporary world."

1232 D., E.K. "The Irish Theatre Society." DIAL, 16 December 1911, p. 521.

> Letter to the editor.

1233 Dague, Roswell. "The London Stage of Today." FORUM, 65 (April 1921), 447-54.

> Most London productions echo concern with World War I.

1234 Dale, Alan. "The Sad Case of the Society Play; How the Selfishness and Folly of the Actor-Managers of London Are Perverting the Art of the Playwright and Revolutionizing All Ideas of Dramatic Chivalry." COSMOPOLITAN (New York), 43 (September 1907), 526-28.

1235 _____. "A Chronicle of New Plays." COSMOPOLITAN, 46 (May 1909), 677-80.

1236 Darlington, W.A. "Accent on Age." THEATRE ARTS MONTHLY (New York), 21 (April 1937), 276-80.

> On the living British dramatists who have written serious and successful plays.

1237 _____. "Actor-Dramatists." THEATRE ARTS MONTHLY (New York), 23 (September 1939), 639-41.

> On the advantages of pursuing both professions.

1238 _____. "Hits from Britain." NEW YORK TIMES MAGAZINE, 17 September 1950, pp. 26-27.

> "On an invasion of Broadway this season by plays which have been notably successful in London."

1239 _____. See also his regular contributions to DAILY TELEGRAPH (London; 1920-68), NEW YORK TIMES (1939-60), and the collected and critical works cited in this bibliography (Nos. 443-46.)

1240  Davis, Richard Harding. "Going to the Play in London." COLLIER'S, 44 (23 October 1909), 15.

> Comparison between British and American methods at the theatre.

1241  Dean, Basil. "An Inquiry into the British Theatre." WORLD REVIEW (London), November 1948, pp. 48-50.

> The present condition "is a complex one for which no single prescription can provide a remedy."

1242  "Death-Bed of the Theater." LITERARY DIGEST, 92 (5 March 1927), 25-26.

1243  DeBlaghd, Earnan. "Amharclann Na Mainstreach." IRIS HIBERNIA (Fribourg, Switzerland), 4, no. 3 (1960), 43-45.

> On Irish drama.

1244  "The Decadence of the Abbey." SATURDAY HERALD (Dublin), 19 July 1913, magazine page.

> Condemns the "protracted absences of the Abbey Company.

1245  DeGruyter, Dom. "Toneel in Engeland." NIEUW VLAAMS TIJDSCHRIFT, June 1952, pp. 1089-106.

> Survey of the theatre in England.

1246  deSmet, Robert. "Le Theatre anglais depuis la guerre." REVUE DE PARIS, 1 December 1931, pp. 616-34.

> Survey.

1247  _____. "Le Mouvement dramatique en angleterre." REVUE DE PARIS,
-8  15 September 1932, pp. 456-70; 1 September 1933, pp. 682-99; 1 October 1934, pp. 185-201; 1 October 1935, pp. 688-704.

> Survey.

1249  _____. "La Litterature dramatique en angleterre." REVUE DE PARIS, 1 November 1936, pp. 190-209.

> Survey.

1250  _____. "Le Theatre en Irlande." REVUE DE PARIS, 15 October 1937, pp. 903-19.

> Survey.

1251-   ____. "Le Theatre en angleterre." REVUE DE PARIS, 1 December
52  1937, pp. 658-74; 1 December 1939, pp. 969-83.

   Survey.


1253 Desmond, Shaw. "The Irish Renaissance." OUTLOOK (New York), 138
   (15 October 1924), 247-49.

   Answers the questions: "Whence sprang the Irish Renaissance?
   Why its existence? Whither is it trending?"


1254 "De Valera As Play Censor." MANCHESTER GUARDIAN WEEKLY, 30
   (13 April 1934), 296.

   The President of the Irish Republic "held strong views on the
   plays to be presented."


1255 Dickinson, Thomas H. "The Drama of Intellectualism." DRAMA (Chicago), no. 7 (1912), 148-62.

   Review article.


1256 Dietrich, Margret. "Die Rebellion gegen das Überlebte in der Dramatik
   des 20. Jahrhunderts--von Shaw bis Ionesco." UNIVERSITAS (Stuttgart),
   16 (1961), 955-65.

   The rebellion against the "survivor" in twentieth-century drama.


1257 Digges, Dudley. "A Theatre Was Made." IRISH DIGEST (Dublin), 4
   (October 1939), 11-14.

   The beginning of the Irish theatre from an actor's point of view.


1258 Disher, M. Willson. "The Influence of the Nursery on the Stage."
   FORTNIGHTLY REVIEW, 117 (1925), 108-16.

   "Argues that we have not altogether lost the faculty of taking
   enjoyment in what we do not believe--DEAR BRUTUS and
   MARY ROSE are proofs of that."


1259 Dobree, Bonamy. "The Idea of Drama." NATION AND ATHENAEUM
   (London), 5 (5 February 1927), 628-29.

   Review article.


1260   ____. "Contemporary English Drama." QUEEN'S QUARTERLY, 41
   (August 1934), 397-404.

   "English drama has compelled itself to the trivial."


1261   ____. "Poetic Drama in England Today." SOUTHERN REVIEW, 4

(Winter 1939), 581-99.

Poetic drama is "arousing popular interest; it is no longer academic."

1262 _____. "Drama in England." SEWANEE REVIEW, 64 (Summer 1956), 470-84.

"Not 'English Drama'; for at the moment the theater in London is a pallid patient, kept alive by brisk frequent injections of foreign plays."

1263 Donn, Uilliam. "The Ulster Literary Theatre." ULAD: A LITERARY & CRITICAL MAGAZINE (Belfast), 1 (November 1904), 7-8.

Survey.

1264 Donoghue, Denis. "Theatre Poetry and Dramatic Verse." STUDIES (Dublin), 47 (Autumn 1958), 305-23.

"Twentieth century verse drama in English has been very slow in becoming a 'modern' movement.

1265 Downer, Alan S. "The Life of Our Design." HUDSON REVIEW, 2 (1949), 242-63.

The function of imagery in poetic drama.

1266 "Drama in the Dark." TIMES LITERARY SUPPLEMENT (London), 12 October 1940, p. 519.

Editorial.

1267 "The Drama of Captivity." TIMES LITERARY SUPPLEMENT, 28 July 1927, pp. 509-10.

Current plays are not contributions to dramatic literature.

1268 Drew, Elizabeth A. "The Prospects for Tragic Drama." FREEMAN, 5 (10 May 1922), 199-201.

"The English disciples of Ibsen have not given our theatre very much to remember in the realm of tragedy."

1269 Dukes, Ashley. "The English Scene--1926." THEATRE ARTS MONTHLY (New York), 10 (December 1926), 839-43.

The urgent need of London is not a dramatist's theatre, "but the theatre that will prove to be his impulse and inspiration."

1270 _____. "The Irish Scene: Dublin Plays and Playhouses." THEATRE ARTS

MONTHLY (New York), 14 (May 1930), 378-84.

Survey.

1271 _____. "The English Scene." THEATRE ARTS MONTHLY (New York), 16 (January 1932), 27-30.

On the productions of the Stage Society.

1272 _____. "The English Scene; Then and Now." THEATRE ARTS MONTHLY (New York), 16 (September 1932), 698-704.

"Twenty years ago the interest of the English stage was focussed on its playwrights, who were in a phase of new and exceptional productivity."

1273 _____. "In the Dramatist's Eye." THEATRE ARTS MONTHLY (New York), 17 (August 1933), 587-92; (September 1933), 674-78.

Tries to discover what the modern dramatist is fixing his eye on and whither he will lead the drama.

1274 _____. "The Scene in Europe." THEATRE ARTS MONTHLY (New York), 18 (February 1934), 98-105.

Survey.

1275 _____. "The English Scene." THEATRE ARTS MONTHLY (New York), 20 (January 1936), 23-26; (April 1936), 264-69; (May 1936), 344-48; (July 1936), 511-16; (December 1936), 936-40.

Survey.

1276 _____. "The Little Professional Theatre." THEATRE ARTS MONTHLY (New York), 21 (July 1937), 533-42.

The advantages and drawbacks of the little theatre compared to the larger theatre.

1277 _____. "The English Scene; New Plays and National Theatre." THEATRE ARTS MONTHLY (New York), 21 (November 1937), 845-53.

Survey plus proposed National Theatre.

1278 _____. "Der neue Geist im englischen Drama." THEATER DER WELT, 1 (1937), 29-32.

The new spirit in English drama.

1279 _____. "The Scene in Europe." THEATRE ARTS MONTHLY (New York), 22 (March 1938), 181-86.

Survey.

1280 _____. "The English Scene." THEATRE ARTS MONTHLY (New York), 22 (April 1938), 256-62; (June 1938), 407-11; (October 1938), 718-24; (November 1938), 787-91.

Survey.

1281 _____. "Re-enter the Chorus." THEATRE ARTS MONTHLY (New York), 22 (May 1938), 335-40.

Deals with the use of the chorus in some modern plays.

1282 _____. "National Comedy." THEATRE ARTS MONTHLY (New York), 22 (September 1938), 657-62.

A growing international sophistication will unite countries in an understanding of social life and character.

1283- _____. "The London Scene." THEATRE ARTS MONTHLY (New York),
84 November 1938, pp. 787-91.

Survey.

1285 _____. "In Paris and London." THEATRE ARTS MONTHLY (New York), 23 (January 1939), 18-26.

Survey.

1286 _____. "The English Scene." THEATRE ARTS MONTHLY (New York), 23 (January 1939), 99-105.

Survey.

1287 _____. "In London." THEATRE ARTS MONTHLY (New York), 23 (March 1939), 175-79.

Survey.

1288 _____. "The British Isles." THEATRE ARTS MONTHLY (New York), 23 (April 1939), 252-56.

Survey.

1289 _____. "National Theatres." THEATRE ARTS MONTHLY (New York), 23 (May 1939), 329-33.

Comparison of the English National Theatre with other national theatres.

1290 _____. "Summer Season: English Scene." THEATRE ARTS MONTHLY (New York), 23 (October 1939), 704-8.

Survey.

1291 _____. "London Blackout: The English Scene." THEATRE ARTS MONTHLY (New York), 23 (November 1939), 780-84.

Survey.

1292 _____. "Theatre in the Dark." THEATRE ARTS MONTHLY (New York), 23 (December 1939), 865-68.

Survey.

1293 _____. "Wartime Theatre; As the Playgoer Sees It." THEATRE ARTS (New York), 26 (January 1942), 19-26.

Theatres have to contend with many difficulties.

1294 _____. "Wartime Theatre; Backstage View." THEATRE ARTS (New York), 26 (February 1942), 91-96.

Difficulties of producing plays during the war.

1295 _____. "English Notes." THEATRE ARTS (New York), 26 (May 1942), 295.

Survey.

1296 "Dull Gaelic Plough." NEWSWEEK, 24 November 1947, p. 84.

Result of the policy that "Gaelic plays and Gaelic-speaking actors and actresses have precedence over all else at the Abbey."

1297 Duncan, Ronald. "Write With Both Hands." DRAMA (London), Winter 1953, pp. 17-20.

"I believe that poets can find their place in the theatre again, if they will learn to discipline their verse to the drama."

1298 _____. "The Language of Theatre Today." DRAMA (London), Autumn 1958, pp. 26-27.

"Poetry is not served when it is written at one remove from the spoken word."

1299 Dunn, Stanley Gerald. "The Revival of Drama." WESTMINSTER REVIEW, 171 (March 1909), 330-35.

Discusses the need for drama "that deals faithfully with some incident or problem of actual life."

1300 Dunsany, Lord Edward John Moreton Drax Plunkett. "Romance and the Modern Stage." NATIONAL REVIEW (London), July 1911, pp. 827-35.

Realism "has come in romance's place."

1301 _____. "Good Plays and Bad--Why?" THEATRE MAGAZINE (New York), 48 (1928), 7-8.

Criticizes the practice of writing plays for particular actors.

1302 Dunton, Edith Kellogg. "The Englishman as a Playgoer." BOOKMAN (New York), 25 (May 1907), 276-81.

1303 Eadie, Dennis. "What Is the Matter with the Theatre?" FORTNIGHTLY REVIEW, 110 (November 1918), 724-28.

The majority of theatres are either run entirely as money-making concerns, or with the actor-partners controlled by the business partners.

1304 Eastman, Fred. "The Why and How of Religious Drama." DRAMA (Chicago), 19 (January 1929), 115-16.

Why and how it is taught.

1305 Eaton, Walter Prichard. "Great Acting and the Modern Drama." SCRIBNER'S (New York), 47 (1910), 209-12.

There are practically "no great parts in modern drama."

1306 _____. "Viewing Irish Players in the Light of Reason." SUNDAY RECORD-HERALD (Chicago), 17 December 1911, part 7, p. 3.

On the Abbey Players' first American tour.

1307 _____. "Some Plays Worth While." AMERICAN MAGAZINE, 73 (February 1912), 487-96.

On Irish plays presented by the Abbey Players.

1308 _____. "Revolt from Realism." VIRGINIA QUARTERLY REVIEW, 10 (October 1934), 515-22.

Examines likely lines of escape from realism.

1309 _____. "The Drama in 1933." AMERICAN SCHOLAR, 3 (Winter 1934), 96-101.

Review article.

1310 _____. "The Plight of the Dramatist." HARPER'S, 182 (March 1941), 417-21.

"The themes this age offers [the dramatist] are too difficult or too bewildering for his grasp."

1311 Ebenhack, Arthur. "Take the Play to the Audience." THEATRE ARTS MONTHLY (New York), 20 (July 1936), 543-44.

On travelling theatres.

1312 Eliot, T.S. "Dramatis Personae." CRITERION, 1 (April 1923), 303-6.

"The chaos of the modern stage is a chaos of styles of acting as much as of types of play."

1313 _____. "Audiences, Producers, Plays, Poets." NEW VERSE, 18 (1935), 3-4.

Thoughts on verse drama.

1314 _____. "Five Points on Dramatic Writing." TOWNSMAN: A QUAR-TERLY REVIEW, July 1938, p. 10; rpt. included in AN ASSESSMENT OF TWENTIETH-CENTURY LITERATURE. Ed. Jacob Isaacs. London: Secker & Warburg, 1951. Pp. 159-60.

Excerpt from a letter to Ezra Pound.

1315 _____. "The Aims of Poetic Drama." ADAM INTERNATIONAL REVIEW, 200 (1949), 10-16.

This original essay is substantially different from the well known version included in Eliot's SELECTED ESSAYS.

1316 Ellehauge, Martin. "The Initial Stages in the Development of the English Problem-Play." ENGLISCHE STUDIEN, 66 (1932), 371-401.

"The development of the problem-play is allied with a movement towards realism in action, characters, and dialogue."

1317 Ellis-Fermor, Una. "Dramatic Notes: The Abbey Theatre Festival (7-20 August 1938)." ENGLISH, 2 (Autumn 1938), 174-77.

Survey.

1318 Elvin, Rene. "Le Theatre en Angleterre." LE MOIS, January 1937, pp. 179-89.

Survey.

1319 Emmet, Alfred. "Britain's 'Little Theatres.'" LISTENER (London), 42 (15 December 1949), 1036-37.

Survey.

1320 "The English Invasion of Our Stage." THE LITERARY DIGEST (New York), 10 March 1934, p. 21.

> Hospitality to products of the British stage "seems more generous in New York than the contrary in London."

1321 "English National Theatre." THEATRE ARTS MONTHLY (New York), 21 (November 1937), 830-32.

> On the English National Theatre project and the present state of drama.

1322 Ervine, St. John. "The Irish Dramatist and the Irish People." FORUM (New York), 51 (June 1914), 940-48.

> "The Irish dramatist writes his plays round peasant characters because peasant life is the national life."

1323 _____. "The Future of the Theatre." BOOKMAN (London), March 1921, pp. 244-46.

> "I foresee a great development in the purely mechanical side of the theatre."

1324 _____. "The Realistic Test in Drama." YALE REVIEW, 11 (1922), 285-303.

> "The playgoer . . . should ask himself of a play, 'Is it true?' That is the realistic test which I apply to drama."

1325 _____. "Daring New Plays in London." THEATRE MAGAZINE (New York), 43 (June 1926), 20-21, 58.

> Survey of theatre productions.

1326 _____. "The Drama in the Doldrums." SHAKESPEARE REVIEW, 1 (June 1928), 83-88.

> Observations on the state of the English theatre.

1327 _____. "Exit, the Theatre!" SATURDAY REVIEW OF LITERATURE (New York), 23 February 1929, pp. 705-7.

> "The theatrical season of 1928-29 so far as the English-speaking world is concerned, was calamitous."

1328 _____. "The Plight of the Little Theatre." THEATRE ARTS MONTHLY (New York), 15 (July 1931), 538-46.

> Comparison between little theatres in America and in England.

1329 _____. "New Vics for Old." LONDON MERCURY, 37 (January 1938), 315-18.

On the repertory theatre.

1330 _____. "The Wars and the Drama." FORTNIGHTLY REVIEW, n.s. 148 (July 1940), 61-70.

The drama has been affected by the mood of exhausted Europe between 1918 and 1939.

1331 _____. "The Wars and the Actor." FORTNIGHTLY REVIEW, n.s. 148, (August 1940), 165-73.

The mood of exhausted Europe during 1918-39 has affected the actor.

1332 Escott, T.H.S. "Theatrical Landmarks." EDINBURGH REVIEW, 207 (January 1918), 85-96.

Review article.

1333 Esslin, Martin. "Contemporary English Drama and the Mass Media." ENGLISH, 18 (Spring 1969), 5-11.

In the age of mass media, "drama no longer is synonymous with live theatre."

1334 Eustis, Morton. "On Time and the Theatre. Priestley Talks about Playwriting." THEATRE ARTS MONTHLY (New York), 22 (January 1938), 45-55.

The playwright-novelist makes observations about the theatre.

1335 Evans, [Sir] B. Ifor. "The Arts in England: A London Letter." SATURDAY REVIEW (New York), 30 (15 March 1947), 11-12.

Survey.

1336 Everson, Ida G. "Young Lennox Robinson and the Abbey Theatre's First American Tour (1911-1912)." MODERN DRAMA, 9 (May 1966), 74-89.

Also includes the programme of the tour.

1337 Falkner, Edward. "The Play's the Thing." QUARTERLY REVIEW, 248 (January 1927), 36-46.

"Undoubtedly, the primal cause of the recent and actual decay of the Drama was due to the influence of the merely commercial manager."

1338 Fallon, Gabriel. "The Aging Abbey." IRISH MONTHLY (Dublin), 66 (April 1938), 265-72; (May 1938), 339-44.

"The decline of the Abbey Theatre in things of the theatre . . . began with the going out of the Fays and their players."

1339 _____. "Tribute to the Fays." IRISH MONTHLY (Dublin), 73 (January 1945), 18-24.

The contribution of William and Frank Fay to the Abbey Theatre.

1340 _____. "Why Is There No Irish Claudel or Mauriac?" EVENING PRESS (Dublin), 5 February 1955, p. 5.

Irish dramatists do not concern themselves specifically with religious or spiritual themes.

1341 _____. "The Future of the Irish Theatre." STUDIES; AN IRISH QUARTERLY REVIEW (Dublin), 44 (Spring 1955), 92-100.

"It is possible that we will return to the first principles of Yeats and use them as he intended they should be used--to bring upon the stage the deeper thoughts and emotions of Ireland."

1342 _____. "Dublin Letter." AMERICA (New York), 98 (12 October 1957), 46-47.

Survey.

1343 _____. "The Abbey Theatre Today." THRESHOLD, 3, no. 4 (1959), 24-32.

Reflections on the Abbey Theatre during its fifty-six years.

1344 _____. "All This and the Abbey Too." STUDIES; AN IRISH QUARTERLY REVIEW (Dublin), 48 (Winter 1959), 434-42.

Implies that only an upsurge of Irish dramatic talent will effect the rebirth of Irish theatre.

1345 Farjeon, Herbert. "An Apology for 'Bad' Plays." SATURDAY REVIEW (London), 27 October 1923, pp. 463-65.

There is room in the theatre for melodramas.

1346 Farrell, James T. "The Irish Cultural Renaissance in the Last Century." IRISH WRITING (Cork), December 1953, pp. 50-53.

"Synge, Yeats, Lady Gregory and their contemporaries helped bring a note of reality into Irish writing."

1347 Fay, Frank J. "The Irish Literary Theatre." UNITED IRISHMAN (Dublin), 5 (4 May 1901).

"I would prefer to see a Theatre inaugurated here that would abolish English completely, and conduct its operations outside of the uncongenial atmosphere of an English commercial theatre."

1348 _____. "An Irish National Theatre." UNITED IRISHMAN (Dublin), 5 (11 May 1901); (18 May 1901).

The Irish language should be used as a medium for Irish drama.

1349 _____. "SAMHAIN." UNITED IRISHMAN (Dublin), 6 (26 October 1901).

Discusses material in the Irish Literary Theatre's journal.

1350 _____. "The Irish Literary Theatre." UNITED IRISHMAN (Dublin), 6 (2 November 1901).

Argues against English actors performing Irish plays.

1351 _____. "The Irish Literary Theatre." UNITED IRISHMAN (Dublin), 6 (23 November 1901).

The Irish Literary Theatre "has been conducted on too large a scale and . . . its performances were too far apart to have the rousing effect they should have on the public mind."

1352 Fay, Gerald. "The British Theatre Today." WORLD REVIEW (London), November 1948, pp. 50-55.

No boom in the West-End theatres.

1353 _____. "The West-End Theatre in the Television Age." LISTENER (London), 70 (12 September 1963), 381-83.

The radical changes taking place in the London West-End theatres are not attributable to the spread of television.

1354 "Feeding the English Stage." LITERARY DIGEST, 101 (29 June 1929), 24.

"The 'Little Theatre' in England is helping Broadway to survive."

1355 Ferrar, Harold. "Robert Emmet in Irish Drama." EIRE-IRELAND, 1 (Summer 1966), 19-28.

Surveys the treatment of the Emmet legend from Dion Boucicault to Paul Vincent Carroll.

1356 Field, Lauraine, ed. "A Hundred Years of Lovemaking." THEATRE ARTS MONTHLY (New York), 14 (June 1930), 499-514.

Extracts from plays representing popular taste through ten decades from 1830 to 1930.

1357 Filon, Augustin. "Le Reveil de l'ame celtique." JOURNAL DES DEBATS (Paris), 19 April 1905, pp. 740-43.

Deals with the beginnings of the Irish dramatic movement.

1358 Findlater, Richard. "The Empty Site." DRAMA (London), Autumn 1957, pp. 23-25.

The case for a National Theatre.

1359 _____. "The Shrinking Theatre." TWENTIETH CENTURY, 165 (May 1959), 493-500.

Current protection for playhouses is inadequate.

1360 Findon, B.W. "A Plea for the Religious Drama." FORTNIGHTLY REVIEW, 84 (October 1905), 708-15.

Steps towards a "rapprochement" between religion and drama.

1361 Finn, Seamus. "The Abbey Theatre." IRISH TIMES (Dublin), 29 July 1944, p. 3.

Letter to the editor on the condition of the Theatre.

1362 Finnian. "Gael-Linn Agus An Dramaiocht." IRIS HIBERNIA (Fribourg, Switzerland), 4, no. 3 (1960), 58-62.

On Irish drama.

1363 Fiske, Minnie Maddern. "The Matter of the Play." INTERNATIONAL MONTHLY, 5 (1902), 629-44.

Concerned with the stage interpretation of the problem play.

1364 Fitz-Gerald, W.G. "The Dramatic Censorship in England." HARPER'S WEEKLY, 51 (29 June 1907), 947.

1365 Forbes-Robertson, Johnston. "The Theatre of Yesterday, Today, and Tomorrow." CENTURY MAGAZINE, 87 (1914), 505-10.

"Things are undoubtedly better all round . . . than they were forty years ago."

1366 "Forty Years of Irish Drama: Yeats, Synge and Lady Gregory; From the

Visionaries to the Realists." TIMES LITERARY SUPPLEMENT (London), 13 April 1940, pp. 182–86.

> Review article.

1367 Fox, R.M. "Realism in Irish Drama." IRISH STATESMAN (Dublin), 23 June 1928, pp. 310–12.

> "The drama of low life is only now being written. Previously it was sentimentalised."

1368 _____. "The Theatre Goes On." THEATRE ARTS (New York), 24 (November 1940), 783–90.

> Survey in Ireland and England.

1369 _____. "Ups and Downs in the Irish Theatre." THEATRE ARTS (New York), 25 (May 1941), 353–58.

> Survey of Irish drama during World War II.

1370 _____. "What Next in Irish Drama?" THEATRE ARTS (New York), 26 (April 1942), 245–49.

> Answers the question: "What has Irish drama to say to the conflict in Europe and the world?"

1371 _____. "Wild Riders of Irish Drama." THEATRE ARTS (New York), 28 (May 1944), 301–4.

> Survey of the year's productions.

1372 _____. "Irish Theatre." THEATRE ARTS (New York), 29 (May 1945), 286–93.

> "When we look at the past year there is nothing very original to record."

1373 _____. "Irish Drama in War and Peace." THEATRE ARTS (New York), 30 (April 1946), 231–35.

> "Luckily the Irish theatre was not submerged in the chaos of world conflict as happened elsewhere in Europe."

1374 _____. "Twilight over Irish Drama." THEATRE ARTS (New York), 30 (December 1946), 706–8.

> The theatre in Ireland has been fighting desperately to retain its finest actors against the coaxings of the film companies.

1375 _____. "The Theatre in Eire." THEATRE ARTS (New York), 31 (November 1947), 30.

Survey.

1376 _____. "Irish Drama Knocks at the Door." LIFE AND LETTERS (London), 61 (April 1949), 16-21.

"The Irish theatre is beginning to express the complexity of modern life and thought in Ireland though the traditional approach still hampers this and imposes a time-lag."

1377 _____. "Same Program, Fifty Years Later." AMERICAN MERCURY, 81 (July 1955), 43-44.

The Abbey Theatre on the occasion of its Golden Jubilee.

1378 Frank, Waldo. "Modern Drama." DIAL (Chicago), 85 (July 1928), 45-50.

A broad sweep of the great modern drama contrasting it with the drama of all time.

1379 Friel, Brian. "Plays Pleasant and Unpleasant." TIMES LITERARY SUPPLEMENT (London), 17 March 1972, pp. 305-6.

On the subjects of Irish drama, past and present.

1380 Fry, Christopher. "The Contemporary Theatre; A Playwright Speaks." LISTENER (London), 23 February 1950, pp. 331-32.

Deals with the problems of the playwright who uses verse for his working language.

1381 _____. "The Play of Ideas." NEW STATESMAN AND NATION (London), 39 (22 April 1950), 458.

Letter to the editor.

1382 _____. "Comedy." ADELPHI, 27 (1950), 27-29.

Deals only with the theory.

1383 _____. "Poetry in the Theatre." SATURDAY REVIEW (New York), 21 March 1953, pp. 18-19, 33.

Taken from a talk presented on the BBC Third Programme.

1384 Fyfe, H. Hamilton. "The Censor's Duty." NINETEENTH CENTURY (London), 52 (August 1902), 282-88.

1385 _____. "Why I Gave Up Writing Plays." NATIONAL REVIEW (London), 94 (November 1929), 412-20.

"I quickly discovered that one should belong to the inner ring of the theatrical profession if one is to make a trade of writing for the stage."

1386 _____. "Why We Need a National Theatre." FORTNIGHTLY REVIEW, n.s. 154, (August 1943), 127-32.

1387 Gaffney, Fannie Hemphreys. "Modern Dramatic Realism." ARENA (Boston), 29 (April 1903), 391-96.

"The trend toward realism on the part of certain modern playwrights seems to gather momentum with each succeeding theatrical season."

1388 Galitzine, Prince Nicolas. "The Theatre: A Revue of 1933. Why the Theatres Are Losing to the Talkies." SATURDAY REVIEW (London), 156 (23 December 1933), 665.

Three reasons: "exorbitant prices," "bother of booking," and "irritating and arbitrary regulations."

1389 Galsworthy, John. "The New Spirit in the Drama." LIVING AGE, 277 (1913), 259-66.

Defends the "new drama" which is "the expression of the sincere moods of men who ask no more than to serve an art." Reprinted from THE HIBBERT JOURNAL.

1390 Garnett, Edward. "The Repertory Theatre in England." NATION (New York), 89 (5 August 1909), 125-26.

1391 Gassner, John. "The Theatre Arts." FORUM (Philadelphia), 109 (April 1948), 212-14.

On the Dublin Gate Theatre.

1392 _____. "Fabianism and the British Playwrights." THEATRE ARTS (New York), 35 (November 1951), 30-31, 92-93.

"The British social play generally displays a moderation as unfortunate in the theatre as it is theoretically admirable in politics."

1393 _____. "The Trifurcation of Drama and Theatre in English." QUARTERLY JOURNAL OF SPEECH, 39 (1953), 323-34.

On the advantages and disadvantages of having distinctive theatre in England, Ireland, and America.

1394 _____. "Forms of Modern Drama." COMPARATIVE LITERATURE, 7 (Spring 1955), 129-43.

1395 _____. "Modern Drama and Society." WORLD THEATRE, 4 (Winter 1955), 21-34.

> Social drama has had many modes and styles at its disposal and its interest has been largely the result of individual creation.

1396 Geddes, Virgil. "The Rebirth of Drama." DRAMA (Chicago), 21 (March 1931), 7.

> Discussion of the relationship between drama and the stage. The return to "real drama" is advocated.

1397 Geier, Woodrow A. "Exile and Salvation in Modern Drama." RELIGION IN LIFE, 30 (Autumn 1961), 589-602.

> Includes discussions of Christopher Fry, W.H. Auden, Graham Greene, and T.S. Eliot.

1398 Gerstenberger, Donna. "The Saint and the Circle: The Dramatic Potential of an Image." CRITICISM, 1 (1960), 336-41.

> The turning wheel and the still point in plays by W.B. Yeats, T.S. Eliot, and Stephen Spender.

1399 _____. "Perspectives of Modern Verse Drama." MODERN DRAMA, 3 (May 1960), 24-29.

> "The conception of verse drama as a formal experience was what had been lost as a result of the increasingly rigid separation on the stage of the domain of poetry and the world of real and vital concerns."

1400 Gibbs, Patrick. "Wanted: Plays of Quality." WORLD REVIEW (London), February 1948, pp. 60-64.

1401 Gibson, Wilfrid Wilson. "Some Thoughts on the Future of Poetic-Drama." POETRY REVIEW, 1 (1912), 119-22.

> In the future, "dramatic verse will be the medium which the energy of life will shape into its most effectual means of expression."

1402 Gielgud, John. "A Living Theatre." NEW STATESMAN AND NATION (London), 21 (19 April 1941), 409-10.

> On the need for a National Theatre. See also the correspondence in the issues for 26 April 1941 (pages 435-36) and 3 May 1941 (page 460).

1403 _____. "The Haymarket and the New: London Flocks to Repertory." THEATRE ARTS (New York), 29 (March 1945), 166-71.

> "Classical repertory has taken London by storm in the sixth year of war."

1404 Gielgud, Val. "Side Lights on the Broadcast Play." THEATRE ARTS MONTHLY (New York), 15 (June 1931), 479-84.

> "The rather peculiar machinery at Savoy Hill . . . in England, is, I believe unique."

1405 Gilder, Rosamond. "New Forms for Old." THEATRE ARTS MONTHLY (New York), 11 (July 1927), 513-20.

> Comments on the increasingly dynamic and varied dramatic fare of today.

1406 _____. "'Smile, Demmit, Smile': War-Time Theatre in Review." THEATRE ARTS (New York), 23 (November 1939), 768-79.

1407 Gill, Michael J. "Neo-Paganism and the Stage." NEW IRELAND REVIEW (Dublin), 27 (May 1907), 179-87.

> Claims that Irish plays are vulgar and brutal.

1408 Gillett, Eric. "Contemporary Prose Forms VI. The Drama." FORTNIGHTLY REVIEW, n.s. 152 (November 1942), 341-47.

> Survey.

1409 Glicksberg, Charles Irving. "The Modern Playwright and the Absolute." QUEEN'S QUARTERLY, 65 (Autumn 1958), 459-71.

> The decline of tragedy.

1410 Goacher, Denis. "Modern Poetic Drama." LISTENER (London), 52 (16 December 1954), 1067-68.

> "The practical test of a verse play is whether it is actable."

1411 Goldsmith, Anthony. "Playwrights of the Future." HORIZON, 7 (March 1943), 195-203.

> Serious modern authors seldom write for the theatre.

1412 Goodhart-Rendel, H.S. "Edwardian Musical Comedy." LISTENER (London), 42 (17 November 1949), 864-65.

> Survey.

1413 Goodwin, Michael. "A Month in the Theatre: The Slump." NINE-
TEENTH CENTURY (London), 142 (July 1947), 26-28.

> Discusses economic pressure and the theatre's failure to keep
> "ahead of our spiritual and intellectual needs."

1414 Graham, Joe. "The Stage: Yesterday, Today, and Tomorrow." QUAR-
TERLY REVIEW, 255 (October 1930), 315-30.

> "The most smashing blow as yet given to the theatrical industry
> has been . . . delivered by the modern cinema."

1415 Granville-Barker, Harley. "The Coming of Ibsen." THEATRE ARTS
MONTHLY (New York), 14 (October 1930), 866-74; (November 1930),
931-39.

> Ibsen gave modern English drama "its intellectual liberty."

1416 _____. "Le Theatre britannique d'aujourd'hui." FRANCE-GRANDE
BRETAGNE, April 1934, pp. 105-17.

> Survey of the contemporary British drama.

1417 Gray, Ken. "T.E. on the Abbey." IRISH TIMES (Dublin), 21 July 1966,
p. 8.

> Telefis Eireann's film about the Abbey Theatre.

1418 Greenwood, George A. "'This England' on the Contemporary Stage; The
Play As a Mirror of Modern Life." WORLD TODAY, 45 (June 1925),
605-9.

> During the past six years the British stage has improved.

1419 Gregory, Lady Isabella Augusta. "The Coming of the Irish Players."
COLLIER'S (Springfield, Ohio), 48 (21 October 1911), 15, 24.

> On the Abbey Players' first American tour.

1420 _____. "A Repertory Theatre." HERALD TRIBUNE (New York), 26
November 1911, part V, pp. 6-7.

> Gives information about the Abbey Theatre.

1421 _____. "The Irish Theatre and the People." YALE REVIEW, 1 (January
1912), 188-91.

> How the Irish theatre came into being.

1422 Grein, J.T. "Twenty-Five Years' Cavalcade of Drama." ILLUSTRATED
LONDON NEWS, 11 May 1935, p. 837.
Survey.

1423 _____. See also Grein's regular contributions to ILLUSTRATED LONDON NEWS (1927-35) and the collections cited in this bibliography (nos. 582-85).

1424 Griffith, Hubert. "What Will the Labour Government Do about Censorship?" THEATRE ARTS MONTHLY (New York), 14 (January 1930), 81-83.

Letter to the editor.

1425 _____. "Can the Drama Have Social Significance?" FORTNIGHTLY REVIEW, 143 (1938), 429-37.

Reasons for curtailing the censor's powers.

1426 Grinberg, M. "Bezobidnaya drob'nasmeshek [A harmless faction of gibes]." TEATR, 2 (1968), 147-57.

On Noel Coward, Terence Rattigan, and Peter Ustinov.

1427 Grossudgel, David I. "The Plight of the Comic Author and Some New Departures in Contemporary Comedy." ROMANTIC REVIEW, 45 (December 1954), 259-70.

Survey.

1428 Gunning, G. Hamilton. "The Decline of Abbey Theatre Drama." IRISH REVIEW (Dublin), 1 (February 1912), 606-9.

Claims that the dramatists who heralded and developed the decline of the Abbey Theatre are Lennox Robinson, T.C. Murray, and St. John Ervine.

1429 Guthrie, Tyrone. "Where Is the Brontosaurus Now?" LONDON MERCURY, 38 (June 1938), 126-29.

On the need for theatrical cooperation.

1430 _____. "The Uncommercial Theatre." BRITAIN TODAY, 135 (June 1948), 11-15.

"Side by side with [a] formidable concentration of financial power, there was no corresponding growth of artistic organization."

1431 Gwynn, Stephen. "The Irish Literary Theatre and Its Affinities." FORTNIGHTLY REVIEW (London), n.s. 70 (December 1901), 1050-62.

Survey.

1432 _____. "An Uncommercial Theatre," FORTNIGHTLY REVIEW (London), n.s. 72 (September 1902), 1044-54.

"What Mr. Yeats and his friends have done is to kindle in Ireland the desire for an art which is an art of ideas."

1433 _____. "Poetry and the Stage." FORTNIGHTLY REVIEW, n.s. 85 (February 1909), 337-51.

Discusses the plays of Stephen Phillips and W.B. Yeats.

1434 Hahanloser-Ingold, Margrit. "Spuren Brechts im englischen Theater." NEUE ZUERCHER ZEITUNG, 2 March 1969, p. 53.

On the influence of Brecht on English drama.

1435 Hall, W. Glenvil. "The Labour Party and the Provincial Theatre." NEW THEATRE MAGAZINE (Bristol), October 1959, pp. 5-7.

Welcomes "the efforts now being made to spread love of the drama in this country."

1436 Halpern, Martin. "Verse in the Theater: The Language of Tragedy." MASSACHUSETTS REVIEW, 8 (1967), 137-48.

What has been accomplished in verse drama "is at least good encouragement to the watchers and waiters for such a revival."

1437 Hamilton, Clayton. "Going to the Theatre in London." BOOKMAN (New York), 31 (August 1910), 601-10.

1438 _____. "The Irish National Theatre." BOOKMAN (New York), 34 (January 1912), 508-16; rpt. included in STUDIES IN STAGECRAFT. London: Grant Richards; New York: Henry Holt, 1914. Pp. 123-44.

Discusses the aims and achievements of the Irish National Theatre Society.

1439 _____. "The Players." EVERYBODY'S MAGAZINE (New York), 28 (May 1913), 678-80.

Survey of the new Irish plays.

1440 Hamilton, Iain. "Poetry and Poeticality." TWENTIETH CENTURY, 151 (June 1952), 533-37.

Contemporary English drama lacks "the poetic quality."

1441 Hankin, St. John. "How to Run an Art Theatre for London." FORT-NIGHTLY REVIEW, 88 (November 1907), 814-18.

1442 _____. "The Need for an Endowed Theatre in London." FORTNIGHTLY REVIEW, 90 (December 1908), 1038-47.

1443 Hanmer, G.V. "The Theatre's Malady." SATURDAY REVIEW (London), 20 (22 July 1933), 101-2.

> The general trade depression, prices of admission, unattractive plays, and counter-attractions.

1444 Hassall, C. "Verse Drama." MASQUE (London), 6 (1948), 3-36.

> Discusses the reasons for the revival of interest in poetic plays and the problems of the poetic dramatist.

1445 Hatcher, Harlan. "Drama in Verse: Anderson, Eliot, MacLeish." ENGLISH JOURNAL, 25 (January 1936), 1-9.

1446 Hawkins, A. Desmond. "The Poet in the Theatre." CRITERION, 14 (October 1934), 29-39.

> The last generation produced no dramatist of a stature in any way comparable with that of contemporary novelists and poets.

1447 Hayes, J.J. "The Little Theatre Movement in Ireland." DRAMA (Chicago), 16 (April 1926), 261-62.

> "The Little Theatre movement in Ireland has a past behind it, but it also has a future before it."

1448 _____. "Who Will Go to Ireland for Aonach Tailteann?" THEATRE ARTS MONTHLY (New York), 15 (January 1931), 78-80.

> Drama in the ancient Gaelic celebration inaugurated some 3,000 years ago in memory of Queen Tailte.

1449 _____. "The Irish Scene." THEATRE ARTS MONTHLY (New York), 16 (November 1932), 922-26.

> Survey.

1450 Hayman, Ronald. "Theatre and Theatres." DRAMA (London), Spring 1972, pp. 50-59.

> Examines "how far the activity of theatre is affected by the buildings available for it and by the prevailing structure of theatrical society."

1451 "Heart-Searchings in the British Theatre." LIVING AGE, 317 (30 June 1923), 795-96.

> The British Theatre "is in a poor way."

1452 Henderson, Archibald. "The New Drama in England." FORUM (New York), 45 (June 1911), 707-24.

> "The New Drama in England today . . . is essentially an experimental school."

1453 Henderson, Gordon. "An Interview with Denis Johnston." JOURNAL OF IRISH LITERATURE, 2 (May-September 1973), 30-44.

> On Irish drama.

1454 _____. "An Interview with Hilton Edwards and Micheal MacLiammoir." JOURNAL OF IRISH LITERATURE, 2 (May-September 1973), 79-97.

> On the Dublin Gate Theatre.

1455 Henderson, W.A. "The Irish Theatre Movement." SUNDAY INDEPENDENT (Dublin), 17 (17 September 1922), 6.

> Survey.

1456 Highet, Gilbert. "The Reinterpretation of the Myths." VANCOUVER QUARTERLY REVIEW, 25 (1949), 520-40.

> Many modern dramatists have gone to Greek mythology for their plots.

1457 "A History of the Abbey." SUNDAY INDEPENDENT (Dublin), 44, (23 January 1949), 3.

> Discusses a history to be written by Lennox Robinson.

1458 Hoare, John Edward. "Ireland's National Drama." NORTH AMERICAN REVIEW (New York), 194 (October 1911), 566-75.

> Review article.

1459 Hobson, Harold. "The British Theater Today; With a Renaissance of Public Interest in Full Swing and Sustained Runs the Rule, the World of the Stage Looks for New Dramatists to Match New Artists." CHRISTIAN SCIENCE MONITOR WEEKLY MAGAZINE SECTION, 23 September 1936, p. 6.

1460 _____. "Laughter Rules in British Theaters." CHRISTIAN SCIENCE MONITOR WEEKLY MAGAZINE SECTION, 30 December 1939, p. 6.

> The English theatre "is recovering from the immediate effects of the outbreak of war."

1461 _____. "Britain's Theater Carries On." CHRISTIAN SCIENCE MONITOR

WEEKLY MAGAZINE SECTION, 23 August 1941, p. 3.

1462 _____. "A National Theater Comes to Britain." CHRISTIAN SCIENCE MONITOR WEEKLY MAGAZINE SECTION, 17 April 1943, p. 4.

1463 _____. "Arts Council Takes a Bow; British Find State Grants to Music and Theater Highly Successful." CHRISTIAN SCIENCE MONITOR WEEKLY MAGAZINE SECTION, 14 February 1948, p. 7.

1464 _____. "State Patronage of the Theater; Britain Stirred by Moral Indignation and Practical Effects of Subsidy Issue." CHRISTIAN SCIENCE MONITOR WEEKLY MAGAZINE SECTION, 7 January 1950, p. 7.

1465 _____. "Poetic Drama Ascendant." CHRISTIAN SCIENCE MONITOR WEEKLY MAGAZINE SECTION, 25 March 1950, p. 4.

1466 _____. "Drama--And Taxes." CHRISTIAN SCIENCE MONITOR WEEKLY MAGAZINE SECTION, 19 August 1950, p. 18.

1467 _____. "Christians on the Stage." DRAMA (London), September 1954, pp. 20-23.

On religious drama.

1468 _____. See also his regular contributions to SUNDAY TIMES (London; 1947-52), and his collected and critical works cited in this bibliography (Nos. 627-31).

1469 Holder, Owen. "The Value and Values of Criticism." DRAMA (London), Summer 1957, pp. 31-33.

"The responsibility of cultivating, maintaining and protecting the arts lies not with their practitioners, but with those outside them."

1470 Holt, Roland. "Plays That Count." FORUM, 69 (May 1923), 1553-61.

Survey of the theatrical season 1922-23.

1471 Hope-Wallace, Philip. "Plays in Performance." DRAMA (London), Summer 1946, pp. 3-5.

Survey.

1472 _____. "An Age of Smartness." PLAYS AND PLAYERS (London), 8 (November 1960), 4-5.

On the English theatre during the 1920s and 1930s.

1473 Hopkins, Charles. "From Piccadilly to Broadway; Sometimes More Than an Ocean Separates Those Two Rialtos." THEATRE MAGAZINE (New York), 53 (March 1931), 18.

> English plays, on the average, are inferior to American offerings but the best of the English plays are considerably better than the finest of the American dramas.

1474 Horn, Robert D. "For Export Only--the London Theater." WESTERN HUMANITIES REVIEW, 5 (Spring 1951), 137-41.

> Survey.

1475 Hornsell, Horace. "The Drama, 1927." OUTLOOK (London), 60 (31 December 1927), 874.

> Survey.

1476 Houghton, Norris. "National Theatres of the World: I. Great Britain." THEATRE ARTS (New York), 30 (September 1946), 529-30.

1477 "How We Spoiled the Irish Actors." LITERARY DIGEST (New York), 45 (13 July 1912), 63.

> Excerpts from English papers on the Irish Players' American visit.

1478 Howe, P.P. "England's New Dramatists." NORTH AMERICAN REVIEW, 198 (August 1913), 218-26.

> Survey.

1479 Howells, W.D. "Some New English Plays." HARPER'S WEEKLY, 48 (23 January 1904), 124-26.

> Survey.

1480 Hughes, Glenn. "Concerning a Theatre of the People." DRAMA (Chicago), 11 (1920), 45-46.

> On W.B. Yeats's lecture "A Theatre of the People."

1481 _____. "The Modern Drama." SCRIPPS COLLEGE PAPERS, 11 (1930), 35-47.

> "England, France, Germany and America yield in varying degrees to the new wave of ritual--England least of all."

1482 Hughes, Richard. "New Trends in the Theatre, VII--England." FORUM, 73 (June 1925), 869-76.

> General survey of the theatre since the war, giving its salient features.

1483 Hunter, Frederick J. "The Value of Time in Modern Drama." JOURNAL OF AESTHETICS AND ART CRITICISM, 16 (December 1957), 194-201.

Considers the factor of time as a variable in the organization of dramatic action and as a variable in the effects of a variety of plays.

1484 Hurd, Michael. "The Glastonbury Festivals, 1914-1926." THEATRE NOTEBOOK, 17 (1963), 51-61.

Survey of the music drama venture by Rutland Boughton.

1485 Hutchinson, Horace G. "People Who Go to Plays." LIVING AGE, 261 (5 June 1909), 613-19.

Reprinted from CORNHILL MAGAZINE.

1486 "In the Theatre, 1936-1956; Some First Impressions." ENGLISH, 11 (Summer 1956), 54-56.

Reprints of reviews.

1487 Irial. "Has the Irish Literary Theatre Failed?" UNITED IRISHMAN (Dublin), 6 (9 November 1901), 3.

"To produce a play or two every twelve months . . . does not seem really the proper method of founding a school of native Irish drama."

1488 "The Irish National Theatre." SAMHAIN (Dublin), October 1903, pp. 34-36.

The Irish Theatre's productions in London.

1489 "The Irish Play of Today." OUTLOOK (New York), 99 (4 November 1911), 561-63.

Reflections on Irish drama.

1490 "The Irish Players in New York." OUTLOOK (New York), 99 (2 December 1911), 801.

The prime characteristics of Irish plays are "their freedom from the purely theatrical and their sincerity and naturalness."

1491 "Irish Plays and Players." OUTLOOK (New York), 98 (29 July 1911), 704.

The Abbey Players to perform in America.

1492 Irving, Laurence. "The Plight of the Serious Drama." FORTNIGHTLY

REVIEW, 95 (April 1911), 641-47.

1493 Ivanof, Viacheslaf. "The Theatre of the Future." ENGLISH REVIEW, 10 (1912), 634-50.

> "The artists who shall re-form the theatre must anticipate and articulate the demands of society, struggling not so much for the sake of their own personal new creativeness as for the very principle and essence of change itself."

1494 Jankovic, Mira. "Engleska poetska drama dvadesetog stoljeca." UMJET-NOST RIJECI (Zagreb), 2 (1957), 143-55.

> Survey of English poetic drama in the twentieth century.

1495 Jenkins, Alan. "Thirty Years Ago." DRAMA (London), 15 (1937), 55-56.

> "The English Theatre of 1906 compares interestingly with present-day drama."

1496 Jennings, Richard. "Do We Want a National Theatre?" SPECTATOR (London), 144 (31 May 1930), 895-96.

1497 Jerome, Jerome K. "The Problem of the Problem Play." HARPER'S WEEKLY, 48 (10 December 1904), 56-58.

1498 John, Victor. "The Festival Theatre in England." THEATRE ARTS MONTHLY (New York), 13 (November 1929), 853-62.

1499 Johnston, Denis. "What Has Happened to the Irish?" THEATRE ARTS (New York), 43 (July 1959), 11-12, 72.

> "Today there are probably as many good Irish authors as ever, but the atmosphere of the country is centrifugal rather than the reverse."

1500 _____. "That's Show Business." THEATRE ARTS (New York), 44 (February 1960), 82-83, 95.

> Reflections by an Irish playwright on the production of plays.

1501 _____. "Humor--Hibernian Style." NEW YORK TIMES, 5 February 1961, Drama Section, p. 3.

> Observations on humor in Irish writing.

1502 Jones, Henry Arthur. "The Drama in the English Provinces." NINE-TEENTH CENTURY (London), 49 (March 1901), 431-44.

1503 _____. "The Recognition of the Drama by the State." NINETEENTH CENTURY (London), 55 (March 1904), 449-66.

The necessity of establishing an English national theatre.

1504 _____. "The Corner Stones of Modern Drama." FORTNIGHTLY REVIEW, n.s. 80 (December 1906), 1084-94.

Part of a lecture delivered at Harvard University on 31 October 1906.

1505 _____. "Literature and the Modern Drama." ATLANTIC MONTHLY, 98 (December 1906), 796-807.

Lecture delivered at Yale University.

1506 _____. "The Foundations of a National Drama." NORTH AMERICAN REVIEW, 186 (November 1907), 384-93.

A lecture, delivered at the Royal Institution of England, explaining why "it is desirable to have a national drama."

1507 _____. "The Urgent Question of the British Theatre." LIVING AGE, 301 (12 April 1919), 95-97.

Reprinted from THE MORNING POST. A "new spirit must be awakened in the English drama."

1508 _____. "Plays with a Purpose." LIVING AGE, 320 (1924), 78-80.

The chief aim of drama should be to interest or amuse.

1509 Jones, Jean Brady. "The 'New Deal' Demanded by Modern Drama." QUARTERLY JOURNAL OF SPEECH, 19 (November 1933), 492-502.

Discusses those plays which treat primarily of political or governmental injustice.

1510 Jones, Leonard A. "The Workers' Theatre Movement in the 'Twenties.'" ZEITSCHRIFT FUER ANGLISTIK UND AMERIKANISTIK (East Berlin), 14 (1966), 259-81.

An excerpt from the author's doctoral dissertation, "The British Workers' Theatre, 1917-1935," submitted to the Karl-Marx-Universitaet, Leipzig.

1511 _____. "The Group Theatre in Britain." ZEITSCHRIFT FUER ANGLISTIK UND AMERIKANISTIK (East Berlin), 19 (1971), 284-87.

Review article on this avant-garde theatre movement from its foundation in 1932 to its demise in 1939.

1512   Jonson, G.C. Ashton.  "The Drama in London."   DRAMA (Chicago), 1
-13    (May 1911), 169-73; 1 (August 1911), 145-51.

   Surveys.

1514   Jurak, Mirko.  "English Political Verse Drama of the Thirties:  Revision
   and Alteration."  ACTA NEOPHILOLOGICA (Ljubljana), 1 (1968), 67-68.

   Includes discussion of W.H. Auden, Christopher Isherwood,
   Louis MacNeice, Stephen Spender, and others.

1515   _____.  "The Group Theatre:  Its Development and Significance for the
   Modern English Theatre."  ACTA NEOPHILOLOGICA (Ljubljana), 2 (1969),
   3-43.

   The Group Theatre existed in London between 1932 and 1939.

1516   _____.  "Dramaturgic Concepts of the English Group Theatre:  The To-
   tality of Artistic Involvement."  MODERN DRAMA, 16 (June 1973), 81-
   86.

   Stresses W.H. Auden and Christopher Isherwood.

1517   _____.  "Commitment and Character Portrayal in the British Politico-
   Poetic Drama of the 1930s."  EDUCATIONAL THEATRE JOURNAL, 26
   (October 1974), 342-51.

   Deals with W.H. Auden, Christopher Isherwood, Stephen Spender, and Louis MacNeice.

1518   K., Q.  "After the Play."   NEW REPUBLIC, 17 (25 January 1919), 377.

   Survey of drama of the last thirty years.

1519   Kelly, Seamus.  "Where Motley Is Worn."  SPECTATOR (London), 196
   (20 April 1956), 538, 540.

   While "there is no dearth of acting or writing talent in the
   Dublin theatre today, there is equally no very adequate economic encouragement for either."

1520   Kenny, M.  "The Plays of the 'Irish' Players."  AMERICA (New York),
   6 (4 November 1911), 78-79.

   Productions of Irish plays denounced in America.

1521   Keohler, Thomas.  "The Irish National Theatre."  DANA (Dublin), 1
   (February 1905), 319-20; (March 1905), 351-52.

   On the opening performances of the Irish National Theatre
   Society at the Abbey Theatre.

1522 Kernodle, George R. "Good Theatre." YALE REVIEW, 28 (Autumn 1938), 112-29.

   The theatre "is no longer subservient to the demands of naturalistic literature and literary content."

1523 _____. "England's Religious-Drama Movement." COLLEGE ENGLISH, 1 (February 1940), 414-26.

   "Like many other revolutions in the theater, the religious-drama movement broke away from the routine of the professional theater by seeking new authors, new actors, and a new audience."

1524- _____. "Time-Frightened Playwrights." AMERICAN SCHOLAR, 18
25 (Autumn 1949), 446-56.

   "The most terrifying plays show man in the twentieth century caught in a speeding whirl of time." Also appeared in MEANJIN 9 (Winter 1950), 118-26.

1526 Kerr, S.P. "What Are Immoral Plays?" WESTMINSTER REVIEW, 155 (April 1901), 444-50.

   Answer to Allan Laidlaw's article, "What Are Immoral Plays?" (No. 1543), challenging his theory and presenting a more solid and tempered argument.

1527 Kilroy, Thomas. "Groundwork for an Irish Theatre." STUDIES; AN IRISH QUARTERLY REVIEW (Dublin), 48 (Summer 1959), 192-98.

   Suggests that the new Abbey Theatre should try to create a workshop atmosphere where aspiring playwrights would receive an apprenticeship in modern stagecraft and learn by practical experience the requirements of a particular body of actors.

1528 Kindermann, Heinz. "Das europaiesche Theater der Jahrhundertwende: eine Umriss-Skizze." MASKE UND KOTHURN (Graz-Wien), 5 (1959), 167-78.

   On the European theatre at the turn of the century.

1529 Kingston, Gertrude. "The Public as Seen from the Stage." NINETEENTH CENTURY (London), 57 (April 1905), 601-14.

1530 _____. "How We Came to Be Censored by the State." NINETEENTH CENTURY (London), 64 (December 1908), 1030-49; 65 (March 1909), 504-20.

   Survey.

1531 _____. "Of Things Theatrical in Germany and England: A Comparison."
NINETEENTH CENTURY (London), 66 (December 1909), 990-1007.

1532 Kitchin, Lawrence. "Realism in the English Mid-Century Drama." WORLD
THEATRE (UNESCO), 14 (January-February 1965), 17-26.

Survey from Robertson to the present.

1533 Knapp, Juliet Lee. "Symbolistic Drama of Today." POET LORE, 32
(1921), 201-33.

Detailed consideration of the subject.

1534 Knight, G. Wilson. "Britain As Dramatic Artist." TIMES LITERARY
SUPPLEMENT (London), 5 April 1941, pp. 164, 166.

Suggests "something of England's national quality."

1535 Knoblock, Edward. "The Playwright's Progress." LISTENER (London),
53 (2 June 1955), 981, 983; rpt. included in his KISMET AND OTHER
PLAYS. London: Chapman, 1957.

Practical notes on playwriting.

1536 Kosok, Heinz. "Englische und amerikanische Kurzdramen im Englischun-
terricht der Oberstufe." DIE NEUEREN SPRACHEN, 14 (1965), 520-29.

On the teaching of drama in universities.

1537 _____. "Die Anfaenge der modernen Repertoire-theaterbewegung in
England und Schottland." MASKE UND KOTHURN (Graz-Wien), 14
(1968), 318-40.

Deals with the beginnings of modern repertory theatre movement
in England and Scotland.

1538 _____. "Das moderne englische Kurzdrama." NEUSPRACHLICHE MIT-
TEILUNGEN AUS WISSENSCHAFT UND PRAXIS (Berlin), 23 (1970),
131-41.

Considers modern English one-act plays.

1539 Krause, David. "The Barbarous Sympathies of Antic Irish Comedy."
MALAHAT REVIEW, 22 (April 1972), 99-117.

Examines J.M. Synge, Sean O'Casey, George Fitzmaurice,
and W.B. Yeats.

1540 Krutch, Joseph Wood. "The Drama as a Social Force." NATION (New
York), 20 April 1932, pp. 467-68.

The propaganda play is usually unsuccessful because "its authors fail to understand the way in which the drama exerts its influence."

1541 L., J. "The Theatre." CHURCH TIMES (London), 23 May 1919, p. 508.

The position, in the main, is "disquieting."

1542 LaBarre, H. "Great Theatres of the World--Abbey: Dublin." COSMO-POLITAN (New York), November 1959, pp. 68-69.

Describes the Abbey as "Ireland's National Theatre showcase for Irish playwrights."

1543 Laidlaw, Allan. "What Are Immoral Plays?" WESTMINSTER REVIEW, 154 (August 1900), 212-16.

The argument is against repression of these plays on the stage. See No. 1526.

1544 Lambert, J.W. "The Critic and the Producer." DRAMA (London), Winter 1954, pp. 53-57.

A talk given at the Malvern Theatre Week, 1954.

1545 Landstone, Charles. "Town and Gown: The British Theatre in the Television Age." LISTENER, 72 (2 July 1964), 13-15.

The importance of provincial theatres is "keeping the taste for theatre alive among the local population, while providing a vitally important training ground for the artists, who will later find their way to . . . the West End."

1546 "The Languishing British Stage." LITERARY DIGEST, 54 (17 February 1917), 405.

"A dubious record for 1916 is reported by the London stage."

1547 Lapham, Jerrold H. "What Hope Radio Drama." THEATRE ARTS MONTHLY (New York), 18 (January 1934), 44-50.

Discussion of the problems of radio drama and speculation as to its possibilities.

1548 Lavery, Emmet. "The Plays Are on the Shelves." COMMONWEAL, 26 (6 August 1937), 361-62.

On Catholic drama.

1549 Lawrence, W.J. "Dublin As a Play-Producing Centre." WEEKLY FREE-

MAN (Dublin), 91 (14 December 1907), 25.

The last part of the article evaluates the eight years' record of the Irish National Society.

1550 _____. "The Abbey Theatre: Its History and Mystery." WEEKLY FREE-MAN (Dublin), 96 (7 December 1912), 11-12.

1551 Leclercq, Raoul. "Le Jeaune theatre ecossais." EUROPE, 21 (December 1929), 567-71.

The young Scottish theatre.

1552 Lenormand, H.R. "Le Theatre d'aujourd'hui et les Elizabethains." CAHIERS DU SUD, 10 (1933), 83-90.

On the Elizabethans and the modern English stage.

1553 Letts, Winifred. "The Fays at the Abbey Theatre." FORTNIGHTLY REVIEW, June 1948, pp. 420-23.

Reflections by an Irish dramatist.

1554 _____. "Young Days at the Abbey Theatre." IRISH WRITING (Cork), September 1951, pp. 43-46.

Memories.

1555 Lewisohn, Ludwig. "The British Drama of Today." NATION (New York), 5 July 1922, p. 23.

Review article.

1556 "The Limits of Stage Illusion." LIVING AGE, 267 (3 December 1910), 587-91.

The atmosphere of illusion should be uniform and convincing.

1557 Linklater, Eric. "The Language of the Theatre Today." DRAMA (London), Autumn 1958, pp. 25-26.

Reprinted from the appendix to his play BREAKSPEAR IN GASCONY (London: Macmillan, 1958). It is difficult to write a great drama in our contemporary idiom.

1558 Littlefield, Joan. "A British 'National Theater.'" CHRISTIAN SCIENCE MONITOR WEEKLY MAGAZINE SECTION, 15 December 1945, pp. 10, 20.

Laurence Olivier and Ralph Richardson are launching "the most theatrical scheme ever planned for Britain's theater-going public."

1559 Littlewood, S.R. "Drama of the Year: Plays That Were--and Might Have Been." REVIEW OF REVIEWS, January 1922, pp. 46-48.

> The general output of plays for the year "has been not altogether without its comparatively good points."

1560 _____. "War-Time--And Afterwards." ENGLISH, 5, no. 26 (1944), 53-55.

> After five years of war "the English theatre is alive, popular, and hopeful."

1561 _____. "Theatre in War--And After." ENGLISH, 5, no. 28 (1945), 120-22.

> It is difficult to find very much high creative purpose among war-time dramatic products.

1562 _____. "Theatre in Victory." ENGLISH, 5, no. 29 (1945), 157-59.

> The drama of the future is likely to be a drama of the people.

1563 _____. "Great Chances for New Playwrights." ENGLISH, 6, no. 34 (1947), 200-202.

> There is urgent demand for new genius in authorship.

1564 _____. "The Drama of the Folk." ENGLISH, 6, no. 35 (1947), 251-53.

> There is a return to folk-drama.

1565 _____. "Fifty Years of Criticism." DRAMA (London), Spring 1948, pp. 15-19.

> Reflections on dramatic criticism by the editor of THE STAGE.

1566 _____. "The Harvest of Forty-Nine." ENGLISH, 7, no. 42 (1949), 284-86.

> There were "many festivals but few great and memorable new plays."

1567 _____. "Towards the National Theatre." ENGLISH, 9, no. 48 (1952), 287-89.

1568 "A Lively Discussion Over the 'Irish Plays.'" BOSTON SUNDAY POST, 8 October 1911, p. 37.

> Statements by W.B. Yeats, Lady Gregory, and others on the controversy over the production of Irish plays in America.

1569 Lyons, J.B. "Play-Going in the 'Forties." DUBLIN MAGAZINE, 9, no. 4 (1972), 80–86.

It was "the golden age of Dublin theatre."

1570 M. "The London Stage in September." BOOKMAN (London), 85 (October 1933), 33.

"Unfortunately there was no London theatre in September."

1571 Macardle, Dorothy. "Experiment in Ireland." THEATRE ARTS MONTHLY (New York), 18 (February 1934), 124–32.

In Dublin "there is a quickened interest in the theatre; dramatists are experimenting with new methods; plays by new writers appear."

1572 MacBride, Maud Gonne. "A National Theatre." UNITED IRISHMAN (Dublin), 10 (24 October 1903), 2–3.

In Ireland a National Theatre "must draw its vitality from that hidden spring from which the seven fountains of Gaelic inspiration flow."

1573 McBrien, Peter [F.]. "Dramatic Ideals of Today." STUDIES: AN IRISH QUARTERLY REVIEW (Dublin), 11 (June 1922), 235–42.

On modern Irish drama.

1574 _____. "Ibsenism." CATHOLIC WORLD, 118 (1923), 192–96.

On the influence of Ibsen on some modern British dramatists.

1575 MacCall, Ewan. "Grass Roots of Theatre Workshop." THEATRE QUARTERLY (London), 3 (January–March 1973), 58–68.

Records the facts about the early years of Joan Littlewood's Theatre Workshop.

1576 MacCarthy, Desmond. "The Gate Theatre." NEW STATESMAN (London), 5 April 1930, pp. 836–37.

Survey of productions by the Gate Theatre, London.

1577 _____. "The Theatre during the Last War." NEW STATESMAN AND NATION (London), 18 (23 September 1939), 425–26.

"The dramatic harvest of 1914 was a rich one." See also the correspondence in the following issue, 30 September 1939.

1578 _____. "Drama." NEW STATESMAN AND NATION (London), 11

September 1943, pp. 167-68.

On the Cambridge Arts Theatre.

1579 _____. "Murder in the Theatre." NEW STATESMAN AND NATION (London), 29 April 1944, pp. 287-88.

Contends that there are too many plays about murders.

1580 McCollom, William G. "Illusion in Poetic Drama." JOURNAL OF AESTHETICS AND ART CRITICISM, 5 (1948-49), 183-88.

"One can find no warrant for the belief that over-all image-patterns may form the real core of a play. The meaning of a play must be derived first of all from the story and the characters."

1581 McCormick, Jane L. "Drive That Man Away: The Theme of the Artist in Society in Celtic Drama, 1890-1950." SUSQUEHANNA UNIVERSITY STUDIES (Selingrove, Pa.), 8 (1969), 213-29.

Discusses the relationship of the artist to society as an important theme in certain plays by W.B. Yeats, J.M. Synge, and Sean O'Casey.

1582 McDermott, Hubert. "The Background to Anglo-Irish Drama." TOPIC, 24 (Fall 1972), 69-76.

Concerned with the 1890s.

1583 MacDonagh, John. "Acting in Dublin." COMMONWEAL (New York), 10 (19 June 1929), 185-86.

On the players and directors of the Abbey Theatre.

1584 Macdonald, John F. "English Life and the English Stage." FORT-NIGHTLY REVIEW, n.s. 95 (April-May 1914), 734-36.

"The English national characteristics upon which English play-wrights base their works do not lend themselves to the intensely dramatic treatment that French national characteristics so lavish-ly afford."

1585 Macdonell, A.G. "What Is Wrong with the Commercial Theatre?" LON-DON MERCURY, 18 (October 1928), 604-14.

Contends that "high rents" and "a shortage of playwrights" flaw the commercial theatre.

1586 Macfall, Haldane. "The Puritan and the Theatre." ENGLISH REVIEW, 10 (1912), 320-35.

"Puritanism, in its enmity to the arts, would fling them to the corrupt and the vile."

1587 MacGowan, Kenneth. "The Living Stage." FREEMAN, 6 (1 November 1922), 184–86.

Realism on the modern European stage.

1588 McHugh, Roger. "Yeats, Synge and the Abbey Theatre." STUDIES; AN IRISH QUARTERLY REVIEW (Dublin), 41 (September–December 1952), 333–40.

Review article.

1589 McIntyre, Clara F. "The Word 'Universality' as Applied to Drama." PMLA, 44 (1929), 927–29.

The difference between tragedy and melodrama is in the treatment of character.

1590 Mackay, Constance D'Arcy. "The Independent Theatres of England." INDEPENDENT, 115 (22 August 1925), 213–14, 224.

The independent noncommercial theatre "makes its way along three distinct avenues: the repertory theatres; the little theatres; and the experimental societies."

1591 McNeill, W.E. "Shakespeare and the Modern Drama." QUEEN'S QUARTERLY, 19 (1912), 214–30.

The hope of the modern drama "lies in its freedom from conventionality and traditional devices."

1592 MacOwan, Michael. "This Age of Discovery." PLAYS AND PLAYERS (London), 1 (October 1953), 10.

"The dramatist of today is more often asking a question than telling us the answer."

1593 Malkani, M.U. "Expressionist Drama in Europe and America." SUNDAY HINDUSTAN STANDARD (Calcutta), 23 May 1954, p. 5.

Includes discussions of C.K. Munro and Sean O'Casey.

1594 Mallinson, Vernon. "The English Theatre." REVUE DES LANGUES VIVANTES, 13 (1947), 174–78.

An examination of the work achieved in the theatre over the last ten years.

1595 Malone, Andrew E. "The Decline of the Irish Drama." NINETEENTH

CENTURY AND AFTER (London), April 1925, pp. 578–88.

"Of the host of playwrights whose work has been produced at the Abbey Theatre in recent years very few give promise of important work in the future."

1596 _____. "The Coming of Age of the Irish Drama." DUBLIN REVIEW, July 1927, pp. 101–14; partial rpt. CATHOLIC WORLD (New York), October 1927, pp. 109–10.

The Abbey Theatre celebrated its 21st birthday on 27 December 1925.

1597 _____. "The Abbey Theatre Season." DUBLIN MAGAZINE, October–December 1927, pp. 30–38.

Survey.

1598 _____. "Some Younger English Dramatists." DUBLIN MAGAZINE, April 1928, pp. 33–43.

"English drama looks like migrating from the stage to the study."

1599- _____. "Ireland." DRAMA (Chicago), November 1930, pp. 14, 34;
1600 December 1930, pp. 19, 24; January 1931, p. 18; February 1931, pp. 16–17, 40; March 1931, pp. 16–17; April 1931, pp. 17–18, 24; May 1931, p. 14; June 1931, p. 11.

The first part of the essay, published in November 1930, concerns the Dublin Gate Theatre; the following seven parts are surveys of theatre productions.

1601 _____. "The Irish Theatre in 1933." DUBLIN MAGAZINE, 9 (July–September 1934), 45–54.

"The year 1933 was merely a good average year in the Irish theatre, with a dozen new plays by Irish authors in Dublin's two repertory theatres."

1602 _____. "Some Recent Plays." DUBLIN MAGAZINE, 10 (January–March 1935), 49–60.

English playwrights are consciously literary artists first and playwrights only at moments or by accident.

1603 Manning, Mary. "In Dublin Today." SATURDAY REVIEW OF LITERATURE (New York), 6 (17 May 1930), 1048–50.

The last part of the article deals with a survey of the theatrical season.

1604 Marshall, Norman. "Plays of the Year [1931]." BOOKMAN (London), 81 (December 1931), 176.

> The majority of playwrights and producers "have been suffering from the obsession of Realism."

1605 _____. "The Theatre in 1933." BOOKMAN (London), 85 (December 1933), 161-63.

> Melodrama "has suddenly burst in upon the theatre again."

1606 _____. "Avantgarde or Rearguard?" LONDON MAGAZINE, 7 (July 1960), 22-25.

> In England "we persist in ignoring what has been going on for many years in the theatres of other countries."

1607 _____. "Banned!" DRAMA (London), Summer 1967, pp. 30-33.

> Review article on censorship.

1608 Martyn, Edward. "A Comparison between Irish and English Theatrical Audiences." BELTAINE (London), February 1900, pp. 11-13.

> "Dublin audiences have awakened to the insipidity of the modern English theatre."

1609 _____. "A Plea for a National Theatre in Ireland." SAMHAIN (Dublin), October 1901, pp. 14-15.

> The strolling English companies contribute to "Anglicising and corrupting the taste of the Irish people."

1610 _____. "A Plea for the Revival of the Irish Literary Theatre." IRISH REVIEW (Dublin), 4 (April 1914), 79-84.

> Stresses the importance of producing "native Irish drama other than the peasant species."

1611 Mason, Harold J. "Classical Myth in Modern Drama." EMORY UNIVERSITY QUARTERLY, 10 (1954), 256-65.

> The limited use of legends in the British theatre.

1612 Mathieson, Andrew. "The Dark East." DRAMA (London), Summer 1969, pp. 45-49.

> Survey of Stratford East productions from 1884 to the present.

1613 Maugham, Somerset. "Maugham Discusses the Drama; Interview." LIVING AGE, 340 (May 1931), 305.

Informal remarks on the differences between the old and the modern play and on the future of the theatre.

1614 Maxwell, Gerald. "The Player and the Public." FORTNIGHTLY RE-VIEW, n.s. 110 (September 1921), 511-18.

Audiences "desert the playhouse for the palace of variety that . . . makes no demand on the intelligence.

1615 May, Frederick. "Drama in the Universities." UNIVERSITIES QUARTERLY, February 1951, pp. 155-61.

Should drama be taught in the universities?

1616 _____. "Practical Drama [in the Universities]." UNIVERSITIES QUAR-TERLY, February 1956, pp. 166-71.

1617 Mayne, Rutherford. "The Ulster Literary Theatre." DUBLIN MAGAZINE, 31 (April-June 1955), 15-21.

This theatre, which celebrated its Golden Jubilee in 1954, has a tradition of presenting fine actors and unique plays, with 1904-9 being a particularly rich period in its history.

1618 Meissner, Paul. "Kulturprobleme des modernen englischen Dramas." ZEITSCHRIFT FUER FRANZOESISCHEN UND ENGLISCHEN UNTERRICHT, 29 (1930), 9-25.

Culture problems of the modern English drama.

1619 Melchiori, Giorgio. "Panorama del teatro di poesia in Inghilterra." LO SPETTATORE ITALIANO, 5 (January 1952), 65-69.

Survey of modern poetic drama in England.

1620 Menlock, Walter. "Dramatic Values." IRISH REVIEW (Dublin), 1 (September 1911), 325-29.

On Irish drama.

1621 Menon, Aubrey. "The Theatre--Living or Dead." BOOKMAN (London), 85 (January 1934), 395.

1622 Mercier, Vivian. "The Dublin Tradition." NEW REPUBLIC (New York), 135 (6 August 1956), 21-22.

Argues that in Dublin "a healthy theatre is living off its traditions."

1623 Middleton, George. "The Earnings of the Dramatised Novel." BOOK-

MAN (New York), 28 (November 1908), 233-39.

1624 Miller, Liam. "Eden and After: The Irish Theatre 1945-1966." STUDIES, AN IRISH QUARTERLY REVIEW (Dublin), 55 (Autumn 1966), 231-35.

> Surveys the Irish theatre since the end of World War II and concludes that "however one looks at the situation today, it is on the National Theatre that our hopes for the future of the theatre in Ireland must be based."

1625 Milligan, Alice. "Literary Theatre Week in Dublin." GAEL (New York), December 1901, pp. 363-65.

> Survey.

1626 Milne, A.A. "Dramatic Art and Craft." NATION AND THE ATHE-NAEUM (London), 27 October 1923, pp. 149-51.

> Review article.

1627 Milstead, John. "The Structure of Modern Tragedy." WESTERN HU-MANITIES REVIEW, 12 (1958), 365-69.

> "The dramatist who can help direct the frenetic energy of our culture to a truer conception of life performs an incalculable service, and in so doing he may create tragedy."

1628 Minton, E.E. "Some Aspects of the Drama." PAPERS OF THE MAN-CHESTER LITERARY CLUB, 41 (1915), 393-402.

> The outlook upon the drama was never more hopeful.

1629 Mizener, Arthur. "Poetic Drama and the Well-Made Play." ENGLISH INSTITUTE ESSAYS, 1949. New York: Columbia University Press, 1950. Pp. 33-54.

> "We are left, for the most part, with unplayable plays by genuine poets and skillfully made plays by men who are, at best, serious journalists."

1630 Monkhouse, A.N. "The Words and the Play." ESSAYS AND STUDIES, 11 (1924), 32-48.

> "If you take the list of English plays published during the last few years you may be reassured about the vitality, the per-manence of the word."

1631 Montgomery, K.L. "Some Writers of the Celtic Renaissance." FORT-NIGHTLY REVIEW (London and New York), n.s. 90 (September 1911), 545-61.

"Perhaps the most original achievement of this Celtic Renaissance has been the organisation of the National Library Theatre."

1632 Moore, George. "The Irish Literary Theatre." SAMHAIN (Dublin), October 1901, pp. 11-13.

"Our three years have shown that an endowed theatre may be of more intellectual service to a community than a university or a public library."

1633 Moore, T[homas]. Sturge. "The Renovation of the Theatre." MONTHLY REVIEW, 7 (April 1902), 102-16.

Renovation is accomplished by addressing a cultivated audience, playing the simplest and most aesthetic plays, and impressing on the performance of them an open and obvious sincerity.

1634 Morgan, Margery M. "Strindberg and the English Theatre." MODERN DRAMA, 7 (September 1964), 161-73.

"The impact of Strindberg even on the most 'advanced' corners of the English theatre came slowly and late."

1635 Morris, Lloyd [R.] "The Changing Art of the Modern Playwright." LITERARY DIGEST INTERNATIONAL BOOK REVIEW, 1 (1923), 44, 46, 48.

Review article.

1636 Mortimer, Raymond. "Theatre." NEW STATESMAN AND NATION (London), 34 (16 August 1947), 129.

Amateurs can give better productions than professionals.

1637 Moses, Montrose J. "W.B. Yeats and the Irish Players." METROPOLITAN MAGAZINE (New York), 35 (January 1912), 23-25, 61-62.

Survey.

1638 _____. "Dramatists without a Country." BOOK-NEWS MONTHLY (Philadelphia), 30 (February 1912), 408-9.

The intensity of the Irish players "is born of that very desire to be individual from England, to stand upon their own tradition."

1639 Moult, Thomas. "The New Dramatist." BOOKMAN (London), July 1921, pp. 189-90.

"Only here and there can be found the dramatist who has persisted in the struggle to express his own artistic vision, and he, obviously, has had little or no place on the post-war stage."

1640 "Mr. Roosevelt as a Critic." LITERARY DIGEST (New York), 44 (24 February 1912), 375-76.

Discusses Roosevelt's "enthusiastic championship of the players who have been badly treated in a foreign country."

1641 Murphy, Daniel J. "Yeats and Lady Gregory: A Unique Dramatic Collaboration." MODERN DRAMA, 7 (December 1964), 322-28.

1642 Murphy, Sheila A. "A Political History of the Abbey Theatre." LITERATURE AND IDEOLOGY (Montreal), 16 (1973), 53-60.

Survey.

1643 Myers, Henry Alonzo. "The Tragic Attitude Toward Value." INTERNATIONAL JOURNAL OF ETHICS, 45 (1935), 337-55.

Examines our aesthetic pleasure in tragedy, but uses no illustrations from modern British drama.

1644 N., N. "An Episode in the London Theatre." NATION (New York), 81 (14 December 1905), 481-83.

Mainly on the Court Theatre productions.

1645 _____. "London Theatres." NATION (New York), 97 (2 October 1913), 316-17.

"The British theatre is sadly deteriorating."

1645A Nares, Owen. "Two Views on a National Theatre." LISTENER (London), 15 December 1938, p. 1311.

1646 Nash, Paul. "I Look at the Theatre." THEATRE ARTS MONTHLY (New York), 14 (December 1930), 1051-55.

English audiences are "incapable of discrimination."

1647 Nathan, George Jean. "The English Theatre." AMERICAN MERCURY, 12 (November 1927), 373-75.

"The British stage is the saddest on view in the world at this moment."

1648 _____. "Nathan Goes to the Theater in London." LITERARY DIGEST, 25 July 1931, p. 19.

Excerpts from reviews.

1649 \_\_\_\_. "Art of the Night." SATURDAY REVIEW OF LITERATURE (New York), 15 (3 April 1937), 30.

On imported English plays.

1650 \_\_\_\_. "Lament for Irish Playwrights." AMERICAN MERCURY (New York), 52 (April 1941), 483-89.

"Except for O'Casey . . . the quondam rich vein appears to have run dry."

1651 "The National Theatre." PLAYS AND PLAYERS (London), 1 (October 1953), 3.

Editorial.

1652 Nethercot, Arthur H. "The Drama of Ideas." SEWANEE REVIEW, 49 (July-September 1941), 370-84.

"The 'drama of ideas' has become a large part of the theater today and has played an important role in our modern culture."

1653 \_\_\_\_. "The Quintessence of Idealism; or, the Slaves of Duty." PMLA, 62 (1947), 844-59.

Traces the progressive repudiation of the concept of moral duty and its implications in plays of the quarter-century before 1914.

1654 "New Poetic Drama." TIMES LITERARY SUPPLEMENT (London), 24 January 1935, pp. 37-38.

Review article. See also the article by R. Doone in the 31 January 1935 issue of TLS (page 62).

1655 "A New Status for English Actors." LITERARY DIGEST, 53 (23 December 1916), 1659.

1656 "A New Thing in the Theater: Some Impressions of the Much-Discussed 'Irish Players.'" HARPERS WEEKLY (New York), 4 (9 December 1911), 19.

Productions of Irish plays as seen by American audiences.

1657 Nicholson, Norman. "Modern Verse-Drama and the Folk Tradition." CRITICAL QUARTERLY, Summer 1960, pp. 166-70.

This essay is part of a symposium entitled "The Living Theatre" to which Roy Walker and Val Gielgud also contributed. Nicholson argues in this essay that, since Eliot's MURDER IN THE CATHEDRAL did not successfully establish a new form, "the folk tradition will have to look elsewhere for a medium."

1658 Nicoll, Allardyce. "London's Laggard Stage." THEATRE ARTS MONTHLY (New York), 12 (November 1928), 835-39.

> "We cannot see beyond the dramatist; we cannot feel the true art of the theatre."

1659 _____. "Wartime Drama in the British Empire--United Kingdom." THE-ATRE ANNUAL FOR 1944. New York: Theatre Library Association, 1944. Pp. 5-11.

> Survey.

1660 "No National Theater for London." LITERARY DIGEST, 72 (4 February 1922), 27-28.

1661 Norwood, Gilbert. "The Present Renaissance of English Drama." WELSH OUTLOOK, 1 (March 1914), 122-27; (April 1914), 165-70; (May 1914), 212-17.

> Survey.

1662 _____. "English Drama between Two Wars." DALHOUSIE REVIEW, 22 (January 1943), 405-20.

> "Future historians of drama will decline to acknowledge that these years form any real epoch."

1663 O'Brien, E.D. "The Theatre." ENGLISH REVIEW, 56 (March 1933), 331-34.

> The "deplorable state of affairs" are due to "high rents, and the absurdly high salaries commanded by the better-known actors."

1664 O'Casey, Sean. "The Play of Ideas." NEW STATESMAN AND NATION (London), 49 (8 April 1950), 397-98.

> "The plays written around the new life must be currents in the mainstream of drama."

1665 O'Connor, Frank. "All the Olympians." SATURDAY REVIEW (New York), 49 (10 December 1966), 30-32, 99; rpt. included in THE BACKWARD LOOK; A SURVEY OF IRISH LITERATURE. London: Macmillan, 1967. Pp. 183-93.

> Synge, Yeats, and Lady Gregory.

1666 O'Connor, Ulick. "Dublin's Dilemma." THEATRE ARTS (New York), 40 (July 1956), 64-65, 96.

> Comparison between the Irish theatre now and "the golden years of the Abbey."

1667 O'D., D. "The Irish National Theatre Company." UNITED IRISHMAN (Dublin), 9 April 1904, p. 6.

See reply by James Connolly, "Some Plays and a Critic," in the 7 May 1904 issue of the same periodical (page 6).

1668 Odle, E.V. "Literary Drama and the Theatre." BOOKMAN (London), August 1922, pp. 228-30.

Why literary plays are not actable.

1669 O'Donnell, Donat. "The Abbey: Phoenix Infrequent." COMMONWEAL (New York), 57 (30 January 1953), 423-24.

"Social calm, literary indolence and dialect conventions" are some of the reasons "why the flame of the Abbey burns low just now."

1670 O'Faolain, Sean. "The Abbey Festival." NEW STATESMAN AND NATION (London), 16 (20 August 1938), 281-82.

The Festival, held 6-20 August 1938, was planned as a "recapitulation of the history of the theatre over some thirty-five years or so."

1671 _____. "Ireland after Yeats." BOOKS ABROAD (Norman, Okla.), 26 (Autumn 1952), 325-33; rpt. BELL (Dublin), 18 (Summer 1953), 37-48.

Contends that the decline in Irish writing after Yeats was due to the shift from the individualistic, aristocratic attitude of Yeats to the social, democratic attitudes of the dramatists who succeeded him.

1672 O'Hegarty, P[atrick]. S[arsfield]. "The Abbey Theatre." IRISH TIMES (Dublin), 6 September 1944, p. 3.

Long letter to the editor on the general condition of the theatre.

1673 O'Mahony, T.P. "Theatre in Ireland." EIRE-IRELAND, 4 (Summer 1969), 93-100.

Comparison between the Irish theatre past and present.

1674 O'Malley, Mary. "Theatre in Belfast." IRIS HIBERNIA (Fribourg, Switzerland), 4, no. 3 (1960), 55-57.

Survey of theatrical activities in Belfast past and present.

1675 _____. "Irish Theater Letter." MASSACHUSETTS REVIEW, 6 (1965), 181-86.

On the Lyric Players Theatre, Belfast.

1676 "On Stage Verse." TIMES LITERARY SUPPLEMENT (London), 5 July 1963, p. 493.

Review article.

1677 O'Neill, George. "The Inauguration of the Irish Literary Theatre." NEW IRELAND REVIEW (Dublin), 11 (June 1899), 246-52.

Survey.

1678 _____. "Recent Irish Drama and Its Critics." NEW IRELAND REVIEW (Dublin), 25 (March 1906), 29-36.

On the controversy over the prevalence "of certain unpleasant types of the Irish peasant in various plays produced during the last few years by writers hailed as representative and eminent Irish dramatists."

1679 _____. "Some Aspects of Our Anglo-Irish Poets: The Irish Literary Theatre; Foreign Inspiration of Alleged Irish Plays." IRISH CATHOLIC (Dublin), 24 (23 December 1911), 5.

Text of a lecture delivered before the Students' National Literary Society in Dublin.

1680 _____. "Irish Drama and Irish Views." AMERICAN CATHOLIC QUARTERLY REVIEW (Philadelphia), 37 (April 1912), 322-32; rpt. IRISH CATHOLIC (Dublin), 25 (31 August 1912), 6; (7 September 1912), 6.

Inquires "how far Ireland has refused . . . to recognize in the new drama a fair portrait of herself."

1681 O'Ryan, Agnes. "The Drama of the Abbey Theatre." IRISH EDUCATIONAL REVIEW (Dublin), 6 (December 1912), 154-63.

Observations on the Irish dramatic movement.

1682 Otten, Kurt. "Die Ueberwindung des Realismus im modernen englischen Drama." DIE NEUEREN SPRACHEN, 1960, pp. 265-78.

The dominance of realism in modern English drama.

1683 Ould, Hermon. "The Contemporary Theatre." ENGLISH REVIEW, 34 (April 1922), 345-47; (June 1922), 548-50; 35 (August 1922), 144-46; (September 1922), 232-35.

Survey.

1684 _____. "Das englische Theater seit dem Kriege." DIE LITERATUR, 27

(1925), 206-12.

Survey of English drama since World War I.

1685 Page, Sean. "The Abbey Theatre." DUBLIN MAGAZINE, 5 (Autumn-Winter 1966), 6-14.

Examines the Abbey as a national theatre.

1686 Palfy, Istvan. "Modern English Drama Through Hungarian Eyes." HUNGARIAN STUDIES IN ENGLISH (L. Kossuth University, Debrecen), 5 (December 1971), 137-49.

How English drama is received by Hungarian critics and audiences.

1687 Pallette, Drew B. "Eliot, Fry, and Broadway." ARIZONA QUARTERLY, 11 (Winter 1955), 342-47.

Examines their work as poetic drama.

1688 Palmer, John. "The Rediscovery of a Famous Author." SATURDAY REVIEW (London), 28 October 1911, pp. 549-50.

Aristotle and the modern drama.

1689 _____. "Footlights and the Super-Doll." SATURDAY REVIEW (London), 20 January 1912, pp. 74-76.

Review article.

1690 _____. "If I Were Still a Dramatic Critic." NINETEENTH CENTURY (London), April 1927, pp. 594-604.

"The English theatre is for the moment not very obviously affected by recent literary developments."

1691 Pattisson, A.L. "Which Is the Opposite of Prose?" DRAMA (London), Summer, 1954, pp. 30-32.

On verse drama.

1692 Peacock, Ronald. "Public and Private Problems in Modern Drama." JOHN RYLANDS LIBRARY BULLETIN, 36 (September 1953), 38-55; rpt. TULANE DRAMA REVIEW, 3 (March 1959), 58-72.

Modern drama is created by a particular imagination, but it is never simply a personal statement. "It is always about men-in-society."

1693 Pearson, Hesketh. "A Great Theatrical Management." LISTENER (London), 52 (28 October 1954), 715-16.

Granville-Barker and J.E. Vedrenne at the Court Theatre.

1694 _____. "The Edwardian Era: A High Old Time." THEATRE ARTS (New York), 45 (July 1961), 54-55.

It was a period of plushy Shakespearean productions, stylish actor-managers, and fancy-dress audiences, but it also provided a dedicated public for Shaw and Galsworthy.

1695 Peinert, Dietrich. "Interpretationshilfen zum neueren englischen und amerikanischen Drama." LITERATUR IN WISSENSCHAFT UND UNTERRICHT (Kiel), 4 (1971), 52-65.

Interpretations to some modern British plays.

1696 Pettet, Edwin Burr. "Report on the Irish Theatre." EDUCATIONAL THEATRE JOURNAL, 8 (May 1956), 109-14.

Survey.

1697 Phelps, William Lyon. "A First Night at a London Theater." INDEPENDENT, 53 (31 January 1901), 271-72.

The experience of a first night at the St. James's Theatre.

1698 Pierce, Roger. "'Intimacy' in the Theatre." EDUCATIONAL THEATRE JOURNAL, 20 (May 1968), 147-51.

1699 Pilcher, Velona. "All Work and No Play." THEATRE ARTS MONTHLY (New York), 13 (July 1929), 506-16.

Playwrights "do not write for the theatre."

1700 _____. "Testament of Theatre." THEATRE ARTS MONTHLY (New York), 31 (March 1947), 45-47.

Reflections on modern drama by the director of the Gate Theatre in London.

1701 "The Players." EVERYBODY'S MAGAZINE (New York), 26 (February 1912), 231-40.

"The monotony of the current theatre season in America was emphatically interrupted by the advent of the Irish Players from the Abbey Theatre, Dublin."

1702 Playfair, Giles. "Theatre of Cowardice." NEW SOCIETY, 7 January 1965, p. 22.

On the importance of theatres outside the West End.

1703 Playfair, Nigel. "Towards Simplicity." ENGLISH REVIEW, 34 (January 1922), 43-46.

Extracted from a paper read to the Architectural Association on simplicity in dramatic scenery.

1704 _____. "The Case for a National Theatre." NINETEENTH CENTURY (London), 104 (August 1928), 217-24.

1705 _____. "The 'Talkies' and a National Theatre." SATURDAY REVIEW (London), 148 (20 July 1929), 69-70.

A National Theatre "could now be made not only a self-supporting but even a paying proposition."

1706 "Plays for Middle-Brows." TIMES LITERARY SUPPLEMENT (London), 29 June 1973, pp. 747-48.

Review article on English drama from 1900-1930.

1707 "Plays in Performance." DRAMA (London), quarterly, 1917-- .

Review in every issue.

1708 Plowman, Max. "Hopes and Fears for Modern Drama." ACADEMY (London), 90 (25 March 1911), 365-67.

"Regarded from the standpoint of art, nothing is more deplorable than the present condition of English drama."

1709 Poel, William. "Poetry in Drama." CONTEMPORARY REVIEW, 104 (1913), 699-707.

Poetry is seldom spoken on the English stage because managers think the public do not appreciate it in drama.

1710 _____. "Trade in Drama." CONTEMPORARY REVIEW, 106 (1914), 209-14.

The tendency of the day is to turn theatres into picture-houses and plays into music-hall sketches.

1711 _____. "A Theatre Reform Association." CONTEMPORARY REVIEW, 111 (January 1917), 108-12.

1712 _____. "The Truth about the Stage." CONTEMPORARY REVIEW, 115 (May 1919), 563-67.

"The grip which commercialism has obtained over the English theatre is not likely to be relaxed."

1713 _____. "Poetry in Drama." MASK, 12 (1927), 7-9.

"Today Commercialism sits as watch-dog at the stage-door, determined to keep out everything but the commonplace."

1714 Pollock, John. "The Censorship." FORTNIGHTLY REVIEW, n.s. 91 (May 1912), 880-94.

1715 "The Position of the Theatre; A Symposium." MASK, 4 (1911), 124-33.

Participants are Ellen Terry, Arthur Pinero, Martin Harvey, Gordon Craig, Walter Crane, John Balance, Christopher St. John, George Calderon, and Allen Carric.

1716 Potter, Helen. "The Drama of the Twentieth Century." ARENA (Boston), 23 (February 1900), 157-66.

Attempts to show the evolution toward the realization of a new ideal--that of a "conditioned stage with a conditioned audience."

1717 Poulenard, E. "Le Modernisme au theatre." ETUDES ANGLAISES, 10 (1957), 392-99.

Review article.

1718 Price, Cecil. "Towards a National Theatre for Wales." ANGLO-WELSH REVIEW (Pembroke Dock, Wales), 12, no. 29 (1962), 12-25.

Survey.

1719 Priestley, J.B. "The State and the Theatre." NEW STATESMAN AND NATION (London), 8 (17 November 1934), 717-18.

Contends that the state should support the serious theatre. See the reply by R. Hope in the same periodical for 24 November 1934 (page 752).

1720 _____. "Audiences and Critics." SPECTATOR (London), 19 April 1935, pp. 649-50.

Maintains that "quite a number of our dramatic critics are busy hindering and not helping the serious Theatre."

1721 _____. "A Dramatist's View." NEW STATESMAN AND NATION (London), 26 (25 September 1943), 198-99.

Up to now dramatic criticism "has been a grave hindrance."

1722 _____. "The Theatre Conference." NEW STATESMAN AND NATION

(London), 35 (21 February 1948), 151–52.

On the first British Theatre Conference which opened at the Caxton Hall on 5 February. See the discussion in the issues for 6 March 1948 (page 194) and 13 March 1948 (page 216).

1723 _____. "The Art of the Dramatist." LISTENER (London), 5 December 1957, pp. 917–19; 12 December 1957, pp. 975–77; 19 December 1957, pp. 1025–27.

Reflections.

1724 Prior, Moody E. "Poetic Drama: An Analysis and a Suggestion." ENGLISH INSTITUTE ESSAYS, 1949. New York: Columbia University Press, 1950. Pp. 3–32.

The modern poet who aspires to be a serious playwright has formidable artistic and psychological difficulties to overcome.

1725 Pryce-Jones, Alan. "Is a National Theatre Necessary?" LONDON MAGAZINE, 7 (July 1960), 25–30.

1726 _____. "The British National Theatre." THEATRE ARTS (New York), 47 (November 1963), 20–21, 78–79.

The National Theatre has become "a fact after a century of frustration."

1727 Quinn, John. "Lady Gregory and the Abbey Theater." OUTLOOK (New York), 94 (16 December 1911), 916–19.

Deals also with W.B. Yeats and J.M. Synge.

1728 Rattigan, Terence. "Concerning the Play of Ideas." NEW STATESMAN AND NATION (London), 39 (4 March 1950), 241–42.

"I believe that the best plays are about people and not about things." See reply by G. Lewis (11 March 1950, page 274) and the rejoinder (13 May 1950, pages 545–46).

1729 Rattray, R.F. "The Modern Drama Renaissance." QUARTERLY REVIEW, 283 (April 1945), 176–87.

Review article.

1730 Read, Herbert. "Modern Drama: The Architectural Hold-Up." LONDON MERCURY, 32 (September 1935), 427–32.

"It is as poetry that the drama today is dead."

1731 Rebora, Piero. "Teatro inglese contemporaneo." NUOVA ANTOLOGIA,

February 1956, pp. 281-90.

Survey.

1732 Recouly, Raymond. "The London Stage As Seen by a Frenchman." SCRIB-NER'S, 73 (May 1923), 521-28.

Survey.

1733 "Red Ladder Now." NEW THEATRE MAGAZINE (Bristol), 12, no. 3 (1973), 23-29.

An account of the Red Ladder Theatre, London.

1734 Redgrave, Michael. "The Present State of the London Stage." CAM-BRIDGE REVIEW, 51 (13 June 1930), 497-98.

Playwrights "produce more and more plays in which the indi-viduality of the characters is stressed at the expense of struc-tural merits."

1735 _____. "An Actor to the Critics." NEW STATESMAN AND NATION (London), 26 (4 September 1943), 151.

Contends that the majority of dramatic critics do not criti-cize. See the ensuing discussion in the issues for 11 Sep-tember 1943 (page 170), 18 September 1943 (page 186), 2 October 1943 (pages 217-18), and 9 October 1943 (page 233).

1736 Reed, Edward. "Playwrights Afield." THEATRE ARTS MONTHLY (New York), 18 (June 1934), 446-54.

On play transplantation between London and New York.

1737 _____. "Prefaces, Parentheses, Poetry." THEATRE ARTS MONTHLY (New York), 20 (March 1936), 224-32.

Review article.

1738 Reid, Alec. "Dublin's Abbey Theatre Today." DRAMA SURVEY, 3 (Fall 1964), 507-19.

A brief history of the Abbey Theatre plus some observations on its organization today and its plans for the future.

1739 Rentoul, Gervais. "Some Problems of the Modern Theatre." EMPIRE RE-VIEW (London), March 1936, pp. 138-44.

The theatre is having to adapt itself to altogether novel condi-tions.

1740 "Repertory." PLAYS AND PLAYERS (London), 5 (August 1958), 22.

Editorial on the fiftieth anniversary of repertory theatres in England.

1741 Reynolds, George F. "Literature for an Audience." STUDIES IN PHILO-
LOGY, 28 (1931), 278-87.

As distinct from literature for the solitary reader.

1742 _____. "British and American Theater: A Personal Tour." WESTERN
HUMANITIES REVIEW, 4 (Winter 1949), 35-38.

Survey.

1743 Rhodes, Raymond Crompton. "The Irish National Theatre." T.P.'S WEEK-
LY (London), 21 (18 April 1913), 504.

Letter to the editor.

1744 Robinson, Lennox. "Recipe for a National Theatre." REALIST (London),
June 1929, pp. 130-41.

Argues that "our recipe for a National Theatre could only have
been cooked over an Irish fire."

1745 Robinson, Robert. "The Lively Art." NEW STATESMAN (London), 56
(29 November 1958), 763.

Review article.

1746 Roosevelt, Theodore. "The Irish Theatre." OUTLOOK (New York), 16
December 1911, pp. 915-16.

On the Abbey Players' first American tour.

1747 Rosenberg, Harold. "Character Change and the Drama." SYMPOSIUM,
3 (1932), 348-69.

"Dramatic and religious thought . . . retrace the steps which
social legality overleaps; they reconstruct the entire individual
to fit him into their schemes of justice."

1748 Rosenfield, John. "The Well-Made Play." SOUTHWEST REVIEW, 42
(Autumn 1957), viii ff.

Frederick Lonsdale, Bernard Shaw, and Somerset Maugham all
learned from the tradition of the well-made play.

1749 Ross, Clarendon. "A Note on the Lack of Theatricality in Modern Realistic Drama." DRAMA (Chicago), 10 (1920), 156-58.

"The true modern realist carries over actual life to the stage, and in so doing he necessarily sweeps the conventionalized theatrical cobwebs off the stage."

1750 Ross, Malcolm Mackenzie. "The Theatre and the Social Confusion." UNIVERSITY OF TORONTO QUARTERLY, 5 (January 1936), 197-215.

"In the contemporary theatre there is apparent a vigorous effort to break away from the social-realistic tradition."

1751 Rosseli, John. "The Importance of Writing Good Plays." REPORTER, 36 (18 May 1967), 44-49.

The public "has had enough of unpleasant plays" and prefers revivals--particularly of Wilde's plays and those of the 1920s.

1752 Rothe, Hans. "Das moderne englische Theater." TAGEBUCH, 5 (June 1924), 848-53, 879-84.

Survey.

1753 Russell, John W. "A Tory and the Provincial Drama." NEW THEATRE (Bristol), January 1960, pp. 11-14.

On the policy of the Conservative government toward the theatre.

1754 Ruttledge, Paul. "Stage Management in the Irish National Theatre." DANA (Dublin), September 1904, pp. 150-52.

1755 Ryan, Stephen P. "Theatre in Dublin." AMERICA (New York), 92 (30 October 1954), 128-29.

Survey.

1756 _____. "Crisis in Irish Letters; Literary Life in Dublin." COMMON-WEAL (New York), 71 (18 December 1959), 347-49.

"The present crop of dramatists includes men of more than average talent . . . but simply not endowed with the touch of genius necessary for enduring fame in the theater."

1757 Saint-Denis, Michel. "The English Theatre in Gaelic Eyes." TEXAS QUARTERLY, 4 (Autumn 1961), 26-45.

Reflections on the English theatre by a French director.

1758 Salerno, Henry F. "The Problem Play: Some Aesthetic Considerations." ENGLISH LITERATURE IN TRANSITION, 11, no. 4 (1968), 195-205.

Examines the work of Bernard Shaw, John Galsworthy, and J.M. Barrie.

1759 Sampson, Martin W. "The Irish Literary Theatre." NATION (New York), 73 (21 November 1901), 395-96.

Survey.

1760 Sayers, Michael. "Poetry and English Theatre." LIFE AND LETTERS TODAY (London), Spring 1936, pp. 75-78.

"The trouble with our poetic plays is that they are frequently boring, not to the intellect, but to the eye."

1761 _____. "A Year in Theatre." CRITERION (London), July 1936, pp. 648-62.

Survey.

1762 Schmidt, Dietmar. "Ueber die Inselkultur: mit einem Blick auf den Niedergang des englischen Theaters." BUEHNE, 4 (1941), 74-75.

A view of the decline of the British theatre.

1763 Schwartz, Barry N. "And the Wall Came Tumbling Down." MIDWEST QUARTERLY, 11 (1969), 83-89.

On naturalism in the modern theatre.

1764 Schwarz, Alfred. "Toward a Poetic of Modern Realistic Tragedy." MODERN DRAMA, 9 (September 1966), 136-46.

A number of general characteristics of modern tragedy as the realists and naturalists conceived it.

1765 Scotney, Norman. "Theatre Prospect." SPECTATOR (London), 173 (22 December 1944), 571-72.

"The war has fostered a keener community-sense and a readiness for new ideas and experiences which . . . provide a very favourable opportunity for an increase of theatrical activity."

1766 Scott, Clement. "Dramatic Art in England and America." MUNSEY'S (New York), 24 (November 1900), 194-99.

A firm and cordial friendship has been established between America and England in relation to dramatic art.

1767 Scott, Harold. "What Can We Do for the Theatre?" SOCIALIST REVIEW, 45 (September 1929), 26-28.

A well-known actor makes some original suggestions for encouraging the theatre proper.

1768 Scott-James, R.A. "The Popular Theatre in War-Time and After." RE-
VIEW OF REVIEWS, 63 (April 1921), 283-86.

> "The popular theatre has . . . shown some susceptibility to change
> in the midst of world change."

1769 _____. "Stimulus for the Drama." CHRISTIAN SCIENCE MONITOR
WEEKLY MAGAZINE SECTION, 19 February 1936, p. 9.

> "A National Theater in Britain, long favored by cultural lead-
> ers as providing new opportunities in the arts, appears to re-
> quire only a united public support to become a reality."

1770 _____. "Temple of the Drama." CHRISTIAN SCIENCE MONITOR
WEEKLY MAGAZINE SECTION, 6 April 1938, p. 6.

> "A National Theater for Great Britain, long a subject of dis-
> cussion, again is finding advocates who believe it will nourish
> talent and foster greater appreciation of good plays."

1771 Scott-Kilvert, Ian. "The Play of Ideas." NEW STATESMAN AND NA-
TION (London), 39 (29 April 1950), 486.

1772 Scudder, Vida D. "The Irish Literary Drama." POET LORE (Philadelphia), 16 (1905), 40-53.

> Survey.

1773 Sears, William P., Jr. "New Dublin Players' Group Challenges Abbey
Theater." LITERARY DIGEST (New York), 117 (9 June 1934), 26.

> The Dublin Gate Theatre.

1774 "Secundus, Flavus." "Anti-Drama: A Diatribe." WESTMINSTER REVIEW,
177 (April 1912), 445-51.

> "It is the inveterate and inevitable defect of stage drama, that
> the properties overpower the poet."

1775 Selle, Carl M. "Dramatic Revolt and Conservatism." CARRELL, 5, no.
2 (1964), 16-22.

> On the influence of Ibsen.

1776 Semar, John. "To Save the Theatre of England." MASK, 4 (1911), 4-
7.

> The need for a school "in which shall be developed fine-cut
> incisive brains and beings to produce the ideal."

1777 Seton, Marie. "Television Drama." THEATRE ARTS MONTHLY (New

York), 22 (December 1938), 878-85.

Survey of the BBC's play productions.

1778 "The Shadow on the Stage." BLACKWOOD'S MAGAZINE, 169 (June 1901), 851-60; rpt. LIVING AGE, 230 (3 August 1901), 276-83.

The theatre is "ailing."

1779 Shanks, Edward. "The Position in the Theatre." LONDON MERCURY, 5 (December 1921), 172-79; rpt. LIVING AGE, 312 (18 February 1922), 421-27.

On the cleavage between "commercial drama" and "artistic drama."

1780 Shaw, Bernard. "The Play of Ideas." NEW STATESMAN AND NATION (London), 39 (6 May 1950), 510-11.

1781 Shaw, Robert. "A New English Theatre?" LONDON MAGAZINE, 7 (July 1960), 30-34.

An actor-dramatist talks about the state of the theatre.

1782 Sherek, Henry. "Why Not a Subsidy for the Theatre?" NEW YORK TIMES MAGAZINE, 16 April 1950, pp. 27, 54-56.

A suggestion for improving the drama under the system of tax-exempt, nonprofit production of cultural plays.

1783 Sherriff, R[obert]. C[edric]. "In Defense of Realism." THEATRE ARTS MONTHLY (New York), 14 (1930), 164-66.

"I defend reality in the theatre because the playwright, with all his ingenuity, has found no substitute for its compelling interest."

1784 Sherriffs, Ronald E. "Governmental Support to the Theatre in Great Britain." THEATRE SURVEY, 6 (November 1965), 91-115.

General acceptance of the concept of theatre as an institution possessing positive values worthy of public support is a comparatively recent development in the history of the British theatre.

1785 Shipp, Horace. "A Critique of Criticism." ENGLISH REVIEW, 34 (January 1922), 47-54.

"Present-day dramatic criticism usually concerns itself with a lengthy recital of the story of the play and a selected list of the players dutifully besprinkled with adjectives."

1786 _____. "The Contemporary Theatre." ENGLISH REVIEW, 34 (May 1922), 439-41.

Survey.

1787 _____. "Old Clothes and New Needs." ENGLISH REVIEW, 35 (July 1922), 47-52.

On the International Theatre Exhibition, South Kensington.

1788 _____. "First Aid to Managers; A Review of Tendencies in 1922." ENGLISH REVIEW, 36 (January 1923), 64-70.

"Theatre art, poetic and imaginative drama, music drama, literary drama: these things have more than held their own in nineteen twenty-two."

1789 _____. "Reality and the Theatre." ENGLISH REVIEW, 45 (1927), 110-12.

Survey.

1790 _____. "The Theatre Today." NATIONAL REVIEW, 97 (1931), 249-57.

Finds "something rotten in the state of the theatre today."

1791 Short, Ernest. "The British Drama Grows Up." QUARTERLY REVIEW, 295 (1957), 216-28.

Review article.

1792 Simpson, Alan. "Paddy in Shaftesbury Avenue." SPECTATOR (London), 21 December 1962, pp. 963-64.

Comparison between English and Irish theatrical tastes by an Irishman living in London.

1793 Skeffington, F. Sheehy. "The Irish National Theatre." T.P.'S WEEKLY (London), 21 (2 May 1913), 566.

Letter to the editor.

1794 Sladen-Smith, F. "Drama and the People." SPECTATOR (London), 18 August 1933, pp. 212-13.

On the ideals and methods of the British Drama League.

1795 _____. "One-Act Plays Galore." DRAMA (London), Autumn 1952, pp. 46-49.

Reviews some recently published one-act plays.

1796 Smith, Hugh. "Twilight of the Abbey?" NEW YORK TIMES, 31 March 1935, Section 11, p. 2.

"The past two years have seen a decline in both the quality and output of the Abbey."

1797 Smith, Paul. "Dublin's Lusty Theater." HOLIDAY (Philadelphia), 33 (April 1963), 119 ff.

Reflections on the Irish theatre then and now.

1798 Smith, Winifred. "Mystics in the Modern Theatre." SEWANEE REVIEW, 50 (January 1942), 35-48.

"The return to mysticism . . . has nowhere been more variously expressed than in the contemporary drama."

1799 Sobel, Bernard. "Propaganda and the Play." SATURDAY REVIEW OF LITERATURE (New York), 25 (7 March 1942), 13.

1800 "Some Modern Plays." TIMES LITERARY SUPPLEMENT (London), 28 June 1923, p. 430.

Review article.

1801 Soper, Paul L. "Representationalism versus Formalism in the Theatre." QUARTERLY JOURNAL OF SPEECH, 27 (October 1941), 404-10.

Examines the conflict between the two theories in the light of philosophy. No references to modern English plays are made.

1802 Speckbaugh, Paul F. "Poetic Drama." SPIRIT, 8 (1941), 93-96.

"Poetic drama, it seems quite certain, has taken its permanent place."

1803 Splendore, Paola. "Il Teatro Politico in Inghilterra, 1930-1940." AN-NALI ISTITUTO UNIVERSITARIO ORIENTALE, NAPOLI, SEZIONE GER-MANICA, 12 (1969), 429-49.

Survey of the political theatre in England.

1804 "Spotlight on the Footlights." ECONOMIST, 3 July 1954, pp. 11-13.

Argues that "this glittering profession, for all its frequent con-comitants of disappointment and poverty, will always attract too many people."

1805 "The Stage of the Future." ACADEMY (London), 53 (27 May 1911), 664.

Sums up the principles of the Futurists.

1806 "Stage Workshop." TIMES LITERARY SUPPLEMENT (London), 28 August 1959, p. 495.

> Editorial on the Abbey Theatre's need to create a workshop atmosphere.

1807 Stallbaumer, Virgil. "Modern Groundlings and the Aims of Drama." AMERICAN BENEDICTINE REVIEW, 21 (1970), 335-50.

> Modern drama has "run into serious trouble on moral grounds."

1808 Stamm, Rudolf. "Rueckgriffe auf die griechische Tragoedie im modernen anglo-amerikanischen Drama." NEUE SORCHER ZEITUNG, 6 (26 January 1958), literary section.

> On the influences of Greek tragedy on modern British and American drama.

1809 "A State Theatre." IRISH PRESS (Dublin), 22 May 1947, p. 4.

> Editorial on the need for a suitable building for the Abbey Theatre.

1810 Stegmeyer, F. "Das englische Theater von heute." DEUTSCHE ALLGE-MEINE ZEITUNG, 11 October 1938.

> The English theatre today.

1811 Stevenson, W.B. "Plays and Poetry in 1934." LIBRARY ASSISTANT, January 1935, pp. 9-15.

> Review article.

1812 _____. "Poetry and Drama in 1937." LIBRARY ASSISTANT, February 1938, pp. 32-39.

> Review article.

1813 Stewart, Andrew J. "The Acting of the Abbey Theatre." THEATRE ARTS MONTHLY (New York), 17 (March 1933), 243-45.

> Actors from the Abbey Theatre in Dublin are "noted for sincerity, naturalness, and simplicity."

1814 Stokes, Leslie. "The English Spotlight: A Joyful Birth." THEATRE ARTS (New York), 30 (February 1946), 111-16.

> On the National Theatre.

1815 Storer, Edward. "Dramatists of Today." LIVING AGE (Boston), 280 (24 January 1914), 225-33; (14 Feburary 1914), 410-17; (28 March 1914),

777-84; 281 (11 April 1914), 88-95; (9 May 1914), 329-36.

New dramatists, considered individually.

1816 "The Stormy Debut of the Irish Players." CURRENT LITERATURE (New York), 51 (December 1911), 675-76.

Productions of Irish plays denounced in America.

1817 "The Story of the Irish Players." SUNDAY RECORD-HERALD (Chicago), 4 February 1912, part 7, p. 1.

As told by George Moore, Sara Allgood, T.W. Rolleston, Lady Gregory, and W.B. Yeats.

1818 Stratton, Clarence. "Diary of a Modern Playgoer." DRAMA (Chicago), 11 (November 1920), 47-49.

1819 Strauss, George. "National Theatre." NEW STATESMAN AND NATION (London), 46 (1 August 1953), 124-25.

See also the correspondence in the issues from 8 August-September 1953, pp. 158, 181, 208, 234, 260, 289, 316-17, 347.

1820 _____. "Theatre Censorship: Exit the Lord Chamberlain." TIMES (London), 24 September 1968, p. 9.

The Labour M.P. discusses the Theatres Act which he introduced into the House of Commons as a Private Member's Bill.

1821 Subbotina, K.A. "Chekhovskie p'esy v tvorchestve angliiskikh dramaturgov XX veka [Chekhov's plays in the work of 20th-century English dramatists]." U.Z.: TYUMENSKII GOSUDARSTVENNYI PEDAGOGICHESKII INSTITUT, TYUMEN', 31 (1967), 82-105.

1822 "Sunday Theatres." SPECTATOR (London), 166 (11 April 1941), 396.

1823 Sutton, Graham. "The Art of the Grand Guignol." BOOKMAN (London), August 1921, pp. 228-29.

1824 _____. "The Theatre of Experiment." BOOKMAN (London), April 1928, pp. 68-70.

On expressionism and modernizing Shakespeare.

1825 _____. "Plays of the Year." BOOKMAN (London), December 1932, pp. 174-75.

Survey.

1826 Swart, J. "Het Engelse toneel en de poezie." RAAM, 6-7 (1964), 41-52.

   On modern British poetic drama.

1827 Swears, Herbert. "A National Theatre." EMPIRE REVIEW, March 1938, pp. 154-59.

   Based on two pamphlets issued by the National Theatre Appeal Committee, together with A NATIONAL THEATRE (No. 289 in this bibliography), a book which outlines what the Committee pronounces to be an "ideal scheme."

1828 Tarn, Adam. "Major Dramatic Trends: 1948-1968." WORLD THEATRE (UNESCO), 17, nos. 1 & 2 (1969), 9-33.

   "I doubt whether there has ever been in the history of the theatre such a turbulent period, such a whirlpool of ideas and of dramatic works, as the past twenty years."

1829 Tennyson, Charles. "Irish Plays and Playwrights." QUARTERLY REVIEW (London), 215 (July 1911), 219-43.

   Review article.

1830 _____. "The Rise of the Irish Theatre." CONTEMPORARY REVIEW (London), 100 (August 1911), 240-47.

   Survey.

1831 "The Theatre Since the War." TIMES LITERARY SUPPLEMENT (London), 24 April 1930, pp. 341-42.

   Leading article.

1832 "Theatres on Sundays?" SPECTATOR (London), 170 (15 January 1943), 46.

   See reply by St. John Ervine in the issue for 22 January 1943, (page 76).

1833 Thevenot, E. "Le drame anglais contemporain." LAROUSSE MENSUEL, October 1929, pp. 229-31.

   Survey.

1834 Thompson, William I[rwin]. "Freedom and Comedy." TULANE DRAMA REVIEW, 9 (Spring 1965), 216-30.

   Examines the hero in the farce, the comedy, and the absurd drama.

1835 Thorogood, Horace. "The Theatre and the Jubilee." ENGLISH REVIEW, 60 (1935), 548-56.

> Changes that have occurred since 1910, principally the disappearance of the actor-manager and the coming of the cinema.

1836 Tildesley, Beatrice. "The British Theatre Conference." AUSTRALIAN QUARTERLY, 20 (June 1948), 51-58.

> Explains why "the performance of stage plays is part of the general life of the people" in Great Britain.

1837 Tobin, Michael. "The Ponderings of a Playgoer." IRIS HIBERNIA (Fribourg, Switzerland), 4, no. 3 (1960), 27-39.

> Remarks about the Irish theatre past and present.

1838 Toller, Ernst. "A British Free People's Theatre." NEW STATESMAN AND NATION (London), 12 September 1936, pp. 350-51.

> "The time has come to build up a true Free People's Theatre in England." See discussion in the following two issues.

1839 Tomkinson, Constance. "The Old Vic Reopened." DALHOUSIE REVIEW, 31 (Summer 1951), 104-12.

> Examines the Old Vic Company as a National Theatre.

1840 Tonson, Jacob [Arnold Bennett]. "Books and Persons." NEW AGE (London), 9 (17 August 1911), 374-75.

> On the Abbey Theatre Company.

1841 "Towards a National Theatre." ENCORE (London), Summer 1956, pp. 13-22.

> A symposium with Kenneth Tynan, Benn W. Levy, Tyrone Guthrie, Peter Hall, and Flora Robson.

1842 Townshend, George. "The Irish Drama." DRAMA (Chicago), August 1911, pp. 93-104.

> Survey.

1843 Tree, Herbert Beerbohm. "Some Aspects of the Drama of Today." NORTH AMERICAN REVIEW, 164 (January 1897), 66-74.

> Critical outline of the essentials of the art of the stage.

1844 Trewin, J.C. "Plays with a Purpose." ILLUSTRATED LONDON NEWS, 210 (4 January 1947), 18.

1845 _____. "The World of the Theatre." ILLUSTRATED LONDON NEWS, 210 (29 March 1947).

This review is continued in subsequent issues.

1846 _____. "Plays in Performance." DRAMA (London), Winter 1949, pp. 7-8.

Survey.

1847 _____. "To Call Oneself a Playgoer." BOOKS, 375 (1968), 124-29.

What one ought to read to call oneself a playgoer.

1848 _____. "Theatre Between the Wars." PLAYS AND PLAYERS (London), 16 (January 1969), 60-65, 76-77; (February 1969), 74; (March 1969), 58-59; (April 1969), 62-63, 72-73; (May 1969), 68-72; (July 1969), 66-71; (August 1969), 68-71.

Looks back at the London theatre between 1918-39.

1849 _____. See also Trewin's regular contributions to MORNING POST (London), 1932-37; OBSERVER (London), 1937-53; and ILLUSTRATED LONDON NEWS, 1947-48, and his collections and critical works cited in this bibliography (Nos. 950-64).

1850 Trussler, Simon. "All Our Yesterdays--1941." PLAYS AND PLAYERS (London), 13 (August 1966), 58-59.

Looks at Shaftesbury Avenue and the blitz.

1851 Turner, W.J. "The Poetic Drama." LONDON MERCURY, 1 (December 1919), 240-44.

Answers the question, "Is there a future for poetic drama?"

1852 _____. "Two Views on a National Theatre." LISTENER (London), 15 December 1938, pp. 1310-11.

1853 _____. "Artistic Direction." NEW STATESMAN AND NATION (London), 18 (8 July 1939), 48-49.

Drawbacks of not possessing a National Theatre.

1854 "The Twentieth Century Theatre." GREAT BRITAIN AND THE EAST (London), 50 (9 June 1938), 622.

1855 Twist, Norman. "Growth As Dramatic Form." THEATRE ARTS (New York), 30 (February 1946), 104-10.

Discusses the significance of this particular conception of form from the point of view of the need for a revival in drama.

1856 Tynan, Kenneth. "Prose and the Playwright." ATLANTIC MONTHLY, 194 (December 1954), 72-76.

Refutes the assumption that the upper reaches of dramatic experience are the exclusive province of poetry, for dramatic intensity is compatible with prose, the most versatile medium of expression that the stage has ever had.

1857 _____. "The National Theatre." WORLD THEATRE, 13 (Summer 1964), 33-36.

1858 _____. "The National Theatre." THEATRE, 2 (1965), 75-87.

1859 Ustinov, Peter. "Crisis in the Theatre." HORIZON, January 1944, pp. 7-12.

"The blame must be shared by everyone interested in the theatre."

1860 Vallette, Jacques. "Note sur la poesie dans le theatre anglais contemporain." MERCURE DE FRANCE, 35 (April 1949), 724-27.

On poetic drama.

1861 Van Druten, John. "The Sex Play." THEATRE ARTS MONTHLY (New York), 11 (January 1927), 23-27.

"The separation of the physical and romantic elements of love necessitated a large cleavage in the drama and a deliberate falsifying of its interpretation of life."

1862 _____. "Small Souls and Great Plays." THEATRE ARTS MONTHLY (New York), 11 (July 1927), 493-98.

"The first problem of the play is how is a dramatist to deal with the really tedious small-talk of really tedious people."

1863 Van Hamel, A.G. "On Anglo-Irish Syntax." ENGLISCHE STUDIEN, 45 (1912), 272-92.

Draws examples from the plays of W.B. Yeats and J.M. Synge.

1864 Van Heyningen, Christina. "The Theatre in England." STANDPUNKTE, 4 (April 1949), 66-75.

Survey of theatrical productions from December 1946 to June 1947.

1865 "Vital Drama." TIMES LITERARY SUPPLEMENT (London), 13 April 1940, p. 183.

Editorial on Irish drama.

1866 W., J. "The Ulster Literary Theatre." ULAD: A LITERARY AND CRITICAL MAGAZINE (Belfast), 1 (February 1905), 4-8.

Survey.

1867 _____. "The Theatre and the People." ULAD: A LITERARY AND CRITICAL MAGAZINE (Belfast), 1 (May 1905), 13-14.

The theatre in Northern Ireland.

1868 Walbrook, H.M. "Irish Dramatists and Their Countrymen." FORTNIGHTLY REVIEW, 94 (November 1913), 957-61; rpt. LIVING AGE (Boston), 279 (27 December 1913), 789-93.

Examines modern Irish drama as a picture of Irishmen.

1869 _____. "The Drama in Clement Scott's Day." FORTNIGHTLY REVIEW, 141 (April 1934), 472-80.

Comparison between British drama in the 1930s and the 1880s.

1870 _____. "The Condition of the Theatre." ENGLISH REVIEW, 64 (July 1937), 812-17.

"While there are about forty playhouses in London today, the number of those which are personally directed in obedience to a definite artistic policy year in and year out by men of practical theatre experience is almost negligible."

1871 Waldman, Milton. "The Present State of English Theatrical Productions." LONDON MERCURY, 15 (January 1927), 289-300.

There is "something dowdy about the English stage." See correspondence in the issue for March 1927 (page 532).

1872 Walker, Roy. "The Body of the Time." WORLD THEATRE, 3, no. 3, (1952), 31-37.

"Eliot, Fry, Priestley, and Ustinov give us a composite dramatic picture of what is most significant in British experience in recent years."

1873 Walkley, A.B. "The Theatre and the War." CORNHILL, 47, no. 280, n.s. (1919), 425-34.

The war "had changed our 'values' and shifted our points of view."

1874 _____. "Drama with a Mission." FORUM (New York), 66 (1921), 489-94.

> "Though a play may contain a lesson, it should not be di-·dactic."

1875 _____. See also Walkley's regular contributions to TIMES (London), 1900-26, and the critical works cited in this bibliography (Nos. 982-86).

1876 Walbrook, H.M. "Irish Dramatists and Their Countrymen." FORTNIGHTLY REVIEW, 94 (November 1913), 957-61; rpt. LIVING AGE (Boston), 279 (27 December 1913), 789-93.

> Survey.

1877 Wanderscheck, H. "Englands Dramatiker schweigen." LEIPZIGER NEUESTE NACHRICHTEN, 216 (1941).

> England's dramatists are silent.

1878 Watkins, Ann. "The Irish Players in America: Their Purpose and Their Art." CRAFTSMAN (New York), 21 (January 1912), 352-63.

> Points out differences between productions of Irish plays and conventional Broadway ones and tells the story of the Irish dramatic movement.

1879 Watson, E.H. Lacon. "Literature and the Stage." DIAL, 52 (16 April 1912), 306-8.

> "Of late years there has been a steady procession of novelists towards the theatre."

1880 Watts, Guy Tracey. "The Tradition of the Theatre." ENGLISHWOMAN, November 1916, pp. 140-48.

> "Something must be done to arouse the mind of the public from its atrophying indifference."

1881 Weales, Gerald. "Theatre Literature and Criticism." EDUCATIONAL THEATRE JOURNAL, 19 (June 1967), 301-7.

> Considers the methods and matter of criticism; the tools of the critic and their availability; and the educational implications.

1882 Webber, John E. "The Irish Players." CANADIAN MAGAZINE (Toronto), 38 (March 1912), 471-81.

> "The visit of the Irish Players to New York has provided one of the most interesting experiences of the theatrical season."

1883 Wedmore, Frederick. "Literature and the Theatre." NINETEENTH CENTURY (London), 51 (April 1902), 568-80.

Compares the English and French stage.

1884 West, Algernon. "Some Notes as to London Theatres Past and Present." NINETEENTH CENTURY (London), 55 (January 1904), 60-68.

1885 West, Anthony. "Actor and Critic." NEW STATESMAN AND NATION (London), 26 (9 October 1943), 231.

See reply by H. Willson in the issue for 16 October 1943 (page 251).

1886 West, Kenyon. "Dramatic Criticism." ERA MAGAZINE, 12 (July 1903), 39-44.

On the ideal dramatic critic and playwright and their responsibilities in interpreting the public taste.

1887 Weygandt, Cornelius. "The Irish Literary Revival." SEWANEE REVIEW, 12 (October 1904), 420-31.

Part of the article deals with the Irish National Theatre.

1888 _____. "The Art of the Irish Players and a Comment on Their Plays." BOOK NEWS MONTHLY (Philadelphia), 30 (February 1912), 379-81.

The Irish Players' visit to America "is revealing to us a new art of the stage."

1889 "What Ails the Theatre?" BLACKWOOD'S, 213 (June 1923), 848-50.

On the responsibilities of the manager, author, actor, and public.

1890 "What Can Be Done To Help the British Stage?" FORTNIGHTLY REVIEW, n.s. 75 (1 February 1904), 187-93.

1891 Whitaker, Thomas R. "Notes on Playing the Player." CENTENNIAL REVIEW (Michigan State University), 16 (1972), 1-22.

Tries to discover whether or not modern drama has "any real unity, any major direction."

1892 Whiting, John. "The Popular Theatre." LONDON MAGAZINE, 1 (February 1962), 84-87.

"Conservatism is the life-blood of the popular theatre; radicalism its death."

1893 Whitworth, Geoffrey. "Hopes for the Theatre." FORTNIGHTLY REVIEW, 118 (July 1922), 163-73.

> "Our best hope for the drama lies in a conscious submission to the ideal."

1894 _____. "The Amateur Movement in England." THEATRE ARTS MONTHLY (New York), 15 (July 1931), 572-78.

1895 _____. "A National Theatre?" NINETEENTH CENTURY (London), 113 (February 1933), 227-40.

1896 _____. "National Theatre." THEATRE ARTS MONTHLY (New York), 19 (August 1935), 581-84.

1897 Whitworth, Robin. "Do We Need a National Theatre?" DRAMA (London), Autumn 1959, pp. 38-40.

> The Deputy Chairman of the British Drama League and member of the Joint Council of the National Theatre and Old Vic talks about the latest developments in the National Theatre Scheme.

1898 Wickham, Glynne. "The Study of Drama in the British Universities, 1945-1966." THEATRE NOTEBOOK, 21, no. 1 (1966), 15-20.

1899 Willcox, Louise Collier. "The Poetic Drama." NORTH AMERICAN REVIEW, 186 (September 1907), 91-97.

1900 Williams, Raymond. "Criticism into Drama 1888-1950." ESSAYS IN CRITICISM, 1 (1951), 120-38.

> A chapter from his book, DRAMA FROM IBSEN TO ELIOT (No. 1010). "Much of the important dramatic criticism of the last seventy years has been what is usually called destructive."

1901 _____. "Drama and the Left." ENCORE (London), March 1959, pp. 6-12.

> Believes that a major difficulty is that the majority theatre in England has been for some time a predominantly middle-class institution.

1902 Williams-Ellis, A. "Unlikely Drama." SPECTATOR (London), 134 (10 January 1925), 41.

> On societies producing plays on Sundays.

1903 Williamson, Hugh Ross. "The Theatre of Tomorrow." FORTNIGHTLY RE-
VIEW, n.s. 138 (December 1935), 727-31.

> A variety of circumstances have combined to force the theatre
> toward becoming "an aristocratic entertainment."

1904 Willis, Ted. "The Play of Ideas." NEW STATESMAN AND NATION
(London), 39 (15 April 1950), 426-27.

1905 Wilmot, Seamus. "The Gaelic Theatre." EIRE-IRELAND, 3 (Summer
1968), 63-71.

> Survey of the drama in the Irish language.

1906 "The World and the Theatre." THEATRE ARTS (New York), 19 (December
1935), 886.

> "On the season's programs of the Abbey and the Gate are
> only three new plays by Irish dramatists."

1907 "The World and the Theatre." THEATRE ARTS MONTHLY (New York),
21 (November 1937), 830-32.

> On the National Theatre.

1908 "The World and the Theatre." THEATRE ARTS (New York), 28 (May
1944), 260.

> "War Novels and the Lag in War Plays--Moving Day for The-
> atre Arts."

1909 Worsley, T.C. "The Domestic Interior." NEW STATESMAN AND NA-
TION (London), 39 (14 January 1950), 34-35.

> Reflections about drama in the last fifty years.

1910 ____. "A Good Year." NEW STATESMAN AND NATION (London),
41 (6 January 1951), 10.

> Survey.

1911 ____. "The Task of the Dramatic Critic." LISTENER (London), 12
November 1953, pp. 810-12.

> "What is required of the critic . . . is that he should not lag
> behind the rest of the theatre-going public, that he should
> lead and not merely follow."

1912 ____. See also Worsley's regular contributions to NEW STATESMAN
AND NATION (London), 1948-49, collected under FUGITIVE ART (No.
1021).

1913 Wreford, Reynell J.R.G. "The Influence of Actors upon Plays." NINE-
TEENTH CENTURY, 100 (November 1926), 783-92.

1914 Yeats, W[illiam]. B[utler]. "Mr. Moore, Mr. Archer, and the Literary
Theatre." DAILY CHRONICLE (London), 30 January 1899, p. 3.

Letter to the editor.

1915 _____. "The Irish Literary Theatre, 1900." DOME (London), 5 (January 1900), 234-36; rpt. BELTAINE (London), February 1900, pp. 22-24.

Because Ireland's moral nature has been aroused by political
sacrifices, and her imagination by a political preoccupation
with her own destiny, she is ready to be moved by profound
thoughts that are a part of the unfolding of herself."

1916 _____. "The Theatre, the Pulpit, and the Newspapers." UNITED IRISH-
MAN (Dublin), 10 (17 October 1903), 2.

Reply to an attack on the Irish National Theatre.

1917 _____. "The Irish National Theatre and Three Sorts of Ignorance."
UNITED IRISHMAN (Dublin), 10 (24 October 1903), 2.

Letter to the editor and the editor's reply.

1918 _____. "Aims of the Irish Theatre." SUN (New York), 18 November
1911, p. 12.

Considers the educational aspect.

1919 _____. "The Irish Drama." TWENTIETH CENTURY (Boston), 5 (1911),
12-15.

An address before the Drama League of Boston.

1920 _____. "A People's Theatre; A Letter to Lady Gregory." IRISH STATES-
MAN (Dublin), 6 December 1919, pp. 572-73; rpt. DIAL (Chicago), 68
(April 1920), 458-68.

"I did not know until very lately that there are certain things,
dear to both our hearts, which no 'People's Theatre' can ac-
complish."

1921 _____. "A Defence of the Abbey Theatre." DUBLIN MAGAZINE, 1
(April-June 1926), 8-12.

A speech delivered at a meeting of the Dublin Literary Society
on 23 February 1926.

1922 Yeats, W[illiam]. B[utler]., and Lady [Isabella Augusta] Gregory. "The

Irish Theatre." NATION (London), 18 June 1910, p. 425.

Letter to the editor.

1923 Young, Stark. "Realism in the Theatre." YALE REVIEW, 16 (1926), 112-24.

"The richness, the variety, of the theatrical medium ends only with the complete resource of life."

1924 _____. "Transatlantic Minorities." NEW REPUBLIC, 78 (21 February 1934), 50.

British and American plays compared.

1925 Zangwill, Israel. "The Theatre Slump." NEW REPUBLIC, 15 (25 May 1918), 119.

Reflections on the state of the theatre.

# Chapter 5
## INDIVIDUAL DRAMATISTS

The reader is reminded that lists of plays by individual dramatists will be found in those bibliographies listed under their names and annotated as "primary." Criticism on playwrights will be included in those items designated as "secondary." Furthermore, the researcher is advised to turn to the index at the end of the book to see which general books and articles (in Chapters 3 and 4, respectively) contain additional material on a particular dramatist. The index also directs the researcher to material on such important topics as the Irish Dramatic Movement, the National Theatre, the Abbey Theatre, modern poetic drama, modern religious drama, and censorship in the British theatre.

## ABERCROMBIE, LASCELLES (1881-1938)

An extensive collection of manuscripts is held in the Brotherton Library, University of Leeds; one of the manuscripts of THE SALE OF ST. THOMAS, Act 1, and those of THE STAIRCASE, THE OLYMPIANS, and the first act of an unfinished, untitled play are held in Bodley.

1926 Batho, Edith Clara, and Bonamy Dobree. THE VICTORIANS AND AFTER, 1830-1914. Introductions to English Literature, vol. IV. General ed. Bonamy Dobree. London: Cresset Press; New York: R.M. McBride, 1938. P. 257.

> Primary.

1927 Cooper, Jeffrey. A BIBLIOGRAPHY AND NOTES ON THE WORKS OF LASCELLES ABERCROMBIE. London: Kaye and Ward, 1968; Hamden, Conn.: Archon Books, 1969.

> Primary.

1928 Daiches, David. THE PRESENT AGE, AFTER 1920. Introductions to English Literature, vol. V. General ed. Bonamy Dobree. London: Cresset Press; Bloomington: Indiana University Press, 1958. Pp. 193-94.

> Primary.

1929 Elton, Oliver. LASCELLES ABERCROMBIE. London: Humphrey Milford, 1939.

> Reprinted from the PROCEEDINGS OF THE BRITISH ACADEMY, 25 (1939).

1930 Gawsworth, John [T.I.F. Armstrong]. TEN CONTEMPORARIES; NOTES TOWARDS THEIR DEFINITIVE BIBLIOGRAPHY. London: Ernest Benn, 1932.

> Primary, with bibliographical notes.

1931 Longaker, Mark, and Edwin C. Bolles. CONTEMPORARY ENGLISH LITERATURE. New York: Appleton-Century-Crofts, 1953. Pp. 150–52.

> Primary. Secondary selected.

1932 Millett, Fred B. CONTEMPORARY BRITISH LITERATURE; A CRITICAL SURVEY AND 232 AUTHOR BIBLIOGRAPHIES. New York: Harcourt, Brace, 1935. Pp. 113–14.

> Primary. Secondary selected.

1933 Temple, Ruth Z., and Martin Tucker. TWENTIETH CENTURY BRITISH LITERATURE; A REFERENCE GUIDE AND BIBLIOGRAPHY. New York: Frederick Ungar, 1968. P. 127.

> Primary. Secondary selected.

1934 Willison, I.R., ed. THE NEW CAMBRIDGE BIBLIOGRAPHY OF ENGLISH LITERATURE. Vol. 4: 1900–1950. Cambridge: At the University Press, 1972. Cols. 995–97.

> Primary. Secondary selected.

## A E   SEE RUSSELL, GEORGE WILLIAM

## AUDEN, W[YSTAN]. H[UGH]. (1907-73)

Bloomfield's bibliography (No. 1936) includes a list of manuscripts which "cannot pretend to be complete; it merely records the existence of manuscripts located during the completion of the bibliography."

1935 Adelman, Irving, and Rita Dworkin. MODERN DRAMA; A CHECKLIST OF CRITICAL LITERATURE ON 20TH CENTURY PLAYS. Metuchen, N.J.: Scarecrow Press, 1967. P. 35.

> Secondary selected.

1936 Bloomfield, B[arry]. C[ambray]. W.H. AUDEN; A BIBLIOGRAPHY: THE

EARLY YEARS THROUGH 1955. Charlottesville: University of Virginia Press, 1964.

Primary. Secondary selected.

1937 Breed, Paul F., and Florence M. Sniderman, comps. DRAMATIC CRITI-CISM INDEX; A BIBLIOGRAPHY OF COMMENTARIES ON PLAYWRIGHTS FROM IBSEN TO THE AVANT-GARDE. Detroit, Mich.: Gale Research Co., 1972. Pp. 58-60.

Secondary selected.

1938 Callan, Edward. "An Annotated Checklist of the Works of W.H. Auden." TWENTIETH CENTURY LITERATURE, 4 (1958), 30-50.

1939 _____. "W.H. Auden; Annotated Checklist II (1958-1969)." TWENTI-ETH CENTURY LITERATURE, 16 (1970), 27-56.

Supplements earlier bibliographies by Callan and Bloomfield.

1940 Clancy, Joseph P. "A W.H. Auden Bibliography 1924-1955." THOUGHT, 30 (Summer 1955), 260-70.

Secondary.

1941 Coleman, Arthur, and Gary R. Tyler. DRAMA CRITICISM. Vol. I: A CHECKLIST OF INTERPRETATION SINCE 1940 OF ENGLISH AND AMERI-CAN PLAYS. Denver, Colo.: Alan Swallow, 1966. Pp. 23-24.

Secondary selected.

1942 Palmer, Helen H., and Anne Jane Dyson. EUROPEAN DRAMA CRITI-CISM. Hamden, Conn.: Shoe String Press, 1968. Pp. 25-26.

Secondary selected.

1943 Salem, James M. A GUIDE TO CRITICAL REVIEWS. Part III: BRITISH AND CONTINENTAL DRAMA FROM IBSEN TO PINTER. Metuchen, N.J.: Scarecrow Press, 1968. P. 21.

Secondary selected.

1944 Stoll, John E. W.H. AUDEN: A READING. Muncie, Ind.: Ball State University, 1970. Pp. 38-40.

Secondary.

1945 Wright, George T. W.H. AUDEN. New York: Twayne Publishers, 1969. Pp. 170-73.

Secondary annotated.

## BARING, MAURICE (1874-1945)

1946 Batho, Edith, Clara, and Bonamy Dobree. THE VICTORIANS AND AFTER, 1830-1914. Introductions to English Literature, vol. IV. General ed. Bonamy Dobree. London: Cresset Press; New York: R.M. McBride, 1938. P. 353.

   Primary.

1947 "Bibliographies of Modern Authors. The Hon. Maurice Baring." LONDON MERCURY, 2 (1920), 346.

   Primary, 1899-1920.

1948 Chaigne, Louis. MAURICE BARING; BIOGRAPHIE. Paris: J. de Gigord, 1935. Pp. 67-72.

   Primary. Secondary selected.

1949 Chaundy, Leslie. A BIBLIOGRAPHY OF THE FIRST EDITIONS OF THE WORKS OF MAURICE BARING. Intro. Desmond MacCarthy. London: Dulan, 1925.

   Primary, with brief notes.

1950 Cutler, Bradley D., and Villa Stiles. MODERN BRITISH AUTHORS; THEIR FIRST EDITIONS. New York: Greenberg; London: G. Allen, 1930; rpt. Folcroft, Pa.: Folcroft Press, 1969. Pp. 3-6.

   Primary.

1951 Daiches, David. THE PRESENT AGE, AFTER 1920. Introductions to English Literature, vol. V. General ed. Bonamy Dobree. London: Cresset Press; Bloomington: Indiana University Press, 1958. Pp. 253-54.

   Primary.

1952 Horgan, Paul, ed. MAURICE BARING RESTORED; SELECTIONS FROM HIS WORK. New York: Farrar, Straus, and Giroux, 1970. Pp. 439-40.

   Primary.

1953 Millett, Fred B. CONTEMPORARY BRITISH LITERATURE; A CRITICAL SURVEY AND 232 AUTHOR BIBLIOGRAPHIES. New York: Harcourt, Brace, 1935. Pp. 119-22.

   Primary. Secondary selected.

1954 Temple, Ruth Z., and Martin Tucker. TWENTIETH CENTURY BRITISH

LITERATURE; A REFERENCE GUIDE AND BIBLIOGRAPHY. New York: Frederick Ungar, 1968. Pp. 130-31.

Primary. Secondary selected.

1955 Willison, I.R., ed. THE NEW CAMBRIDGE BIBLIOGRAPHY OF ENGLISH LITERATURE. Vol. 4: 1900-1950. Cambridge: At the University Press, 1972. Cols. 517-19.

Primary. Secondary selected.

## BARRIE, [SIR] JAMES M[ATTHEW]. (1860-1937)

1956 Adelman, Irving, and Rita Dworkin. MODERN DRAMA; A CHECKLIST OF CRITICAL LITERATURE ON 20TH CENTURY PLAYS. Metuchen, N.J.: Scarecrow Press, 1967. Pp. 38-41.

Secondary selected.

1957 Block, Andrew. SIR JAMES M. BARRIE; HIS FIRST EDITIONS: POINTS AND VALUES. London: Foyle, 1933.

Primary.

1958 Breed, Paul F., and Florence M. Sniderman, comps. DRAMATIC CRITI-CISM INDEX; A BIBLIOGRAPHY OF COMMENTARIES ON PLAYWRIGHTS FROM IBSEN TO THE AVANT-GARDE. Detroit, Mich.: Gale Research Co., 1972. Pp. 66-69.

Secondary selected.

1959 Coleman, Arthur, and Gary R. Tyler. DRAMA CRITICISM. Vol. I: A CHECKLIST OF INTERPRETATION SINCE 1940 OF ENGLISH AND AMERI-CAN PLAYS. Denver, Colo.: Alan Swallow, 1966. Pp. 25-26.

Secondary selected.

1960 Cutler, Bradley D. SIR JAMES M. BARRIE; A BIBLIOGRAPHY, WITH FULL COLLATIONS OF THE AMERICAN UNAUTHORIZED EDITIONS. New York: Greenberg, 1931.

Supplements Garland (No. 1962).

1961 Cutler, Bradley D., and Villa Stiles. MODERN BRITISH AUTHORS; THEIR FIRST EDITIONS. New York: Greenberg; London: G. Allen, 1930; rpt. Folcroft, Pa.: Folcroft Press, 1969. Pp. 7-11.

Primary.

1962 Garland, Herbert. A BIBLIOGRAPHY OF THE WRITINGS OF SIR JAMES

M. BARRIE. London: Bookman's Journal, 1928.

Primary. Secondary selected.

1963 Geduld, Harry M. SIR JAMES BARRIE. New York: Twayne Publishers, 1971. Pp. 180-84.

Secondary annotated.

1964 Green, Roger Lancelyn. JAMES M. BARRIE. London: Bodley Head, 1960. Pp. 59-64.

Primary. Secondary selected.

1965 Palmer, Helen H., and Anne Jane Dyson. EUROPEAN DRAMA CRITICISM. Hamden, Conn.: Shoe String Press, 1968. Pp. 28-32.

Secondary selected.

1966 Salem, James M. A GUIDE TO CRITICAL REVIEWS. Part III: BRITISH AND CONTINENTAL DRAMA FROM IBSEN TO PINTER. Metuchen, N.J.: Scarecrow Press, 1968. Pp. 24-30.

Secondary selected.

1967 Shields, Katharine G. "Sir James M. Barrie, Bart., Being a Partial Bibliography." BULLETIN OF BIBLIOGRAPHY, 16 (1937), 44-46.

Secondary selected and annotated.

1968 Watson, George, ed. THE NEW CAMBRIDGE BIBLIOGRAPHY OF ENGLISH LITERATURE. Vol. 3: 1800-1900. Cambridge: At the University Press, 1969. Cols. 1188-92.

Primary. Secondary selected.

## BAX, CLIFFORD (1886-1962)

1969 Temple, Ruth Z., and Martin Tucker. TWENTIETH CENTURY BRITISH LITERATURE; A REFERENCE GUIDE AND BIBLIOGRAPHY. New York: Frederick Ungar, 1968. Pp. 132-33.

Primary. Secondary selected.

1970 Willison, I.R., ed. THE NEW CAMBRIDGE BIBLIOGRAPHY OF ENGLISH LITERATURE. Vol. 4: 1900-1950. Cambridge: At the University Press, 1972. Cols. 910-11.

Primary. Secondary selected.

## BENNETT, [ENOCH] ARNOLD (1867-1931)

The chief collections of Bennett manuscripts are in the New York Public Library (Berg Collection), Indiana University, University College London (C.K. Ogden Collection), and The Arnold Bennett Museum, Keele University.

1971 Adelman, Irving, and Rita Dworkin. MODERN DRAMA; A CHECKLIST OF CRITICAL LITERATURE ON 20TH CENTURY PLAYS. Metuchen, N.J.: Scarecrow Press, 1967. Pp. 54-55.

Secondary selected.

1972 Batho, Edith Clara, and Bonamy Dobree. THE VICTORIANS AND AFTER, 1830-1914. Introductions to English Literature, vol. IV. General ed. Bonamy Dobree. London: Cresset Press; New York: R.M. McBride, 1938. Pp. 319-20.

Primary.

1973 Emery, N. ARNOLD BENNETT 1867-1931: A BIBLIOGRAPHY. Stoke-on-Trent: Horace Banks Reference Library, 1967.

Primary.

1974 Gordan, John D. "Arnold Bennett; The Centenary of His Birth. An Exhibition in the Berg Collection." BULLETIN OF THE NEW YORK PUBLIC LIBRARY, 72 (1968), 72-122.

Primary. Secondary selected.

1975 Hepburn, James G. THE ART OF ARNOLD BENNETT. Bloomington: Indiana University Press, 1963. Pp. 222-38.

Primary. Secondary selected.

1976 Hepburn, James G., et al. "Bibliography." ENGLISH FICTION [title changed to ENGLISH LITERATURE IN TRANSITION], 1 (1957).

The bibliography of secondary material begun in this issue has been continued in each subsequent issue to date.

1977 Lafourcade, Georges. ARNOLD BENNETT; A STUDY. London: Frederick Muller, 1939. Pp. 281-93.

Primary. Secondary selected.

1978 Longaker, Mark, and Edwin C. Bolles. CONTEMPORARY ENGLISH LITERATURE. New York: Appleton-Century-Crofts, 1953. Pp. 197-202.

Primary. Secondary selected.

1979 Millett, Fred B. CONTEMPORARY BRITISH LITERATURE; A CRITICAL SURVEY AND 232 AUTHOR BIBLIOGRAPHIES. New York: Harcourt, Brace, 1935. Pp. 133-37.

    Primary. Secondary selected.

1980 Palmer, Helen H., and Anne Jane Dyson. EUROPEAN DRAMA CRITI-CISM. Hamden, Conn.: Shoe String Press, 1968. Pp. 51-52.

    Secondary selected.

1981 Temple, Ruth Z., and Martin Tucker. TWENTIETH CENTURY BRITISH LITERATURE; A REFERENCE GUIDE AND BIBLIOGRAPHY. New York: Frederick Ungar, 1968. Pp. 135-36.

    Primary. Secondary selected.

1982 Willison, I.R., ed. THE NEW CAMBRIDGE BIBLIOGRAPHY OF ENGLISH LITERATURE. Vol. 4: 1900-1950. Cambridge: At the University Press, 1972. Cols. 429-36.

    Primary. Secondary selected.

## BESIER, RUDOLPH (1878-1942)

1983 Adelman, Irving, and Rita Dworkin. MODERN DRAMA; A CHECKLIST OF CRITICAL LITERATURE ON 20TH CENTURY PLAYS. Metuchen, N.J.: Scarecrow Press, 1967. P. 56.

    Secondary selected.

1984 Palmer, Helen H., and Anne Jane Dyson. EUROPEAN DRAMA CRITI-CISM. Hamden, Conn.: Shoe String Press, 1968. Pp. 52-53.

    Secondary selected.

1985 Salem, James M. A GUIDE TO CRITICAL REVIEWS. Part III: BRITISH AND CONTINENTAL DRAMA FROM IBSEN TO PINTER. Metuchen, N.J.: Scarecrow Press, 1968. Pp. 37-39.

    Secondary selected.

1986 Willison, I.R., ed. THE NEW CAMBRIDGE BIBLIOGRAPHY OF ENGLISH LITERATURE. Vol. 4: 1900-1950. Cambridge: At the University Press, 1972. Cols. 912-13.

    Primary. Secondary selected.

## BINYON, [ROBERT] LAURENCE (1869-1943)

1987 "Bibliographies of Modern Authors: Laurence Binyon." LONDON MER-

CURY, 2 (1920), 114-15.

 Primary, 1890-1919.

1988 Longaker, Mark, and Edwin C. Bolles. CONTEMPORARY ENGLISH LIT-
ERATURE. New York: Appleton-Century-Crofts, 1953. Pp. 109-11.

 Primary. Secondary selected.

1989 Millett, Fred B. CONTEMPORARY BRITISH LITERATURE; A CRITICAL
SURVEY AND 232 AUTHOR BIBLIOGRAPHIES. New York: Harcourt,
Brace, 1935. Pp. 141-44.

 Primary. Secondary selected.

1990 Temple, Ruth Z., and Martin Tucker. TWENTIETH CENTURY BRITISH
LITERATURE; A REFERENCE GUIDE AND BIBLIOGRAPHY. New York:
Frederick Ungar, 1968. P. 137.

 Primary.

1991 Watson, George, ed. THE NEW CAMBRIDGE BIBLIOGRAPHY OF EN-
GLISH LITERATURE. Vol. 3: 1800-1900. Cambridge: At the University
Press, 1969. Cols. 612-13.

 Primary. Secondary selected.

## BOTTOMLEY, GORDON (1874-1948)

1992 Abbott, Claude Colleer. "Introduction." POEMS AND PLAYS. By Gordon Bottomley. London: Bodley Head, 1953. Pp. 9-19.

 Bibliographical information in text.

1993 Abbott, Claude Colleer, and Anthony Bertram, eds. POET AND PAINT-
ER, BEING THE CORRESPONDENCE BETWEEN GORDON BOTTOMLEY
AND PAUL NASH, 1910-1946. London: Oxford University Press, 1955.

 Bibliographical information in "Introduction" and in various
 places throughout text.

1994 Batho, Edith Clara, and Bonamy Dobree. THE VICTORIANS AND AFTER,
1830-1914. Introductions to English Literature, vol. IV. General ed.
Bonamy Dobree. London: Cresset Press; New York: R.M. McBride,
1938. P. 254.

 Primary.

1995 Breed, Paul F., and Florence M. Sniderman, comps. DRAMATIC CRITI-
CISM INDEX; A BIBLIOGRAPHY OF COMMENTARIES ON PLAYWRIGHTS

FROM IBSEN TO THE AVANT-GARDE. Detroit, Mich.: Gale Research Co., 1972. P. 115.

Secondary selected.

1996 Longaker, Mark, and Edwin C. Bolles. CONTEMPORARY ENGLISH LIT-ERATURE. New York: Appleton-Century-Crofts, 1953. Pp. 152-54.

Primary. Secondary selected.

1997 Millett, Fred B. CONTEMPORARY BRITISH LITERATURE; A CRITICAL SURVEY AND 232 AUTHOR BIBLIOGRAPHIES. New York: Harcourt, Brace, 1935. Pp. 148-49.

Primary. Secondary selected.

1998 Muir, Percival Horace. "Gordon Bottomley; A Check List." POINTS, 1874-1930; BEING EXTRACTS FROM A BIBLIOGRAPHER'S NOTEBOOK. London: Constable, 1931. Pp. 93-98.

Primary, with some bibliographical notes.

1999 Temple, Ruth Z., and Martin Tucker. TWENTIETH CENTURY BRITISH LITERATURE; A REFERENCE GUIDE AND BIBLIOGRAPHY. New York: Frederick Ungar, 1968. P. 139.

Primary. Secondary selected.

2000 Willison, I.R., ed. THE NEW CAMBRIDGE BIBLIOGRAPHY OF ENGLISH LITERATURE. Vol. 4: 1900-1950. Cambridge: At the University Press, 1972. Cols. 238-39.

Primary. Secondary selected.

## BOYLE, WILLIAM (1853-1922)

2001 Breed, Paul F., and Florence M. Sniderman, comps. DRAMATIC CRITI-CISM INDEX; A BIBLIOGRAPHY OF COMMENTARIES ON PLAYWRIGHTS FROM IBSEN TO THE AVANT-GARDE. Detroit, Mich.: Gale Research Co., 1972. P. 116.

Secondary selected.

2002 Watson, George, ed. THE NEW CAMBRIDGE BIBLIOGRAPHY OF EN-GLISH LITERATURE. Vol. 3: 1800-1900. Cambridge: At the University Press, 1969. Col. 1939.

Primary.

## BRIDIE, JAMES [OSBORNE HENRY MAVOR] (1888-1951)

2003 Adelman, Irving, and Rita Dworkin. MODERN DRAMA; A CHECKLIST OF CRITICAL LITERATURE ON 20TH CENTURY PLAYS. Metuchen, N.J.: Scarecrow Press, 1967. P. 68.

Secondary selected.

2004 Bannister, Winifred. JAMES BRIDIE AND HIS THEATRE. London: Rockliff, 1955. P. ix.

List of Bridie's plays, published and unpublished.

2005 Breed, Paul F., and Florence M. Sniderman, comps. DRAMATIC CRITICISM INDEX; A BIBLIOGRAPHY OF COMMENTARIES ON PLAYWRIGHTS FROM IBSEN TO THE AVANT-GARDE. Detroit, Mich.: Gale Research Co., 1972. Pp. 130-31.

Secondary selected.

2006 Coleman, Arthur, and Gary R. Tyler. DRAMA CRITICISM. Vol. I: A CHECKLIST OF INTERPRETATION SINCE 1940 OF ENGLISH AND AMERICAN PLAYS. Denver, Colo.: Alan Swallow, 1966. Pp. 32-33.

Secondary selected.

2007 Daiches, David. THE PRESENT AGE, AFTER 1920. Introductions to English Literature, vol. V. London: Cresset Press; Bloomington: Indiana University Press, 1958. P. 326.

Primary.

2008 Luyben, Helen L. JAMES BRIDIE, CLOWN AND PHILOSOPHER. Philadelphia: University of Pennsylvania Press, 1965. Pp. 177-78.

Primary. Secondary selected.

2009 Salem, James M. A GUIDE TO CRITICAL REVIEWS. Part III: BRITISH AND CONTINENTAL DRAMA FROM IBSEN TO PINTER. Metuchen, N.J.: Scarecrow Press, 1968. Pp. 51-52.

Secondary selected.

2010 Temple, Ruth Z., and Martin Tucker. TWENTIETH CENTURY BRITISH LITERATURE; A REFERENCE GUIDE AND BIBLIOGRAPHY. New York: Frederick Ungar, 1968. Pp. 140-41.

Primary. Secondary selected.

2011 Willison, I.R., ed. THE NEW CAMBRIDGE BIBLIOGRAPHY OF ENGLISH

LITERATURE. Vol. 4: 1900-1950. Cambridge: At the University Press, 1972. Cols. 914-17.

Primary. Secondary selected.

## BRIGHOUSE, HAROLD (1882-1958)

2012 Brighouse, Harold. WHAT I HAVE HAD; CHAPTERS IN AUTOBIOGRAPHY. London: Harrap, 1953.

Bibliographical information in text.

2013 Longaker, Mark, and Edwin C. Bolles. CONTEMPORARY ENGLISH LITERATURE. New York: Appleton-Century-Crofts, 1953. Pp. 413-14.

Primary.

2014 Millett, Fred B. CONTEMPORARY BRITISH LITERATURE; A CRITICAL SURVEY AND 232 AUTHOR BIBLIOGRAPHIES. New York: Harcourt, Brace, 1935. Pp. 154-55.

Primary. Secondary selected.

2015 Willison, I.R., ed. THE CAMBRIDGE BIBLIOGRAPHY OF ENGLISH LITERATURE. Vol. 4: 1900-1950. Cambridge: At the University Press, 1972. Cols. 917-19.

Primary. Secondary selected.

## CANNAN, GILBERT (1884-1955)

2016 Batho, Edith Clara, and Bonamy Dobree. THE VICTORIANS AND AFTER, 1830-1914. Introductions to English Literature, vol. IV. General ed. Bonamy Dobree. London: Cresset Press; New York: R.M. McBride, 1938. P. 323.

Primary.

2017 Millett, Fred B. CONTEMPORARY BRITISH LITERATURE; A CRITICAL SURVEY AND 232 AUTHOR BIBLIOGRAPHIES. New York: Harcourt, Brace, 1935. Pp. 162-64.

Primary. Secondary selected.

2018 Temple, Ruth Z., and Martin Tucker. TWENTIETH CENTURY BRITISH LITERATURE; A REFERENCE GUIDE AND BIBLIOGRAPHY. New York: Frederick Ungar, 1968. P. 144.

Primary.

2019 Willison, I.R., ed. THE NEW CAMBRIDGE BIBLIOGRAPHY OF ENGLISH LITERATURE. Vol. 4: 1900-1950. Cambridge: At the University Press, 1972. Cols. 547-48.

Primary. Secondary selected.

## CARROLL, PAUL VINCENT (1900-1968)

2020 Adelman, Irving, and Rita Dworkin. MODERN DRAMA; A CHECKLIST OF CRITICAL LITERATURE ON 20TH CENTURY PLAYS. Metuchen, N.J.: Scarecrow Press, 1967. P. 73.

Secondary selected.

2021 Breed, Paul F., and Florence M. Sniderman, comps. DRAMATIC CRITICISM INDEX; A BIBLIOGRAPHY OF COMMENTARIES ON PLAYWRIGHTS FROM IBSEN TO THE AVANT-GARDE. Detroit, Mich.: Gale Research Co., 1972. Pp. 147-48.

Secondary selected.

2022 Moses, Montrose J., and Oscar J. Campbell, eds. DRAMAS OF MODERNISM AND THEIR FORERUNNERS. Boston: Little, Brown, 1941. Pp. 933-34, 945.

Primary. Secondary selected.

2023 Palmer, Helen H., and Anne Jane Dyson. EUROPEAN DRAMA CRITICISM. Hamden, Conn.: Shoe String Press, 1968. Pp. 77-79.

Secondary selected.

2024 Salem, James M. A GUIDE TO CRITICAL REVIEWS. Part III: BRITISH AND CONTINENTAL DRAMA FROM IBSEN TO PINTER. Metuchen, N.J.: Scarecrow Press, 1968. Pp. 25-60.

Secondary selected.

2025 Temple, Ruth Z., and Martin Tucker. TWENTIETH CENTURY BRITISH LITERATURE; A REFERENCE GUIDE AND BIBLIOGRAPHY. New York: Frederick Ungar, 1968. P. 144.

Primary. Secondary selected.

2026 Willison, I.R., ed. THE NEW CAMBRIDGE BIBLIOGRAPHY OF ENGLISH LITERATURE. Vol. 4: 1900-1950. Cambridge: At the University Press, 1972. Cols. 921-22.

Primary. Secondary selected.

## COLUM, PADRAIC (1881-1972)

2027 Breed, Paul F., and Florence M. Sniderman, comps. DRAMATIC CRITI-
CISM INDEX; A BIBLIOGRAPHY OF COMMENTARIES ON PLAYWRIGHTS
FROM IBSEN TO THE AVANT-GARDE. Detroit, Mich.: Gale Research
Co., 1972. Pp. 176-77.

Secondary selected.

2028 Bowen, Zack. PADRAIC COLUM; A BIOGRAPHICAL-CRITICAL INTRO-
DUCTION. Carbondale: Southern Illinois University Press, 1970. Pp.
155-57.

Primary.

2029 Denson, Alan. "Padraic Colum: An Appreciation with a Checklist of
His Publications." DUBLIN MAGAZINE, 6, no. 1 (1967), 50-67; no.
2 (1967), 83-85.

Primary.

2030 Longaker, Mark, and Edwin C. Bolles. CONTEMPORARY ENGLISH LIT-
ERATURE. New York: Appleton-Century-Crofts, 1953. Pp. 49-50.

Primary.

2031 Millett, Fred B. CONTEMPORARY BRITISH LITERATURE; A CRITICAL
SURVEY AND 232 AUTHOR BIBLIOGRAPHIES. New York: Harcourt,
Brace, 1935. Pp. 175-77.

Primary. Secondary selected.

2032 Temple, Ruth Z., and Martin Tucker. TWENTIETH CENTURY BRITISH
LITERATURE; A REFERENCE GUIDE AND BIBLIOGRAPHY. New York:
Frederick Ungar, 1968. Pp. 147-48.

Primary. Secondary selected.

2033 Watson, George, ed. THE NEW CAMBRIDGE BIBLIOGRAPHY OF EN-
GLISH LITERATURE. Vol. 3: 1800-1900. Cambridge: At the University
Press, 1969. Cols. 1942-43.

Primary. Secondary selected.

## CONNELL, NORREYS. SEE O'RIORDAN,
## CONAL HOLMES O'CONNELL

## CORKERY, DANIEL (1878-1967)

2034 Millett, Fred B. CONTEMPORARY BRITISH LITERATURE; A CRITICAL

SURVEY AND 232 AUTHOR BIBLIOGRAPHIES. New York: Harcourt, Brace, 1935. Pp. 185-86.

Primary. Secondary selected.

2035 Willison, I.R., ed. THE NEW CAMBRIDGE BIBLIOGRAPHY OF ENGLISH LITERATURE. Vol. 4: 1900-1950. Cambridge: At the University Press, 1972. Cols. 923-24.

Primary. Secondary selected.

## COWARD, [SIR] NOEL [PIERCE] (1899-1973)

2036 Adelman, Irving, and Rita Dworkin. MODERN DRAMA; A CHECKLIST OF CRITICAL LITERATURE ON 20TH CENTURY PLAYS. Metuchen, N.J.: Scarecrow Press, 1967. Pp. 85-86.

Secondary selected.

2037 Breed, Paul F., and Florence M. Sniderman, comps. DRAMATIC CRITI-CISM INDEX; A BIBLIOGRAPHY OF COMMENTARIES ON PLAYWRIGHTS FROM IBSEN TO THE AVANT-GARDE. Detroit, Mich.: Gale Research Co., 1972. Pp. 178-79.

Secondary selected.

2038 Coleman, Arthur, and Gary R. Tyler. DRAMA CRITICISM. Vol. I: A CHECKLIST OF INTERPRETATION SINCE 1940 OF ENGLISH AND AMERI-CAN PLAYS. Denver, Colo.: Alan Swallow, 1966. P. 45.

Secondary selected.

2039 Daiches, David. THE PRESENT AGE, AFTER 1920. Introductions to En-glish Literature, vol. V. General ed. Bonamy Dobree. London: Cres-set Press; Bloomington: Indiana University Press, 1958. P. 328.

Primary.

2040 Levin, Milton. NOEL COWARD. New York: Twayne Publishers, 1968. Pp. 149-53.

Primary. Secondary selected and annotated.

2041 Longaker, Mark, and Edwin C. Bolles. CONTEMPORARY ENGLISH LIT-ERATURE. New York: Appleton-Century-Crofts, 1953. Pp. 417-20.

Primary. Secondary selected.

2042 Mander, Raymond, and Joe Mitchenson. THEATRICAL COMPANION TO COWARD. London: Rockliff, 1957. Pp. 391-96.

Primary.

2043  Millett, Fred B.  CONTEMPORARY BRITISH LITERATURE; A CRITICAL
SURVEY AND 232 AUTHOR BIBLIOGRAPHIES.  New York:  Harcourt,
Brace, 1935.  Pp. 186-87.

Primary.  Secondary selected.

2044  Morley, Sheridan.  "Bibliography."  A TALENT TO AMUSE; A BIBLIOG-
RAPHY OF NOEL COWARD.  London:  Heinemann, 1969.  Pp. 345-48.

Primary.  Secondary selected.

2045  Palmer, Helen H., and Anne Jane Dyson.  EUROPEAN DRAMA CRITI-
CISM.  Hamden, Conn.:  Shoe String Press, 1968.  Pp. 104-14.

Secondary selected.

2046  Salem, James M.  A GUIDE TO CRITICAL REVIEWS.  Part III:  BRITISH
AND CONTINENTAL DRAMA FROM IBSEN TO PINTER.  Metuchen, N.J.:
Scarecrow Press, 1968.  Pp. 73-80.

Secondary selected.

2047  Temple, Ruth Z., and Martin Tucker.  TWENTIETH CENTURY BRITISH
LITERATURE; A REFERENCE GUIDE AND BIBLIOGRAPHY.  New York:
Frederick Ungar, 1968.  P. 150.

Primary.  Secondary selected.

2048  Willison, I.R., ed.  THE NEW CAMBRIDGE BIBLIOGRAPHY OF ENGLISH
LITERATURE.  Vol. 4:  1900-1950.  Cambridge:  At the University Press,
1972.  Cols. 924-27.

Primary.  Secondary selected.

## DANE, CLEMENCE [WINIFRED ASHTON] (1888-1965)

2049  Adelman, Irving, and Rita Dworkin.  MODERN DRAMA; A CHECKLIST
OF CRITICAL LITERATURE ON 20TH CENTURY PLAYS.  Metuchen, N.J.:
Scarecrow Press, 1967.  P. 88.

Secondary selected.

2050  Millett, Fred B.  CONTEMPORARY BRITISH LITERATURE; A CRITICAL
SURVEY AND 232 AUTHOR BIBLIOGRAPHIES.  New York:  Harcourt,
Brace, 1935.  Pp. 190-91.

Primary.  Secondary selected.

2051  Salem, James M.  A GUIDE TO CRITICAL REVIEWS.  Part III:  BRITISH
AND CONTINENTAL DRAMA FROM IBSEN TO PINTER.  Metuchen,

N.J.: Scarecrow Press, 1968. Pp. 80-82.

Secondary selected.

2052 Temple, Ruth Z., and Martin Tucker. TWENTIETH CENTURY BRITISH LITERATURE; A REFERENCE GUIDE AND BIBLIOGRAPHY. New York: Frederick Ungar, 1968. Pp. 151-52.

Primary. Secondary selected.

## DRINKWATER, JOHN (1882-1937)

2053 Cutler, Bradley D., and Villa Stiles. MODERN BRITISH AUTHORS; THEIR FIRST EDITIONS. New York: Greenberg; London: G. Allen, 1930; Folcroft, Pa.: Folcroft Press, 1969. Pp. 44-47.

Primary.

2054 Daiches, David. THE PRESENT AGE, AFTER 1920. Introductions to English Literature, vol. V. General ed. Bonamy Dobree. London: Cresset Press; Bloomington: Indiana University Press, 1958. Pp. 194-95.

Primary.

2055 Danielson, Henry. BIBLIOGRAPHIES OF MODERN AUTHORS. London: Bookman's Journal, 1921. Pp. 41-60.

Primary.

2056 Longaker, Mark, and Edwin C. Bolles. CONTEMPORARY ENGLISH LITERATURE. New York: Appleton-Century-Crofts, 1953. Pp. 156-58.

Primary. Secondary selected.

2057 Millett, Fred B. CONTEMPORARY BRITISH LITERATURE; A CRITICAL SURVEY AND 232 AUTHOR BIBLIOGRAPHIES. New York: Harcourt, Brace, 1935. Pp. 210-12.

Primary. Secondary selected.

2058 Roeder, Alois Wilhelm. JOHN DRINKWATER ALS DRAMATIKER. Giessen: Verlag des Englischen Seminars der Universitaet Giessen, 1927. Pp. 40-44.

Primary. Secondary selected.

2059 Salem, James M. A GUIDE TO CRITICAL REVIEWS. Part III: BRITISH AND CONTINENTAL DRAMA FROM IBSEN TO PINTER. Metuchen, N.J.: Scarecrow Press, 1968. Pp. 85-87.

Secondary selected.

2060 [Smith, Timothy d'Arch]. JOHN DRINKWATER, 1882-1937. CATALOGUE OF AN EXHIBITION. London: Times Bookshop, 1962.

 Primary. Also manuscripts, association items, and iconography.

2061 Temple, Ruth Z., and Martin Tucker. TWENTIETH CENTURY BRITISH LITERATURE; A REFERENCE GUIDE AND BIBLIOGRAPHY. New York: Frederick Ungar, 1968. Pp. 156-57.

 Primary. Secondary selected.

2062 Willison, I.R., ed. THE NEW CAMBRIDGE BIBLIOGRAPHY OF ENGLISH LITERATURE. Vol. 4: 1900-1950. Cambridge: At the University Press, 1972. Col. 263-66.

 Primary. Secondary selected.

## DUKES, ASHLEY (1885-1959)

2063 Dukes, Ashley. THE SCENE IS CHANGED. London: Macmillan, 1942.

 Autobiography. Bibliographical information in the text.

2064 Millett, Fred B. CONTEMPORARY BRITISH LITERATURE; A CRITICAL SURVEY AND 232 AUTHOR BIBLIOGRAPHIES. New York: Harcourt, Brace, 1935. Pp. 212-13.

 Primary. Secondary selected.

2065 Willison, I.R., ed. THE NEW CAMBRIDGE BIBLIOGRAPHY OF ENGLISH LITERATURE. Vol. 4: 1900-1950. Cambridge: At the University Press, 1972. Cols. 934-35.

 Primary. Secondary selected.

## DUNSANY [EDWARD JOHN MORETON DRAX PLUNKETT], LORD (1878-1957)

2066 Adelman, Irving, and Rita Dworkin. MODERN DRAMA; A CHECKLIST OF CRITICAL LITERATURE ON 20TH CENTURY PLAYS. Metuchen, N.J.: Scarecrow Press, 1967. P. 91.

 Secondary selected.

2067 Breed, Paul F., and Florence M. Sniderman, comps. DRAMATIC CRITI-CISM INDEX; A BIBLIOGRAPHY OF COMMENTARIES ON PLAYWRIGHTS FROM IBSEN TO THE AVANT-GARDE. Detroit, Mich.: Gale Research Co., 1972. P. 193.

 Secondary selected.

2068 Cutler, Bradley D., and Villa Stiles. MODERN BRITISH AUTHORS; THEIR FIRST EDITIONS. New York: Greenberg; London: G. Allen, 1930; Folcroft, Pa.: Folcroft Press, 1969. Pp. 48-49.

Primary.

2069 Danielson, Henry. BIBLIOGRAPHIES OF MODERN AUTHORS. London: Bookman's Journal, 1921. Pp. 67-75.

Primary, 1905-20.

2070 Millett, Fred B. CONTEMPORARY BRITISH LITERATURE; A CRITICAL SURVEY AND 232 AUTHOR BIBLIOGRAPHIES. New York: Harcourt, Brace, 1935. Pp. 213-15.

Primary. Secondary selected.

2071 Salem, James M. A GUIDE TO CRITICAL REVIEWS. Part III: BRITISH AND CONTINENTAL DRAMA FROM IBSEN TO PINTER. Metuchen, N.J.: Scarecrow Press, 1968. Pp. 89-90.

Secondary selected.

2072 Stoddard, F.G. "The Lord Dunsany Collection." LIBRARY CHRONICLE OF THE UNIVERSITY OF TEXAS, 9, no. 3 (1967), 27-32.

Discursive essay with particular attention to manuscripts at the University of Texas.

2073 Watson, George, ed. THE NEW CAMBRIDGE BIBLIOGRAPHY OF ENGLISH LITERATURE. Vol. 3: 1800-1900. Cambridge: At the University Press, 1969. Cols. 1945-48.

Primary. Secondary selected.

## ELIOT, T[HOMAS]. S[TEARNS]. (1888-1965)

There are significant collections of Eliot's manuscripts in Houghton Library, Harvard; in Texas University Library; in the John Hayward Bequest, King's College Cambridge; and in New York Public Library.

2074 Adelman, Irving, and Rita Dworkin. MODERN DRAMA; A CHECKLIST OF CRITICAL LITERATURE ON 20TH CENTURY PLAYS. Metuchen, N.J.: Scarecrow Press, 1967. Pp. 93-103.

Secondary selected.

2075 Bentz, Hans Willi. T.S. ELIOT IN UBERSETZUNGEN. Frankfurt-am-Main: Hans W. Bentz, 1963.

List of 222 translations of Eliot published after 1945.

2076 Breed, Paul F., and Florence M. Sniderman, comps. DRAMATIC CRITI-
CISM INDEX; A BIBLIOGRAPHY OF COMMENTARIES ON PLAYWRIGHTS
FROM IBSEN TO THE AVANT-GARDE. Detroit, Mich.: Gale Research
Co., 1972. Pp. 202-14.

Secondary selected.

2077 Coleman, Arthur, and Gary R. Tyler. DRAMA CRITICISM. Vol. I: A
CHECKLIST OF INTERPRETATION SINCE 1940 OF ENGLISH AND AMERI-
CAN PLAYS. Denver, Colo.: Alan Swallow, 1966. Pp. 56-67.

Secondary selected.

2078 Gallup, Donald Clifford. T.S. ELIOT: A BIBLIOGRAPHY. 2nd rev.
ed. London: Faber and Faber, 1969.

Primary.

2079 Jones, David E. THE PLAYS OF T.S. ELIOT. London: Routledge, 1960;
Toronto: University of Toronto Press, 1961. Pp. 223-38.

Secondary selected.

2080 Longaker, Mark, and Edwin C. Bolles. CONTEMPORARY ENGLISH LIT-
ERATURE. New York: Appleton-Century-Crofts, 1953. Pp. 267-72.

Primary. Secondary selected.

2081 Ludwig, Richard M. "T.S. Eliot." FIFTEEN MODERN AMERICAN AU-
THORS; A SURVEY OF RESEARCH AND CRITICISM. Ed. Jackson R.
Bryer. Durham, N.C.: Duke University Press, 1969. Pp. 139-74.

Survey and evaluation of the Eliot bibliographies, editions,
manuscripts, letters, biographies, and criticism.

2082 Malawsky, Beryl York. "T.S. Eliot: A Check-List, 1952-1964." BUL-
LETIN OF BIBLIOGRAPHY, 25 (May-August 1967), 59-61, 69.

Primary, supplementing Gallup (No. 2078).

2083 Millett, Fred B. CONTEMPORARY BRITISH LITERATURE; A CRITICAL
SURVEY AND 232 AUTHOR BIBLIOGRAPHIES. New York: Harcourt,
Brace, 1935. Pp. 215-17.

Primary. Secondary selected.

2084 Palmer, Helen H., and Anne Jane Dyson. EUROPEAN DRAMA CRITI-
CISM. Hamden, Conn.: Shoe String Press, 1968. Pp. 130-39.

Secondary selected.

2085 Salem, James M. A GUIDE TO CRITICAL REVIEWS. Part III: BRITISH AND CONTINENTAL DRAMA FROM IBSEN TO PINTER. Metuchen, N.J.: Scarecrow Press, 1968. Pp. 90-93.

    Secondary selected.

2086 Schwartz, Jacob. 1100 OBSCURE POINTS: THE BIBLIOGRAPHIES OF 25 ENGLISH AND 21 AMERICAN AUTHORS. Bristol, Eng.: Chatford House Press, 1931; rpt., 1969.

    Primary.

2087 Temple, Ruth Z., and Martin Tucker. TWENTIETH CENTURY BRITISH LITERATURE; A REFERENCE GUIDE AND BIBLIOGRAPHY. New York: Frederick Ungar, 1968. P. 159.

    Primary. Secondary selected.

2088 Unger, Leonard, ed. T.S. ELIOT; A SELECTED CRITIQUE. New York: Rinehart, 1948. Pp. 463-78.

    Secondary.

2089 Willison, I.R., ed. THE NEW CAMBRIDGE BIBLIOGRAPHY OF ENGLISH LITERATURE. Vol. 4: 1900-1950. Cambridge: At the University Press, 1972. Cols. 157-201.

    Primary. Secondary selected.

## ERVINE, ST. JOHN [GREER] (1883-1971)

2090 Adelman, Irving, and Rita Dworkin. MODERN DRAMA; A CHECKLIST OF CRITICAL LITERATURE ON 20TH CENTURY PLAYS. Metuchen, N.J.: Scarecrow Press, 1967. P. 104.

    Secondary selected.

2091 Batho, Edith Clara, and Bonamy Dobree. THE VICTORIANS AND AFTER, 1830-1914. Introductions to English Literature, vol. IV. General ed. Bonamy Dobree. London: Cresset Press; New York: R.M. McBride, 1938. P. 272.

    Primary.

2092 Breed, Paul F., and Florence M. Sniderman, comps. DRAMATIC CRITI-CISM INDEX; A BIBLIOGRAPHY OF COMMENTARIES ON PLAYWRIGHTS FROM IBSEN TO THE AVANT-GARDE. Detroit, Mich.: Gale Research Co., 1972. Pp. 215-16.

    Secondary selected.

2093 Longaker, Mark, and Edwin C. Bolles. CONTEMPORARY ENGLISH LIT-
ERATURE. New York: Appleton-Century-Crofts, 1953. P. 63.

> Primary.

2094 Millett, Fred B. CONTEMPORARY BRITISH LITERATURE; A CRITICAL
SURVEY AND 232 AUTHOR BIBLIOGRAPHIES. New York: Harcourt,
Brace, 1935. Pp. 220-22.

> Primary. Secondary selected.

2095 Salem, James M. A GUIDE TO CRITICAL REVIEWS. Part III: BRITISH
AND CONTINENTAL DRAMA FROM IBSEN TO PINTER. Metuchen, N.J.:
Scarecrow Press, 1968. Pp. 93-95.

> Secondary selected.

2096 Temple, Ruth Z., and Martin Tucker. TWENTIETH CENTURY BRITISH
LITERATURE; A REFERENCE GUIDE AND BIBLIOGRAPHY. New York:
Frederick Ungar, 1968. P. 160.

> Primary. Secondary selected.

2097 Watson, George, ed. THE NEW CAMBRIDGE BIBLIOGRAPHY OF EN-
GLISH LITERATURE. Vol. 3: 1800-1900. Cambridge: At the University Press, 1969. Col. 1945.

> Primary. Secondary selected.

## FITZMAURICE, GEORGE (1877-1963)

2098 Breed, Paul F., and Florence M. Sniderman, comps. DRAMATIC CRITI-
CISM INDEX; A BIBLIOGRAPHY OF COMMENTARIES ON PLAYWRIGHTS
FROM IBSEN TO THE AVANT-GARDE. Detroit, Mich.: Gale Research
Co., 1972. Pp. 220-21.

> Secondary selected.

2099 THE PLAYS OF GEORGE FITZMAURICE. Vol. I: DRAMATIC FANTA-
SIES. Ed. Austin Clarke; Vol. II: FOLK PLAYS. Ed. Howard K. Slaugh-
ter; Vol. III: REALISTIC PLAYS. Ed. Howard K. Slaughter. Dublin:
Dolmen Press, 1967, 1969, 1970.

> The introductions to each of these three volumes include refer-
> ences to secondary material.

2100 Watson, George, ed. THE NEW CAMBRIDGE BIBLIOGRAPHY OF EN-
GLISH LITERATURE. Vol. 3: 1800-1900. Cambridge: At the University Press, 1969. Cols. 1941-42.

> Primary. Secondary selected.

## FLECKER, JAMES ELROY (1884-1915)

The corrected typescript of HASSAN is in Bodley, and the manuscript of DON JUAN is in Cheltenham Public Library. There is other manuscript material in the British Museum; Fitzwilliam Museum; Lockwood Memorial Library, Buffalo; and British Embassy, Beirut.

2101 Batho, Edith Clara, and Bonamy Dobree. THE VICTORIANS AND AFTER, 1830-1914. Introductions to English Literature, vol. IV. General ed. Bonamy Dobree. London: Cresset Press; New York: R.M. McBride, 1938. P. 259.

Primary.

2102 Cutler, Bradley D., and Villa Stiles. MODERN AUTHORS; THEIR FIRST EDITIONS. New York: Greenberg; London: G. Allen, 1930; Folcroft, Pa.: Folcroft Press, 1969. Pp. 51-52.

Primary.

2103 Danielson, Henry. BIBLIOGRAPHIES OF MODERN AUTHORS. London: Bookman's Journal, 1921. Pp. 81-89.

Primary, 1906-21.

2104 Goldring, Douglas. JAMES ELROY FLECKER; AN APPRECIATION WITH SOME BIOGRAPHICAL NOTES. London: Chapman and Hall, 1922. Pp. 191-95.

Primary.

2105 Longaker, Mark, and Edwin C. Bolles. CONTEMPORARY ENGLISH LITERATURE. New York: Appleton-Century-Crofts, 1953. Pp. 154-56.

Primary. Secondary selected.

2106 Mercer, Thomas Stanley. JAMES ELROY FLECKER; FROM SCHOOL TO SAMARKAND. Thames Ditton, Surrey: Merle Press, 1952. Pp. 47-56.

Primary.

2107 Millett, Fred B. CONTEMPORARY BRITISH LITERATURE; A CRITICAL SURVEY AND 232 AUTHOR BIBLIOGRAPHIES. New York: Harcourt, Brace, 1935. Pp. 224-25.

Primary. Secondary selected.

2108 Temple, Ruth Z., and Martin Tucker. TWENTIETH CENTURY BRITISH LITERATURE; A REFERENCE GUIDE AND BIBLIOGRAPHY. New York: Frederick Ungar, 1968. P. 162.

Primary. Secondary selected.

2109 Willison, I.R., ed. THE NEW CAMBRIDGE BIBLIOGRAPHY OF ENGLISH LITERATURE. Vol. 4: 1900–1950. Cambridge: At the University Press, 1972. Cols. 274–76.

Primary. Secondary selected.

## FRY, CHRISTOPHER (1907-   )

2110 Adelman, Irving, and Rita Dworkin. MODERN DRAMA; A CHECKLIST OF CRITICAL LITERATURE ON 20TH CENTURY PLAYS. Metuchen, N.J.: Scarecrow Press, 1967. Pp. 107–11.

Secondary selected.

2111 Breed, Paul F., and Florence M. Sniderman, comps. DRAMATIC CRITI-CISM INDEX; A BIBLIOGRAPHY OF COMMENTARIES ON PLAYWRIGHTS FROM IBSEN TO THE AVANT-GARDE. Detroit, Mich.: Gale Research Co., 1972. Pp. 227–31.

Secondary selected.

2112 Coleman, Arthur, and Gary R. Tyler. DRAMA CRITICISM. Vol. I: A CHECKLIST OF INTERPRETATION SINCE 1940 OF ENGLISH AND AMERI-CAN PLAYS. Denver, Colo.: Alan Swallow, 1966. Pp. 76–79.

Secondary selected.

2113 Daiches, David. THE PRESENT AGE, AFTER 1920. Introductions to En-glish Literature, vol. V. General ed. Bonamy Dobree. London: Cres-set Press; Bloomington: Indiana University Press, 1958. P. 330.

Primary.

2114 Palmer, Helen H., and Anne Jane Dyson. EUROPEAN DRAMA CRITI-CISM. Hamden, Conn.: Shoe String Press, 1968. Pp. 147–52.

Secondary selected.

2115 Salem, James M. A GUIDE TO CRITICAL REVIEWS. Part III: BRITISH AND CONTINENTAL DRAMA FROM IBSEN TO PINTER. Metuchen, N.J.: Scarecrow Press, 1968. Pp. 98–101.

Secondary selected.

2116 Schear, Bernice Larson, and Eugene C. Prater. "A Bibliography on Christopher Fry." TULANE DRAMA REVIEW, 4 (March 1960), 88–98.

Primary. Secondary.

2117 Stanford, Derek. CHRISTOPHER FRY. London: Longmans, Green, 1962. P. 44.

   Primary.

2118 Temple, Ruth Z., and Martin Tucker. TWENTIETH CENTURY BRITISH LITERATURE; A REFERENCE GUIDE AND BIBLIOGRAPHY. New York: Frederick Ungar, 1968. P. 164.

   Primary. Secondary selected.

2119 Willison, I.R., ed. THE NEW CAMBRIDGE BIBLIOGRAPHY OF ENGLISH LITERATURE. Vol. 4: 1900-1950. Cambridge: At the University Press, 1972. Cols. 938-41.

   Primary. Secondary selected.

## GALSWORTHY, JOHN (1867-1933)

2119A Adelman, Irving, and Rita Dworkin. MODERN DRAMA; A CHECKLIST OF CRITICAL LITERATURE ON 20TH CENTURY PLAYS. Metuchen, N.J.: Scarecrow Press, 1967. Pp. 111-14.

   Secondary selected.

2120 Bennett, J.W. "Galsworthy and H.G. Wells." YALE UNIVERSITY LI-BRARY GAZETTE, 28 (1953).

   On the Yale Galsworthy collection.

2121 Birmingham. University Library. GALSWORTHY CENTENARY EXHIBI-TION: CATALOGUE. Birmingham, Eng.: 1967.

   Duplicated typescript.

2122 Breed, Paul F., and Florence M. Sniderman, comps. DRAMATIC CRITI-CISM INDEX; A BIBLIOGRAPHY OF COMMENTARIES ON PLAYWRIGHTS FROM IBSEN TO THE AVANT-GARDE. Detroit, Mich.: Gale Research Co., 1972. Pp. 232-34.

   Secondary selected.

2123 Coleman, Arthur, and Gary R. Tyler. DRAMA CRITICISM. Vol. I: A CHECKLIST OF INTERPRETATION SINCE 1940 OF ENGLISH AND AMERI-CAN PLAYS. Denver, Colo.: Alan Swallow, 1966. Pp. 79-80.

   Secondary selected.

2124 Cutler, Bradley D., and Villa Stiles. MODERN BRITISH AUTHORS; THEIR FIRST EDITIONS. New York: Greenberg; London: G. Allen,

1930; rpt. Folcroft, Pa.: Folcroft Press, 1969. Pp. 53-58.

Primary.

2125 Evans, D. Wyn, comp. JOHN GALSWORTHY: CATALOGUE OF THE
COLLECTION. Birmingham, Eng.: Birmingham University Library, 1967.

2126 Fabes, Gilbert H. JOHN GALSWORTHY: HIS FIRST EDITIONS; POINTS
AND VALUES. London: Foyle, 1932.

Primary.

2127 Gerber, Helmut [E.], et al. "John Galsworthy." ENGLISH LITERATURE
IN TRANSITION, 1 (1957), 23-24; 2 (1958), 7-29; 7 (1964), 93-110.

Continued in subsequent issues. Secondary annotated.

2128 McGirr, Alice T[hurston]. "Reading List of John Galsworthy."
BULLETIN OF BIBLIOGRAPHY, 7 (1913), 113.

Secondary.

2129 Marrot, H.V. A BIBLIOGRAPHY OF THE WORKS OF JOHN GALS-
WORTHY. London: Elkin Matthews and Marrot; New York: Scribner's,
1928.

Primary. Secondary selected.

2130 Mikhail, E.H. JOHN GALSWORTHY THE DRAMATIST; A BIBLIOGRAPHY
OF CRITICISM. Troy, N.Y.: Whitston Publishing Co., 1971.

Secondary.

2131 Mottram, Ralph. JOHN GALSWORTHY. London: Longmans, Green,
1953. Pp. 37-40.

Primary.

2132 Palmer, Helen H., and Anne Jane Dyson. EUROPEAN DRAMA CRITICISM.
Hamden, Conn.: Shoe String Press, 1968. Pp. 155-56.

Secondary selected.

2133 Salem, James M. A GUIDE TO CRITICAL REVIEWS. Part III: BRITISH
AND CONTINENTAL DRAMA FROM IBSEN TO PINTER. Metuchen,
N.J.: Scarecrow Press, 1968. Pp. 101-5.

Secondary selected.

2134 Schwartz, Jacob. 1100 OBSCURE POINTS: THE BIBLIOGRAPHIES OF

25 ENGLISH AND 21 AMERICAN AUTHORS. Bristol, Eng.: Chatford House Press, 1931; rpt., 1969.

Primary.

2135 Takahashi, Genji. STUDIES IN THE WORKS OF JOHN GALSWORTHY. Tokyo: Shinozki Shorin, 1954.

Primary. Bibliography of translations.

2136 Willison, I.R., ed. THE NEW CAMBRIDGE BIBLIOGRAPHY OF ENGLISH LITERATURE. Vol. 4: 1900-1950. Cambridge: At the University Press, 1972. Cols. 579-86.

Primary. Secondary selected.

## GARNETT, EDWARD [WILLIAM] (1868-1937)

2137 Heilbrun, Carolyn G. THE GARNETT FAMILY. London: George Allen & Unwin, 1961. Pp. 202-10.

Primary.

2138 Millett, Fred B. CONTEMPORARY BRITISH LITERATURE; A CRITICAL SURVEY AND 232 AUTHOR BIBLIOGRAPHIES. New York: Harcourt, Brace, 1935. Pp. 240-41.

Primary. Secondary selected.

## GIBSON, W[ILFRID]. W[ILSON]. (1878-1962)

2139 Daiches, David. THE PRESENT AGE, AFTER 1920. Introductions to English Literature, vol. V. General ed. Bonamy Dobree. London: Cresset Press; Bloomington: Indiana University Press, 1958. Pp. 186-87.

Primary.

2140 Gawsworth, John [T.I.F. Armstrong]. TEN CONTEMPORARIES; NOTES TOWARD THEIR DEFINITIVE BIBLIOGRAPHY. London: Ernest Benn, 1932. Pp. 74-94.

Primary, 1902-32, with bibliographical notes.

2141 Longaker, Mark, and Edwin C. Bolles. CONTEMPORARY ENGLISH LITERATURE. New York: Appleton-Century-Crofts, 1953. Pp. 237-40.

Primary. Secondary selected.

2142 Millett, Fred B. CONTEMPORARY BRITISH LITERATURE; A CRITICAL SURVEY AND 232 AUTHOR BIBLIOGRAPHIES. New York: Harcourt,

Brace, 1935. Pp. 244-46.

Primary. Secondary selected.

2143 Temple, Ruth Z., and Martin Tucker. TWENTIETH CENTURY BRITISH
LITERATURE; A REFERENCE GUIDE AND BIBLIOGRAPHY. New York:
Frederick Ungar, 1968. P. 167.

Primary.

2144 Willison, I.R., ed. THE NEW CAMBRIDGE BIBLIOGRAPHY OF ENGLISH
LITERATURE. Vol. 4: 1900-1950. Cambridge: At the University Press,
1972. Cols. 281-82.

Primary. Secondary selected.

## GRANVILLE-BARKER, HARLEY (1877-1946)

A number of typescripts and manuscripts are held at the British Museum and
elsewhere. See No. 2151.

2145 Adelman, Irving, and Rita Dworkin. MODERN DRAMA; A CHECKLIST
OF CRITICAL LITERATURE ON 20TH CENTURY PLAYS. Metuchen, N.J.:
Scarecrow Press, 1967. Pp. 128-29.

Secondary selected.

2146 Batho, Edith Clara, and Bonamy Dobree. THE VICTORIANS AND AFTER,
1830-1914. Introductions to English Literature, vol. IV. General ed.
Bonamy Dobree. London: Cresset Press; New York: R.M. McBride,
1938. Pp. 267-68.

Primary.

2147 Breed, Paul F., and Florence M. Sniderman, comps. DRAMATIC CRITI-
CISM INDEX; A BIBLIOGRAPHY OF COMMENTARIES ON PLAYWRIGHTS
FROM IBSEN TO THE AVANT-GARDE. Detroit, Mich.: Gale Research
Co., 1972. Pp. 276-77.

Secondary selected.

2148 Coleman, Arthur, and Gary R. Tyler. DRAMA CRITICISM. Vol. I: A
CHECKLIST OF INTERPRETATION SINCE 1940 OF ENGLISH AND AMERI-
CAN PLAYS. Denver, Colo.: Alan Swallow, 1966. P. 84.

Secondary selected.

2149 Davis, Mary Louise. "Reading List on Harley Granville-Barker." BULLE-
TIN OF BIBLIOGRAPHY, 7 (1913), 130-32.

Primary. Secondary.

2150 Longaker, Mark, and Edwin C. Bolles. CONTEMPORARY ENGLISH LIT-
ERATURE. New York: Appleton-Century-Crofts, 1953. Pp. 409-10.

Primary. Secondary selected.

2151 May, Frederick, and Margery M. Morgan. "A List of Writings." HAR-
LEY GRANVILLE-BARKER: MAN OF THE THEATRE, DRAMATIST AND
SCHOLAR. By Charles B. Purdom. London: Rockliff, 1955. Pp. 293-
309.

Primary.

2152 Millett, Fred B. CONTEMPORARY BRITISH LITERATURE; A CRITICAL
SURVEY AND 232 AUTHOR BIBLIOGRAPHIES. New York: Harcourt,
Brace, 1935. Pp. 252-54.

Primary. Secondary selected.

2153 Temple, Ruth Z., and Martin Tucker. TWENTIETH CENTURY BRITISH
LITERATURE; A REFERENCE GUIDE AND BIBLIOGRAPHY. New York:
Frederick Ungar, 1968. Pp. 170-71.

Primary. Secondary selected.

2154 Willison, I.R., ed. THE NEW CAMBRIDGE BIBLIOGRAPHY OF ENGLISH
LITERATURE. Vol. 4: 1900-1950. Cambridge: At the University Press,
1972. Cols. 944-46.

Primary. Secondary selected.

# GREGORY, LADY [ISABELLA AUGUSTA] (1859-1932)

2155 Adelman, Irving, and Rita Dworkin. MODERN DRAMA; A CHECKLIST
OF CRITICAL LITERATURE ON 20TH CENTURY PLAYS. Metuchen, N.J.:
Scarecrow Press, 1967. Pp. 132-33.

Secondary selected.

2156 Batho, Edith Clara, and Bonamy Dobree. THE VICTORIANS AND AFTER,
1830-1914. Introductions to English Literature, vol. IV. General ed.
Bonamy Dobree. London: Cresset Press; New York: R.M. McBride,
1938. P. 271.

Primary.

2157 Breed, Paul F., and Florence M. Sniderman, comps. DRAMATIC CRITI-
CISM INDEX; A BIBLIOGRAPHY OF COMMENTARIES ON PLAYWRIGHTS
FROM IBSEN TO THE AVANT-GARDE. Detroit, Mich.: Gale Research
Co., 1972. Pp. 281-83.

Secondary selected.

2158 Coleman, Arthur, and Gary R. Tyler. DRAMA CRITICISM. Vol. I: A CHECKLIST OF INTERPRETATION SINCE 1940 OF ENGLISH AND AMERICAN PLAYS. Denver, Colo.: Alan Swallow, 1966. P. 87.

Secondary selected.

2159 Coxhead, Elizabeth. JOHN MILLINGTON SYNGE AND LADY GREGORY. London: Longmans, Green, 1962. Pp. 34-35; 2nd rev. ed., 1969. Pp. 28-32.

Primary.

2160 _____. "Lady Gregory's Principal Publications." LADY GREGORY; A LITERARY PORTRAIT. 2nd ed., rev. and enl. London: Secker & Warburg, 1966. Pp. 219-20.

2161 Klenze, Hilda V. LADY GREGORY'S LEBEN UND WERK. Bochum-Langendreer, Germany: Heinrich Poeppinghaus O.H.-G., 1940; rpt. New York: Johnson Reprint, 1966. Pp. 90-91.

Primary.

2162 Longaker, Mark, and Edwin C. Bolles. CONTEMPORARY ENGLISH LITERATURE. New York: Appleton-Century-Crofts, 1953. Pp. 57-59.

Primary. Secondary selected.

2163 Mikhail, E.H. "The Theatre of Lady Gregory." BULLETIN OF BIBLIOGRAPHY, 27 (January-March 1970), 9-10.

Secondary.

2164 Millett, Fred B. CONTEMPORARY BRITISH LITERATURE; A CRITICAL SURVEY AND 232 AUTHOR BIBLIOGRAPHIES. New York: Harcourt, Brace, 1935. Pp. 257-59.

Primary. Secondary selected.

2165 Salem, James M. A GUIDE TO CRITICAL REVIEWS. Part III: BRITISH AND CONTINENTAL DRAMA FROM IBSEN TO PINTER. Metuchen, N.J.: Scarecrow Press, 1968. Pp. 115-16.

Secondary selected.

2166 Temple, Ruth Z., and Martin Tucker. TWENTIETH CENTURY BRITISH LITERATURE; A REFERENCE GUIDE AND BIBLIOGRAPHY. New York: Frederick Ungar, 1968. P. 172.

Primary. Secondary selected.

2167 Watson, George, ed. THE NEW CAMBRIDGE BIBLIOGRAPHY OF EN-
GLISH LITERATURE. Vol. 3: 1800-1900. Cambridge: At the University
Press, 1969. Cols. 1939-41.

Primary. Secondary selected.

## HANKIN, ST. JOHN [EMILE CLAVERING] (1869-1909)

2168 Breed, Paul F., and Florence M. Sniderman, comps. DRAMATIC CRITI-
CISM INDEX; A BIBLIOGRAPHY OF COMMENTARIES ON PLAYWRIGHTS
FROM IBSEN TO THE AVANT-GARDE. Detroit, Mich.: Gale Research
Co., 1972. P. 284.

Secondary selected.

2169 Drinkwater, John, ed. THE DRAMATIC WORKS OF ST. JOHN HAN-
KIN. 3 vols. New York: Mitchell Kennerley, 1912.

Includes bibliographical information in the editor's introduction
to Volume I (pages 3-28). Casts and dates of original performances appear in Volume III (pages 225-31).

2170 Willison, I.R., ed. THE NEW CAMBRIDGE BIBLIOGRAPHY OF ENGLISH
LITERATURE. Vol. 4: 1900-1950. Cambridge: At the University Press,
1972. Cols. 950-51.

Primary. Secondary selected.

## HERBERT, [SIR] A[LAN]. P[ATRICK]. (1890-1971)

2171 Fabes, Gilbert. THE FIRST EDITIONS OF A.E. COPPART, A.P. HER-
BERT, AND CHARLES MORGAN, WITH VALUES AND BIBLIOGRAPHICAL
POINTS. London: Myers, 1933. Pp. 55-125.

Primary.

2172 Millett, Fred B. CONTEMPORARY BRITISH LITERATURE; A CRITICAL
SURVEY AND 232 AUTHOR BIBLIOGRAPHIES. New York: Harcourt,
Brace, 1935. Pp. 268-70.

Primary. Secondary selected.

2173 Temple, Ruth Z., and Martin Tucker. TWENTIETH CENTURY BRITISH
LITERATURE; A REFERENCE GUIDE AND BIBLIOGRAPHY. New York:
Frederick Ungar, 1968. Pp. 177-78.

Primary.

2174 Willison, I.R., ed. THE NEW CAMBRIDGE BIBLIOGRAPHY OF ENGLISH
LITERATURE. Vol. 4: 1900-1950. Cambridge: At the University Press,

1972. Cols. 288-90.

Primary. Secondary selected.

## HOUGHTON, STANLEY (1881-1913)

2175 Batho, Edith Clara, and Bonamy Dobree. THE VICTORIANS AND AFTER, 1830-1914. Introductions to English Literature, vol. IV. General ed. Bonamy Dobree. London: Cresset Press; New York: R.M. McBride, 1938. P. 269.

Primary.

2176 Breed, Paul F., and Florence M. Sniderman, comps. DRAMATIC CRITI-CISM INDEX; A BIBLIOGRAPHY OF COMMENTARIES ON PLAYWRIGHTS FROM IBSEN TO THE AVANT-GARDE. Detroit, Mich.: Gale Research Co., 1972. P. 307.

Secondary selected.

2177 Longaker, Mark, and Edwin C. Bolles. CONTEMPORARY ENGLISH LIT-ERATURE. New York: Appleton-Century-Crofts, 1953. Pp. 412-13.

Primary. Secondary selected.

2178 Salem, James M. A GUIDE TO CRITICAL REVIEWS. Part III: BRITISH AND CONTINENTAL DRAMA FROM IBSEN TO PINTER. Metuchen, N.J.: Scarecrow Press, 1968. Pp. 125-26.

Secondary selected.

2179 Willison, I.R., ed. THE NEW CAMBRIDGE BIBLIOGRAPHY OF ENGLISH LITERATURE. Vol. 4: 1900-1950. Cambridge: At the University Press, 1972. Col. 954.

Primary. Secondary selected.

## HOUSMAN, LAURENCE (1865-1959)

2180 Batho, Edith Clara, and Bonamy Dobree. THE VICTORIANS AND AFTER, 1830-1914. Introductions to English Literature, vol. IV. General ed. Bonamy Dobree. London: Cresset Press; New York: R.M. McBride, 1938. P. 270.

Primary.

2181 Breed, Paul F., and Florence M. Sniderman, comps. DRAMATIC CRITI-CISM INDEX; A BIBLIOGRAPHY OF COMMENTARIES ON PLAYWRIGHTS FROM IBSEN TO THE AVANT-GARDE. Detroit, Mich.: Gale Research Co., 1972. Pp. 307-8.

Secondary selected.

2182 Kemp, Ivor. LAURENCE HOUSMAN, 1865-1959: A BRIEF CATALOGUE OF THE COLLECTION OF BOOKS, MANUSCRIPTS AND DRAWINGS PRESENTED TO THE STREET LIBRARY. Street, Somerset: Somerset County Library, Street Branch, 1967.

2183 Longaker, Mark, and Edwin C. Bolles. CONTEMPORARY ENGLISH LITERATURE. New York: Appleton-Century-Crofts, 1953. Pp. 410-12.

Primary. Secondary selected.

2184 Millett, Fred B. CONTEMPORARY BRITISH LITERATURE; A CRITICAL SURVEY AND 232 AUTHOR BIBLIOGRAPHIES. New York: Harcourt, Brace, 1935. Pp. 278-81.

Primary. Secondary selected.

2185 Rudolf, Anna. DIE DICHTUNG VON LAURENCE HOUSMAN. Breslau, Poland: Priebatschs Buchhandlung, 1930. Pp. 85-89.

Primary. Secondary selected.

2186 Salem, James M. A GUIDE TO CRITICAL REVIEWS. Part III: BRITISH AND CONTINENTAL DRAMA FROM IBSEN TO PINTER. Metuchen, N.J.: Scarecrow Press, 1968. Pp. 126-27.

Secondary selected.

2187 Temple, Ruth Z., and Martin Tucker. TWENTIETH CENTURY BRITISH LITERATURE; A REFERENCE GUIDE AND BIBLIOGRAPHY. New York: Frederick Ungar, 1968. P. 180.

Primary. Secondary selected.

2188 Watson, George, ed. THE NEW CAMBRIDGE BIBLIOGRAPHY OF ENGLISH LITERATURE. Vol. 3: 1800-1900. Cambridge: At the University Press, 1969. Cols. 632, 1098.

Primary. Secondary selected.

## HUGHES, RICHARD [ARTHUR WARREN] (1900-    )

2189 Millett, Fred B. CONTEMPORARY BRITISH LITERATURE; A CRITICAL SURVEY AND 232 AUTHOR BIBLIOGRAPHIES. New York: Harcourt, Brace, 1935. P. 286.

Primary. Secondary selected.

2190 Temple, Ruth Z., and Martin Tucker. TWENTIETH CENTURY BRITISH LITERATURE; A REFERENCE GUIDE AND BIBLIOGRAPHY. New York: Frederick Ungar, 1968. Pp. 181-82.

Primary.

2191 Willison, I.R., ed. THE NEW CAMBRIDGE BIBLIOGRAPHY OF ENGLISH LITERATURE. Vol. 4: 1900-1950. Cambridge: At the University Press, 1972. Col. 607.

    Primary. Secondary selected.

## HYDE, DOUGLAS (1860-1949)

2192 Millett, Fred B. CONTEMPORARY BRITISH LITERATURE; A CRITICAL SURVEY AND 232 AUTHOR BIBLIOGRAPHIES. New York: Harcourt, Brace, 1935. Pp. 290-92.

    Primary. Secondary selected.

2193 O'Hegarty, Patrick Sarsfield. "A Bibliography of Dr. Douglas Hyde." DUBLIN MAGAZINE, 14 (January-March 1939), 57-66; (April-June 1939), 72-78; rpt. as pamphlet, A BIBLIOGRAPHY OF DR. DOUGLAS HYDE. Dublin: Privately printed, 1939.

    Primary.

2194 Watson, George, ed. THE NEW CAMBRIDGE BIBLIOGRAPHY OF EN-GLISH LITERATURE. Vol. 3: 1800-1900. Cambridge: At the University Press, 1969. Cols. 1909-10.

    Primary. Secondary selected.

## ISHERWOOD, CHRISTOPHER [WILLIAM BRADSHAW] (1904-    )

2195 Daiches, David. THE PRESENT AGE, AFTER 1920. Introductions to English Literature, vol. V. General ed. Bonamy Dobree. London: Cressett Press; Bloomington: Indiana University Press, 1958. P. 313.

    Primary.

2196 Palmer, Helen H., and Anne Jane Dyson. EUROPEAN DRAMA CRITICISM. Hamden, Conn.: Shoe String Press, 1968. Pp. 25-26.

    Secondary selected.

2197 Temple, Ruth Z., and Martin Tucker. TWENTIETH CENTURY BRITISH LITERATURE; A REFERENCE GUIDE AND BIBLIOGRAPHY. New York: Frederick Ungar, 1968. P. 183.

    Primary. Secondary selected.

2198 Westby, Selmer, and Clayton M. Brown. CHRISTOPHER ISHERWOOD: A BIBLIOGRAPHY 1923-1967. Los Angeles: California State College, for J.F. Kennedy Memorial Library, 1968. Pp. 3-51.

    Primary and secondary.

2199 Wilde, Alan. CHRISTOPHER ISHERWOOD. New York: Twayne Publishers, 1971. Pp. 161-64.

> Checklist of selected primary material. General secondary annotated bibliography. Eighteen reviews of Isherwood's books.

2200 Willison, I.R., ed. THE NEW CAMBRIDGE BIBLIOGRAPHY OF ENGLISH LITERATURE. Vol. 4: 1900-1950. Cambridge: At the University Press, 1972. Cols. 619-20.

> Primary. Secondary selected.

## JACOBS, WILLIAM WYMARK (1863-1943)

2201 Longaker, Mark, and Edwin C. Bolles. CONTEMPORARY ENGLISH LITERATURE. New York: Appleton-Century-Crofts, 1953. Pp. 219-20.

> Primary. Secondary selected.

2202 Millett, Fred B. CONTEMPORARY BRITISH LITERATURE; A CRITICAL SURVEY AND 232 AUTHOR BIBLIOGRAPHIES. New York: Harcourt, Brace, 1935. Pp. 293-94.

> Primary. Secondary selected.

2203 Osborne, E.A. "Epitome of a Bibliography of W.W. Jacobs." AMERICAN BOOK COLLECTOR, 5 (1934), 201-4, 268-72, 286-88, 331-34, 358-62.

> A bibliographical essay.

2204 Temple, Ruth Z., and Martin Tucker. TWENTIETH CENTURY BRITISH LITERATURE; A REFERENCE GUIDE AND BIBLIOGRAPHY. New York: Frederick Ungar, 1968. P. 183.

> Primary. Secondary selected.

2205 Willison, I.R., ed. THE NEW CAMBRIDGE BIBLIOGRAPHY OF ENGLISH LITERATURE. Vol. 4: 1900-1950. Cambridge: At the University Press, 1972. Cols. 620-21.

> Primary. Secondary selected.

## JESSE, F[RYNIWYD]. [MARSH] TENNYSON
## [MRS. H.M. HARWOOD] (1889-1958)

2206 Daiches, David. THE PRESENT AGE, AFTER 1920. Introductions to English Literature, vol. V. General ed. Bonamy Dobree. London: Cresset Press; Bloomington: Indiana University Press, 1958. Pp. 276-77.

> Primary.

2207 Millett, Fred B. CONTEMPORARY BRITISH LITERATURE; A CRITICAL SURVEY AND 232 AUTHOR BIBLIOGRAPHIES. New York: Harcourt, Brace, 1935. Pp. 296-97.

Primary. Secondary selected.

2208 Willison, I.R., ed. THE NEW CAMBRIDGE BIBLIOGRAPHY OF ENGLISH LITERATURE. Vol. 4: 1900-1950. Cambridge: At the University Press, 1972. Cols. 623-24.

Primary. Secondary selected.

## JOHNSTON, DENIS [WILLIAM] (1901-    )

2209 Breed, Paul F., and Florence M. Sniderman, comps. DRAMATIC CRITI-CISM INDEX; A BIBLIOGRAPHY OF COMMENTARIES ON PLAYWRIGHTS FROM IBSEN TO THE AVANT-GARDE. Detroit, Mich.: Gale Research Co., 1972. Pp. 35-58.

Secondary selected.

2210 Daiches, David. THE PRESENT AGE, AFTER 1920. Introductions to En-glish Literature, vol. V. General ed. Bonamy Dobree. London: Cres-set Press; Bloomington: Indiana University Press, 1958. P. 329.

Primary.

2211 Salem, James M. A GUIDE TO CRITICAL REVIEWS. Part III: BRITISH AND CONTINENTAL DRAMA FROM IBSEN TO PINTER. Metuchen, N.J.: Scarecrow Press, 1968. P. 141.

Secondary selected.

2212 Spinner, Kasper. DIE ALTE DAME SAGT: NEIN! IRISCHE DRAMATIKER. LENNOX ROBINSON, SEAN O'CASEY, DENIS JOHNSTON. Schweizer Anglistische Arbeiten, 52. Bern: A. Francke Verlag, 1961. Pp. 208-10.

Primary selected. Secondary selected.

2213 Temple, Ruth Z., and Martin Tucker. TWENTIETH CENTURY BRITISH LITERATURE; A REFERENCE GUIDE AND BIBLIOGRAPHY. New York: Frederick Ungar, 1968. P. 185.

Primary.

2214 Willison, I.R., ed. THE NEW CAMBRIDGE BIBLIOGRAPHY OF ENGLISH LITERATURE. Vol. 4: 1900-1950. Cambridge: At the University Press, 1972. Cols. 957-58.

Primary. Secondary selected.

## JONES, [SIR] HENRY ARTHUR (1851-1929)

2215 Adelman, Irving, and Rita Dworkin. MODERN DRAMA; A CHECKLIST OF
CRITICAL LITERATURE ON 20TH CENTURY PLAYS. Metuchen, N.J.:
Scarecrow Press, 1967. Pp. 173-74.

Secondary selected.

2216 Breed, Paul F., and Florence M. Sniderman, comps. DRAMATIC CRITI-
CISM INDEX; A BIBLIOGRAPHY OF COMMENTARIES ON PLAYWRIGHTS
FROM IBSEN TO THE AVANT-GARDE. Detroit, Mich.: Gale Research
Co., 1972. Pp. 358-59.

Secondary selected.

2217 Coleman, Arthur, and Gary R. Tyler. DRAMA CRITICISM. Vol. I: A
CHECKLIST OF INTERPRETATION SINCE 1940 OF ENGLISH AND AMERI-
CAN PLAYS. Denver, Colo.: Alan Swallow, 1966. P. 99.

Secondary selected.

2218 Jones, Doris Arthur. THE LIFE AND LETTERS OF HENRY ARTHUR JONES.
London: Victor Gollancz, 1930. Pp. 411-31.

Primary. Play productions.

2219 Millett, Fred B. CONTEMPORARY BRITISH LITERATURE; A CRITICAL
SURVEY AND 232 AUTHOR BIBLIOGRAPHIES. New York: Harcourt,
Brace, 1935. Pp. 298-301.

Primary.

2220 Salem, James M. A GUIDE TO CRITICAL REVIEWS. Part III: BRITISH
AND CONTINENTAL DRAMA FROM IBSEN TO PINTER. Metuchen, N.J.:
Scarecrow Press, 1968. Pp. 141-44.

Secondary selected.

2221 Temple, Ruth Z., and Martin Tucker. TWENTIETH CENTURY BRITISH
LITERATURE; A REFERENCE GUIDE AND BIBLIOGRAPHY. New York:
Frederick Ungar, 1968. P. 186.

Primary. Secondary selected.

2222 Walter, Frank K. "Reading List on Henry Arthur Jones." BULLETIN OF
BIBLIOGRAPHY, 6 (1911), 273-75.

Primary selected. Secondary selected. Annotated.

2223 Watson, George, ed. THE NEW CAMBRIDGE BIBLIOGRAPHY OF ENGLISH

LITERATURE. Vol. 3: 1800-1900. Cambridge: At the University Press, 1969. Cols. 1164-66.

Primary. Secondary selected.

## LAWRENCE, D[AVID]. H[ERBERT]. (1885-1930)

The largest collections of Lawrence manuscripts and typescripts are in the libraries of the University of California and of the University of Texas.

2224 Adelman, Irving, and Rita Dworkin. MODERN DRAMA; A CHECKLIST OF CRITICAL LITERATURE ON 20TH CENTURY PLAYS. Metuchen, N.J.: Scarecrow Press, 1967. P. 184.

Secondary selected.

2225 Beards, Richard D., and G.B. Crump. "D.H. Lawrence: Ten Years of Criticism, 1959-1968; A Checklist." D.H. LAWRENCE REVIEW, 1 (1968), 245-85.

Continued in subsequent issues. Secondary.

2226 Beebe, Maurice, and Anthony Tommasi. "Criticism of D.H. Lawrence: A Selected Checklist with an Index of Studies of Separate Works." MODERN FICTION STUDIES, 5 (Spring 1959), 83-89.

Secondary.

2227 Breed, Paul F., and Florence M. Sniderman, comps. DRAMATIC CRITICISM INDEX; A BIBLIOGRAPHY OF COMMENTARIES ON PLAYWRIGHTS FROM IBSEN TO THE AVANT-GARDE. Detroit, Mich.: Gale Research Co., 1972. P. 380.

Secondary selected.

2228 Coleman, Arthur, and Gary R. Tyler. DRAMA CRITICISM. Vol. I: A CHECKLIST OF INTERPRETATIONS SINCE 1940 OF ENGLISH AND AMERICAN PLAYS. Denver, Colo.: Alan Swallow, 1966. P. 115.

Secondary selected.

2229 Cowan, James C. is preparing a volume on Lawrence for the Annotated Secondary Bibliography Series on English Literature in Transition, edited by Helmut E. Gerber, to be published by Northern Illinois University Press.

2230 Cutler, Bradley D., and Villa Stiles. MODERN BRITISH AUTHORS; THEIR FIRST EDITIONS. New York: Greenberg; London: G. Allen, 1930; rpt. Folcroft, Pa.: Folcroft Press, 1969. Pp. 99-102.

Primary.

2231 Edwards, Lucy I. D.H. LAWRENCE: A FINDING LIST AND HOLDINGS IN THE CITY, COUNTY AND UNIVERSITY LIBRARIES OF NOTTING-HAM. Nottingham: [Nottingham County Library], 1969.

2232 Fabes, Gilbert H. D.H. LAWRENCE; HIS FIRST EDITIONS. London: Foyles, 1933.

Primary.

2233 Hepburn, James G. "D.H. Lawrence's Plays: An Annotated Bibliography." BOOK COLLECTOR, 14 (Spring 1965), 78-81.

Primary.

2234 McDonald, Edward D. A BIBLIOGRAPHY OF THE WRITINGS OF D.H. LAWRENCE. Philadelphia: Centaur Book Shop, 1925; supplement, THE WRITINGS OF D.H. LAWRENCE, 1925-1930. A BIBLIOGRAPHICAL SUPPLEMENT. London: Simpkin; Philadelphia: Centaur Book Shop, 1925.

Primary. Secondary selected.

2235 Palmer, Helen H., and Anne Jane Dyson. EUROPEAN DRAMA CRITI-CISM. Hamden, Conn.: Shoe String Press, 1968. Pp. 234-35.

Secondary selected.

2236 Powell, Lawrence C. THE MANUSCRIPTS OF LAWRENCE. Los Angeles: Public Library, 1937. Pp. 43-44.

Primary.

2237 Roberts, Warren. "The Manuscripts of D.H. Lawrence." LITERARY CHRONICLE OF THE UNIVERSITY OF TEXAS, 5 (1955), 36-43.

Primary.

2238 _____. A BIBLIOGRAPHY OF D.H. LAWRENCE. Soho Bibliographies, no. 13. London: Rupert Hart-Davis, 1963.

Primary. Secondary selected.

2239 Sagar, Keith. THE ART OF D.H. LAWRENCE. Cambridge: At the University Press, 1966. Pp. 248-56.

Primary. Secondary selected, 1959-65.

2240 Tedlock, E.W., Jr. THE FRIEDA LAWRENCE COLLECTION OF D.H. LAWRENCE MANUSCRIPTS; A DESCRIPTIVE BIBLIOGRAPHY. Albuquerque: University of New Mexico Press, 1948.

Primary.

2241 White, William. D.H. LAWRENCE: A CHECKLIST, 1931-1950. Detroit, Mich.: Wayne University Press, 1950.

> Reprinted from BULLETIN OF BIBLIOGRAPHY, 19 (1948-49), 174-77, 209-11, 235-39. Primary. Secondary selected.

2242 Willison, I.R., ed. THE NEW CAMBRIDGE BIBLIOGRAPHY OF ENGLISH LITERATURE. Vol. 4: 1900-1950. Cambridge: At the University Press, 1972. Cols. 481-503.

> Primary. Secondary selected.

## LETTS, WINIFRED M. [MRS. W.H. VERSCHOYLE] (1882-    )

2243 Longaker, Mark, and Edwin C. Bolles. CONTEMPORARY ENGLISH LITERATURE. New York: Appleton-Century-Crofts, 1953. Pp. 50-51.

> Primary. Secondary selected.

## LEVY, BENN [WOLFE] (1900-1974)

2244 Daiches, David. THE PRESENT AGE, AFTER 1920. Introductions to English Literature, vol. V. General ed. Bonamy Dobree. London: Cresset Press; Bloomington: Indiana University Press, 1958. P. 329.

> Primary.

2245 Salem, James M. A GUIDE TO CRITICAL REVIEWS. Part III: BRITISH AND CONTINENTAL DRAMA FROM IBSEN TO PINTER. Metuchen, N.J.: Scarecrow Press, 1968. Pp. 147-49.

> Secondary selected.

2246 Temple, Ruth Z., and Martin Tucker. TWENTIETH CENTURY BRITISH LITERATURE; A REFERENCE GUIDE AND BIBLIOGRAPHY. New York: Frederick Ungar, 1968. P. 193.

> Primary.

2247 Willison, I.R., ed. THE NEW CAMBRIDGE BIBLIOGRAPHY OF ENGLISH LITERATURE. Vol. 4: 1900-1950. Cambridge: At the University Press, 1972. Cols. 960-61.

> Primary. Secondary selected.

## LONSDALE, FREDERICK [LIONEL FREDERICK LEONARD] (1881-1954)

2248 Breed, Paul F., and Florence M. Sniderman, comps. DRAMATIC CRITICISM INDEX; A BIBLIOGRAPHY OF COMMENTARIES ON PLAYWRIGHTS

FROM IBSEN TO THE AVANT-GARDE. Detroit, Mich.: Gale Research Co., 1972. P. 389.

Secondary selected.

2249 Donaldson, Frances. FREDDY LONDSALE. London: Heinemann, 1957. Pp. 247-49.

Primary.

2250 Longaker, Mark, and Edwin C. Bolles. CONTEMPORARY ENGLISH LITERATURE. New York: Appleton-Century-Crofts, 1953. Pp. 420-21.

Primary.

2251 Millett, Fred B. CONTEMPORARY BRITISH LITERATURE; A CRITICAL SURVEY AND 232 AUTHOR BIBLIOGRAPHIES. New York: Harcourt, Brace, 1935. P. 333.

Primary. Secondary selected.

2252 Salem, James M. A GUIDE TO CRITICAL REVIEWS. Part III: BRITISH AND CONTINENTAL DRAMA FROM IBSEN TO PINTER. Metuchen, N.J.: Scarecrow Press, 1968. Pp. 149-52.

Secondary selected.

2253 Temple, Ruth Z., and Martin Tucker. TWENTIETH CENTURY BRITISH LITERATURE: A REFERENCE GUIDE AND BIBLIOGRAPHY. New York: Frederick Ungar, 1968. P. 196.

Primary. Secondary selected.

2254 Willison, I.R., ed. THE NEW CAMBRIDGE BIBLIOGRAPHY OF ENGLISH LITERATURE. Vol. 4: 1900-1950. Cambridge: At the University Press, 1972. Cols. 961-62.

Primary. Secondary selected.

## McEVOY, CHARLES ALFRED (1879-1929)

2255 Millett, Fred B. CONTEMPORARY BRITISH LITERATURE; A CRITICAL SURVEY AND 232 AUTHOR BIBLIOGRAPHIES. New York: Harcourt, Brace, 1935. P. 343.

Primary. Secondary selected.

2256 Willison, I.R., ed. THE NEW CAMBRIDGE BIBLIOGRAPHY OF ENGLISH LITERATURE. Vol. 4: 1900-1950. Cambridge: At the University Press, 1972. Col. 964.

Primary.

## MacNAMARA, BRINSLEY [JOHN WELDON] (1890-1963)

2257 Breed, Paul F., and Florence M. Sniderman, comps. DRAMATIC CRITI-
CISM INDEX; A BIBLIOGRAPHY OF COMMENTARIES ON PLAYWRIGHTS
FROM IBSEN TO THE AVANT-GARDE. Detroit, Mich.: Gale Research
Co., 1972. P. 397.

Secondary selected.

2258 Willison, I.R., ed. THE NEW CAMBRIDGE BIBLIOGRAPHY OF ENGLISH
LITERATURE. Vol. 4: 1900-1950. Cambridge: At the University Press,
1972. Col. 965.

Primary. Secondary selected.

## MARTYN, EDWARD (1859-1923)

2259 Adelman, Irving, and Rita Dworkin. MODERN DRAMA; A CHECKLIST
OF CRITICAL LITERATURE ON 20TH CENTURY PLAYS. Metuchen, N.J.:
Scarecrow Press, 1967. Pp. 192-93.

Secondary selected.

2260 Breed, Paul F., and Florence M. Sniderman, comps. DRAMATIC CRITI-
CISM INDEX; A BIBLIOGRAPHY OF COMMENTARIES ON PLAYWRIGHTS
FROM IBSEN TO THE AVANT-GARDE. Detroit, Mich.: Gale Research
Co., 1972. Pp. 410-12.

Secondary selected.

2261 Coleman, Arthur, and Gary R. Tyler. DRAMA CRITICISM. Vol. I: A
CHECKLIST OF INTERPRETATION SINCE 1940 OF ENGLISH AND AMERI-
CAN PLAYS. Denver, Colo.: Alan Swallow, 1966. P. 135.

Secondary selected.

2262 Watson, George, ed. THE NEW CAMBRIDGE BIBLIOGRAPHY OF EN-
GLISH LITERATURE. Vol. 3: 1800-1900. Cambridge: At the University Press, 1969. Col. 1939.

Primary. Secondary selected.

## MASEFIELD, JOHN (1878-1967)

2263 Breed, Paul F., and Florence M. Sniderman, comps. DRAMATIC CRITI-
CISM INDEX; A BIBLIOGRAPHY OF COMMENTARIES ON PLAYWRIGHTS
FROM IBSEN TO THE AVANT-GARDE. Detroit, Mich.: Gale Research
Co., 1972. P. 412.

Secondary selected.

2264 Coleman, Arthur, and Gary R. Tyler. DRAMA CRITICISM. Vol. I: A CHECKLIST OF INTERPRETATION SINCE 1940 OF ENGLISH AND AMERICAN PLAYS. Denver, Colo.: Alan Swallow, 1966. P. 135.

Secondary selected.

2265 Cutler, Bradley D., and Villa Stiles. MODERN BRITISH AUTHORS; THEIR FIRST EDITIONS. New York: Greenberg; London: G. Allen, 1930; rpt. Folcroft, Pa.: Folcroft Press, 1969. Pp. 111-14.

Primary.

2266 Drew, Fraser Bragg. "Some Contributions to the Bibliography of John Masefield." PAPERS OF THE BIBLIOGRAPHICAL SOCIETY OF AMERICA, 53 (1959), 188-96.

List of 318 book reviews by Masefield in the MANCHESTER GUARDIAN. This list corrects and extends Simmons (No. 2271).

2267 Handley-Taylor, Geoffrey. JOHN MASEFIELD, O.M. THE QUEEN'S POET LAUREATE; A BIBLIOGRAPHY AND EIGHTY-FIRST BIRTHDAY TRIBUTE. London: Cranbrook Tower Press, 1960.

Primary. Secondary selected.

2268 Nevinson, Henry Woodd. JOHN MASEFIELD: AN APPRECIATION. TOGETHER WITH A BIBLIOGRAPHY. London: Heinemann, 1931.

Primary.

2269 Salem, James M. A GUIDE TO CRITICAL REVIEWS. Part III: BRITISH AND CONTINENTAL DRAMA FROM IBSEN TO PINTER. Metuchen, N.J.: Scarecrow Press, 1968. P. 157.

Secondary selected.

2270 Sherman, Clarence. "John Masefield; A Contribution toward a Bibliography." BULLETIN OF BIBLIOGRAPHY, 8 (1915), 158-60.

Includes many early periodical reviews of Masefield.

2271 Simmons, Charles H. A BIBLIOGRAPHY OF JOHN MASEFIELD. New York: Columbia University Press; London: Oxford University Press, 1930.

Primary first editions. Secondary selected.

2272 Williams, I.A. BIBLIOGRAPHIES OF MODERN AUTHORS. NO. 2, JOHN MASEFIELD. London: Chaundy, 1921.

Pamphlet.

2273 Willison, I.R., ed. THE NEW CAMBRIDGE BIBLIOGRAPHY OF ENGLISH LITERATURE. Vol. 4: 1900-1950. Cambridge: At the University Press, 1972. Cols. 306-13.

Primary. Secondary selected.

## MAUGHAM, W[ILLIAM]. SOMERSET (1874-1965)

2274 Adelman, Irving, and Rita Dworkin. MODERN DRAMA; A CHECKLIST OF CRITICAL LITERATURE ON 20TH CENTURY PLAYS. Metuchen, N.J.: Scarecrow Press, 1967. Pp. 193-94.

Secondary selected.

2275 Bason, F.T. WILLIAM SOMERSET MAUGHAM; A BIBLIOGRAPHY OF THE WRITINGS. London: Unicorn Press, 1931.

Primary.

2276 Bender, J. Terry. A COMPREHENSIVE EXHIBITION OF THE WRITINGS OF W.S. MAUGHAM. May-August, 1958. Stanford, Calif.: Stanford University Library, 1958.

Primary. Locates manuscripts.

2277 Breed, Paul F., and Florence M. Sniderman, comps. DRAMATIC CRITI-CISM INDEX; A BIBLIOGRAPHY OF COMMENTARIES ON PLAYWRIGHTS FROM IBSEN TO THE AVANT-GARDE. Detroit, Mich.: Gale Research Co., 1972. Pp. 413-17.

Secondary selected.

2278 Coleman, Arthur, and Gary R. Tyler. DRAMA CRITICISM. Vol. I: A CHECKLIST OF INTERPRETATION SINCE 1940 OF ENGLISH AND AMERI-CAN PLAYS. Denver, Colo.: Alan Swallow, 1966. P. 137.

Secondary selected.

2279 Henry, W.H., Jr. A FRENCH BIBLIOGRAPHY OF W.S. MAUGHAM; A LIST OF HIS WORKS PUBLISHED IN FRANCE, HIS CONTRIBUTIONS TO FRENCH PERIODICALS, THE SWISS, BELGIAN, AND FRENCH CRITI-CISM OF HIS BOOKS, PLAYS AND FILMS. Charlottesville: Biblio-graphical Society of the University of Virginia, 1967.

Primary. Secondary.

2280 Jonas, Klaus W. A BIBLIOGRAPHY OF THE WRITINGS OF W. SOMER-SET MAUGHAM. New Brunswick, N.J.: Rutgers University Press, 1950.

Primary.

2281 Mander, Raymond, and Joe Mitchenson. THEATRICAL COMPANION TO MAUGHAM. London: Rockliff, 1955. Pp. 299–302.

   Published plays.

2282 Mikhail, E.H. "Somerset Maugham and the Theatre." BULLETIN OF BIBLIOGRAPHY, 27 (April–June 1970), 42–48.

   Secondary.

2283 Palmer, Helen H., and Anne Jane Dyson. EUROPEAN DRAMA CRITICISM. Hamden, Conn.: Shoe String Press, 1968. Pp. 261–65.

   Secondary selected.

2284 Salem, James M. A GUIDE TO CRITICAL REVIEWS. Part III: BRITISH AND CONTINENTAL DRAMA FROM IBSEN TO PINTER. Metuchen, N.J.: Scarecrow Press, 1968. Pp. 157–63.

   Secondary selected.

2285 Sanders, Charles, ed. W.S. MAUGHAM: AN ANNOTATED BIBLIOGRAPHY OF WRITINGS ABOUT HIM. De Kalb: Northern Illinois University Press, 1970.

   Primary. Secondary.

2286 Stott, Raymond Toole. THE WRITINGS OF W.S. MAUGHAM; A BIBLIOGRAPHY. London: Bertram Rota, 1956; SUPPLEMENT TO THE WRITINGS OF W.S. MAUGHAM. London: Nicholas Vane, 1961.

   Primary. Extensive bibliographical notes.

2287 Willison, I.R., ed. THE NEW CAMBRIDGE BIBLIOGRAPHY OF ENGLISH LITERATURE. Vol. 4: 1900–1950. Cambridge: At the University Press, 1972. Cols. 661–69.

   Primary. Secondary selected.

## MAYNE, RUTHERFORD [SAMUEL J. WADDELL] (1878–   )

2288 Breed, Paul F., and Florence M. Sniderman, comps. DRAMATIC CRITICISM INDEX; A BIBLIOGRAPHY OF COMMENTARIES ON PLAYWRIGHTS FROM IBSEN TO THE AVANT-GARDE. Detroit, Mich.: Gale Research Co., 1972. P. 419.

   Secondary selected.

2289 Watson, George, ed. THE NEW CAMBRIDGE BIBLIOGRAPHY OF ENGLISH LITERATURE. Vol. 3: 1800–1900. Cambridge: At the University Press,

1969. Col. 1941.

Primary. Secondary selected.

## MILNE, A[LLAN]. A[LEXANDER]. (1882-1956)

2290 Adelman, Irving, and Rita Dworkin. MODERN DRAMA; A CHECKLIST
OF CRITICAL LITERATURE ON 20TH CENTURY PLAYS. Metuchen, N.J.:
Scarecrow Press, 1967. P. 202.

Secondary selected.

2291 Cutler, Bradley D., and Villa Stiles. MODERN BRITISH AUTHORS;
THEIR FIRST EDITIONS. New York: Greenberg; London: G. Allen,
1930; rpt. Folcroft, Pa.: Folcroft Press, 1969. Pp. 115-17.

Primary.

2292 [Hutchinson, B.] "Christopher Robin, Pooh and Piglet; Prices at Sotheby's
Sale of 24 February, 1969." BOOK COLLECTOR AND LIBRARY MONTH-
LY, 13 (May 1969), 20-21.

2293 Moses, Montrose J., and Oscar J. Campbell, eds. DRAMAS OF MOD-
ERNISM AND THEIR FORERUNNERS. Boston: Little, Brown, 1941. Pp.
923-24, 941.

Primary selected. Secondary selected.

2294 Palmer, Helen H., and Anne Jane Dyson. EUROPEAN DRAMA CRITI-
CISM. Hamden, Conn.: Shoe String Press, 1968. Pp. 272-74.

Secondary selected.

2295 Salem, James M. A GUIDE TO CRITICAL REVIEWS. Part III: BRITISH
AND CONTINENTAL DRAMA FROM IBSEN TO PINTER. Metuchen, N.J.:
Scarecrow Press, 1968. Pp. 163-66.

Secondary selected.

2296 Temple, Ruth Z., and Martin Tucker. TWENTIETH CENTURY BRITISH
LITERATURE; A REFERENCE GUIDE AND BIBLIOGRAPHY. New York:
Frederick Ungar, 1968. P. 206.

Primary. Secondary selected.

2297 Willison, I.R., ed. THE NEW CAMBRIDGE BIBLIOGRAPHY OF ENGLISH
LITERATURE. Vol. 4: 1900-1950. Cambridge: At the University Press,
1972. Cols. 671-73.

Primary. Secondary selected.

## MONKHOUSE, ALLAN NOBLE (1853-1936)

2298 Batho, Edith Clara, and Bonamy Dobree. THE VICTORIANS AND AFTER, 1830-1914. Introductions to English Literature, vol. IV. General ed. Bonamy Dobree. London: Cresset Press; New York: R.M. McBride, 1938. P. 268.

Primary.

2299 Longaker, Mark, and Edwin C. Bolles. CONTEMPORARY ENGLISH LIT-ERATURE. New York: Appleton-Century-Crofts, 1953. P. 412-14.

Primary. Secondary selected.

2300 Millett, Fred B. CONTEMPORARY BRITISH LITERATURE; A CRITICAL SURVEY AND 232 AUTHOR BIBLIOGRAPHIES. New York: Harcourt, Brace, 1935. Pp. 368-69.

Primary. Secondary selected.

2301 Temple, Ruth Z., and Martin Tucker. TWENTIETH CENTURY BRITISH LITERATURE; A REFERENCE GUIDE AND BIBLIOGRAPHY. New York: Frederick Ungar, 1968. P. 207.

Primary. Secondary selected.

2302 Willison, I.R., ed. THE NEW CAMBRIDGE BIBLIOGRAPHY OF ENGLISH LITERATURE. Vol. 4: 1900-1950. Cambridge: At the University Press, 1972. Col. 968.

Primary. Secondary selected.

## MOORE, GEORGE (1852-1933)

2303 Breed, Paul F., and Florence M. Sniderman, comps. DRAMATIC CRITI-CISM INDEX; A BIBLIOGRAPHY OF COMMENTARIES ON PLAYWRIGHTS FROM IBSEN TO THE AVANT-GARDE. Detroit, Mich.: Gale Research Co., 1972. Pp. 447-48.

Secondary selected.

2304 Collet, George Paul. MOORE ET LA FRANCE. Geneva: Droz; Paris: Minard, 1957.

Lists uncollected articles and prefaces.

2305 Cutler, Bradley D., and Villa Stiles. MODERN BRITISH AUTHORS; THEIR FIRST EDITIONS. New York: Greenberg; London: G. Allen, 1930; rpt. Folcroft, Pa.: Folcroft Press, 1969. Pp. 118-21.

Primary.

2306 Danielson, Henry. "Moore: A Bibliography 1878-1921." A PORTRAIT OF MOORE IN A STUDY OF HIS WORK. By John Freeman. London: Werner Laurie, 1922. Pp. 231-83.

Primary.

2307 Gerber, Helmut E. "George Moore: An Annotated Bibliography of Writings about Him." ENGLISH FICTION IN TRANSITION, 2, no. 2 (1959), 1-91.

Supplemented in subsequent issues of ENGLISH FICTION (title changed to ENGLISH LITERATURE IN TRANSITION). Secondary.

2308 Gilcher, Edwin. A BIBLIOGRAPHY OF GEORGE MOORE. DeKalb: Northern Illinois University Press, 1970.

Primary annotated.

2309 Noel, Jean C. GEORGE MOORE; L'HOMME ET L'OEUVRE (1852-1933). Paris: Marcel Didier, 1966. Pp. 555-647.

Primary. Secondary selected.

2310 Temple, Ruth Z., and Martin Tucker. TWENTIETH CENTURY BRITISH LITERATURE: A REFERENCE GUIDE AND BIBLIOGRAPHY. New York: Frederick Ungar, 1968. Pp. 207-8.

Primary. Secondary selected.

2311 Watson, George, ed. THE NEW CAMBRIDGE BIBLIOGRAPHY OF ENGLISH LITERATURE. Vol. 3: 1800-1900. Cambridge: At the University Press, 1969. Cols. 1014-19.

Primary. Secondary selected.

2312 Williams, I.A. BIBLIOGRAPHIES OF MODERN AUTHORS. NO. 3, GEORGE MOORE. London: Chaundy, 1921.

Pamphlet.

## MOORE, THOMAS STURGE (1870-1944)

2313 "Bibliographies of Modern Authors: Thomas Sturge Moore." LONDON MERCURY, 3 (1920), 100-101.

Primary.

2314 Daiches, David. THE PRESENT AGE, AFTER 1920. Introductions to English Literature, vol. V. General ed. Bonamy Dobree. London: Cresset Press; Bloomington: Indiana University Press, 1958. Pp. 181-82.

Primary.

2315 Gwynn, Frederick L. STURGE MOORE AND THE LIFE OF ART. Lawrence: Kansas University Press, 1951. Pp. 125–35.

Primary. Secondary selected.

2316 Longaker, Mark, and Edwin C. Bolles. CONTEMPORARY ENGLISH LITERATURE. New York: Appleton–Century–Crofts, 1953. Pp. 116–19.

Primary. Secondary selected.

2317 Millett, Fred B. CONTEMPORARY BRITISH LITERATURE; A CRITICAL SURVEY AND 232 AUTHOR BIBLIOGRAPHIES. New York: Harcourt, Brace, 1935. Pp. 375–76.

Primary. Secondary selected.

2318 Temple, Ruth Z., and Martin Tucker. TWENTIETH CENTURY BRITISH LITERATURE; A REFERENCE GUIDE AND BIBLIOGRAPHY. New York: Frederick Ungar, 1968. P. 208.

Primary. Secondary selected.

2319 Willison, I.R., ed. THE NEW CAMBRIDGE BIBLIOGRAPHY OF ENGLISH LITERATURE. Vol. 4: 1900–1950. Cambridge: At the University Press, 1972. Cols. 315–16.

Primary. Secondary selected.

## MORGAN, CHARLES [LANGBRIDGE] (1894-1958)

2320 Adelman, Irving, and Rita Dworkin. MODERN DRAMA; A CHECKLIST OF CRITICAL LITERATURE ON 20TH CENTURY PLAYS. Metuchen, N.J.: Scarecrow Press, 1967. Pp. 204–5.

Secondary selected.

2321 Breed, Paul F., and Florence M. Sniderman, comps. DRAMATIC CRITICISM INDEX; A BIBLIOGRAPHY OF COMMENTARIES ON PLAYWRIGHTS FROM IBSEN TO THE AVANT–GARDE. Detroit, Mich.: Gale Research Co., 1972. P. 448.

Secondary selected.

2322 Daiches, David. THE PRESENT AGE, AFTER 1920. Introductions to English Literature, vol. V. General ed. Bonamy Dobree. London: Cresset Press; Bloomington: Indiana University Press, 1958. P. 297.

Primary.

2323 Duffin, Henry Charles. THE NOVELS AND PLAYS OF CHARLES MOR-

GAN. London: Bowes and Bowes, 1959.

Index listing plays.

2324 Fabes, Gilbert H. THE FIRST EDITIONS OF A.E. COPPARD, A.P. HER-
BERT, AND CHARLES MORGAN, WITH VALUES AND BIBLIOGRAPHICAL
POINTS. London: Myers, 1933.

A book for dealers or collectors.

2325 Longaker, Mark, and Edwin C. Bolles. CONTEMPORARY ENGLISH LIT-
ERATURE. New York: Appleton-Century-Crofts, 1953. Pp. 361-62.

Primary. Secondary selected.

2326 Millett, Fred B. CONTEMPORARY BRITISH LITERATURE; A CRITICAL
SURVEY AND 232 AUTHOR BIBLIOGRAPHIES. New York: Harcourt,
Brace, 1935. Pp. 376-77.

Primary. Secondary selected.

2327 Temple, Ruth Z., and Martin Tucker. TWENTIETH CENTURY BRITISH
LITERATURE; A REFERENCE GUIDE AND BIBLIOGRAPHY. New York:
Frederick Ungar, 1968. Pp. 208-9.

Primary. Secondary selected.

2328 Willison, I.R., ed. THE NEW CAMBRIDGE BIBLIOGRAPHY OF ENGLISH
LITERATURE. Vol. 4: 1900-1950. Cambridge: At the University Press,
1972. Cols. 676-77.

Primary. Secondary selected.

## MUNRO, CHARLES KIRKPATRICK
### [CHARLES WALDEN KIRKPATRICK MACMULLAN] (1889-   )

2329 Daiches, David. THE PRESENT AGE, AFTER 1920. Introductions to English Literature, vol. V. General ed. Bonamy Dobree. London: Cresset Press; Bloomington: Indiana University Press, 1968. P. 327.

Primary.

2330 Millett, Fred B. CONTEMPORARY BRITISH LITERATURE; A CRITICAL
SURVEY AND 232 AUTHOR BIBLIOGRAPHIES. New York: Harcourt,
Brace, 1935. Pp. 380-81.

Primary. Secondary selected.

2331 Salem, James M. A GUIDE TO CRITICAL REVIEWS. Part III: BRITISH
AND CONTINENTAL DRAMA FROM IBSEN TO PINTER. Metuchen, N.J.:
Scarecrow Press, 1968. Pp. 172-73.

Secondary selected.

2332 Temple, Ruth Z., and Martin Tucker. TWENTIETH CENTURY BRITISH
LITERATURE; A REFERENCE GUIDE AND BIBLIOGRAPHY. New York:
Frederick Ungar, 1968. P. 210.

   Primary. Secondary selected.

2333 Willison, I.R., ed. THE NEW CAMBRIDGE BIBLIOGRAPHY OF ENGLISH
LITERATURE. Vol. 4: 1900-1950. Cambridge: At the University Press,
1972. Col. 969.

   Primary. Secondary selected.

## MURRAY, THOMAS CORNELIUS (1873-1959)

2334 Adelman, Irving, and Rita Dworkin. MODERN DRAMA; A CHECKLIST
OF CRITICAL LITERATURE ON 20TH CENTURY PLAYS. Metuchen, N.J.:
Scarecrow Press, 1967. P. 205.

   Secondary selected.

2335 Breed, Paul F., and Florence M. Sniderman, comps. DRAMATIC CRITI-
CISM INDEX; A BIBLIOGRAPHY OF COMMENTARIES ON PLAYWRIGHTS
FROM IBSEN TO THE AVANT-GARDE. Detroit, Mich.: Gale Research
Co., 1972. Pp. 451-52.

   Secondary selected.

2336 Millett, Fred B. CONTEMPORARY BRITISH LITERATURE; A CRITICAL
SURVEY AND 232 AUTHOR BIBLIOGRAPHIES. New York: Harcourt,
Brace, 1935. P. 385.

   Primary. Secondary selected.

2337 Salem, James M. A GUIDE TO CRITICAL REVIEWS. Part III: BRITISH
AND CONTINENTAL DRAMA FROM IBSEN TO PINTER. Metuchen, N.J.:
Scarecrow Press, 1968. Pp. 173-74.

   Secondary selected.

2338 Watson, George, ed. THE NEW CAMBRIDGE BIBLIOGRAPHY OF EN-
GLISH LITERATURE. Vol. 3: 1800-1900. Cambridge: At the University Press, 1969. Cols. 1944-45.

   Primary. Secondary selected.

## O'CASEY, SEAN (1880-1964)

The major collection of manuscripts, and typescript drafts of plays and prose
writings is in the Berg Collection, New York Public Library. Important letters
are in the Cornell University and Texas University Libraries.

2339 Adelman, Irving, and Rita Dworkin. MODERN DRAMA; A CHECKLIST OF CRITICAL LITERATURE ON 20TH CENTURY PLAYS. Metuchen, N.J.: Scarecrow Press, 1967. Pp. 206-10.

   Secondary selected.

2340 Armstrong, William A. SEAN O'CASEY. Writers and Their Works, no. 198. 2nd ed. London: Longmans, Green, 1971. Pp. 33-38.

   Primary. Secondary selected.

2341 Ayling, Ronald, ed. SEAN O'CASEY. Modern Judgements Series. London: Macmillan, 1969. Pp. 261-69.

   Primary. Secondary selected.

2342 _____. "Sean O'Casey." THE NEW CAMBRIDGE BIBLIOGRAPHY OF ENGLISH LITERATURE. Vol. 4: 1900-1950. Ed. I.R. Willison. Cambridge: At the University Press, 1972. Cols. 879-85.

   Primary. Secondary selected.

2343 Ayling, Ronald, and Michael J. Durkan are completing a bibliography of the writings of Sean O'Casey for Macmillan, London.

2344 Brandstaedter, Otto. "Ein O'Casey-Bibliographie." ZEITSCHRIFT FUR ANGLISTIK AND AMERIKANISTIK (Berlin), 2 (1954), 240-54.

   Secondary.

2345 Breed, Paul F., and Florence M. Sniderman, comps. DRAMATIC CRITICISM INDEX; A BIBLIOGRAPHY OF COMMENTARIES ON PLAYWRIGHTS FROM IBSEN TO THE AVANT-GARDE. Detroit, Mich.: Gale Research Co., 1972. Pp. 459-70.

   Secondary selected.

2346 Carpenter, Charles A. "Sean O'Casey Studies Through 1964." MODERN DRAMA, 10 (May 1967), 17-23.

   Secondary.

2347 Coleman, Arthur, and Gary R. Tyler. DRAMA CRITICISM. Vol. I: A CHECKLIST OF INTERPRETATION SINCE 1940 OF ENGLISH AND AMERICAN PLAYS. Denver, Colo.: Alan Swallow, 1966. Pp. 154-56.

   Secondary selected.

2348 Levidova, I.M., and V.M. Parchevskaia. SEAN O'CASEY BIBLIOGRAPHIC GUIDE. Writers of Foreign Countries Series. Moscow: Knigna

Publishing House, 1964.

Primary. Secondary. In Russian.

2349 Mikhail, E.H. SEAN O'CASEY: A BIBLIOGRAPHY OF CRITICISM. London: Macmillan, 1972.

Primary. Secondary.

2350 Palmer, Helen H., and Anne Jane Dyson. EUROPEAN DRAMA CRITICISM. Hamden, Conn.: Shoe String Press, 1968. Pp. 300-305.

Secondary selected.

2351 Salem, James M. A GUIDE TO CRITICAL REVIEWS. Part III: BRITISH AND CONTINENTAL DRAMA FROM IBSEN TO PINTER. Metuchen, N.J.: Scarecrow Press, 1968. Pp. 174-78.

Secondary selected.

## O'KELLY, SEAMUS (1881-1918)

2352 Breed, Paul F., and Florence M. Sniderman, comps. DRAMATIC CRITICISM INDEX; A BIBLIOGRAPHY OF COMMENTARIES ON PLAYWRIGHTS FROM IBSEN TO THE AVANT-GARDE. Detroit, Mich.: Gale Research Co., 1972. Pp. 476-77.

Secondary selected.

2353 O'Hegarty, Patrick Sarsfield. "Bibliographies of 1916 and the Irish Revolution, IV. Seamus O'Kelly." DUBLIN MAGAZINE, 9 (October-December 1934), 47-51.

Primary, with bibliographical notes.

2354 Willison, I.R., ed. THE NEW CAMBRIDGE BIBLIOGRAPHY OF ENGLISH LITERATURE. Vol. 4: 1900-1950. Cambridge: At the University Press, 1972. Cols. 687-88.

Primary. Secondary selected.

## O'RIORDAN, CONAL HOLMES O'CONNELL (1874-1950)

2355 Bateson, F.W., ed. THE CAMBRIDGE BIBLIOGRAPHY OF ENGLISH LITERATURE. Vol. III: 1800-1900. Cambridge: At the University Press, 1940. Col. 1965.

Primary.

2356 Longaker, Mark, and Edwin C. Bolles. CONTEMPORARY ENGLISH LIT-

ERATURE. New York: Appleton-Century-Crofts, 1953. Pp. 62-63.

Primary.

2357 Millett, Fred B. CONTEMPORARY BRITISH LITERATURE; A CRITICAL
SURVEY AND 232 AUTHOR BIBLIOGRAPHIES. New York: Harcourt,
Brace, 1935. Pp. 406-7.

Primary. Secondary selected.

## PHILLIPS, STEPHEN (1868-1915)

2358 Batho, Edith Clara, and Bonamy Dobree. THE VICTORIANS AND AFTER,
1830-1914. Introductions to English Literature, vol. IV. General ed.
Bonamy Dobree. London: Cresset Press; New York: R.M. McBride,
1938. Pp. 266-67.

Primary.

2359 Hale, Edward Everett, Jr. DRAMATISTS OF TODAY. New York:
Henry Holt; London: G. Bell, 1905. P. 220.

Plays. Brief annotations.

2360 Longaker, Mark, and Edwin C. Bolles. CONTEMPORARY ENGLISH LIT-
ERATURE. New York: Appleton-Century-Crofts, 1953. Pp. 107-9.

Primary. Secondary selected.

2361 Milliken, Clara A. "Reading List on Modern Dramatists: Stephen Phillips." BULLETIN OF BIBLIOGRAPHY, 5 (1907), 51.

Primary. Secondary.

2362 Salem, James M. A GUIDE TO CRITICAL REVIEWS. Part III: BRITISH
AND CONTINENTAL DRAMA FROM IBSEN TO PINTER. Metuchen, N.J.:
Scarecrow Press, 1968. P. 185.

Secondary selected.

2363 Temple, Ruth Z., and Martin Tucker. TWENTIETH CENTURY BRITISH
LITERATURE; A REFERENCE GUIDE AND BIBLIOGRAPHY. New York:
Frederick Ungar, 1968. P. 215.

Primary. Secondary selected.

2364 Watson, George, ed. THE NEW CAMBRIDGE BIBLIOGRAPHY OF EN-
GLISH LITERATURE. Vol. 3: 1800-1900. Cambridge: At the University Press, 1969. Cols. 1194-96.

Primary. Secondary selected.

## PHILLPOTTS, EDEN (1862-1960)

2365 Girvan, Waveney. EDEN PHILLPOTTS; AN ASSESSMENT AND A TRIB-
UTE. London: Hutchinson, 1953. Pp. 153-59.

English first editions.

2366 Hinton, Percival. EDEN PHILLPOTTS; A BIBLIOGRAPHY OF FIRST EDI-
TIONS. Birmingham, Eng.: Greville Worthington, 1931.

Primary, 1888-1931.

2367 Millett, Fred B. CONTEMPORARY BRITISH LITERATURE; A CRITICAL
SURVEY AND 232 AUTHOR BIBLIOGRAPHIES. New York: Harcourt,
Brace, 1935. Pp. 410-13.

Primary. Secondary selected.

2368 Temple, Ruth Z., and Martin Tucker. TWENTIETH CENTURY BRITISH
LITERATURE; A REFERENCE GUIDE AND BIBLIOGRAPHY. New York:
Frederick Ungar, 1968. Pp. 215-16.

Primary selected. Secondary selected.

2369 Willison, I.R., ed. THE NEW CAMBRIDGE BIBLIOGRAPHY OF ENGLISH
LITERATURE. Vol. 4: 1900-1950. Cambridge: At the University Press,
1972. Cols. 699-704.

Primary. Secondary selected.

## PINERO, [SIR] ARTHUR WING (1855-1934)

2370 Adelman, Irving, and Rita Dworkin. MODERN DRAMA; A CHECKLIST
OF CRITICAL LITERATURE ON 20TH CENTURY PLAYS. Metuchen, N.J.:
Scarecrow Press, 1967. Pp. 239-41.

Secondary selected.

2371 Breed, Paul F., and Florence M. Sniderman, comps. DRAMATIC CRITI-
CISM INDEX; A BIBLIOGRAPHY OF COMMENTARIES ON PLAYWRIGHTS
FROM IBSEN TO THE AVANT-GARDE. Detroit, Mich.: Gale Research
Co., 1972. Pp. 532-33.

Secondary selected.

2372 Coleman, Arthur, and Gary R. Tyler. DRAMA CRITICISM. Vol. I: A
CHECKLIST OF INTERPRETATION SINCE 1940 OF ENGLISH AND AMERI-
CAN PLAYS. Denver, Colo.: Alan Swallow, 1966. Pp. 174-75.

Secondary selected.

2373 Dunkel, Wilbur Dwight. SIR ARTHUR WING PINERO; A CRITICAL BIOG-
RAPHY WITH LETTERS. Chicago: University of Chicago Press, 1941.
Pp. 137-38.

> Cogent discussion of sources of primary and secondary bibliog-
> raphy.

2374 Fyfe, H. Hamilton. ARTHUR WING PINERO, PLAYWRIGHT: A STUDY.
London: Greening, 1902. Pp. 232-50.

> First productions of plays, 1877-1901.

2375 Hale, Edward Everett, Jr. DRAMATISTS OF TODAY. London: G. Bell,
1906. Pp. 212-27.

> First productions of plays, 1877-1904.

2376 Longaker, Mark, and Edwin C. Bolles. CONTEMPORARY ENGLISH LIT-
ERATURE. New York: Appleton-Century-Crofts, 1953. Pp. 393-95.

> Primary. Secondary selected.

2377 Millett, Fred B. CONTEMPORARY BRITISH LITERATURE; A CRITICAL
SURVEY AND 232 AUTHOR BIBLIOGRAPHIES. New York: Harcourt,
Brace, 1935. Pp. 415-17.

> Primary. Secondary selected.

2378 Palmer, Helen H., and Anne Jane Dyson. EUROPEAN DRAMA CRITI-
CISM. Hamden, Conn.: Shoe String Press, 1968. Pp. 311-14.

> Secondary selected.

2379 Salem, James M. A GUIDE TO CRITICAL REVIEWS. Part III: BRITISH
AND CONTINENTAL DRAMA FROM IBSEN TO PINTER. Metuchen, N.J.:
Scarecrow Press, 1968. Pp. 185-88.

> Secondary selected.

2380 Temple, Ruth Z., and Martin Tucker. TWENTIETH CENTURY BRITISH
LITERATURE; A REFERENCE GUIDE AND BIBLIOGRAPHY. New York:
Frederick Ungar, 1968. Pp. 216-17.

> Primary. Secondary selected.

2381 Walter, Frank K. "Reading List on Arthur Wing Pinero." BULLETIN OF
BIBLIOGRAPHY, 6 (1912), 298-300.

> Primary. Secondary selected.

2382 Watson, George, ed. THE NEW CAMBRIDGE BIBLIOGRAPHY OF ENGLISH

LITERATURE. Vol. 3: 1800–1900. Cambridge: At the University Press, 1969. Cols. 1166–69.

Primary. Secondary selected.

## PRIESTLEY, J[OHN]. B[OYNTON]. (1894–    )

A substantial collection of Priestley typescripts is in the University of Texas Humanities Research Center Library.

2383 Adelman, Irving, and Rita Dworkin. MODERN DRAMA; A CHECKLIST OF CRITICAL LITERATURE ON 20TH CENTURY PLAYS. Metuchen, N.J.: Scarecrow Press, 1967. Pp. 249–50.

Secondary selected.

2384 Breed, Paul F., and Florence M. Sniderman, comps. DRAMATIC CRITI-CISM INDEX; A BIBLIOGRAPHY OF COMMENTARIES ON PLAYWRIGHTS FROM IBSEN TO THE AVANT-GARDE. Detroit, Mich.: Gale Research Co., 1972. Pp. 551–53.

Secondary selected.

2385 Brown, Ivor. J.B. PRIESTLEY. Writers and Their Works, no. 84. London: Longmans, Green, 1957. Pp. 35–39.

Primary.

2386 Coleman, Arthur, and Gary R. Tyler. DRAMA CRITICISM. Vol. I: A CHECKLIST OF INTERPRETATION SINCE 1940 OF ENGLISH AND AMERI-CAN PLAYS. Denver, Colo.: Alan Swallow, 1966. Pp. 178–79.

Secondary selected.

2387 Day, A.E. "J.B. Priestley: An Interim Bibliography."

Unpublished typescript in the University of Texas Library. Pri-mary.

2388 Evans, Gareth L. J.B. PRIESTLEY--THE DRAMATIST. London: Heine-mann, 1964. Pp. 226–27.

Secondary.

2389 Jones, L[eonard]. A. "The First Editions of Priestley." BOOKMAN (London), 80 (1931).

Primary.

2390 Loeb, Ladislaus. MENSCH UND GESELLSCHAFT BEI J.B. PRIESTLEY.

Bern: A. Francke Verlag, 1962. Pp. 215-22.

Primary. Secondary.

2391 Palmer, Helen H., and Anne Jane Dyson. EUROPEAN DRAMA CRITI-
CISM. Hamden, Conn.: Shoe String Press, 1968. Pp. 326-31.

Secondary selected.

2392 Salem, James M. A GUIDE TO CRITICAL REVIEWS. Part III: BRITISH
AND CONTINENTAL DRAMA FROM IBSEN TO PINTER. Metuchen, N.J.:
Scarecrow Press, 1968. Pp. 193-96.

Secondary selected.

2393 Teagarden, Lucetta J. "The J.B. Priestley Collection [at the University
of Texas]." LIBRARY CHRONICLE OF THE UNIVERSITY OF TEXAS, 7,
no. 3 (1963), 27-32.

Descriptive essay of this extensive collection.

2394 _____. J.B. PRIESTLEY: AN EXHIBITION OF BOOKS AND MANU-
SCRIPTS. Austin: University of Texas, 1963.

Selective descriptive list.

2395 Willison, I.R., ed. THE NEW CAMBRIDGE BIBLIOGRAPHY OF ENGLISH
LITERATURE. Vol. 4: 1900-1950. Cambridge: At the University Press,
1972. Cols. 712-17.

Primary. Secondary selected.

## RATTIGAN, TERENCE [MERVYN] (1911-    )

2396 Adelman, Irving, and Rita Dworkin. MODERN DRAMA: A CHECKLIST
OF CRITICAL LITERATURE ON 20TH CENTURY PLAYS. Metuchen, N.J.:
Scarecrow Press, 1967. P. 250.

Secondary selected.

2397 Breed, Paul F., and Florence M. Sniderman, comps. DRAMATIC CRITI-
CISM INDEX; A BIBLIOGRAPHY OF COMMENTARIES ON PLAYWRIGHTS
FROM IBSEN TO THE AVANT-GARDE. Detroit, Mich.: Gale Research
Co., 1972. Pp. 555-56.

Secondary selected.

2398 Coleman, Arthur, and Gary R. Tyler. DRAMA CRITICISM. Vol. I: A
CHECKLIST OF INTERPRETATION SINCE 1940 OF ENGLISH AND AMERI-
CAN PLAYS. Denver, Colo.: Alan Swallow, 1966. P. 179.

Secondary. Selected.

2399 Daiches, David. THE PRESENT AGE, AFTER 1920. Introductions to English Literature, vol. V. General ed. Bonamy Dobree. London: Cresset Press; Bloomington: Indiana University Press, 1958. P. 331.

First productions.

2400 Palmer, Helen H., and Anne Jane Dyson. EUROPEAN DRAMA CRITICISM. Hamden, Conn.: Shoe String Press, 1968. Pp. 340–45.

Secondary. Selected.

2401 Salem, James M. A GUIDE TO CRITICAL REVIEWS. Part III: BRITISH AND CONTINENTAL DRAMA FROM IBSEN TO PINTER. Metuchen, N.J.: Scarecrow Press, 1968. Pp. 197–201.

Secondary selected.

2402 Temple, Ruth Z., and Martin Tucker. TWENTIETH CENTURY BRITISH LITERATURE; A REFERENCE GUIDE AND BIBLIOGRAPHY. New York: Frederick Ungar, 1968. Pp. 197–201.

Secondary selected.

2403 Willison, I.R., ed. THE NEW CAMBRIDGE BIBLIOGRAPHY OF ENGLISH LITERATURE. Vol. 4: 1900–1950. Cambridge: At the University Press, 1972. Cols. 976–77.

Primary. Secondary selected.

## ROBINSON, [ESME STUART] LENNOX (1886-1958)

2404 Breed, Paul F., and Florence M. Sniderman, comps. DRAMATIC CRITICISM INDEX; A BIBLIOGRAPHY OF COMMENTARIES ON PLAYWRIGHTS FROM IBSEN TO THE AVANT-GARDE. Detroit, Mich.: Gale Research Co., 1972. Pp. 565–66.

Secondary selected.

2405 Longaker, Mark, and Edwin C. Bolles. CONTEMPORARY ENGLISH LITERATURE. New York: Appleton-Century-Crofts, 1953. Pp. 61–62.

Primary.

2406 Millett, Fred B. CONTEMPORARY BRITISH LITERATURE; A CRITICAL SURVEY AND 232 AUTHOR BIBLIOGRAPHIES. New York: Harcourt, Brace, 1935. Pp. 441–42.

Primary. Secondary selected.

2407 O'Neill, Michael J. LENNOX ROBINSON. New York: Twayne Publishers, 1964. Pp. 15–21, 181–84.

Primary. Secondary annotated.

2408 Salem, James M. A GUIDE TO CRITICAL REVIEWS. Part III: BRITISH
AND CONTINENTAL DRAMA FROM IBSEN TO PINTER. Metuchen, N.J.:
Scarecrow Press, 1968. Pp. 201-3.

Secondary selected.

2409 Spinner, Kaspar. DIE ALTE DAME SAGT: NEIN! DREI IRISCHE DRA-
MATIKER. LENNOX ROBINSON. SEAN O'CASEY. DENIS JOHN-
STON. Bern: A. Francke Verlag, 1961. Pp. 207-8.

Primary.

2410 Temple, Ruth Z., and Martin Tucker. TWENTIETH CENTURY BRITISH
LITERATURE A REFERENCE GUIDE AND BIBLIOGRAPHY. New York:
Frederick Ungar, 1968. P. 223.

Primary. Secondary selected.

2411 Watson, George, ed. THE NEW CAMBRIDGE BIBLIOGRAPHY OF EN-
GLISH LITERATURE. Vol. 3: 1800-1900. Cambridge: At the University
Press, 1969. Cols. 1943-44.

Primary. Secondary selected.

## RUSSELL, GEORGE WILLIAM [A E ] (1867-1935)

Most of AE's manuscripts and letters are in the National Library, Dublin; Indiana
University; Colby College; Yale University; County Museum Armagh; Congres-
sional Library, Washington; Harvard University; and New York Public Library.

2412 Denson, Alan. PRINTED WRITINGS BY GEORGE WILLIAM RUSSELL
(AE); A BIBLIOGRAPHY WITH SOME NOTES ON HIS PICTURES AND
PORTRAITS. Evanston, Ill.: Northwestern University Press, 1961.

Primary. Secondary selected.

2413 Kindilien, Caroline T. "George William Russell ('AE') and the Colby
Collection." COLBY LIBRARY QUARTERLY, 4 (May 1955), 21-24, 31-
55.

The George Russell Collection at Colby College.

2414 Longaker, Mark, and Edwin C. Bolles. CONTEMPORARY ENGLISH LIT-
ERATURE. New York: Appleton-Century Crofts, 1953. Pp. 43-45.

Primary. Secondary selected.

2415 Millett, Fred B. CONTEMPORARY BRITISH LITERATURE; A CRITICAL
SURVEY AND 232 AUTHOR BIBLIOGRAPHIES. New York: Harcourt,
Brace, 1935. Pp. 446-48.

Primary. Secondary selected.

2416 Temple, Ruth Z., and Martin Tucker. TWENTIETH CENTURY BRITISH
LITERATURE; A REFERENCE GUIDE AND BIBLIOGRAPHY. New York:
Frederick Ungar, 1968. Pp. 225-26.

Primary. Secondary selected.

2417 Watson, George, ed. THE NEW CAMBRIDGE BIBLIOGRAPHY OF EN-
GLISH LITERATURE. Vol. 3: 1800-1900. Cambridge: At the University
Press, 1969. Cols. 1912-16.

Primary. Secondary selected.

## SHAW, GEORGE BERNARD (1856-1950)

Most of Shaw's manuscripts are in the British Museum.

2418 Adelman, Irving, and Rita Dworkin. MODERN DRAMA; A CHECKLIST
OF CRITICAL LITERATURE ON 20TH CENTURY PLAYS. Metuchen, N.J.:
Scarecrow Press, 1967. Pp. 264-89.

Secondary selected.

2419 Bosworth, R.F. "Shaw Recordings at the B.B.C.: SHAW REVIEW, 7 (May
1964), 42-46.

An essay describing ten recordings.

2420 Breed, Paul F., and Florence M. Sniderman, comps. DRAMATIC CRITI-
CISM INDEX; A BIBLIOGRAPHY OF COMMENTARIES ON PLAYWRIGHTS
FROM IBSEN TO THE AVANT-GARDE. Detroit, Mich.: Gale Research
Co., 1972. Pp. 605-56.

Secondary selected.

2421 Broad, C. Lewis, and Violet M. Broad. DICTIONARY TO THE PLAYS
AND NOVELS OF BERNARD SHAW, WITH BIBLIOGRAPHY OF HIS WORKS
AND OF THE LITERATURE CONCERNING HIM, WITH A RECORD OF
THE PRINCIPAL SHAVIAN PLAY PRODUCTIONS. London: A. and C.
Block; New York: Macmillan, 1929. Pp. 87-112.

Chronological list of primary works. Chronological lists of
other writings and of reported speeches. Play productions.

2422 Coleman, Arthur, and Gary R. Tyler. DRAMA CRITICISM. Vol. I: A

CHECKLIST OF INTERPRETATION SINCE 1940 OF ENGLISH AND AMERI-CAN PLAYS. Denver, Colo.: Alan Swallow, 1966. Pp. 186-95.

Secondary selected.

2423 Cutler, Bradley D., and Villa Stiles. MODERN BRITISH AUTHORS; THEIR FIRST EDITIONS. New York: Greenberg; London: G. Allen, 1930; rpt. Folcroft, Pa.: Folcroft Press, 1969. Pp. 125-31.

Primary.

2424 Farley, Earl, and Marvin Carlson. "George Bernard Shaw: A Selected Bibliography (1945-1955)." MODERN DRAMA, September 1959, pp. 188-202; December 1959, pp. 295-325.

The September issue lists secondary books, the December secondary periodicals.

2425 Heydet, Xavier. "Bibliographisches." SHAW-KOMPENDIUM. Paris, 1936, pp. 151-224.

Primary. Secondary selected.

2426 Keough, Lawrence C. "George Bernard Shaw, 1946-1955: A Selected Bibliography." BULLETIN OF BIBLIOGRAPHY, 22 (1959), 224-26; 23 (1960), 20-24, 36-41.

Primary. Secondary.

2427 Laurence, Dan H. has a Shaw bibliography in preparation.

2428 Lewis, Arthur O., Jr., and Stanley Weintraub. "Bernard Shaw--Aspects and Problems of Research." SHAW REVIEW, 3 (1960), 18-26.

Survey of secondary bibliographies.

2429 Lowenstein, F.E. THE REHEARSAL COPIES OF BERNARD SHAW'S PLAYS. London: Reinhardt and Evans, 1950.

Primary. Extensive bibliographical, textual, and historical notes.

2430 Milliken, Clara A. "Reading List of Modern Dramatists . . . Shaw." BULLETIN OF BIBLIOGRAPHY, 5 (October 1907), 52-53.

Secondary.

2431 Palmer, Helen H., and Anne Jane Dyson. EUROPEAN DRAMA CRITI-CISM. Hamden, Conn.: Shoe String Press, 1968. Pp. 368-88.

Secondary selected.

2432 Salem, James M. A GUIDE TO CRITICAL REVIEWS. Part III: BRITISH
AND CONTINENTAL DRAMA FROM IBSEN TO PINTER. Metuchen, N.J.:
Scarecrow Press, 1968. Pp. 213-25.

> Secondary selected.

2433 SHAW BULLETIN, 1-2 (1951-59); title changed to SHAW REVIEW, 3
(1960-- ).

> Almost every issue contains "A Continuing Check-List of Sha-
> viana" by various editors. Primary. Secondary.

2434 Smith, Winifred. "Bernard Shaw and His Critics (1892-1938)." POET
LORE, 47 (1941), 76-83.

> Secondary selected.

2435 Spencer, T[heodore]. J. "An Annotated Check-List of Criticism of the
post-SAINT JOAN Plays." SHAW REVIEW, 2 (1959), 45-48.

> Secondary selected.

2436 Ward, Alfred C. BERNARD SHAW. Writers and Their Work, no. 1.
London: Longmans, Green, 1951. Pp. 41-56.

> Primary.

2437 Wells, Geoffrey H. A BIBLIOGRAPHY OF THE BOOKS AND PAMPHLETS
OF GEORGE BERNARD SHAW. London: Bookman's Journal, 1928.

> Reprinted from BOOKMAN'S JOURNAL, March 1925, and
> April 1925. Primary.

## SHERRIFF, ROBERT CEDRIC (1896-1975)

2438 Breed, Paul F., and Florence M. Sniderman, comps. DRAMATIC CRITI-
CISM INDEX; A BIBLIOGRAPHY OF COMMENTARIES ON PLAYWRIGHTS
FROM IBSEN TO THE AVANT-GARDE. Detroit, Mich.: Gale Research
Co., 1972. P. 657.

> Secondary selected.

2439 Daiches, David. THE PRESENT AGE, AFTER 1920. Introductions to English Literature, vol. V. General ed. Bonamy Dobree. London: Cresset
Press; Bloomington: Indiana University Press, 1958. P. 327.

> Primary.

2440 Palmer, Helen H., and Anne Jane Dyson. EUROPEAN DRAMA CRITI-
CISM. Hamden, Conn.: Shoe String Press, 1968. Pp. 391-93.

> Secondary selected.

2441 Salem, James M. A GUIDE TO CRITICAL REVIEW. Part III: BRITISH AND CONTINENTAL DRAMA FROM IBSEN TO PINTER. Metuchen, N.J.: Scarecrow Press, 1968. Pp. 235-36.

Secondary selected.

2442 Temple, Ruth Z., and Martin Tucker. TWENTIETH CENTURY BRITISH LITERATURE; A REFERENCE GUIDE AND BIBLIOGRAPHY. New York: Frederick Ungar, 1968. P. 230.

Primary. Secondary selected.

2443 Willison, I.R., ed. THE NEW CAMBRIDGE BIBLIOGRAPHY OF ENGLISH LITERATURE. Vol. 4: 1900-1950. Cambridge: At the University Press, 1972. Col. 979.

Primary. Secondary selected.

## SHIELS, GEORGE [GEORGE MORSHIEL] (1886-1949)

2444 Breed, Paul F., and Florence M. Sniderman, comps. DRAMATIC CRITI-CISM INDEX; A BIBLIOGRAPHY OF COMMENTARIES ON PLAYWRIGHTS FROM IBSEN TO THE AVANT-GARDE. Detroit, Mich.: Gale Research Co., 1972. Pp. 661-62.

Secondary selected.

2445 Salem, James M. A GUIDE TO CRITICAL REVIEWS. Part III: BRITISH AND CONTINENTAL DRAMA FROM IBSEN TO PINTER. Metuchen, N.J.: Scarecrow Press, 1968. Pp. 236-37.

Secondary selected.

2446 Willison, I.R., ed. THE NEW CAMBRIDGE BIBLIOGRAPHY OF ENGLISH LITERATURE. Vol. 4: 1900-1950. Cambridge: At the University Press, 1972. Cols. 979-80.

Primary. Secondary selected.

## SMITH, DODIE [DOROTHY GLADYS SMITH] (1896-    )

2447 Breed, Paul F., and Florence M. Sniderman, comps. DRAMATIC CRITI-CISM INDEX; A BIBLIOGRAPHY OF COMMENTARIES ON PLAYWRIGHTS FROM IBSEN TO THE AVANT-GARDE. Detroit, Mich.: Gale Research Co., 1972. P. 664.

Secondary selected.

2448 Salem, James M. A GUIDE TO CRITICAL REVIEWS. Part III: BRITISH AND CONTINENTAL DRAMA FROM IBSEN TO PINTER. Metuchen, N.J.:

Scarecrow Press, 1968. Pp. 238-39.

Secondary selected.

2449 Willison, I.R., ed. THE NEW CAMBRIDGE BIBLIOGRAPHY OF ENGLISH LITERATURE. Vol. 4: 1900-1950. Cambridge: At the University Press, 1972. Cols. 979-80.

Primary. Secondary selected.

## SUTRO, ALFRED (1863-1933)

2450 Millett, Fred B. CONTEMPORARY BRITISH LITERATURE; A CRITICAL SURVEY AND 232 AUTHOR BIBLIOGRAPHIES. New York: Harcourt, Brace, 1935. Pp. 483-84.

Primary. Secondary selected.

2451 Temple, Ruth Z., and Martin Tucker. TWENTIETH CENTURY BRITISH LITERATURE; A REFERENCE GUIDE AND BIBLIOGRAPHY. New York: Frederick Ungar, 1968. Pp. 237-38.

Primary.

2452 Willison, I.R., ed. THE NEW CAMBRIDGE BIBLIOGRAPHY OF ENGLISH LITERATURE. Vol. 4: 1900-1950. Cambridge: At the University Press, 1972. Cols. 983-84.

Primary. Secondary selected.

## SYNGE, JOHN MILLINGTON (1871-1909)

Synge's manuscripts, diaries, notebooks, etc., are in Dublin, in the possession of his estate. Some letters are in the Berg Collection of the New York Public Library.

2453 Adelman, Irving, and Rita Dworkin. MODERN DRAMA; A CHECKLIST OF CRITICAL LITERATURE ON 20TH CENTURY PLAYS. Metuchen, N.J.: Scarecrow Press, 1967. Pp. 306-9.

Secondary selected.

2454 Bourgeois, Maurice. JOHN MILLINGTON SYNGE AND THE IRISH THEATRE. London: Constable, 1913; rpt. New York: Benjamin Blom, 1965. Pp. 251-314.

Primary. Secondary annotated.

2455 Breed, Paul F., and Florence M. Sniderman, comps. DRAMATIC CRITICISM INDEX; A BIBLIOGRAPHY OF COMMENTARIES ON PLAYWRIGHTS

FROM IBSEN TO THE AVANT-GARDE. Detroit, Mich.: Gale Research Co., 1972. Pp. 685-93.

Secondary selected.

2456 Coleman, Arthur, and Gary R. Tyler. DRAMA CRITICISM. Vol. I: A CHECKLIST OF INTERPRETATION SINCE 1940 OF ENGLISH AND AMERICAN PLAYS. Denver, Colo.: Alan Swallow, 1966. Pp. 202-5.

Secondary selected.

2457 Gerstenberger, Donna. JOHN MILLINGTON SYNGE. New York: Twayne Publishers, 1964. Pp. 142-52.

Primary. Secondary annotated.

2458 Greene, David H., and E.M. Stephens. "A List of the Published Writings of Synge." JOHN MILLINGTON SYNGE, 1871-1909. New York: Macmillan, 1959. Pp. 308-10.

2459 McGirr, Alice Thurston. "Reading List on John Millington Synge." BULLETIN OF BIBLIOGRAPHY, 7 (1913), 114-15.

Secondary.

2460 MacPhail, Ian, and M. Pollard. JOHN MILLINGTON SYNGE 1871-1909: A CATALOGUE OF AN EXHIBITION HELD AT TRINITY COLLEGE LIBRARY DUBLIN ON THE OCCASION OF THE FIFTIETH ANNIVERSARY OF HIS DEATH. Dublin: Dolmen Press, 1959.

Primary, with bibliographical notes. List of periodical contributions, annotated. List of manuscripts.

2461 _____. "John Millington Synge: Some Bibliographical Notes." IRISH BOOK, 1 (1960), 3-10.

Surveys the bibliographical problems connected with Synge.

2462 Mikhail, E.H. "Sixty Years of Synge Criticism, 1907-1967; A Selective Bibliography." BULLETIN OF BIBLIOGRAPHY, 27 (January-March 1970), 11-13; 27 (April-June 1970), 53-56.

Secondary.

2463 _____. J.M. SYNGE; A BIBLIOGRAPHY OF CRITICISM. London: Macmillan, 1975.

Secondary.

2464 Palmer, Helen H., and Anne Jane Dyson. EUROPEAN DRAMA CRITICISM. Hamden, Conn.: Shoe String Press, 1968. Pp. 407-10.

Secondary selected.

2465 Price, Alan. SYNGE AND ANGLO-IRISH DRAMA. London: Methuen, 1961. Pp. 229-31.

Secondary.

2466 Salem, James M. A GUIDE TO CRITICAL REVIEWS. Part III: BRITISH AND CONTINENTAL DRAMA FROM IBSEN TO PINTER. Metuchen, N.J.: Scarecrow Press, 1968. Pp. 244-46.

Secondary selected.

2467 Watson, George, ed. THE NEW CAMBRIDGE BIBLIOGRAPHY OF EN-GLISH LITERATURE. Vol. 3: 1800-1900. Cambridge: At the University Press, 1969. Cols. 1934-38.

Primary. Secondary selected.

## VAN DRUTEN, JOHN [WILLIAM] (1901-57)

2468 Adelman, Irving, and Rita Dworkin. MODERN DRAMA; A CHECKLIST OF CRITICAL LITERATURE ON 20TH CENTURY PLAYS. Metuchen, N.J.: Scarecrow Press, 1967. Pp. 314-15.

Secondary selected.

2469 Breed, Paul F., and Florence M. Sniderman, comps. DRAMATIC CRITI-CISM INDEX; A BIBLIOGRAPHY OF COMMENTARIES ON PLAYWRIGHTS FROM IBSEN TO THE AVANT-GARDE. Detroit, Mich.: Gale Research Co., 1972. P. 704.

Secondary selected.

2470 Daiches, David. THE PRESENT AGE, AFTER 1920. Introductions to En-glish Literature, vol. V. General ed. Bonamy Dobree. London: Cresset Press; Bloomington: Indiana University Press, 1958. Pp. 329-30.

Primary.

2471 Temple, Ruth Z., and Martin Tucker. TWENTIETH CENTURY BRITISH LITERATURE; A REFERENCE GUIDE AND BIBLIOGRAPHY. New York: Frederick Ungar, 1968. P. 245.

Primary. Secondary selected.

2472 Willison, I.R., ed. THE NEW CAMBRIDGE BIBLIOGRAPHY OF ENGLISH LITERATURE. Vol. 4: 1900-1950. Cambridge: At the University Press, 1972. Cols. 986-88.

Primary. Secondary selected.

## VANE, SUTTON (1888-1963)

2473 Breed, Paul F., and Florence M. Sniderman, comps. DRAMATIC CRITI-
CISM INDEX; A BIBLIOGRAPHY OF COMMENTARIES ON PLAYWRIGHTS
FROM IBSEN TO THE AVANT-GARDE. Detroit, Mich.: Gale Research
Co., 1972. P. 704.

   Secondary selected.

2474 Coleman, Arthur, and Gary R. Tyler. DRAMA CRITICISM. Vol. I: A
CHECKLIST OF INTERPRETATION SINCE 1940 OF ENGLISH AND AMERI-
CAN PLAYS. Denver, Colo.: Alan Swallow, 1966. P. 212.

   Secondary selected.

2475 Palmer, Helen H., and Anne Jane Dyson. EUROPEAN DRAMA CRITICISM.
Hamden, Conn.: Shoe String Press, 1968. P. 417.

   Secondary selected.

2476 Salem, James M. A GUIDE TO CRITICAL REVIEWS. Part III: BRITISH
AND CONTINENTAL DRAMA FROM IBSEN TO PINTER. Metuchen, N.J.:
Scarecrow Press, 1968. Pp. 253-54.

   Secondary selected.

2477 Willison, I.R., ed. THE NEW CAMBRIDGE BIBLIOGRAPHY OF ENGLISH
LITERATURE. Vol. 4: 1900-1950. Cambridge: At the University Press,
1972. Col. 988.

   Primary.

## WILLIAMS, EMLYN (1905-    )

2478 Adelman, Irving, and Rita Dworkin. MODERN DRAMA; A CHECKLIST
OF CRITICAL LITERATURE ON 20TH CENTURY PLAYS. Metuchen, N.J.:
Scarecrow Press, 1967. P. 324.

   Secondary selected.

2479 Breed, Paul F., and Florence M. Sniderman, comps. DRAMATIC CRITI-
CISM INDEX; A BIBLIOGRAPHY OF COMMENTARIES ON PLAYWRIGHTS
FROM IBSEN TO THE AVANT-GARDE. Detroit, Mich.: Gale Research
Co., 1972. Pp. 738-39.

   Secondary selected.

2480 Coleman, Arthur, and Gary R. Tyler. DRAMA CRITICISM. Vol. I: A
CHECKLIST OF INTERPRETATION SINCE 1940 OF ENGLISH AND AMERI-
CAN PLAYS. Denver, Colo.: Alan Swallow, 1966. P. 224.

Secondary selected.

2481 Longaker, Mark, and Edwin C. Bolles. CONTEMPORARY ENGLISH LIT-
ERATURE. New York: Appleton-Century-Crofts, 1953. P. 491.

Primary.

2482 Palmer, Helen H., and Anne Jane Dyson. EUROPEAN DRAMA CRITI-
CISM. Hamden, Conn.: Shoe String Press, 1968. Pp. 428-30.

Secondary selected.

2483 Salem, James M. A GUIDE TO CRITICAL REVIEWS. Part III: BRITISH
AND CONTINENTAL DRAMA FROM IBSEN TO PINTER. Metuchen, N.J.:
Scarecrow Press, 1968. Pp. 263-65.

Secondary selected.

2484 Temple, Ruth Z., and Martin Tucker. TWENTIETH CENTURY BRITISH
LITERATURE; A REFERENCE GUIDE AND BIBLIOGRAPHY. New York:
Frederick Ungar, 1968. P. 252.

Primary. Secondary selected.

## YEATS, WILLIAM BUTLER (1865-1939)

Most of Yeats's manuscripts and personal papers are in the possession of his family. There are manuscripts and letters in the National Library Dublin, the Berg
Collection of the New York Public Library, and the University of Texas.

2485 Adams, Hazard. "Yeats Scholarship and Criticism: A Review of Research."
TEXAS STUDIES IN LITERATURE AND LANGUAGE, 3 (Winter 1962),
439-51.

Essay-survey of primary material and secondary writings.

2486 Adelman, Irving, and Rita Dworkin. MODERN DRAMA; A CHECKLIST
OF CRITICAL LITERATURE ON 20TH CENTURY PLAYS. Metuchen, N.J.:
Scarecrow Press, 1967. Pp. 332-40.

Secondary selected.

2487 Alspach, Russell K. "Additions to Allan Wade's Bibliography of W.B.
Yeats." IRISH BOOK, 2, nos. 3-4 (1963), 91-114.

2488 Breed, Paul F., and Florence M. Sniderman, comps. DRAMATIC CRITI-
CISM INDEX; A BIBLIOGRAPHY OF COMMENTARIES ON PLAYWRIGHTS
FROM IBSEN TO THE AVANT-GARDE. Detroit, Mich.: Gale Research
Co., 1972. Pp. 762-76.

Secondary selected.

2489 Coleman, Arthur, and Gary R. Tyler. DRAMA CRITICISM. Vol. I: A CHECKLIST OF INTERPRETATION SINCE 1940 OF ENGLISH AND AMERICAN PLAYS. Denver, Colo.: Alan Swallow, 1966. Pp. 232-35.

Secondary selected.

2490 Cross, K.G.W. "The Fascination of What's Difficult: A Survey of Yeats Criticism and Research." IN EXCITED REVERIE: A CENTENARY TRIBUTE TO WILLIAM BUTLER YEATS, 1865-1939. Ed. A. Norman Jeffares and K.G.W. Cross. London and New York: Macmillan, 1965. Pp. 315-37.

Essay on the history of Yeats scholarship.

2491 Cross, K.G.W., and R.T. Dunlop. A BIBLIOGRAPHY OF YEATS CRITICISM, 1887-1965. London: Macmillan, 1971.

Secondary.

2492 Cutler, Bradley D., and Villa Stiles. MODERN BRITISH AUTHORS; THEIR FIRST EDITIONS. New York: Greenberg; London: G. Allen, 1930; rpt. Folcroft, Pa.: Folcroft Press, 1969. Pp. 164-67.

Primary.

2493 Gerstenberger, Donna. "Yeats and the Theater: A Selected Bibliography." MODERN DRAMA, 6 (May 1963), 64-71.

Secondary selected.

2494 Jochum, K.P.S. W.B. YEATS'S PLAYS; AN ANNOTATED CHECKLIST OF CRITICISM. Saarbrucken: Anglistisches Institut der Universitat des Saarlandes, 1966.

Secondary.

2495 McGirr, Alice Thurston. "Reading List on William Butler Yeats." BULLETIN OF BIBLIOGRAPHY, 7 (1913), 82-83.

Secondary annotated.

2496 OhAodha, Michael. "Unrecorded Yeats Contributions to Periodicals." IRISH BOOK, 2, nos. 3-4 (1963), 129.

Primary.

2497 Palmer, Helen, H., and Anne Jane Dyson. EUROPEAN DRAMA CRITICISM. Hamden, Conn.: Shoe String Press, 1968. Pp. 433-39.

Secondary selected.

2498 Salem, James M. A GUIDE TO CRITICAL REVIEWS. Part III: BRITISH

AND CONTINENTAL DRAMA FROM IBSEN TO PINTER. Metuchen, N.J.: Scarecrow Press, 1968. P. 266.

Secondary selected.

2499 Saul, George B[randon]. "Thread to a Labyrinth: A Selective Bibliography in Yeats." BULLETIN OF THE NEW YORK PUBLIC LIBRARY, 58 (July 1954), 344-37.

A severely restricted list of books.

2500 _____. PROLEGOMENA TO THE STUDY OF YEATS'S PLAYS. Philadelphia: University of Pennsylvania Press, 1958; rpt., 1971.

Secondary.

2501 Schwartz, Jacob. 1100 OBSCURE POINTS: THE BIBLIOGRAPHIES OF 25 ENGLISH AND 21 AMERICAN AUTHORS. Bristol, Eng.: Chatford House Press, 1931; rpt., 1969.

Primary.

2502 Stoll, John E. THE GREAT DELUGE: A YEATS BIBLIOGRAPHY. Troy, N.Y.: Whitston, 1971.

Primary. Secondary.

2503 Symons, Arthur. A BIBLIOGRAPHY OF THE FIRST EDITIONS OF BOOKS BY WILLIAM BUTLER YEATS. London: First Edition Club; New York: R.R. Bowker, 1924.

Primary.

2504 Wade, Allan. A BIBLIOGRAPHY OF THE WRITINGS OF W.B. YEATS. Soho Bibliographies, no. 1. 3rd ed., rev. ed. Russell K. Alspach. London: Rupert Hart-Davis, 1968.

Primary. Secondary selected.

# AUTHOR INDEX

This index is alphabetized letter by letter and references are to entry numbers. It includes authors, translators, compilers, and contributors.

## A

Aas, L. 1042
Abbott, Claude Colleer 1992-93
Abdur Rub Choudhury, Khan Sahib 260
Abercrombie, Lascelles 1048
Adams, Hazard 2485
Adams, J. Donald 1049
Adams, W.D. 195
Adcock, A. St. John 261-62
Adelman, Irving 2, 1935, 1956, 1971, 1983, 2003, 2020, 2036, 2049, 2066, 2074, 2090, 2110, 2119A, 2145, 2155, 2215, 2224, 2259, 2274, 2290, 2320, 2334, 2339, 2370, 2383, 2396, 2418, 2453, 2468, 2478, 2486
AE. See Russell, George William
Agate, James 263-82, 1050-51
Aiken, Conrad 283
Aldington, Richard 284
Alldridge, John 1052
Allen, Charles 3
Allen, John 285
Allen, Percy 1053
Allen, Ralph G. 555
Allensworth, Josephine 1054
Alspach, Russell K. 2487, 2504
Altick, Richard D. 394
Anderson, John 1056
Anderson, Michael 196

Andreades, A. 1057
Andrews, Charlton 286
Andrews, Irene Dwen 1058
Angus, William 1059
Ansorge, Peter 1060
Archer, William 287-89, 481, 867, 1061-76, 1207
Armstrong, T.I.F. See Gawsworth, John
Armstrong, William A. 290-92, 370, 996, 1077, 2340
Arnold, Sidney 1078
Arns, Karl 293, 1079-83
Atkinson, Brooks 1086
Auden, W.H. 1088
Aylen, Leo 295
Ayling, Ronald 809, 2341-43

## B

B 1089-90
Bab, Julius 296
Baker, Blanch M. 8
Baker, Denys Val 297-98
Baker, George Pierce 299, 1091-92
Bakshy, Alexander 300, 1093
Balance, John 1715
Ball, Robert Hamilton 200
Balmforth, Ramsden 301-2
Bannister, Winifred 2004
Barbor, H.R. 1094
Barley, Joseph Wayne 303

# Author Index

# Author Index

# Author Index

Hobson, Bulmer  626
Hobson, Harold  627-31, 995, 1459-68
Hodson, James Landsdale  632
Hogan, Robert  512, 633-67
Holden, David F.  77
Holden, Michael  218
Holder, Owen  1469
Holloway, John  219
Holloway, Joseph  636-37
Holt, Roland  1470
Hooper, W.E.  638
Hope, R.  1719
Hope-Wallace, Philip  639, 995, 1471-72
Hopkins, Charles  1473
Hopper, Stanley Romaine  916
Horgan, Paul  1952
Hormann, Wilhelm  640
Horn, Robert D.  1474
Hornby, Richard  78-79
Hornsell, Horace  1475
Houghton, Norris  641, 1476
Howard, Diana  80, 220
Howard-Hill, T.H.  81
Howarth, Herbert  642
Howe, P.P.  643, 1478
Howells, W.D.  1479
Hoy, Cyrus  644
Hubbell, Jay B
Hudson, Lynton  646-48
Hughes, Glenn  649-50, 1480-81
Hughes, Richard  1482
Huneker, James Gibbons  651
Hunt, Elizabeth R.  652
Hunter, Frederick J.  82-83, 1483
Hunter, G.K.  653
Hurd, Michael  1484
Hurt, James  654
Hutchinson, B.  2292
Hutchinson, Horace G.  1485
Hyman, Alan  655

## I

International Association for the Study of Anglo-Irish Literature  89
International Federation of Library Associations  90
International Theatre Institute  221

Ireland, Norma Olin  92-93
Irial  1487
Irving, Laurence  1492
Isaacs, Jacob  495, 656, 1314
Ivanof, Viacheslaf  1493

## J

Jackson, Sir Barry  703
Jacquot, Jean  657
James, D.G.  658
Jameson, Storm  659
Jankovic, Mira  1494
Jeans, Ronald  660
Jeffares, Norman  2490
Jellicoe, Ann  661
Jenkins, Alan  1495
Jennings, Humphrey  662
Jennings, Richard  1496
Jerome, Jerome K.  1497
Jochum, K.P.S.  2494
John, Victor  1498
Johnson, Albert E.  94-95
Johnston, Denis  1499-1501
Jonas, Klaus W.  2280
Jones, David E.  2079
Jones, Doris Arthur  2218
Jones, Henry Arthur  663-65, 781, 1502-8
Jones, Jean Brady  1509
Jones, Leonard A.  1510-11, 2389
Jonson, G.C. Ashton  1512-13
Jordon, John  666
Joyce, James  304, 667
Junge, Ewald  97
Jurak, Mirko  668, 1514-17

## K

K., Q.  1518
Kahn, A.M.C.  98-99
Kain, Richard M.  669
Kavanagh, Peter  670-71
Keller, Dean H.  100
Kelly, Blanche Mary  672
Kelly, Seamus,  1519
Kemp, Ivor  2182
Kennedy, Andrew  673
Kennedy, David  674

# Author Index

McBrien, Peter F.  716, 1573-74
McCaan, Sean  717
MacCall, Ewan  1575
MacCarthy, Desmond  718-20, 867, 1576-79, 1949
MacCarthy, Justin  597
McCarthy, Mary  721
McCollom, William G.  722-23, 1580
McCormick, Jane L.  1581
McDermott, Hubert  1582
MacDonagh, John  1583
MacDonagh, Thomas  724
McDonald, Edward D.  2234
Macdonald, John F.  1584
Macdonell, A.G.  1585
Macfall, Haldane  1586
McGirr, Alice Thurston  2128, 2459, 2495
MacGowan, Kenneth  725-28, 1587
McHenry, Margaret  729
McHugh, Roger  578, 1588
McIntyre, Clara F.  1589
Mackay, Constance D'Arcy  1590
MacKenna, Stephen  730
McLeod, Stuart R.  731
MacLiammoir, Michael  732-35
MacNamara, Brinsley  110
McNamee, Lawrence F.  111
McNeill, W.E.  1591
MacOwan, Michael  1592
MacPhail, Ian  2460-61
Macqueen-Pope, W.  736-40
Mais, S.P.B.  741-42
Malawsky, Beryl York  2082
Malevinsky, Moses L.  743
Malkani, M.U.  1593
Mallinson, Vernon  1594
Malone, Andrew E.  744, 861, 1595-1602
Malye, Jean  745
Mandel, Oscar  746
Mander, Raymond  227, 747, 2042, 2281
Manly, John M.  118
Manning, Mary  1603
Mantle, Burns  198, 748-52
Marrot, H.V.  2129
Marshall, Norman  753, 1604-7
Martin, Wallace  754

Martyn, Edward  1608-10
Martz, Louis L.  755
Marx, Milton  756
Mason, A.E.W.  757
Mason, Eugene  758
Mason, Harold J.  1611
Mathieson, Andrew  1612
Matlaw, Myron  228
Matthews, Brander  759-60
Matthison, Wynne  1207
Maugham, Somerset  908, 1613
Maxwell, Gerald  1614
May, Frederick  1615-16, 2151
May, Robin  229, 761
Mayne, Rutherford  1617
Meier, Erika  762
Meissner, Paul  1618
Melchinger, Siegfried  230-31
Melchiori, Giorgio  1619
Mellown, Elgin  112
Melnitz, William W.  113, 727-28
Menlock, Walter  1620
Menon, Aubrey  1621
Mercer, Thomas Stanley  2106
Merchant, W. Moelwyn  763
Mercier, Vivian  764-65, 1622
Mersand, Joseph  114
Metwally, Abdalla A.  766
Middleton, George  1623
Mikhail, E.H.  115-17, 2130, 2163, 2282, 2349, 2462-63
Miller, Anna Irene  767
Miller, J. William  768
Miller, Liam  1624
Miller, Nellie Burget  769
Millett, Fred B.  118, 770-71, 775, 1932, 1953, 1979, 1989, 1997, 2014, 2017, 2031, 2034, 2043, 2050, 2057, 2064, 2070, 2083, 2094, 2107, 2138, 2142, 2152, 2164, 2172, 2184, 2189, 2192, 2202, 2207, 2219, 2251, 2255, 2300, 2317, 2326, 2330, 2336, 2357, 2367, 2377, 2406, 2415, 2450
Milligan, Alice  1625
Milliken, Clara A.  2361, 2430
Milne, A.A.  1626
Milne, George Heron  109
Milstead, John  1627

Minton, E.E. 1628
Mitchell, Langdon 294
Mitchenson, Joe 227, 747, 2042, 2281
Mizener, Arthur 1629
Moderwell, Hiram Kelly 772
Monahan, Michael 773
Monkhouse, A.N. 1630
Montague, C.E. 268, 774
Montgomery, K.L. 1631
Moody, William Vaughan 775
Moore, George 776, 1632
Moore, Harry T. 284
Moore, Thomas Sturge 1633
Morgan, A.E. 777
Morgan, Louise 778
Morgan, Margery M. 1634, 2151
Morley, Malcolm 779
Morley, Sheridan 735, 2044
Morris, Adah V. 130
Morris, Lloyd R. 780, 1635
Morrison, G.E. 781
Mortimer, Raymond 1636
Moses, Montrose, J. 1637-38, 2022, 2293
Mottram, Ralph 2131
Moult, Thomas 1639
Mueller, William R. 232
Muir, Kenneth 782
Muir, Percival Horace 1998
Mulliken, Clara A. 122
Munro, C.K. 783
Murphy, Daniel J. 1641
Murphy, Sheila A. 1642
Murray, Gilbert 481, 1207
Murray, T.C. 861
Myers, Henry Alonzo 1643
Myers, Paul 68

N

N., N. 1644-45
Nares, Owen 1645A
Nash, Paul 1646
Nathan, George Jean 233, 784-90, 1647-50
Nethercot, Arthur H. 1652-53
Nevinson, Henry Woodd 791, 2268
Newman, Evelyn 792
New York Public Library 124

New York Public Library. Reference Department 125
Nichols, Beverley 793
Nicholson, Norman 1657
Nicoll, Allardyce 127-29, 794-803, 854, 1658-59
Nic Shiubhlaigh, Marie 804
Noble, Peter 235, 805
Noel, Jean C. 2309
Norman, C.H. 806
Norton, Clara 131
Norton, Elizabeth Towne 132
Norwood, Gilbert 1661-62

O

O'Brien, E.D. 1663
O'Casey, Sean 304, 807-9, 1664
O'Connor, Frank 304, 810-11, 861, 1665
O'Connor, Norreys Jephson 812
O'Connor, Ulick 1666
O'D., D. 1667
Odle, E.V. 1668
O'Donnel, Frank, Hugh 813
O'Donnell, Donat 1669
O'Donoghue, D.J. 133
O'Driscoll, Robert 715, 814
O'Faolain, Sean 1670-71
O'Hagan, Thomas 815
OhAodha, Michael 816-17, 2496
O'Hegarty, Patrick Sarsfield 134, 1672, 2193, 2353
Oliver, D.E. 818
Oliver, William I. 333
Olivier, Laurence 805, 877
Olson, Elder 819
O'Mahony, Mathew 236
O'Mahony, T.P. 1673
O'Malley, Mary 1674-75
O'Neill, George 1677-80
O'Neill, James J. 135, 820
O'Neill, Michael J. 636-37, 2407
Oppel, Horst 70, 821
Oppenheimer, George 822
O'Ryan, Agnes 1681
Osborne, E.A. 2203
Ottemiller, John H. 136
Otten, Kurt 1682
Ould, Hermon 823, 1683-84

# Author Index

Owen, Harrison 824

## P

Page, Sean 1685
Palfy, Istvan 1686
Pallette, Drew B. 1687
Palmer, D.J. 825
Palmer, Frank 531
Palmer, Helen H. 137, 1942, 1965,
  1980, 1984, 2023, 2045, 2084,
  2114, 2132, 2196, 2235, 2283,
  2294, 2350, 2378, 2391, 2400,
  2431, 2440, 2464, 2475, 2482,
  2497
Palmer, John 826-27, 1688-90
Parchevskaia, V.M. 2348
Parker, William 634, 851
Patterson, Charlotte A. 138
Pattisson, A.L. 1691
Paul-Dubois, L. 828
Peacock, Ronald 829-30, 1692
Peake, Dorothy Margaret 139, 191
Pearson, Hesketh 831-33, 1693-94
Peinert, Dietrich 1695
Pellizzi, Camillo 834
Percy, Edward 835
Perry, Henry Ten Eyck 836
Pettet, Edwin Burr 1696
Phelps, William Lyon 837-39, 1697
Phipps, Hulda Mossberg 458
Pierce, Roger 1698
Pilcher, Velona 1699-1700
Pinero, Arthur 1715
Platt, Agnes 840
Playfair, Giles 1702
Playfair, Nigel 841, 1703-5
Plowman, Max 1708
Plunkett, Edward John Moreton Drax.
  See Dunsany, Lord Edward John
  Moreton Drax Plunkett
Poel, William 842, 1709-13
Pogson, Rex 140, 843
Pohle, Helen Loudora 141
Pollak, Felix 3
Pollard, M. 2460-61
Pollock, John 844, 1714
Popkin, Henry 142
Popot, Raymonde 634, 851
Porter, Raymond J. 845
Potter, Helen 1716

Poulenard, E. 1717
Powell, Lawrence C. 2236
Power, Patrick C. 846
Prater, Eugene C. 2116
Price, Alan 937, 2465
Price, Cecil 1718
Pride, Leo B. 237
Priestley, J.B. 847-49, 1719-23
Prior, Moody, E. 850, 1724
Pryce-Jones, Alan 1725-26
Purdom, Charles B. 2151

## Q

Queant, G. 238
Quinn, Edward 211
Quinn, John 1727

## R

Rae, Kenneth 239
Rafroidi, Patrick 634, 851
Raphaelson, Samson 852
Rattigan, Terence 1728
Rattray, R.F. 1729
Rawson, C.J. 973
Raymond, John 639
Read, Herbert 1730
Reaske, Christopher R. 853
Rebora, Piero 1731
Recouly, Raymond 1732
Redgrave, Michael 1734-35
Reed, Edward 1736-37
Reeves, John A. 536-37
Reid, Alec 1738
Rentoul, Gervais 1739
Reynolds, Ernest 854
Reynolds, George F. 1741-42
Rhodes, Raymond Crompton 1743
Rickert, Edith 118
Rickword, Edgell 855
Rivoallan, Anatole 856
Roberts, Peter 240
Roberts, Warren 2237-38
Robinson, Lennox 857-61, 1744
Robinson, Robert 1745
Robson, Flora 1841
Rodgers, W.R. 862
Roeder, Alois Wilhelm 2058
Roosevelt, Theodore 1746

# Author Index

Simons, Eric N.   167
Simpson, Alan   1792
Skeffington, F. Sheehy   1793
Skelton, Robin   904-5
Skinner, R. Dana   906
Sladen-Smith, F.   1794-95
Slater, Derek   907
Slater, Guy   908
Slaughter, Howard K.   2099
Smith, Gus   622
Smith, Hugh   1796
Smith, Paul   1797
Smith, Timothy d'Arch   2060
Smith, Winifred   1798, 2434
Snider, Rose   909
Sniderman, Florence M.   19, 1937,
   1958, 1995, 2001, 2005, 2021,
   2027, 2037, 2067, 2076, 2092,
   2098, 2111, 2122, 2147, 2157,
   2168, 2176, 2181, 2209, 2216,
   2227, 2248, 2257, 2260, 2263,
   2277, 2288, 2303, 2321, 2335,
   2345, 2352, 2371, 2384, 2397,
   2404, 2420, 2438, 2444, 2447,
   2455, 2469, 2473, 2479, 2488
Sobel, Bernard   168, 247, 1799
Soper, Paul L.   1801
Sorell, Walter   910
Southern, Richard   239
Spanos, William V.   911
Speaight, Robert   912-13
Speckbaugh, Paul F.   1802
Speer, Rev. J.C.   914
Spence, E.F.   915
Spencer, Terence John Bew   248
Spencer, Theodore J.   916, 2435
Spinner, Kaspar   917, 2212, 2409
Splendore, Paola   1803
Sprinchorn, Evert   249
Stallbaumer, Virgil   1807
Stallings, Roy   68
Stallman, R.W.   252
Stamm, Rudolf   918-19, 1808
Stanford, Derek   920, 2117
Starkie, Enid   921
Starkie, Walter   861
Stegmeyer, F.   1810
Stein, Walter   922
Steiner, George   923

Stephens, E.M.   2458
Stevenson, W.B.   1811-12
Stewart, Andrew J.   1813
Stewart, J.I.M.   924
Stiles, Villa   50, 1950, 1961, 2053,
   2068, 2102, 2124, 2230, 2265,
   2291, 2305, 2423, 2492
Stoddard, F.G.   2072
Stokes, Leslie   1814
Stoll, John E.   1944, 2502
Storer, Edward   1815
Stott, Raymond Toole   2286
Stratman, Carl J.   170-73
Stratton, Clarence   1818
Strauss, George   1819-20
Streatfeild, G.S.   925
Strong, L.A.G.   926-29
Styan, J.L.   930-33
Subbotina, K.A.   1821
Sutherland, A.C.   64
Sutton, Graham   934, 1823-25
Swart, J.   1826
Swears, Herbert   1827
Swinnerton, Frank   935
Symons, Arthur   936, 2503
Synge, J.M.   481, 555, 937

# T

Takahashi, Genji   2135
Talbot, A.J.   938
Tarn, Adam   1828
Taylor, Alison   939
Taylor, Estella Ruth   940
Taylor, George   941
Taylor, John Russell   253, 942
Teagarden, Lucetta J.   2393-94
Tedlock, E.W., Jr.   2240
Temple, Ruth Z.   175, 1933, 1954,
   1969, 1981, 1990, 1999, 2010,
   2018, 2025, 2032, 2047, 2052,
   2061, 2087, 2096, 2108, 2118,
   2143, 2153, 2166, 2173, 2187,
   2190, 2197, 2204, 2213, 2221,
   2253, 2296, 2301, 2310, 2318,
   2327, 2332, 2363, 2368, 2380,
   2402, 2410, 2416, 2442, 2446,
   2451, 2471, 2484
Tennyson, Charles   1829-30
Tennyson, G.B.   943

# Author Index

Wedmore, Frederick 1883
Weintraub, Stanley 2428
Welland, Dennis 996
Welcher, Jeanne K. 26
Welker, David 190
Wells, Geoffrey H. 2437
Wells, Stanley 129, 153
Wellwarth, George 231
West, Algernon 1884
West, Anthony 1885
West, Dorothy Herbert 139, 191
West, Kenyon 1886
Westby, Selmer 2198
Weygandt, Cornelius 997-98, 1887-88
Whitaker, Thomas R. 1891
White, Terence de Vere 999
White, William 2241
Whitfield, George 1000
Whiting, Frank M. 1001
Whiting, John 1002, 1892
Whitley, Alvin 503
Whitworth, Geoffrey 1003-5, 1893-96
Whitworth, Robin 1897
Wickham, Glynne 1898
Wieczorek, Hubert 1006
Wild, Friedrich 1007
Wilde, Alan 2199
Wilde, Oscar 481
Wilde, Percival 1008
Williams, Emlyn 959
Williams, Harold 1009
Williams, I.A. 2272, 2312
Williams, Jesse Lynch 294
Williams, Rowan 834
Williams, Raymond 1010-12, 1900-1901
Williams, Stephen 1013
Williams, T.G. 1014

Williams-Ellis, A. 1902
Williamson, Audrey 1015
Williamson, Hugh Ross 1903
Willcox, Louise Collier 1899
Willis, Ted 1904
Willson, H. 1885
Willison, I.R. 192, 1934, 1955, 1970, 1982, 1986, 2000, 2011, 2015, 2019, 2026, 2035, 2048, 2062, 2065, 2089, 2109, 2119, 2136, 2144, 2154, 2170, 2179, 2191, 2200, 2205, 2208, 2214, 2242, 2247, 2254, 2256, 2258, 2273, 2287, 2297, 2302, 2319, 2328, 2333, 2354, 2369, 2395, 2403, 2443, 2446, 2449, 2454, 2472, 2477
Wilmot, Seamus 1905
Wilson, A.E. 1016-18
Wilson, N. Scarlyn 1019
Wimsatt, W.K., Jr. 1020
Worsley, T.C. 995, 1021-22 1909-12
Worth, Katharine J. 1023
Wreford, Reynell J.R.G. 1913
Wright, Edward A. 1024
Wright, George T. 1945

## Y

Yamamoto, Shuji 1025
Yeats, William Butler 304, 481, 555, 702, 1026-38, 1190, 1568, 1914-22
Young, Ella 1039
Young, Stark 1040-41, 1923-24

## Z

Zangwill, Israel 1925

# TITLE INDEX

This index is alphabetized letter by letter and references are to entry numbers. In some cases, titles have been shortened.

# Title Index

# Title Index

## M

# SUBJECT INDEX

This index is alphabetized letter by letter. References are to entry numbers and underlined numbers refer to major entries on a topic.

502, 515, 541, 565, 575,
579, 598, 620, 633-35, 642,
645, 669, 674, 676, 690,
693, 702, 712, 724, 730,
744-45, 760, 764-65, 773,
776, 780, 787-88, 791, 804,
808, 810, 812, 814, 828,
845-46, 856-57, 859, 862,
872, 875-76, 880, 898, 904,
937, 946, 967, 979, 990,
997, 999, 1001, 1006-7,
1010, 1025, 1039
critical periodical articles 1053,
1058, 1098, 1119, 1199,
1206, 1243, 1253, 1307,
1322, 1340, 1348, 1355,
1362, 1366-67, 1369-71,
1373-74, 1379, 1407, 1439,
1449, 1453, 1489, 1499,
1501, 1519-20, 1539, 1549,
1568, 1573, 1582, 1595-96,
1620, 1650, 1671, 1678-80,
1756, 1772, 1829, 1842,
1865, 1868, 1876, 1919
reference books on 208, 215, 236
See also Drama, Gaelic; Irish Dramatic Movement; Literary
drama
Drama, post-Elizabethan 1552
Drama, psychological 369, 581
bibliography of 104, 189
See also Personality in drama
Drama, religious 303, 496, 763, 863,
913, 992, 1171, 1173, 1304,
1360, 1467, 1523, 1548
bibliography of 60, 95
See also Morality and drama; Religion in drama; Saints in drama
Drama, Victorian 346, 461, 500,
520, 567, 800, 867. See
also Theater, Victorian
"Drama of ideas" 1652, 1728, 1771,
1780
Drama of the absurd 1834
Dramatic criticism. See Drama, critical material; Press and dramatic criticism; Theater, critical
material; names of specific
playwrights

Dramatists. See Drama, critical
material; Novelists as playwrights; Playwrights; names
of specific playwrights
Drinkwater, John 52, 261, 264-66,
269, 434, 478, 497, 564,
758, 777, 934, 948, 1042,
2053-62
Dublin Gate Theatre 489, 707, 732,
1118, 1201, 1391, 1454,
1599, 1773
Dublin Literary Society 1921
Dukes, Ashley 2063-65
Dunsany, Lord 52, 341, 397, 434,
607, 611, 777, 812, 998,
2066-73
"Night at an Inn" 864
Durrell, Lawrence 543

E

Editors, bibliography of 38
Edwardian drama. See Drama, Edwardian
Edwards, Hilton 1201, 1454
Eireann, Telefis 1417
Eliot, T. S. 160, 297, 333, 343,
370, 438, 441, 462, 517-
18, 533, 538, 543, 549-50,
564, 568, 589, 620, 640,
656-57, 673, 697, 731, 746,
763, 766, 821, 823, 868,
911, 916, 919-20, 922, 930,
1000, 1010, 1012, 1015,
1020, 1023, 1397, 1445,
1687, 1872, 2074-89
"Murder in the Cathedral" 1657
Elizabethan drama. See Drama,
Elizabethan
Emmet, Robert 1355
Ervine, St. John 262, 265, 302,
434, 462, 478, 625, 742,
777, 934, 1042, 1428,
2090-97
Experimental drama and theater 753,
1012, 1590, 1824. See also
"New drama" school
Expressionist drama 650, 1059, 1593,
1824

320

# Subject Index

One-act plays 338, 612, 698, 751,
1008, 1169, 1226, 1538,
1795
index to 187
in teaching oral reading 1054
Opera
bibliography 131
reference works 205
Oratory, study and teaching 1054
O'Riordan, Conal Holmes O'Connell
2355-57

## P

Pantomine 278
influence on drama 451
Peasants in drama 1322, 1610, 1678
"People's Theatre." See Society and
drama
Performers. See Actors and acting
Performing arts. See Drama; Theater
Personality in drama 886
Phillips, Stephen 122, 269, 599, 607,
831, 945, 948, 1015, 1433,
2358-64
Phillpots, Eden 2365-69
Pinero, Arthur Wing 285, 538, 599,
742, 762, 1715, 2370-82
Pirandello, Luigi 708
Playgoing 271, 314, 372, 470, 474,
664, 783, 1024, 1214, 1240,
1302, 1437, 1485, 1847
Playhouses. See Music halls; Theaters
Play of ideas 552, 665, 825, 1142,
1381, 1652, 1664, 1728,
1771, 1780, 1904
Plays. See Drama
Playwrights
bibliography 19, 38, 52, 160,
168, 186
critical material
in books and eassys 259-1041
by individual author 1926-2504
in periodicals 1042-925
portraits 638
reference works 195, 211, 214,
223, 230-31, 245, 249, 257
See also Novelists as playwrights;
names of specific playwrights
Playwriting 294, 381, 491, 495, 506,

521, 602, 604, 660, 679,
694, 726, 743, 824, 835,
848, 852, 864, 928, 938,
941, 976, 1102, 1128,
1301, 1314, 1334, 1385,
1527, 1535, 1692, 1699,
1751, 1879. See also
Drama, theory and techni-
que
Plots 976, 1580
use of Greek mythology in 1456
outlines of 203, 244, 247, 249
Poetic drama 335, 358, 365-66,
370, 390, 395, 467, 492-
94, 528, 534, 567, 573,
635, 656, 668, 689, 731,
782, 829, 861, 905, 948,
956, 996, 1048, 1088,
1120, 1125-26, 1170, 1175,
1196, 1261, 1264-65, 1297-
98, 1313, 1315, 1380,
1383, 1399, 1401, 1410,
1436, 1440, 1444-46,
1465, 1494, 1514, 1517,
1580, 1619, 1629, 1654,
1657, 1676, 1679, 1687,
1691, 1709, 1713, 1724,
1730, 1760, 1788, 1802,
1811-12, 1826, 1851,
1856, 1860, 1899. See
also Language in drama,
rhythm of
Poetry, bibliography of taped 37
Poetry, Irish 773
bibliography of 133
Politics and drama 291, 364, 668,
946, 1509, 1514, 1517,
1642, 1753, 1803, 2353.
See also Democratic atti-
tude in drama; Propaganda
in drama; Sinn Fein rebellion in drama
Pound, Ezra 495, 1314
Press and dramatic criticism 1160,
1163
Priestley, J. B. 297, 326, 354,
416, 441, 462, 517, 543,
564, 568, 589, 640, 786,
1015, 1334, 2383-95
Problem plays 302, 1316, 1497,